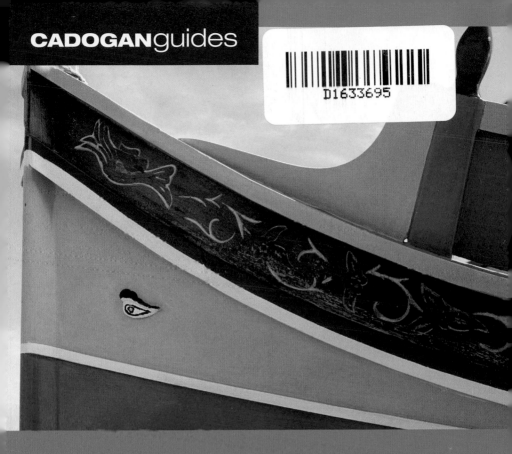

# CADOGANguides

D1633695

# MALTA,
## GOZO & COMINO

'On either side of the high prow of every Maltese fishing boat or luzzu
you will see an inky oval blob, the reverentially painted open and ever-
watchful Eye of Osiris, a simple superstition to ward off evil spirits.
Catholic names and shrines also found on board show how the strands
of the island's different cultures entwine.'

Simon Gaul

# About the Guide

The **full-colour introduction** gives the author's overview of the region, together with suggested **itinerary** and a regional **'where to go' map** and **feature** to help you plan your trip.

Illuminating and entertaining **cultural chapters** on history, topics, food and drink, art and architecture give you a rich flavour of the region.

**Planning Your Trip** covers the basics of **getting there** and **getting around**, plus entry formalities. The **Practical A–Z** deals with all the **essential information** and **contact details** that you may need, including a section for disabled travellers.

The **regional chapters** are arranged in a loose touring order, with plenty of public transport and driving information. The author's top **'Don't Miss'** ⭐ sights are highlighted at the start of each chapter.

A short **language guide**, a **glossary** of cultural terms, a **chronology** of dates, a who's who of **architects and artists**, ideas for **further reading** and a comprehensive **index** can be found at the end of the book.

### Hotel Price Guide (*see also* p.74)

| | | |
|---|---|---|
| Luxury | €€€€ | Over Lm60 (€140) |
| Expensive | €€€ | Lm35–60 (€80–140) |
| Moderate | €€ | Lm20–34 (€47–79) |
| Inexpensive | € | Under Lm20 (€47) |

### Restaurant Price Guide (*see also* p.79)

| | | |
|---|---|---|
| Expensive | €€€€ | Over Lm15 (€35) |
| Moderate | €€€ | Lm8–15 (€18–35) |
| Inexpensive | €€ | Lm5–8 (€12–18) |
| Budget | € | Under Lm5 (€12) |

# About the Author

Simon Gaul was born in London and spent much of his childhood idly but happily sailing the shores of the Central Mediterranean. He is the father of three children, and lives and works in Monaco.

**4th Edition Published 2007**

# INTRODUCING
# MALTA, GOZO
## 01 & COMINO

*Above: Senglea, Malta*
*pp.134–5*

You are lucky if you travel to Malta by boat. That is how the Phoenician traders, in their small rounded vessels, first encountered the archipelago nearly three thousand years ago. Today, the bastions of the fortress capital Valletta skim welcomingly into view out of the hazy Mediterranean light, but time has barely altered the landfall.

From the air, the archipelago is the last splutter of Europe before Africa, and the bare limestone topography hints at the arid sands 200 miles (300km) beyond. Flying north from Africa, the islands are like a tentative toe-print from the outsize body of the dark continent as it stretches towards Europe. That's Malta: an untethered outcrop at the crossroads of the Mediterranean; a devoutly Roman Catholic country, but with Allah as its name for the father of Christ.

Think of Malta, and two very different ideas may come to mind: 'an unconscionably romantic history', to quote Evelyn Waugh, and, more prosaically, a holiday destination under a baking sun. The Order of St John ruled supreme here for nearly 270 years, and its crusading knights, 'the flower of European aristocracy', left part of the magic of their era in towering fortifications, stately *palazzi* and noble Baroque churches and cathedrals whose walls are adorned still with the art of Caravaggio, Antoine de Favray and Mattia Preti – a disproportionately grand legacy for such a small island. In addition, just about every major player in European history – from Count Roger the Norman, to Napoleon, to Hitler – has squabbled over this isolated but valuable piece of real estate, and left a mark in some corner. The only visitors who came in peace were St Luke and St Paul, who planted the banner of Christianity.

*Above: The resort of Sliema, Malta, pp.153–8*

*Opposite: The Baroque splendour of the Auberge de Castile et Leon, Valletta, Malta, pp.102–3*

Yet, of course, the-times-they-are-a-changing. The current dilemma is the ugly face of commercialism. Since independence in 1964, Malta has fluttered towards tourism like a moth towards light. In 2002, just under a million people visited the islands – almost three times their combined population. Only now, and possibly too late, are the authorities trying to take their holiday destination 'upmarket', with the marketing men doing everything in their power to lose the reputation (and unprintable sobriquets) the islands earned in the 1970s. New services, communications and hotels have been built, and tariffs have, inevitably and markedly, risen.

Malta is now trying to compete as a destinational five-star resort; but the jury is still out, and will remain so for some time. The spin is no longer 'give them a cold Coke beside a pool'; sites and museums – notably the Museum of Archaeology and the Hypogeum – are slowly being restored. Notwithstanding that, the 'crane' is still the national bird. Drive or sail along the northern coast and cranes are just about all you will see. For some reason, probably a combination of avarice and 'Keeping Up With The Grechs', the Maltese will always be a nation of builders, and they'll only cease when the southern quarries run dry. Sadly, there will be August snow before the national bird takes a dive off the northern shore skyline.

One of the few things that has not changed, so far, is the cheeky grin the Maltese always sport, except when behind the wheel of a car – beware, their driving is anything but Catholic. The islanders, both Maltese and Gozitan (and there is a difference, you will discover), are an energetic, industrious and wealthy people. Yet, for a much-invaded people they are almost naïvely welcoming, and the only timidity you may find is on Gozo.

# Geography and Where to Go

The islands which constitute the Republic of Malta lie almost dead centre of the Mediterranean: Sicily is just 60 miles (96km) to the north, North Africa 170 miles (290km) to the south, Gibraltar 1,100 miles (1,825km) to the west and Alexandria 900 miles (1,510km) to the east. The archipelago consists of three principal inhabited islands: Malta, Gozo and Comino; and three uninhabited islets, Cominotto, Filfla and St Paul's Island. Malta, the largest landmass, covers 95 square miles (245 sq km) with 82 miles (136km) of coastline; the sister island, Gozo, is approximately 8 by 4 miles (13.5 by 6.5km) and has about 26 miles (43km) of coastline; and tiny Comino covers only 1 square mile (2.5 sq km). Combined, the islands are no bigger than the Isle of Wight; Malta itself is no bigger than Martha's Vineyard.

The total population of the islands – the fourth-highest per square mile in the world – is approximately 376,500, of whom 28,000 are Gozitan. In addition, there are 580,000 Maltese nationals dotted throughout the world, predominantly in Australia and North America. The language is Malti but most people speak English and Italian.

The islands are primarily sedimentary rock, two-thirds being the soft pale honey-coloured globigerina limestone from which the majority of local stone buildings are made. The landscape is unremarkable, neither flat nor hilly, with moderate contours and open valleys. From the air it can look barren, especially in summer, redeemed only by the pinks, reds and whites of the oleander bushes. The limestone buildings and the dry-stone walls built to protect crops from the extremes of the weather don't flatter the landscape either, but in spring it is surprisingly verdant. Gozo, only 3 miles (5km) away, is perennially greener due to its clay soil and hillier, more compact contours. None of the islands have mountains, rivers or natural minerals. The highest point on Malta is Dingli Cliffs at approximately 850ft (260m) above sea level: Gozo's little summit is the hill at Ta'Dbiegi (about 600ft/180m).

**Valletta and the Three Cities** focuses mainly on Valletta itself, designated a World Heritage Site: the capital is a mightily impressive fortified city with a magnificent cathedral, and the palace of the Grand Master of the Order of St John. Its similarly fortified suburb Floriana contains the Argotti Botanical Gardens. **The Northeast Coast**'s busy resorts of Sliema and St Julian's outstrip the capital in terms of size, and from Sliema are some of the very best views of Valletta, which lies across the water. Paceville is one of Malta's hottest nightspots. The holiday development continues along **The North Coast**, which offers some tempting diving spots and boat trips. **The Southwest Coast** is far less developed and has wild landscapes made for walking such as Dingli Cliffs, some prehistoric sites such as Clapham Junction, Hagar Qim and Mnajdra, and Siġġiewi, perhaps the most enchanting Maltese village. **The South** encompasses the fishing village of Marsaxlokk, the ancient sites of the Hypogeum and Tarxien Temples, and the cave of Għar Dalam, which has yielded a rich array of prehistoric animal bones. In **Mdina, Rabat and the Inland Towns**, Mdina itself is a tiny medieval walled city full of shadowy alleys, snoozing cats and a history spanning Roman and Arabic occupations; St Paul's Cathedral is a grand moment of Maltese Baroque elegance. **Gozo and Comino** are easily reached from mainland Malta, and make a wonderful contrast, highly rewarding for exploring on foot, with quiet green farmland inland, and some towering cliffs and rock formations along the coast.

# Chapter Divisions

Map showing chapter divisions of Malta, Gozo and Comino, including Valletta and the Three Cities (07, p.95), The Northeast Coast (08, p.145), The North Coast (09, p.171), The Southwest Coast (10, p.191), The South (11, p.211), Mdina, Rabat and the Inland Towns (12, p.233), and Gozo and Comino (13, p.263). Scale: 5 km / 3 miles.

*Above: Ramla Bay, Gozo, p.298*

*Left: St Julian's Bay, Malta, pp.159–61*

## Shorelines

North and south of Malta are two different worlds. Sandy bays and spreading resorts, and the capital city of Valletta in the north contrast with the more remote, rugged terrain of the south. Views change at every turn: caves and coves, cliffs and concrete high-rise. Pick your way round carefully, head off in a boat, dive into the depths of the startlingly clear waters, seek out a waterfront eatery offering fresh sea food, or venture out to Gozo, where life trundles along at an amiably slower pace.

Above: Festa at Kirkop, Malta

Opposite from top: Niche of the Madonna outside Carmelite Church, Mdina, Malta, p.244; painted dome of St Paul's Shipwreck, Valletta, Malta, p.111

## Festa

Village festivals don't come much louder or more ebullient than the Maltese *festa*. Firecrackers jolt the community into a weekend of action, but the preparation takes months as funds are raised, the village tidied up and decorated, and the holy statues polished in preparation for their journey through the streets. Locals dress up, fireworks adorn the night sky, bells are rung, the band plays and everyone joins in to honour whichever saint is being honoured. Nadur and St Julian's are among the most spectacular events, but you can encounter the *festa* virtually anywhere.

## Churches

For those who don't wish to grill themselves under the relentless sun there are over 350 churches to snoop around. In the villages are some marvellously unchanged places of worship, such as the Immaculate Conception at Għarb on Gozo, the Annunciation at Ħal Millieri and St Gregory's at Żejtun. Statelier by far are the Baroque cathedrals of St Paul's, Mdina, and St John's Co-Cathedral, Valletta, with its frescoes, Flemish tapestries, and Caravaggio's painting of *The Beheading of St John the Baptist*. The 20th century added some eccentric curios: an eggcup-shaped Church of the Assumption – invariably known as the Egg Church – in Mġarr, and the extraordinary Rotunda Church at Xewkija.

# Ancient Sites

A journey round the Maltese archipelago reveals the oldest freestanding structures yet discovered in the world, notably Ġgantija, Tarxien, Ħagar Qim and Mnajdra. Massive walled structures of huge boulders enclose enigmatic curved chambers, often linked to the worship of curvaceous female figurines thought to be fertility goddesses. Elsewhere are strange Bronze Age cart ruts etched into the rock some 3,500 years ago, the best-known being the unforgettably named Clapham Junction. Try to book a ticket to see the underground marvels of the Hypogeum. A trip over to Sicily takes you to Syracuse and Taormina, with their wealth of Roman remains.

*Below: Tarxien goddess of fertility, Malta, p.227*

*Opposite: Ġgantija, Gozo, pp.277–8*

*Above: Valletta, Malta,*
*pp.95–130*

# Itinerary and Best of...

## Malta, Gozo and Comino in 7 Days

**Day 1** Valletta: explore the streets, cathedral and Grand Master's Palace.

**Day 2** A cruise from Sliema Creek. Shop in Sliema or discover Rabat and the Ta'Qali Crafts Village.

**Day 3** Siġġiewi, Dingli and a stroll on Dingli Cliffs, and seek out the medieval churches at Ħal Millieri, or go diving at Għar Lapsi.

**Day 4** A day trip to Gozo. Browse the market for picnic items, take in the views from the Citadel, and visit the prehistoric site of Ġgantija. Visit the village of Xagħra and stroll by Ta'Ċenċ Cliffs.

**Day 5** Venture to the southeastern corner of Malta, to the Tarxien Temples or (if you have booked in advance) the Hypogeum. Call at the fishing village of Marsaxlokk and look into the Church of St Gregory at Żejtun.

**Day 6** Spend a day on a sandy beach such as Mellieħa Bay, go diving or snorkelling, or plump for a walk.

**Day 7** Take a day trip to Ionian Sicily and spend the day with the Romans in Syracuse, visiting the catacombs, archaeological museum and Neapolis Archaeological Park. Or venture further north to Mount Etna and the hill village resort of Taormina.

## The Best of Malta, Gozo and Comino

**Anchorages:** Dwejra Bay, Gozo; (after 4pm) The Blue Lagoon, Comino

**Archaeological sites:** Ġgantija; Hypogeum

**Art gallery:** St James's Cavalier, Valletta

**Bars:** Gleneagles, Mġarr Harbour, Gozo; Café Jubilee, Valletta (especially in winter)

**Baroque cathedrals:** (exterior) St Paul's, Mdina); (interior) St John's Co-Cathedral, Valletta

**Cave:** Għar Dalam

**Day trip:** Sicily (for Taormina, Mount Etna, Catania market and Syracuse)

**Dotty legend:** Il-Maqluba, Qrendi

**Dive:** Blue Hole, off Fungus Rock, Gozo

**Evening entertainments:** Manoel Theatre, Valletta; various functions at St James's Cavalier, Valletta

**Escutcheon:** Grand Master Pinto's, Auberge de Castile et Leon, Valletta

**Excursion:** A Captain Morgan cruise

*Festas*: Nadur, Gozo; St Julian's

**Fishing**: Within 20 yards of the two fish farms at Mistra Bay and Fort St Lucian

**Garden**: San Anton Palace, Attard

**Grand Master's indulgence**: Verdala Palace

**Impressive ruin**: Fort Manoel (but undergoing restoration)

**Kids' distractions**: Eden Superbowl, Ice Arena, cinema and amusement arcade, St George's Bay; water sports at the Hilton Hotel, St Julian's

**Lace**: Sannat, Gozo

**Market**: St James's Ditch, Valletta

**Marina**: Lazzaretto Creek, Ta'Xbiex

**Medieval church**: The Annunciation, Ħal Millieri

**Museums**: Maritime Museum, Vittoriosa; Folklore Museum, Għarb, Gozo

**Old village**: Siġġiewi

**Outrageous souvenir**: suit of armour from the Crafts Village, Ta'Qali

**Religious artefact**: Flemish tapestries, St John's Co-Cathedral Museum, Valletta

**Sight**: Mdina city itself

**Snacks**: Bread from local baker, eaten with warm, dark red tomatoes; *pastizzi* (little peacakes and cheesecakes) from local bars and confectioners

**Swimming**: The Blue Lagoon, Comino (before 10.30am or after 4pm); off the rocks at Fomm ir-Riħ; Għasri Valley Beach, Gozo

**View**: From Dingli Cliffs

**Village churches**: The Immaculate Conception, Għarb, Gozo; St Gregory's, Żejtun

**Village square**: Xagħra, Gozo

**Walk**: Ta'Ċenċ Cliffs, Gozo

*Below: The turquoise waters of Blue Lagoon, Comino, pp.302–3*

# CONTENTS

**01 Introducing Malta, Gozo and Comino 1**
Where to Go 6
Itinerary 16

**02 History 19**

**03 Topics 39**
Driving 40
Of Churches 40
Dom Mintoff 41
A Little More about
Local Politics 43
The Maltese Cross 44
The Festa 45
Hunting and Trapping 46
De la Valette and
Dragut Rais 47
St Paul 49
The Eye of Osiris 52

**04 Food and Drink 53**
Eating Out, the
Maltese Way 54
Maltese Tastes 54
Maltese Drinks 56

**05 Planning Your Trip 57**
When to Go 58
Tourist Information 60
Embassies and Consulates 61
Entry Formalities 61
Disabled Travellers 61
Insurance and EHIC Cards 62
Money 62
Getting There 63
Getting Around 65
Tour Operators 72
Where to Stay 73

**06 Practical A–Z 75**
Conversion Tables 76
Children 77
Crime and the Police 78
Eating Out 79
Electricity 80
Health and Emergencies 81
Internet 82
Libraries 82

Living and Working
in Malta 82
Markets and Shopping 82
Marrying in Malta 84
Media 84
Opening Hours 85
Packing 86
Postal Services 86
Religious Affairs 87
Sports and Activities 87
Telephones 91
Time 92
Tipping 92
Toilets 92
VAT 92
Women Travellers 92
Yachting Information 92

**The Guide**

**07 Valletta and the Three Cities 95**
Valletta 97
Valletta City Sights 100
St John's Co-Cathedral
and Museum 104
The Grand Master's
Palace 112
Floriana 124
The Three Cities 130
Senglea (L'Isla) 134
Vittoriosa (Birgu) 135
Copiscua (Bormla) 144

**08 The Northeast Coast 145**
From Ta'Xbiex to
Gwardamanġa 147
Msida and Ta'Xbiex 147
Pieta and
Gwardamanġa 148
Gzira and Manoel Island 149
Sliema, St Julian's, Paceville
and Around 152
St Julian's Bay, Balluta,
Paceville and
St George's Bay 159
Madliena, Għargħur and
Baħar iċ-Ċagħaq 165

Madliena and Għargħur 165
Baħar iċ-Ċagħaq 166

**09 The North Coast 167**
The Great Fault and the
Victoria Lines 169
Salina Bay 169
St Paul's Bay and Around 171
Qawra, Bufjibba, St Paul's Bay,
Xemxija and Mistra Bay 175
Bur Marrad and the
Wardija Ridge 176
West of St Paul's Bay 180
Mellieħa and Mellieħa Bay
(Il-Għadira) 180
The Marfa Peninsula:
Paradise Bay, Ċirkewwa,
Ramla and Armier 182
Għajn Tuffieħa and
Golden Bay 184
Mġarr and Ġnejna Bay 185
Żebbieħ and the
Skorba Temples 187
Fomm ir-Riħ 187

**10 The Southwest Coast 191**
Around Dingli to Mnajdra
via Siġġiewi 194
Ħaġar Qlm and Mnajdra 200
Żurrieq and Around 205

**11 The South 211**
Marsaxlokk Bay 213
Birżebbuġa 214
Għar Dalam 215
Marsaxlokk 217
Delimara Point 219
Marsaskala and
St Thomas Bay 220
Inland: Żabbar, Żejtun
and Around 223
Żabbar 223
Tarxien, Paola and
the Temples 225
Luqa 228
Gudja, Għaxaq and
Around 229
Żejtun 230

**12** Mdina, Rabat and
the Inland Towns **233**
**Mdina and Rabat** 234
Mdina City Sights 237
Rabat 246
**Mosta and Naxxar** 252
Mosta 252
Naxxar and San Pawl
tat-Tarġa 253
**Birkirkara, the Three Villages
and Żebbuġ** 255
Birkirkara 255
The Three Villages 257
Żebbuġ 259

**13** Gozo and Comino **263**
**Victoria (Rabat)** 269
The Citadel 270
Outside the Citadel 273
**North of Victoria** 276
Xagħra 276
Żebbuġ 280
**West of Victoria** 282
San Lawrenz 282
Fungus Rock and
Dwejra Bay 282
Għarb 284
Għasri, Għammar and
Ta'Pinu 286
**South of Victoria** 288

Kerċem and Santa Lucija 288
Sannat and Munxar 288
Xlendi 290
Xewkija 291
Mġarr ix-Xini 292
**East of Victoria** 293
Mġarr and Għajnsielem 293
Qala 296
Nadur 296
**Comino (Kemmuna)** 300
What to see on Comino 301

**14** Trips to Ionian
Sicily **305**
Syracuse 307
Catania and Mount Etna 312
Catania 312
Mount Etna 314
Taormina 316

# Reference

**15** Language **320**
**16** Glossary **322**
**17** Chronology **323**
**18** Architects and
Artists **325**
**19** Further Reading **327**
**20** Index **329**

## Maps and Plans

Malta, Comino and Gozo
*inside front cover*
Chapter Divisions 4
Malta's Military History:
Two Walks 20–1
Bus Routes in Malta 70–1
Around Valletta 96
Valletta 102
St John's Co-Cathedral 106
Grand Master's Palace 114
Floriana 125
Senglea (L'Isla) 134
Vittoriosa (Birgu) 137
The Northeast Coast 146
Sliema and St Julian's 153
The North Coast 168
St Paul's Bay and
Buġibba 172–3
Southwest Coast 192–3
Around Dingli 195
Ħaġar Qim 201
Mnajdra 203
The South 212
Tarxien 227
Mdina, Rabat and the
Inland Towns 234
Mdina 238
St Paul's Cathedral 241
Mdina and Rabat 247
Gozo and Comino 264–5
Victoria (Rabat) 271
Ġgantija 277
Ionian Sicily 306
Colour Touring Maps
*end of guide*

# History

*Malta's Military History: Two Walks* 20
*c. 5000–c. 800 BC: Prehistory* 22
*c. 800–218 BC: Phoenician and
    Carthaginian Periods* 23
*218 BC –AD 318: The Roman Period* 24
*AD 318–1090: The Byzantine and Arab
    Periods* 24
*The Medieval Period: 1090–1530* 24
*1530–1798: The Order of the Knights
    of St John in Malta* 26
*1798–1800: The French* 33
*1800–1939: British Colonial Rule* 34
*1939–45: The Second World War* 35
*1945–64: After the Second World War
    to Independence* 37
*1964–the Present: The Democratic
    Republic of Malta* 37

O2

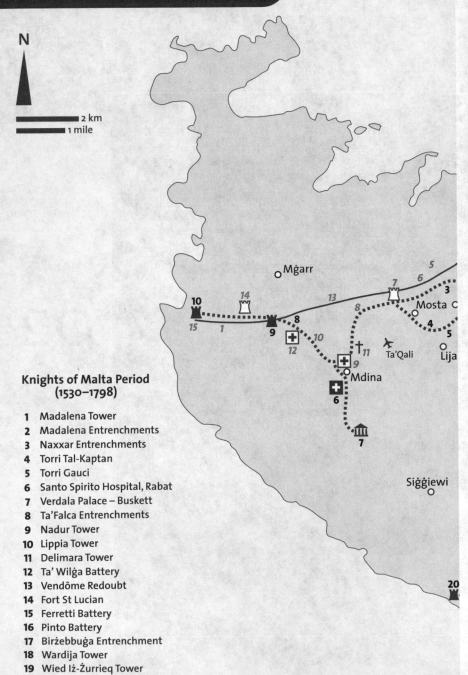

N

2 km
1 mile

Mġarr

Mosta

Ta'Qali

Lija

Mdina

Siġġiewi

## Knights of Malta Period (1530–1798)

1  Madalena Tower
2  Madalena Entrenchments
3  Naxxar Entrenchments
4  Torri Tal-Kaptan
5  Torri Gauci
6  Santo Spirito Hospital, Rabat
7  Verdala Palace – Buskett
8  Ta'Falca Entrenchments
9  Nadur Tower
10  Lippia Tower
11  Delimara Tower
12  Ta' Wilġa Battery
13  Vendôme Redoubt
14  Fort St Lucian
15  Ferretti Battery
16  Pinto Battery
17  Birżebbuġa Entrenchment
18  Wardija Tower
19  Wied Iż-Żurrieq Tower
20  Ħamrija Tower

## British Period (1800–1964)

1 Victoria Lines–NW Front
2 Fort Madalena
3 San Giovanni Battery
4 Gharghur High Angle Battery
5 Sound Mirror–Maghtab
6 Nuclear Underground Command Centre
7 Fort Mosta
8 Targa Battery
9 Connaught Hospital, Mdina
10 St David's Barracks–Mtarfa
11 Mtarfa/Ta'Qali Cemetery
12 Mtarfa Hospital
13 Dwejra Lines
14 Fort Binġemma
15 Fomm ir-Riħ Redoubt
16 St Paul's Battery
17 Fort Tas-Silġ
18 Wolseley Battery
19 Fort Delimari
20 Delimari Lighthouse
21 Fort St Lucian
22 Fort Bengħisa
23 Wied Żnuber Stop Wall and Field Defences
24 Ħas-Sabtan Underground Fuel Depot

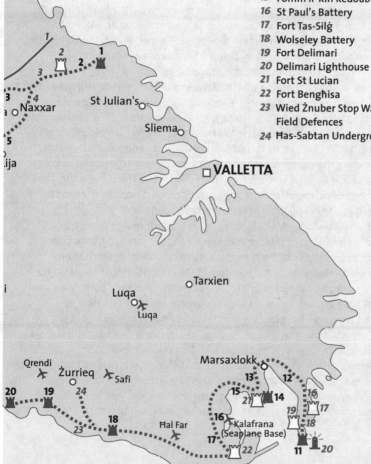

> *The oldest free-standing structures in the world are now believed to be*
> *the megalithic temples at Mġarr and Skorba in Malta. With those at*
> *Ġgantija in Gozo they date from c. 3250 BC.*
>                                    *The Guinness Book of Records, 1998*

# c. 5000–c. 800 BC

## Prehistory

Malta is rich in prehistoric remains. The first period of its prehistory began 10–12,000 years ago when the islands became separated from Sicily and the continental European landmass, at the very beginning of the current Holocene era. The first human inhabitation of the archipelago probably occurred some 7,000 years ago in the **Neolithic period**; there are early pottery relics from the **Skorba phases** in the Museum of Archaeology, Valletta.

The most active settlements established themselves during the long **Temple phase** of the Copper Age, which lasted from c. 4100 BC to c. 2500 BC. Man then would have been no more than a simple subsistence farmer who garnered his vital materials, such as obsidian, from neighbouring Sicily. Yet this civilization constructed the great structures like Ġgantija on Gozo.

The last phase in the Copper Age was the **Tarxien phase**, when the structures at Tarxien were built, and it was the most elaborate. (As the Tarxien phase was ending, c. 2600 BC, the Great Pyramid in Egypt was being constructed – up to 1,000 years after Ġgantija.) The Temple phase, with its idolatrous 'Fat' divinities (possibly symbolizing fertility), came to an abrupt and possibly fiery end soon afterwards. Theories regarding the sudden disappearance of this clever and religious culture range from invasion to mass suicide. There is no evidence of the subsequent, far less artistic and skilled inhabitants having had any connection with the peoples of the Temple phase – they appeared as if from another civilization.

The third and last period in Malta's prehistory is the **Bronze Age**. Bronze, a man-made alloy fused out of molten lead, copper and tin, came to Malta from the eastern Mediterranean. Its discovery revolutionized weaponry, habitation and agriculture here as elsewhere. Little is known of the civilization that occupied the islands over this 1,700-year period until c. 800 BC; similar pieces of pottery, weapons and jewellery have been found as far afield as Greece and southern Italy.

The **Tarxien Cemetery phase** (during which Stonehenge was built in Britain) marked the introduction of cremation. During the later **Borġ in-Nadur** and **Baħrija phases** man began to display more hostile intentions, building fortified hilltop settlements and starting to move about the island. (The mysterious cart ruts which appear on parts of the island date from the Baħrija phase.) By 800–700 BC a primitive society capable of self-sufficiency seems to have evolved, but also appeared ready to embrace new ideas from the larger exploring cultures of the Near East.

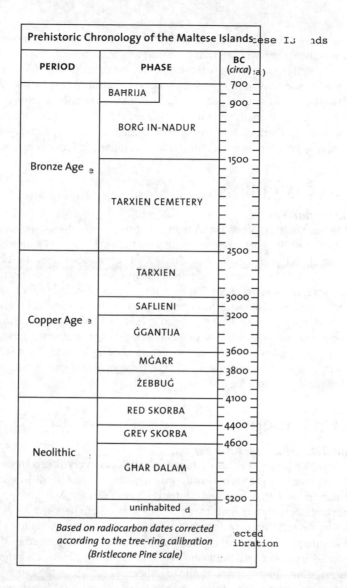

| Prehistoric Chronology of the Maltese Islands | | |
|---|---|---|
| PERIOD | PHASE | BC (circa) |
| Bronze Age | BAĦRIJA | 700 — 900 — |
| | BORĠ IN-NADUR | |
| | | 1500 — |
| | TARXIEN CEMETERY | |
| | | 2500 — |
| Copper Age | TARXIEN | |
| | SAFLIENI | 3000 — 3200 — |
| | ĠGANTIJA | |
| | MĠARR | 3600 — 3800 — |
| | ŻEBBUĠ | |
| Neolithic | RED SKORBA | 4100 — |
| | GREY SKORBA | 4400 — 4600 — |
| | GĦAR DALAM | |
| | uninhabited | 5200 — |

*Based on radiocarbon dates corrected according to the tree-ring calibration (Bristlecone Pine scale)*

# c. 800–218 BC

## Phoenician and Carthaginian Periods

The Phoenicians were bold yet peaceful traders from the Near and Middle East, what is roughly Lebanon today. From c. 1200 BC they began plying their routes through the Mediterranean, exporting Tyrian purple cloth, timber and jewellery while in pursuit of treasures like tin from the rich seams of Cornwall. By 800 BC they had established trading outposts in Birgu (Vittoriosa) and the Grand Harbour.

It was at this time that Malta was first christened *maleth*, which is Phoenician for 'a place of shelter, or haven', and it is from the Phoenician language that Malti has evolved. With the ascendancy of Carthage in North Africa during the 6th century BC, the Phoenician hold waned. Malta became a vital naval base for the **Carthaginians** just as Sicily had been for their enemy, the Greeks, some 200–300 years earlier. The Romans first sacked Malta in 257 BC during the First Punic War. Thereafter, the Carthaginians reoccupied the islands until the Second Punic War in 218 BC when the Roman consul Tiberius Sempronius ended their colonization.

## 218 BC–AD 318

### The Roman Period

The Romans left more of a mark than the previous incumbents; they brought prosperity, albeit under a Roman yoke, during their 536-year occupation but left scant archaeological remains. Malta settled into a European base, one it has never really left, and the island became famous for its honey, cloth and sailcloth. Despite the wholesale pillaging by the Roman Praetor **Verres** (73–71 BC) the island enjoyed peace as a Roman adjunct to Sicily; both Julius Caesar and Augustus invoked laws aimed at helping their colonies, and during Hadrian's reign (AD 117–38) Malta and Gozo were made *municipia*. The single-most important occurrence during Rome's occupation was **St Paul**'s arrival, however unplanned, in AD 60. He and **St Luke** sowed the seeds of Christianity, and converted Roman Governor **Publius** who subsequently became the first bishop of Malta.

## AD 318–1090

### The Byzantine and Arab Periods

The **Dark Ages** are particularly murky in Malta's case. Very little is known of those who occupied the islands or how they were governed. After the division of the Roman Empire into Eastern and Western Empires in AD 395, Malta fell under **Constantinople** (Byzantium) in the east. The **Arab caliphs** deposed the Byzantines in AD 870, 238 years after the death of the Prophet Mohammed. Initially it was a peaceful period, with Christians and Muslims living amicably together. The Maltese adopted aspects of Arab culture (many converted to Islam), including their language and agricultural skills, and together they carried on the earnest trade of slaving. Yet Arab heritage is scant on the islands: essentially they reduced the walls of Mdina, and fortified Birgu (Vittoriosa).

## The Medieval Period: 1090–1530

*Norman 1090–1194, Swabian (Germans) 1194–1266, Angevin (French) 1266–83, Aragonese and Castilian (Spanish) 1283–1530*

Medieval, in historical terms, usually refers to the 1,000-year period from the abdication of Romulus Augustulus in AD 476 to the fall of Constantinople and the

Turkish Empire in 1453. Malta's medieval period is far shorter but extends to the arrival of the Order of St John in 1530.

**Count Roger the Norman** took the islands from the Arabs in 1090, annexing them to his recent conquest of Sicily, just 24 years after his fellow countryman, William, conquered England. (Folklore tells how Roger, needing the help of the Maltese citizens, tore his quartered red-and-white banner in half, thus creating the Maltese flag of today.) He immediately introduced a tripartite feudal system of State, Church and Nobility, all subject to the whim of the ruling fief. Thus, providing the taxes were paid, Malta now enjoyed a hitherto unknown degree of independence; and in spite of their Christian overlord the people remained basically Muslim. The country only began to adopt European mores after a genealogical dispute between the Normans and Swabians made the **Swabian Frederick II** (head of the House of Hohenstaufen) King Frederick I of Sicily in 1197 as well as Holy Roman Emperor. As the new Holy Roman Emperor, Frederick paid little attention to Malta, using it at one time as a penal colony – in 1223 he shipped the entire population of the Italian town of Celano to Malta after its feudal lord committed high treason. Towards the end of his 53-year reign (1197–1250) he indulged in his own brand of 'ethnic cleansing' by expelling Muslims from the islands for ever.

In 1266 **Manfred**, the last of the Swabian kings, was killed in battle by **Charles of Anjou**, brother of Louis IX and King of Naples and Sicily. Thus the Kingdom of Sicily, and therefore Malta, passed to the **French**. This was unfortunate, for as a ruler Charles was half tyrannical despot, half simply mad. Mercifully, the Angevin rule of Malta lasted a mere 17 years. Charles was defeated at sea off Malta by Peter of Aragon's fleet the year after the calamitous uprising of 1282, known as the **Sicilian Vespers**; **Peter of Aragon** was then crowned King of Sicily by a grateful people.

Under the **Aragonese**, Malta remained a fief and not a part of crown land; it became no more than an outsize gaming chip, passed around, mortgaged and bartered among Spanish nobles. The patent disregard the Aragonese had for the overtaxed and exploited islands and their people led to an increase in the already frequent corsair slaving raids. However, the first Maltese noble was created under the Aragonese in 1350, and towards the end of the 14th century both Malta and Gozo established a local governing body, the Università, the head of which, the Hakem or Captain of the Rod, was appointed by the Sicilian monarch. How effective it was at dealing with anything other than local matters is debatable; feudal overlords were rarely interested in the plight of serfs.

In 1412 the Aragonese line became extinct, and the islands passed to the **Castilian Spanish**, but very little changed – the island was still mostly pawn or prey. On one occasion in 1419, and at the request of the Università, **Alphonso V** raised a wine tax to pay for a fort on Comino in an attempt to stem the corsair raids. Yet having collected the money he absconded with it, and the very next year hocked the islands to the Sicilian **Don Antonio Cardona** for 30,000 gold florins. Eight years later in 1428, Alphonso V visited Malta and accepted that the islands would forever remain in the royal domain. In 1436, 10 new parishes were formed, but, until and after the arrival of the Order of St John in 1530, the islands continued to be plagued by famine, North African corsairs, Turks and pestilence.

# 1530–1798

## The Order of the Knights of St John in Malta

Alphonso V's promise in 1428 to maintain Malta as part of the Spanish Empire in perpetuity was broken by his descendant Charles V. In the same way, the Order quickly forswore L'Isle Adam's promise to the Maltese to uphold their interests and nobility. For the Order, Malta was initially somewhere to regroup before attempting to retake the verdant island of Rhodes. A series of Christian defeats shattered all the knights' illusions, however, and so they proceeded to make Malta as safe and congenial a home as possible.

In the ensuing 25 years, while the Maltese aristocracy sulked in Mdina and the knights fortified Birgu, the **Turks** had virtually free run of the central Mediterranean. **Dragut Rais**, Suleyman's de facto mercenary, kept up his marauding ways and in one attack in 1551 depopulated Gozo, hauling 5,000 into slavery. Later that same year, the Order ignominiously lost its unwanted base at Tripoli to Dragut Rais and **Sinan Pasha**. Morale was at a very low ebb by the time de la Valette assumed the magistracy in 1557. Two years later, in a catastrophic attempt to capture Dragut's base, the island of Djerba off the North African coast, the Order and its Christian allies lost over half their fleet; the forces of Islam effectively had won the battle for the central Mediterranean. All that stood in their way was a puny garrison on the obscure sandstone rock of Malta.

### History of the Order Before 1530

The **Order of St John of Jerusalem**, the oldest chivalric Order, was established in 1048 by a group of pious Italian merchants from Amalfi. Its sole purpose was to provide a nursing hospital for the increasing number of pilgrims visiting the Holy Sepulchre in Jerusalem, then a part of the Caliphate of Egypt. It was not until 1099, after the successful **First Crusade** had wrested Jerusalem back, that the nursing brothers began to assume a military role. In 1104 King Baldwin I of Jerusalem offered them land, and in 1113 Pope Paschal II formally recognized the constitution of the **Knights Hospitallers** in a bull and conferred upon them papal protection. (The original bull is in the Bibliotheca in Valletta.)

Under their first leader, Raymond du Puy (1125–58), the transformation from hospitaller to warrior was made; the knights went into battle wearing their distinctive tunics of a white cross emblazoned against a scarlet background – 'the white cross of peace in the bloodstained field of war'. In the 12th and 13th centuries they fought alongside the kings of Jerusalem during the **Second and Third Crusades**. In the course of the bloody Third Crusade of 1191, **Richard Cœur de Lion** took Acre, 80 miles (130km) from Jerusalem on the shores of the east Mediterranean, and the Order established itself there for nearly 100 years. But the rearguard action the Christians waged against the forces of Islam was doomed: the knights were defeated at Acre in 1291 in the last battle of the Crusades and sought refuge in Cyprus, a sojourn that lasted until they captured Rhodes in 1310.

For nearly 200 years the Order of St John fortified **Rhodes** and harried the Turks with needling consistency. The potpourri of intermarried European royalty nurtured its growth (after the suppression of the Knights Templars the mercenary aristocrats of St John were the only effective force preventing Islam from infiltrating westwards). Consequently its wealth and status grew, it developed a navy and strengthened its internal organization. After the **fall of Byzantine Constantinople** to the Turkish Sultan, Mahomet II, in 1453, the **Turks** turned their attention to Rhodes. Their first attempt at invasion in 1480 was repulsed, but the second in 1522 succeeded following a fierce six-month siege. **Grand Master de L'Isle Adam** extracted terms for an honourable surrender from the young Turkish Sultan, Suleyman I (son of Selim the Grim), also known as Suleyman the Magnificent. On 1 January 1523 the Grand Master, 180 knights and upwards of 4,000 Rhodians set sail like refugees for an unknown destination.

For nearly eight years Grand Master de L'Isle Adam knocked on the doors of Europe's rulers. Henry VIII promised the Order 20,000 crowns and Pope Clement VIII gave it temporary refuge in Viterbo. Eventually the shrewd and self-motivated **Charles V**, emperor of Spain, offered them permanent sanctuary in Malta, providing they also assumed the burdensome defence of Tripoli. The Order sent a delegation to recce the island, and received a dismal report: infertile, barren, lacking in water, marauded by corsairs, difficult to defend and populated by 12,000 impoverished people. Yet, with no alternative in sight, de L'Isle Adam accepted the territories as the Order's perpetual sovereign domain. The annual rent was none too steep: a peregrine falcon to be presented annually on All Saints' Day to Charles V's Sicilian viceroy. The **Act of Donation** was signed in April 1530 (it too is in the Bibliotheca's archives in Valletta), and the Order dropped anchor in the Grand Harbour in October of that year.

## The Great Siege of 1565

*If the Turks should prevail against the Isle of Malta it is uncertain what further peril might follow to the rest of Christendom.*
Queen Elizabeth I, 1565

In the theatre of Christian-Muslim attrition that gripped the Mediterranean during the 16th century, Malta, with its vanguard of chivalrous knights, was centre stage. **Grand Master de la Valette** was a perspicacious man: sooner or later, he surmised, the now septuagenarian **Suleyman the Magnificent** would wish to extinguish the Order before he died (something Suleyman regretted not doing 43 years earlier at Rhodes). On the morning of 18 May 1565 the finest Muslim forces, marshalled from every corner of Suleyman's empire, hove into view over the horizon. A formidable armada of 181 ships under the command of Admiral Piali contained a mighty army (in excess of 35,000 warriors) under the command of **Mustapha Pasha**. De la Valette had been able to muster 541 knights and servants-at-arms, a brave but untrained Maltese militia of about 4,500 and a regiment of 1,200 Spanish and Italian foot soldiers; with the other conscripts and slaves his forces totalled 8,500–9,000 men in all. His request to the Sicilian viceroy, Don Garcia de Toledo, for 15,000 reinforcements went initially unheeded. De la Valette had time enough to poison the island's few water wells and harvest the crops before he and his Maltese subjects shut the gates of Birgu, L'Isla and Mdina on that late spring morning and settled down to wait.

From the very first day of the campaign, the Turks were hampered by the fiercest of military enemies: bad luck, petty jealousies and a split command. Suleyman had foolishly divided the command between Admiral Piali and Mustapha Pasha. Fortunately for the knights, Suleyman's military mentor and long-time scourge of Malta, Dragut Rais, was delayed in North Africa. With a long summer ahead, Admiral Piali argued against Mustapha Pasha's wise strategy of attacking Mdina and Birgu overland from the south. Piali demanded the safe haven of Marsamxett for his prized fleet, an obsession which bedevilled the entire campaign, and which meant storming Fort St Elmo first.

When the octogenarian Dragut Rais finally arrived on 2 June with his own band of 1,500 mercenaries, he found a disastrous plan hindered in its execution by a quarrelling and split command. Quickly he galvanized the Turkish troops and, knowing it was too late to withdraw from the attack on St Elmo, established further gun emplacements. The siege of Fort St Elmo carried on relentlessly until, after 31 days of continuous bombardment, it fell on 23 June, the eve of the feast of John the Baptist, the Order's patron saint. Vignettes of the brutality of the siege emerged: the fanatical, hashish-fuelled warriors were slaughtered in such numbers in their repeated assaults on the fort that their corpses became bridges of putrefying flesh; Mustapha Pasha beheaded four knights and placed their torsos on crosses to float across the Grand Harbour; in retaliation de la Valette fired the heads of Turk prisoners from his cannons. Most disastrous of all (for the Turks) was Dragut Rais's accidental death from a rock splinter, which marked the turning point of the siege, in which no quarter was asked, nor ever given.

The Turks continued to pound away at Forts St Angelo and St Michael during the sweltering summer months; the capture of St Elmo at the cost of 8,000 men had just been a Pyrrhic victory. Finally, on 7 September, the meagre and long overdue relief force of 8,000 men arrived from the dilatory viceroy of Sicily, **Don Garcia de Toledo**. The rout of the Turks was completed the following day in a final bloody pitched battle in the shallows of St Paul's Bay. The Turks had lost 30,000 men and of the original 9,000-strong Christian garrison just 600 were standing and able to bear arms. But the toll went far beyond the horror of the mere death count. For the Turkish Empire it marked the beginning of the end; the loss of prestige was immense and its subsequent defeat by the Holy Alliance forces at the Battle of Lepanto in 1571, where 197 of its ships were destroyed, was one from which they were never to recover. Suleyman the Magnificent died in battle the following year while besieging a Hungarian city, both Mustapha Pasha and Piali returned to the Levant and were spared, and Don Garcia faded ignominiously from history. De la Valette died peacefully three years later in his chapel in Fort St Angelo, fêted as a hero by all Europe.

## The Knights of the Order of St John: The Constitution

### The Sovereign Military and Hospitaller Order of St John of Jerusalem of Rhodes and Malta

The **Convent** or official seat (be it in Acre, Rhodes or Malta) held the corpus of the Order. Three principal ranks existed within the Order to mirror its three principal vocations: military, religious and medical – the **Knights of Justice**, the **conventual chaplains** and the **servants-at-arms**. At the head presided the **grand master**, elected for life by his fellow knights within three days of his predecessor's death.

A **Knight of Justice** not only had to be of noble Catholic birth but also had to deliver 'proofs' of his maternal and paternal purity, with 4–16 quarterings. (The Italians were the least strict, with four quarterings lest the 'proofs' revealed too much illegitimacy; while the Teutonic temperament of the Germans forbade admittance even to papal and royal bastards, who were allowed in the other *langues*.) Having been accepted as a novice, a young knight would reside in the *auberge* or hall of residence of his *langue*, and serve a total of five years at the Convent. During these years he had to serve in at least six **caravans** (tours of duty), two a year, in the galleys. Upon the completion of his novitiate the young nobleman attended his investiture at the feet of the grand master. Only after the solemn mass at which he swore oaths of Obedience, Poverty and Chastity did he receive his eight-pointed cross on a black mantle (symbolizing the camel skin worn by the Order's patron saint, John the Baptist) and become a Knight of Justice.

Further down the hierarchy, the **conventual chaplains** who served in the galleys, hospitals and churches had only to prove they were of legitimate and gentle birth and unconnected with 'any vile mechanic business'. **Servants-at-arms** simply had to show legitimate birth and were allowed to serve in a military or secretarial capacity. Further honorary ranks such as **Knight of Grace** were held within the gift of the grand master.

Apart from the conventual church, hospital and other public buildings of this sovereign state, the Convent accommodated what were initially the eight *langues* of knights: of Provence, Auvergne, France, Italy, Aragon, Castile et Leon (once a part of Aragon), Germany and England. Each had its own *auberge*. (After Henry VIII's reformation in 1540 the English *langue* disbanded.) At the head of each was the *pilier*, who also held a high-ranking post within the Order. The *pilier* of the Italian *langue* was also the admiral of the fleet and the *pilier* of Provence was the Order's treasurer. Each *langue* owned properties in its territory and the revenues paid to the Order were called *responsions*. A knight was bound by statute to leave four-fifths of his entire wealth to the Order, but was free to dispose of his quint or one-fifth. Thus the Order grew wealthy from the coffers of European aristocracy.

A newly created knight was at liberty to return to his own country or to remain in the Convent and become eligible to vie for promotion and a position in any of the Order's more than 500 *commanderies*. The larger of these were called **priories** and the smaller **bailiwicks** and *commanderies*. The heads of the *commanderies* held corresponding ranks of priors, bailiffs and commanders. If, on the other hand, a knight chose to return to his own estates he must, if summoned by the grand master in times of threat, make immediate haste to the aid of the Convent. The grand master enjoyed the status and prerogatives of a ruling sovereign. He presided over four separate governing councils responsible for all financial, judicial, religious and military matters. The supreme governing and legislative authority lay in the **Chapter-General**. Headed by the grand master, it comprised the *piliers* of each *langue*, the bishop and other senior distinguished knights, or **Knights Grand Cross**, and could only be convened by either the Pope or the grand master.

The Order still exists today under Grand Master Andrew Bertie, a Scot, and it maintains its seat in Rome as well as an embassy in Valletta. It concentrates on charitable and hospitalling works around the world.

## After the Great Siege: 1565–1798

*The knights neglected to live, but were prepared to die, in the service of Christ.*
Edward Gibbon (1737–94)

The Order had locked the forces of Islam in their eastern Mediterranean basin, and in the euphoric aftermath of the Great Siege contemporary Maltese history begins. In a fit of grateful munificence the Pope and the crowned heads of Europe, including a Protestant Queen Elizabeth I, showered the already wealthy Order with financial rewards. Within six years the knights' new fortified city, **Valletta**, was built. Prosperity came to Malta during the Order's subsequent 233-year reign: new agricultural skills were learnt and new industries created; the population increased fivefold to 100,000; it became a trading post and Europe's largest slave market; and the rich knights spent famously on towns, palaces and defences. Perversely, the Order's victory over its Islamic enemy – its *raison d'être* for so long – combined with subsequent affluence, brought about a cancer which led to its downfall.

## A Succession of Grand Masters

Grand Master de la Valette died in 1568, leaving **Grand Master del Monte** (1568–72) to inaugurate the new city in 1571. His successor, the very pious and aged **Grand Master de la Cassière** (1572–81), was perhaps the first to identify the hazards that lay ahead for a religious order without a real enemy. Offended by the spread of Protestantism, he tried to reaffirm the monastic traditions and counter the exuberant and unmonastic behaviour of the young knights who had replenished the Order's ranks. In desperation he turned to the Pope, who saddled the Order with an inquisitor in an attempt to stamp out those who chose not to obey their vows of Obedience, Poverty and Chastity. De la Cassière still found time to build and pay for St John's Co-Cathedral and the Sacra Infermeria. After his death in Rome he was succeeded by one of the more colourful grand masters, the French **de Verdalle** (1581–95), who was the first to take his sovereign position to heart and to enjoy its trappings. Resolutely hedonistic, he interpreted the enlightenment of his people to mean extra candles at his lavish banquets. He reigned supremely yet shrewdly and was able to marry his lavish tastes with the more tempered ones of his church: he built for himself the Verdala Palace, commissioned his own galley for privateering and still ingratiated himself with Pope Sixtus V who appointed him a cardinal (the only one in the Order's history). But his 14-year reign was unsettled: he curtailed the powers of the Università, endured factional disputes between the different *langues*, reacted to a new Turkish threat by building the two Cavaliers of St John and St James in Valletta, and stood by while 15 per cent of the population was wiped out by bubonic plague. **Grand Master Garzes** (1595–1601) was the opposite – a humble peace-loving man who cared for the poor. His suit of armour is on display in the Palace Armoury.

By the time that **Alof de Wignacourt** (1601–22) assumed the magistracy, Valletta's population was the same as it is today, and the much-needed aqueduct from Rabat to Valletta was one of the many projects he undertook. The 21-year reign of this tall handsome man was marked by humility and compassion. He founded the Monte di Rendenzione degli Schiavi to ransom Christian slaves and built the island's most impressive forts, St Lucian, St Thomas and St Mary's, to guard against the still-prevalent corsair raids. His magnificent suit of armour is displayed in the Palace Armoury and his portrait hangs in the Grand Master's Palace (a Caravaggio portrait of him is in the Louvre). **Grand Master de Vasconcellos** (1622–3) was all but dead when he succeeded de Wignacourt; well into his eighties, he only lasted a matter of months. Another Frenchman with opulent, almost corrupt tastes was **de Paule** (1623–36) who built the San Anton Palace as a summer retreat for hosting none-too-religious gatherings. Fearing a Turkish invasion, he commenced the building of the Floriana Lines and, despite his high living, he too reigned until ripe: he died aged 84.

In spite of the constant threat of a major Turkish invasion, the 17th century was essentially one of peace for Malta. In 1614 the last Turkish raid took place, and from then on only the piratical incursions of the Barbary corsairs had to be tolerated. Yet it was not so for Europe: France and Spain were at war, creating problems for the neutral Order and the *langues* of those countries, while Venice was locked in a fierce struggle with the Turks.

Pug-faced **Grand Master Lascaris** (1636–57) brought a strong measure of puritanism to an idle Order and began the building of defences known as the Margherita Lines. He too hung on to power, eventually relinquishing it at the age of 97. The deterrent effect of the Valletta fortifications helped maintain the peace, and as the century progressed subsequent grand masters strategically reinforced the coastline, thereby encouraging the Maltese to settle the countryside.

Lascaris's Spanish successor, **de Redin** (1657–60), built a series of towers, many of which still stand. **Grand Master Gessan** reigned for a matter of weeks in 1660. The Spanish **Cotoner** brothers, **Rafael** (1660–63) and **Nicolas** (1663–80) commenced, and were nearly bankrupted by, the construction of vast defences known as the Cottonera Lines; they also improved the Sacra Infermeria after a plague which left 12,000 dead. More famously, the brothers commissioned the splendid Baroque vault frescoes by Mattia Preti in St John's Co-Cathedral.

Cotoner's Neapolitan successor **Grand Master Carafa** (1680–90) was a sprightly 66 when elected and was part of the European Alliance which defeated the Turks and forced the abdication of Sultan Mohammed IV. In 1693, during the reign of Alof de Wignacourt's nephew, **Adrien** (1690–97), a cataclysmic earthquake destroyed much of Ionian Sicily, Malta and Gozo.

The Aragonese **Grand Master Perellos** (1697–1720) rebuilt the cathedral in Mdina, one of the finest examples of the local Baroque idiom. Apart from displaying an artistic flair (he acquired the exquisite Gobelin tapestries in the Grand Master's Palace and those in St John's Co-Cathedral), this cultured and good-looking man modernized the Order's navy. His reign ushered in what proved to be for the Order a fateful 18th century.

## The Decline of the Order

By the time of Perellos's death in 1720, the Order had shifted imperceptibly into final decline. Womanizing, drinking, duelling and an unparallelled ostentation had fully supplanted the ideals founded in the Holy Lands; its consciousness of militant Catholicism had expired and its very fabric had become a sham. The knights were now an embarrassing anachronism to all save their equally morally bankrupt protectors, the Popes in Rome. They had become an exotic central Mediterranean police force. Their navy helped to good effect in the Venetian-Turkish war of 1715–18, but mostly it just roamed the sea in search of a diminishing stock of corsairs.

Pope Alexander VII was once an inquisitor in Malta. His nephew, **Grand Master Zondadari** (1720–2), succeeded Perellos and attempted to develop the islands into an entrepôt for trade. His two-year reign was followed by 14 years under the aristocratic Portuguese **de Vilhena**. This wealthy and popular aesthete zealously built many magnificent buildings such as Fort Manoel, the Manoel Theatre and the Palazzo Vilhena.

When de Vilhena died in 1736, King Philip V of Spain's son, the Bourbon **Charles VIII**, united Naples and Sicily and crowned himself the autonomous king of the newly created Kingdom of the Two Sicilies; so Spain no longer had direct administration over what was in effect Malta's breadbasket, Sicily.

Following the somewhat uneventful reign of the Majorcan **Ramon Despuig** (1736–41) was the long 32-year reign of another Iberian, the Portuguese **Grand Master Pinto** (1741–73). The pompous but crafty Pinto assumed considerably more regal airs and traits than the kings of England and France combined, and it was during his tenure at the Grand Master's Palace that the Order's death knell sounded; this, however, went unheard. His self-aggrandizement knew no bounds: for evidence look at either the evocative portrait by de Favray in the sacristy at St John's Co-Cathedral or the strikingly ebullient façade he commissioned for his Auberge de Castile et Leon.

Pinto was not a man to be content with mere titles, so he tried to acquire Corsica from the Genoese in 1763; this shrewd ruse was designed to reduce Malta's dependence on Sicily, and also to enhance his standing with those whom he considered his peers, the monarchs of Europe. Despite much haggling, a price could not be agreed upon and the French bought it in 1768, just one year before the Order's nemesis, **Napoleon Bonaparte**, was born there.

Pinto's despised Spanish successor, **Grand Master Ximenes** (1773–5), struggled along for only two years; his legacy after a third of a century of Pinto's despotism was an empty treasury and an understandably resentful population. Following a commonplace disagreement between the Order and the Maltese clergy, there was a feeble but nevertheless symbolic rebellion in 1775, known as 'the Priests' Revolt'; Ximenes executed the ringleaders. Later that year, but too late to save the Order, the wise and cautious French aristocrat **de Rohan** (1775–97) was elected to the magistracy. He immediately convened a Chapter-General, the first since de Paule's reign 144 years earlier, and put in place a new municipal code, laws and statutes to alleviate tension; the ordinary Maltese had grown weary of their self-destructive and arrogant rulers.

Financially and spiritually impoverished, the Order received its final blow in 1789 with the **French Revolution**. De Rohan, a staunch royalist, financed Louis XVI's unsuccessful flight to Varennes from France in 1791, which resulted in the confiscation of all the Order's French *commanderies* the next year; the *langues* of Auvergne, France and Provence contributed three-quarters of the Order's finances. The reforming and decent de Rohan died in 1797, convinced that he would be the very last grand master to reign in Malta.

Again, and unwittingly, Malta found itself at the centre of the Mediterranean stage. Turmoil and war lay in store for Europe, and the empires of Austria, France, the Two Sicilies, Russia and Britain, and America all watched each other nervously throughout the last decade of the 18th century. For Malta the situation was unique – while on previous occasions the island itself had been prized, its value now was strategic and lay in keeping the island out of the hands of the enemy, whoever that was. In 1797 a compliant, even simple, German – the first in the Order's history – **von Hompesch** (1797–8) was elected. Strapped for cash, this kindly man foolishly accepted **Tsar Paul I**'s offer of 72 *commanderies* to found a Russian Orthodox *langue*. Napoleon was enraged at this move, and while en route to his Egyptian campaign he anchored his incredible armada of 472 ships and 50,000 soldiers off the Grand Harbour; on 9 June 1798 he requested permission to water his ships. While an understandably intimidated von Hompesch vacillated, a fifth column of French knights brought months of subversive scheming into play.

Two days later, and with few shots fired at or from the greatest fortifications in Europe, von Hompesch was 'persuaded' to capitulate ignominiously. Terms were agreed aboard Napoleon's flagship *L'Orient*: the Order would be given three days to pack its possessions and leave, but the French knights were free to stay. The aggrieved and now deserted Maltese meanwhile were treated by the French to the same empty promises with regard to their own status as they had been many times before. Von Hompesch was given sanctuary in Russia, and as a force – nursing, religious or military – the Order was spent.

Ironically, the knights had fortified and defended themselves into provocation and near-extinction; the better and more lavish the defences, the more coveted the island. It was a prize England would not allow France to keep for long.

# 1798–1800

## The French

*I would rather see the British on the heights of Montmartre than in Malta.*

Napoleon

**Napoleon** stayed six days, about half as long as the average modern tourist's sojourn in Malta. Yet during that time he and his governor, **General Vaubois**, descended rather like a plague of republicanizing super-locusts; they despoiled churches, defaced escutcheons, looted *palazzi*, created havoc and basically stole anything that was not nailed to the floor. The Maltese population looked on helplessly.

Napoleon left with 268 years' worth of accumulated treasures and all the silver *L'Orient* could hold (Nelson sank it and its cache of plunder two months later in the Battle of the Nile). General Vaubois remained in charge of a timorously small garrison of 4,000 men. His first mistake, apart from promulgating unpopular new laws, was to upset the clergy. In the wake of an attempt to auction the treasures of the Carmelite church in Mdina, the oppressed Maltese spontaneously killed a French officer and began an **uprising** on 2 September 1798.

Vaubois and his garrison retreated into Valletta, and ironically the Maltese were the only ones ever to lay siege to de la Valette's fortress city. Assistance came from the **Portuguese navy** and the **British**, who were repairing their warships after Nelson's earlier victory at the Battle of the Nile; together their ships blockaded the harbours while the Anglo-Maltese forces attended to the landward front. Dispirited as he was by Napoleon's defeat in Egypt, it still took until 5 September 1800 for General Vaubois to be starved into surrender. In October, **Captain Alexander Ball** assumed temporary administrative responsibility for the islands on behalf of the British.

# 1800–1939

## British Colonial Rule

*Well, when the great cauldron of war is seething, and the nations stand round it striving to fish out something to their purpose from the mess, Britannia always has a great advantage in her trident. Malta is one of the titbits she has impaled with that awful implement.*

James Russell Lowell, 1854

The Treaty of Amiens of 1802 forged a fragile peace between France and England. It was agreed that the Maltese islands should be restored to the Order, a compromise both war-weary countries felt able to tolerate. The astonished Maltese, however, wanted none of it: a bankrupt and essentially leaderless Order could not offer the islands the stability they would have as a British colony. The recently knighted Sir Alexander Ball prevaricated (as the Order waited impatiently in Sicily), while trying to canvass support in London for Britain's de facto occupation of Malta. For 12 years Malta was in limbo as a quasi-British protectorate. The island's future was not officially clarified until Napoleon's abdication and the subsequent **Treaty of Paris** in 1814 when it was formally added to George III's growing list of colonial possessions. Malta's first British governor was **Sir Thomas Maitland**, known as 'King Tom' on account of his imperious manner. One of his first acts was to abolish the Università and bring certain laws into line with British jurisprudence.

For Malta the 19th century was uneventful, the islands simply reflecting the fluctuating fortunes of Britain and her empire. Similarly, the economy was inextricably linked to the naval base and garrison. The **Crimean War** (1854–6) brought a degree of prosperity, as did the opening of the **Suez Canal** in 1869. Defence spending increased with the new dock in French Creek and the construction of the Victoria Lines. As the century progressed the islands were slowly 'anglicized' and English joined Italian as the spoken language (Malti was still a local dialect). By the closing decades of the century Malta had become an important and flourishing coaling station for the imperial steamships plying between Britain and India.

Internal affairs were also of a roller-coaster nature. Ultimate authority rested in London, via the governor, but the beginning of the 19th century saw a flame lit under an erstwhile dormant Maltese political consciousness. The first of many attempts at giving the Maltese a restricted degree of autonomy was in 1835; further efforts were made in 1849 and 1887. All of the implemented local constitutions were argued over between London, Malta and the governor, and subsequently revoked.

At the turn of the 20th century the population approached 185,000. The **First World War** saw the island return to its Hospitaller roots when it became the 'nurse of the Mediterranean' and tended 25,000 sick and wounded from the Dardanelles. Economic and political tensions in an island ever vulnerable to the vicissitudes of war culminated in riots on 7 June 1919 when four Maltese were shot by British troops.

A new diarchic constitution was introduced in 1921: with a local Maltese government for Maltese affairs and an imperial one for foreign and military decisions, and a system of proportional representation (which still prevails today). However, after hiccuping through many trying coalitions and local dissensions, the constitution was again revoked by the British in 1930. It was restored two years later, only to have its mandate finally withdrawn in 1933 – certain strata of Maltese society were undecided if their allegiance lay with a conservative Britain or with a burgeoning fascist Italy.

# 1939–45

## The Second World War: The Second Great Siege

*To Honour her brave People I award the George Cross to the Island Fortress of Malta to bear witness to a Heroism and a Devotion that will long be famous in History.*
King George VI, 15 April 1942

The second Great Siege of Malta was to be a more drawn out and severe test of human resolve than the Turkish attempt in 1565. Both sieges were waged on Malta because it had the misfortune to be a strategic cog in the grand design of the oppressors at the time. Four hundred years on, the strategy of siege warfare had not changed: bomb the enemy mercilessly, cut off supplies and hope to starve the besieged into surrender. Although both campaigns ultimately failed, the Axis powers came perilously close to victory in the summer of 1942.

On 10 June 1940 **Mussolini** and his **Italian army** joined Hitler's war effort. By dawn the following morning Italian bombers were over Malta and the first casualties were incurred; poignantly, they fell at Fort St Elmo. In the six months remaining of 1940 there were 211 air-raid warnings, a modest foretaste of what lay in store.

Almost the sum total of the island's preparedness on 11 June was a few anti-aircraft guns, the antiquated guns of HMS *Terror* lying in Pieta Creek and four Gloucester Gladiator biplanes. Three of the planes, nicknamed Faith, Hope and Charity, flew; the fourth was cannibalized for spares. (Faith, the sole survivor, is on display in the War Museum in Valletta.) On that day the governor, **Lieutenant General Sir William Dobbie**, immediately implemented war restrictions on the population of 250,000 civilians and 30,000 military.

The Allied command had been divided over the fortress island's fate in the event of war; the Army and RAF favoured mass evacuation, while the Royal Navy, with 145 years' experience of Malta's strategic importance, advocated staying put; the Royal Navy's vote was carried solely due to **Winston Churchill**'s influence. Nonetheless, the procrastination meant that Malta was ill equipped to deal with the realities of modern aerial and marine warfare.

In the New Year of **1941**, the Italians were being routed in North Africa. In London the **War Office** had noted that Malta could be an effective base for offensive strikes against Axis shipping. But so too had the Axis high command: crack squadrons of the **German Luftwaffe** were stationed in Sicily and, with serious damage sustained to the HMS *Illustrious*, en route to the Allies' Mediterranean naval base at Alexandria, the conflict intensified. Mussolini's dispirited army of

130,000 was taken prisoner in February, the month **Field Marshal Rommel** assumed command of the North African campaign. Throughout the spring and summer the Allies used Malta like an aircraft carrier to harry Rommel's supply lines, but after the fall of Crete at the end of May the Malta–Alexandria supply line was almost cut off; the base for the convoys of supplies to the besieged island was then switched to Gibraltar.

Hitler's ultimately fatal **invasion of Russia** on 22 June, and the subsequent redeployment of the Luftwaffe, gave Malta a respite from the thrice-daily air raids; the total for 1941 was 963. In the autumn and winter months of that year Malta reached the peak of its disruptive powers and more Axis shipping was destroyed than ever before.

**Rommel**, despite the supply deprivations, enjoyed considerable success in the early months of 1942. Scenting a victory in the desert, the Axis command deployed more aircraft in Sicily; Malta had simply to be bombed and starved into submission. By the end of February 1942, *The Times of Malta* (the newspaper did not miss one day of publication throughout the siege) reported that there had been 80 days of almost continuous alert. In January and February alone there were 499 air-raid alerts and during six weeks of March and April 6,700 tons of bombs fell; Malta endured 157 days of continuous bombing (London had 57 during the 'Blitz'). From January to June (and for a long time thereafter), rationing was way below life-sustaining levels; the staple provisions for a family of two adults and three children for *one month* was: four 10oz (300g) tins of corned beef, four 3oz (100g) tins of fish, 11oz (330g) of rice, 6oz (200g) of sugar plus a daily bread ration of 48oz (1360g). Powdered milk, flour, fruit and eggs just did not exist. It was during this maelstrom of bombs and splintering limestone, when ammunition, food and kerosene were as scarce as typhoid, scurvy and amoebic dysentery were commonplace, that King George VI staged a morale-boosting coup: Malta and its population were awarded the **George Cross**, the highest British civilian award, on 15 April 1942.

In May, an ailing Governor (now Lord) Dobbie was replaced by **Field Marshal Viscount Gort VC**. One of Dobbie's last actions in office was to prepare an inventory of the remaining rations and set an August 'target date' when Malta would have to surrender unless a substantial convoy arrived. Ultimately, and ironically, it was the Allies' catastrophic loss of Tobruk to Rommel in June which saved Malta; the Axis high command blinked and scotched the planned invasion of Malta, 'Operation Herkules'. During this momentary lapse of concentration, the Allies were able to assemble the convoy which was to save the island, '**Operation Pedestal**'. Of the 14 heavily guarded merchantmen, only five made it into the Grand Harbour. (It became known as the Santa Marija convoy after the venerated 15 August *festa* of the Assumption when the final ship, the US oiler *Ohio*, limped into port.) Its comparative success forced the Axis powers to accept that Malta could and would now survive. Two months later, Rommel's February 1941 statement to Berlin, 'Without Malta, the Axis will end by losing control of North Africa', came true. The Axis lost the battle of **El Alamein** and with it North Africa. The cost to Malta had been enormous: from 1941 to 1942 alone there were 2,994 air-raid alerts (an average of over four a day), 30,000 buildings were destroyed, hundreds of thousands of tons of shipping were lost, as were many thousands of civilian and servicemen's lives.

There were better tidings in 1943. The Allies took Tripoli in January, and the final surrender of the Axis forces in North Africa came in May. Air raids still continued, though infrequently, and rations were very marginally increased. King George VI visited Malta and the Allies prepared for the planned invasion of Sicily, 'Operation Husky'; once again the island became a strategic aircraft carrier for over 30 squadrons of aircraft. Following the success of 'Operation Husky', Mussolini's downfall and the surrender of the Italian navy, Malta's role in the Second World War slipped into the shade, as the Allies' cloud began to blanket a hitherto Axis Europe.

# 1945–64

## After the Second World War to Independence

The British Government donated £30 million to help compensate the Maltese for the extensive war damage. The inventiveness demanded by the war years had turned many simple farmers into semiskilled manual workers. The combination of compensation and new skills provided a base for the post-war expansion. In September 1947, a new **constitution**, similar to the 1921 diarchal one, was introduced along with the vote for women. In the same year the flow of emigrants to North America and Australia began; today Maltese emigrants total one and a half times the island's entire population.

By the late 1950s the famous dockyards were economically unviable and had begun to outlive their usefulness to the British. In the 1962 elections the two principal parties (the Malta Labour Party and the Nationalist Party) both placed **independence** for Malta in their manifesto; when the population voted in favour, the Colonial Secretary in London had no alternative but to take heed. Malta was granted independence on 21 September 1964 but signed a ten-year **Mutual Defence Agreement** and remained a part of the **British Commonwealth**.

# 1964–the Present

## The Democratic Republic of Malta

From 1972 NATO and the British maintained a military presence which finally ended in 1979. Malta became a **democratic republic** in 1974 and today the islands are neutral and non-aligned. Malta joined the United Nations in 1964 and the Council of Europe in 1965. But with the demise of British colonial rule came a real need to establish an economy that could survive on its own (the only British financial involvement was the 'rent' paid for military installations and the money its servicemen spent locally). **Tourism** became an obvious target for development.

Politically the internal situation has been and is split almost equally between the ruling **Nationalist Party** (PN) and the **Malta Labour Party** (MLP); relative newcomers to the political arena are the **Green Party** (AD) who have yet to gain a seat in Parliament. The five-yearly elections are always closely run and passionately contested. Each of the first two parties has been in power for similar periods since independence, with the Labour Party, mainly under Mr Dom Mintoff (*see* pp.41–3), ruling continuously (and sometimes fractiously with Britain) for the period 1971–87.

Malta was the first of the new accession countries to hold a referendum on whether to join the **European Union** in 2003. Despite a reasonably clear-cut YES vote of 54 per cent, the NO camp claimed victory, somewhat bizarrely on the grounds that only 91 per cent voted, so the numbers of the electorate who registered a YES vote was just under half. Nevertheless, Malta joined the EU in 2004; it has five MEPs. The euro is to be adopted as the new currency, replacing the Maltese pound in January 2008.

# Topics

Driving 40
Of Churches 40
Dom Mintoff 41
A Little More about Local Politics 43
The Maltese Cross 44
The Festa 45
Hunting and Trapping 46
De la Valette and Dragut Rais 47
St Paul 49
The Eye of Osiris 52

03

# Driving

Local drivers have seven golden rules.

1. Wheels and a semblance of movement are enough to classify something as a vehicle. Age, condition and size of rust holes are immaterial.
2. Exclusive ownership of the road is included in the hire-purchase agreement.
3. Vehicles are fertility symbols and 200-decibel stereos are part of the mating ritual.
4. Once behind the wheel you are immortal. (Many roadside shrines attest to the fallacy of this belief.)
5. Noise is in direct proportion to speed.
6. Courtesy is a small township in the Australian Outback.
7. The Highway Code is something the Axis cracked in 1944; it has no bearing on driving in Malta.

# Of Churches

Venturing off the beaten track onto the even more beaten secondary tracks, you will encounter three contrasting insights into the Maltese and their sometimes bewildering relationship with their Church, as described below.

### Non Gode L'Immunità Ecclesiastica

A small marble tablet set into stone walls by the main door of many wayside chapels eloquently demonstrates how 'economical' interpretation of legal loopholes is not a recent phenomenon. Until the beginning of the 19th century the ecclesiastical authorities had temporal jurisdiction over all church buildings to the complete exclusion of the civil authorities. Wily criminals soon cottoned on to this, and in times of imminent arrest many hapless villains sought sanctuary in a nearby chapel. Understandably, the ecclesiastical authorities became concerned and withdrew these rights of sanctuary in respect of certain churches by affixing the *Non Gode* legends.

After Malta had become a British colony in the early 19th century, the British refused to tolerate the Church's compromise with this old custom, which still enabled old lags to seek refuge in *unmarked* buildings. So in 1828 Governor Sir Frederic Ponsonby proclaimed the end of rights to asylum, 'for wicked and profligate men have often been tempted to commit murders, robberies and similarly atrocious crimes in the hope of escaping punishment by taking refuge in such places'.

### Clocks

Many village churches have a clock affixed to one of their usual twin Baroque towers (invariably it was the only clock the villagers had). Aesthetically a second clock was needed to achieve the all-important symmetry of the building, but often by the time the new church had been completed (sometimes 30 years after work had begun) the parishioners' goodwill (and their purses) had long been exhausted. Frequently, the dilemma was resolved by painting a second *trompe l'œil* clock-face.

All have their hands set steadfastly a few minutes before midnight – traditionally the devil's witching hour.

### Nicci
These are similar to wall-mounted cash dispensers, only in reverse: money is deposited and favours are promised. You will see them in the unlikeliest of places – where roads meet, or in dead-end streets and around blind corners. Each has its own saint, and is often further adorned by a small altar. Prayers are said here and money dropped into the embedded and locked box. In return there are heavenly rewards in the hereafter, but such rewards are entirely dependent on how much money is given. A donation of 10 Malta *liri* (*see* p.62) could ensure you a whole week in heaven.

# Dom Mintoff

It all seems an extremely long time ago, but in fact it was only in 1984 that Dom Mintoff, the leader of the Malta Labour Party (MLP), resigned as the country's longest-serving prime minister.

He was born to a poor family, in Cospicua, in 1916 when the Three Cities were a proletariat backyard of British colonial rule. Malta was then a fortress island, its fate tied to the waning British Empire. His socialist views (like those of many) were formed within the Three Cities and the sweaty lee of the Royal Navy's dockyards. The cold mantle of arrogance worn by the British did not help to foster good relations either.

Between the wars he trained as an architect and engineer in Malta, and in 1939 he won a Rhodes Scholarship to Oxford University. Upon his return he contested the post-war election in 1947, and the MLP won. At the time, his party had a pro-British stance – a *fin d'empire* British chequebook was helping to rebuild the island after the devastations of the Second World War. Furthermore, the 31-year-old Dom (now Minister of Works) had married an English woman. In 1955, after a factional dispute within the MLP (still a pro-British party), he became prime minister on a mandate for full integration with Britain.

Oddly enough, if one fact is to be remembered about Mintoff's foreign policy (apart from the fact that he did not actually have one) it is his taunting and vociferous dislike of the British – the roots of which surely lay in the integration issue. Mintoff adopted the notion of integration with Britain after it was first espoused some years before by Lord Strickland: the Maltese islands were to become, in effect, just another set of parliamentary constituencies sending MPs to the House of Commons at Westminster. In today's more politically aware times his proposal smacks of incomprehensible naïvety. Yet Britain, nervous of the rumblings of Arab nationalism coming from Nasser, appeared to countenance the idea. Much against the wishes of his long-time adversary, the Catholic Church, a referendum was tabled for 1956. The result was conclusive: 74.83 per cent of those who had cast votes ticked the box for full integration with Britain. But the powers in Whitehall fudged the issue and turned the proposal down, saying that the vote did not take into account the wishes of those who had not voted! Loss of face and honour were very important to Mintoff and, amid the pervading aroma of betrayal, a stalemate ensued. He resigned in 1958 and the British suspended the Maltese constitution.

In the bitter aftermath of the debacle, the issue was no longer integration: it was independence or bust. Mintoff now seemed more determined than ever to make Malta over to the Maltese. He wanted to take the people away from the insensitive assertiveness of the British, and out of their state of suppressive ignorance perpetrated by the Church. The general election of 1962 was a disaster for the MLP, however, and it was the right-wing Nationalist Party that ushered in independence in 1964. (Although a greater percentage of the population actually voted at the subsequent independence referendum, only 50.68 per cent voted for independence.) For nine years Mintoff remained as Leader of the Opposition, albeit anything but quietly. It was during this fallow period, and his subsequent premiership in the 1970s, that the dangerous side of his talents began to manifest itself. As a leader he was hated and worshipped in equal measure; in that respect alone he was out of the Reagan-Thatcher mould. Mintoff possessed the two most seductive qualities a politician can: he was both truly charismatic and a forceful orator – a pied piper figure whose clarion call of Malta for the Maltese was followed by the people. But if you were not for him you were against him (apathy and neutrality were not the hallmarks of his era) and sadly he polarized a nation. The MLP was re-elected in 1971 and remained in power until 1987. In March 1979 Mintoff was finally to achieve a somewhat Pyrrhic victory when the last British warship sailed out of the Grand Harbour. Malta now belonged to the Maltese, and then only was he content, a life's work done.

Whatever has been and will be said about him, even his fiercest detractors acknowledge that he was a skilled and maverick politician; he courted controversy and did not mind being cut off from an overbearing Church he despised, any more than he minded going to London to demand more money with forceful ultimatums. He would flirt with the Soviets, or be in cahoots with the palpably deranged Colonel Qaddafi, just as readily as he would beg aid from the Italians. Any action was acceptable providing he saw it as fulfilment of his ideals for Malta; ironically, his single-mindedness was his blind spot.

During the 16 years or more the MLP governed, unsavoury and undemocratic governments like China and North Korea provided aid, labour and training; hospitals and schools were needlessly shut, taxes were burdensomely high, and the Church was baited like a bear in a pit. Worst of all, corruption flourished; it was not the benign backscratching of South American nations, either. Everything required a permit in socialist Malta and there was almost a published tariff of bribes. All this appeared to be lost in Mintoff's blind spot. As a man of humble tastes, he incorrectly presumed his ministers were too. An instinctive player, he rarely watched his own back, let alone anyone else's.

The legacy of his long years in office was contradiction and oddity. Malta was left with little or no debt, but with little or no ability to move forward either; the island's infrastructure had been woefully neglected. Yet, while Mintoff and Malta accumulated more column inches of international press comment than many a country a hundred times larger, living standards for the poor did rise, and the islands were returned to the Maltese.

He knew (and did not mind) that his resignation as prime minister in 1984 – midway through a term of office – would leave a power vacuum. His untimely departure was not on account of a tawdry sex scandal *à l'anglaise*, nor Italian financial *tangenti*; he had simply had enough. After 30 years in politics, he knew that his own and his party's chances of reelection in the evolutionary 1980s were slim. As far as he was concerned, his deputy prime minister could be the fall guy (he was), and the MLP could lose the next election under a different leader (they did, 2½ years later, in 1987).

Again, this time in 1997, Dom Mintoff demonstrated his desire to mix, stir and obfuscate. The ruling Labour Party, led by Dr Alfred Sant (a Harvard graduate who sports an ill-fitting wig), needed to pass an unpopular budget. Suffice it to say, and without delving into the minutiae of Maltese politics, the 82-year-old ex-prime minister held the entire country to ransom for a considerable period. It is often remarked that his voice will be heard from the grave.

Further crises erupted for the beleaguered Dr Sant in November 1997 and June 1998 with Dom Mintoff abstaining on the Cottonera Waterfront project. This forced a general election in 1998, resulting in the Labour Party losing power after just two years in office. At the time of writing, the Nationalist Party is in government, after winning the 2003 general election, and having taken Malta into the European Union the year after. The next general election is due in 2008.

## A Little More about Local Politics

Malta is a very politically aware nation. The islands have approximately one elected representative (MP) per 6,000 of population. (Duplicate that in Britain or America and you would have 11,700 MPs in the House of Commons or 50,000 Members of Congress: chaos would reign and no law would ever be passed.)

The Maltese political system is very similar to the British one. There are two principal parties: the right-wing **Nationalist Party** and the more left-wing **Malta Labour Party**. There is also a green party called **Alternativa Demokratica**. MPs are elected to a single House of Representatives in free democratic elections in five-year cycles on a proportional representation basis. All are fiercely contested and decided by the smallest of margins, and the somewhat overloaded system functions well, despite an aura of self-importance.

The idea of 'the career politician' is an alien phenomenon (MPs' salaries are relatively modest). Here, parliament is not a congenial social club, nor an ivory tower in which to languish. Rewards are more intangible and come from the reverence shown by their followers; walk through any village and at least one street will be named after a politician – it is an honours system in all but name.

The importance of politics in Malta has increased ever since the end of the Second World War, while the Church's erstwhile iron grasp over the conscience of the population (priests would 'advise' their congregation how to vote) has simultaneously diminished. Surprisingly at first, the post-independence generation seemed to approve of the contraction of Malta's power and wealth, but there is no mystery behind the politicizing of the nation. The search by a vulnerable and much-invaded island race for a national and international voice, independence in 1964, and declaration as a neutral republic in 1974 has helped to keep politics on everyone's mind. A somewhat less apparent, but probably no less important, reason for its ascendancy can be spotted in every village. The *zuntier* (forecourt) of the parish church is the traditional end-of-day meeting place, somewhere for the men to sit and talk. Never far away, there were (and still are) the political clubs or *każin*, the blue banners of the Nationalist Party and the red ones of the Malta Labour Party winking invitingly from their ever-open doors. The clubs (together with their bars) pulled people off the church's *zuntier* and into their sphere of influence.

Every day at the most basic level, the Maltese are kept in close touch with their politicos and their antics. Their breakfast-time diet of newsprint is profuse: they digest four daily and six Sunday newspapers, and politics is never off the front page. The local TV and radio stations gleefully report on even the most tedious events. This appetite for politics resulted in the 1993 reintroduction of local government. The islands were divided into 68 **councils**, each with an elected mayor and secretary. Council elections are held every four years.

## The Maltese Cross

While the Order of St John was still in Acre (in the mid-13th century), the eight-pointed cross, known as the Maltese Cross, replaced the Order's simple insignia of a white cross on a scarlet background – 'the white cross of peace in the bloodstained field of war'.

The knights' new insignia enshrined in its four principal arms the Christian tenets of Prudence, Justice, Temperance and Fortitude. The eight points of the cross's four arms represent the Beatitudes as taught by Christ in the Sermon on the Mount. The whiteness of the cross symbolizes the purity required by those who would live, fight and die in the service of the Christian faith.

# The *Festa*

If you can, try to imagine a film set in a Maltese piazza in front of an illuminated and well-dressed Baroque church; families dressed in all their finery are milling about in a bustle of uncoordinated activity. The bunting and pennants quiver gratefully in the breeze, and the lights are respectfully dimmed to a soft Mediterranean dusk. Suddenly, there are several explosive cracks like mortar fire; the young jump like rabbits, while the elderly stoically grip their chests.

Now, study the scene a little closer, and you will perceive that the many Laurel-and-Hardy-style directors appear to be reading from a biblical script (that easily could have been written by Groucho Marx) as a solemn procession appears. There is a frightful din as the band strikes up, and decorations and lighting are supplanted by a seemingly endless and deafening display of gunpowder pyrotechnics, Las Vegas style. Moreover, the scene seems to gather momentum as the hours roll into the black night. If your mind's eye is capable of drawing such a dysfunctional picture, you know how a *festa* might appear. Yet it is only on the surface that the gathering looks anarchic. In reality the villagers' *festa*, held annually in honour of their patron saint, is painstakingly prepared, rehearsed and anticipated – the high point of the year.

The history of the village *festa* dates back to the later years of the Order of St John, when celebrations were encouraged on thin pretexts as an unsophisticated method of diverting the peasant's mind away from his lot. It was under the British in the mid- and late 19th century that local celebrations really started to flourish and civic band clubs (the communities' glue) began to form. Today the *festa* is an important social occasion when families reunite from all over the islands, and the prestige of the village and its clubs are vested in the event's outcome. (Some would say, rather cynically, that it is also a time when the Church can reassert its authority.)

The *festa* lasts a weekend, building throughout Saturday to climax on Sunday. Weeks of volunteer work – spring-cleaning the village, fund-raising, decorating the streets, reverential hanging of red damask and chandeliers in the church, polishing the statues that are to be carried solemnly through the streets – are over. Sometime after dawn on Saturday the brutal noise of the petards heralds the start of the party.

Throughout the celebrations the Maltese, making the boldest of sartorial statements (the women wear all their jewellery), will mooch in and out of relatives' and friends' houses, sing songs and occasionally pause to listen to the less-than-euphonious brass bands, lose teeth to vicious and sweet *qubbajt* (nougat), chomp on *mqaret* (vile-looking hot fritters stuffed with crushed dates) and drink too much. The two high points are the High Mass when the bells are rung with as much rhythm as free verse, and the evening firework displays which signal the end of the day's festivities. The startling fireworks are home-made; Catherine wheels whirr like a hypnotist's eyes, and the rocket tails cascade in exploding rainbows; it is a very unusual year when someone does not blow themselves to pieces in the preceding weeks. But the Maltese have very few cares at *festa* time, and the following Monday, *'xalata*, is the day for hangovers, picnics and lazing by the beach.

If one singular aspect stands out in all the noise, gunpowder and incense of the *festas*, it's the unsophisticatedness of it all – that's what makes them unique. They are traditional and simple celebrations to which all are invited.

*Festas* usually run through the long evenings of June, July, August and September. Many villages have a secondary *festa*; only the primary ones are noted in the text. *See* pp.59–60 for dates.

# Hunting and Trapping

Most nations have their blood sports, and these sometimes have an element of economic, social or conservation responsibility, whatever you may think of them. In Malta, however, the *kaċċa*, or the hunt, has now become killing simply for the sake and thrill of it, and the 'seasons' are so abused that they no longer have any meaning. In mitigation the worn-out plea to 'look at other countries' is trotted out by the hunters, but their principal self-justification rests with tradition – the knights hunted in the islands for 268 years. In reality there is no excuse for the atrocities, and the practices of the lawless minority continue to bring international condemnation on Malta. The island's three principal bird sanctuaries are no longer inviolate – they are often the site of indiscriminate bird slaughter.

The single most disturbing aspect of all is the shooting of migratory birds – whether internationally protected or not – as they fly between habitats. If you walk by Dingli Cliffs in spring when the birds migrate north from Africa, the dawn chorus sounds, without hyperbole, like Beirut of old. Many practices have gone way beyond the boundaries of sportsmanship: semi-automatic shotguns are used and speedboats driven by the *kaċċatur*, the hunters, wait out at sea for the exhausted birds before they even reach landfall.

An important adjunct to hunting is the 'sport' of **bird trapping**. There are about 4,000 registered trappers and their aim is to capture songbirds, such as finches and robins. Visitors to Malta walking in the countryside will invariably come across cleared and levelled strips of land surrounded by poles supporting small platforms. When a trapper is *in situ*, a 'clap-net' is laid on the ground and songbirds in small cages are placed on the poles to attract other migrating birds.

Malta does not have a legal requirement in which the 'bag' is recorded, therefore estimates of birds trapped, netted or shot can be misleading. Nevertheless, figures published in 1992 (and disputed by the Malta Association for Hunting and Conservation) suggest that among the long list of those shot, killed or trapped is an astonishing annual bag of 3 million finches, 500,000 thrushes, 500,000 swallows, 135,000 turtle doves, 80,000 golden orioles and 50,000 birds of prey – an average of 12 birds for every man, woman and child on the islands. (There are no figures at all for those birds caught in illegal mist-nets which you will sometimes come across by the cliffs.) With few exceptions the birds are inedible and the Maltese are not great poultry-eaters. So what happens to them? The larger and rarer species are left with the taxidermist, to appear later as possessions on a mantelpiece, while smaller birds are shot at for target practice (like road signs). Trapped songbirds are put in tiny cages to be hung on the wall or carried around by old men.

To the average holiday-maker or businessman passing through it seems obvious that the time has come to outlaw the *kaċċa*, or at the very least curb and police it. Unfortunately, the authorities (who collect revenues from guns, ammunition, etc.) are either unable or unwilling to grasp the nettle. Even the minority, macho wannabe-Hemingways go scot-free while drawing unwanted attention to those who do hunt only permitted prey within the seasons. Evidently, the hunting lobby is just too powerful in the precariously balanced war of attrition that is local politics. Until Malta's breadwinner, the tourist industry, is very seriously affected, nothing will be done; 'green' tourists and certain conferences already boycott the islands but they are a tiny number compared with a large market.

The migration seasons, March–May and September–November, are the periods when the unsavoury customs of the *kaċċatur* are at their most pronounced. Unlike Japan, where it is highly unlikely that you will stumble across a whaling fleet, in Malta it is impossible during these months not to be concerned or intimidated, or both, in parts of the countryside. Try to avoid, especially in the mornings or early evenings, Dingli, Buskett, Wardija, Delimara, the deserted areas near to Ġaġar Qim and any of the exposed cliffs in Malta and Gozo. The letters 'RTO' painted on the walls of country lanes indicate the hunting area is 'reserved to outsiders', not that you can get in if you are an outsider yourself. Disturbing a hunter or trapper can lead to much shouting and abuse, often with a loaded gun pointed in your direction – confrontation is best avoided.

The EU bans spring hunting in general, but Malta applied for a derogation and spring hunting is allowed for turtle dove and quail. Every year the numbers shot are supposed to be reported to the EU and breeding schemes should be in place. However the sad fact is that regulating species and numbers will never be effective in Malta as it is all so difficult to control. Until the EU puts its foot down and bans hunting and trapping during migratory seasons the massacres will continue, but there is little sign of the political will to do this.

# De la Valette and Dragut Rais

Leaders sometimes epitomize the era in which they live. The 16th century with its religious polarization and brutal warfare brought together two adversaries of similar mettle: the Christian knight Jean Parisot de la Valette, and the Muslim corsair, Dragut Rais, known as 'The Drawn Sword of Islam'.

**Jean Parisot de la Valette** was born in 1494, 'issue of the first hereditary Counts of Toulouse of ancestors who had fought in the Albigensian wars and in the Crusades with St Louis'. He joined the Order of St John (variously described as 'the most remarkable body of religious warriors the world has ever seen' and 'a foreign legion of militant Christians'), at the age of 20 and never returned to his native France, dedicating his life to the Order.

Described by the Abbé de Brantôme as 'a very handsome man, tall, calm and unemotional', he was just 28 when the Order was defeated at Rhodes in 1522 by the Turks and their young sultan, Suleyman the Magnificent. Born in the same year as de la Valette, and together with Dragut, Suleyman was to be his arch enemy. During the Order's subsequent wilderness years, before it was offered Malta in 1530, de la Vallette observed as Grand Master de L'Isle Adam begged for aid from monarchs across Europe. It was then that he acquired the traits that came to symbolize his subsequent magistracy: a bearing which commanded respect and inspiration, patience, iron discipline, rigid observance of vows, a nose for politics and an almost fanatical hatred of Muslims. It was said 'the seal of a hero was on his brow' and furthermore that de la Valette was 'capable of converting a Protestant or of governing a kingdom'. By the time he was elected grand master in 1557 at the age of 63, he had served in all the important positions within the Order, and had even had the unique distinction of being general of the galleys, a sinecure of the Italian *langue*.

It was during one summer trading voyage that the centuries-old Christian-Muslim confict caused the two warriors to meet. In the summer of 1541 de la Valette was wounded during a sea engagement and his ship, *San Giovanni*, was sunk. Dragut was an officer on board the corsair Kust Aly's ship, and it was he who ensured that de la Valette's wounds were properly treated. De la Valette spent more than year chained to an oar as a galley slave until an exchange of prisoners secured his release. In an extraordinary parallel, some years later Dragut was captured and he too was tethered to the rowing benches; fate had again thrown the two men together for a second and last time. 'Dragut, it's the custom of war,' de la Valette is said to have remarked as Dragut pulled on the oar, to which a smiling Dragut replied, 'and a change of fortune!'

Grand Master de la Valette knew that Suleyman the Magnificent would one day try to complete the annihilation of the Order after his uncustomary moment of clemency at Rhodes in 1522, and in the warm May of 1565 the Turkish fleet appeared off Malta and what became known as the Great Siege began in earnest. Throughout the siege the now 70-year-old grand master led from the front. The Christian footsoldier and diarist Francisco Balbi who fought in the siege wrote: 'If it had not been for the constant foresight and preparations made by the grand master, not one of us would have survived.'

With the Muslim enemy routed and Suleyman's expansion into the central Mediterranean halted, plaudits and wealth were heaped on him and the Order. De la Valette lived for a further three years and died a peaceful death in 1568 in the chapel at Fort St Angelo after a day's hunting in the *boschetto*. He is buried in the crypt of St John's Co-Cathedral in the city which bears his name. The Latin inscription on his tomb, composed by his English secretary Sir Oliver Starkey, reads: 'Here lies La Valette, worthy of eternal honour. He who was once the scourge of Africa and Asia, and the shield of Europe, whence he expelled the barbarians by his holy arms, is the first to be buried in this beloved city, whose founder he was.'

If the central Mediterranean had mainstay industries at all in the 15th and 16th centuries it was piracy and slavery. Rounding up Christian slaves to sell or ransom was a highly profitable wheeze for the corsairs whose nesting ground was the north coast of Africa, the Barbary Coast. At the turn of the 16th century the most skilled and feared practitioners were the brothers Khair-ed-din, known as 'Redbeard', and Horuk, and it was with them that **Dragut Rais** learnt his trade.

He was born to an Anatolian peasant family in 1485 in the little village of Charabalac in Turkey. His fate was sealed when as a child the province's governor took him to Egypt where he later enlisted in the military as a bombardier. He soon tired of the conventions of the army corps, however, and went to sea as a gunner on a pirate vessel and later 'acquired' a *galliot* of his own. News of Dragut's exploits reached the ears of the wily Barbarossa brothers who persuaded him to fall in with them at their newly captured base of Algiers in 1529 when he was 44. He sailed as lieutenant of their squadron until 1546 when Redbeard died and the mantle of 'Christian scourge' fell easily upon Dragut's shoulders; by now he was a maverick tactician of audacious cunning with an encyclopaedic knowledge of the Mediterranean.

In 1551, tired of lone piracy and thirsting for war, Dragut put his acumen and galleys at the service of the Turkish sultan, Suleyman the Magnificent. His first campaign as a new admiral in the Turkish navy was to capture the Order's outpost in Tripoli with Sinan Pasha. The battle was swift and decisive (he 'built a pyramid of Christian bones'), and a grateful Suleyman then confirmed him as governor of Tripoli. In the same year he carried off the entire population of Gozo in an act of revenge for the death of his brother who had been killed there in 1544 during one of his numerous raids on the islands.

Dragut was 80 years old when he arrived in Malta on 2 June, just three weeks after the Great Siege of 1565 had commenced. Not even his tactical skill could reverse the disastrous miscalculations of the Turkish commanders, and 16 days later on 18 June he was killed accidentally by a splinter of rock thrown up by a cannon ball. Eleven years earlier, in what proved to be a self-fulfilling prophecy, Dragut had remarked after his brother's death: 'I have felt, in this island, the shadow of the wing of death. One of these days it is written that I, too, shall die in the territory of the knights.' The death of one of de la Valette's arch enemies boosted the flagging morale of the besieged, and Francisco Balbi recorded it thus: 'Dragut laid low, his brains spattered from his mouth, nostrils and ears ... de la Valette was very pleased at this.' His tomb can still be seen in Tripoli and, in Malta, Dragut Point is where he 'left his name with his life'; but perhaps the most fitting epitaph for one of the greatest warriors of the 16th century was written by the French historian Jurien de la Gravière in 1887: *'Il est mort sans déclin, dernière faveur de la fortune pour un homme qu'elle avait toujours gâté.'* ('He died at his peak, one final gift from Fortune, whose favour he had always enjoyed.')

# St Paul

Malta's most famous tourist. The Maltese are very proud of the unscheduled three-month visit he paid them back in AD 60. For a strict Catholic country, it is quite a claim to fame; after Christ himself, there really is no more important figure in early Christian history. It was Paul who, in the middle of the first century AD, organized the disparate set of beliefs and practices that sat uneasily under the umbrella heading 'Christianity' into a coherent whole; who gave the fledgling church purpose and direction and who took it upon himself to spread the new religion throughout the known world. Paul's letters are the earliest extant Christian documents, pre-dating even New Testament Gospels. It is therefore easy to understand why the Maltese are so proud of the association and why they are so irritated by modern theologists who doubt the veracity of the story.

Nothing, of course, can be proved. The historical sources for Paul's life, which include his own letters plus 'The Acts of the Apostles' (probably written by Paul's travelling companion Luke at least 30 years after his death), are often tantalizingly vague regarding dates and places. Nonetheless, they provide enough information for us to be able to piece together the basics of the Apostle's career.

We know that Paul was born into a Jewish family in Tarsus, Cilicia, which, at the time, was part of the Roman province of Asia Minor, and that he inherited Roman citizenship from his father; something which would prove of great value to him during later evangelizing troubles. Roman citizens had certain rights within the Empire (including the right to travel unmolested) which preserved them from the worst excesses of local summary justice. For most of his early life he was a committed Jew and even trained for a while as a rabbi. It is unlikely that he ever met Christ. Indeed, at first, Paul was one of Christ's harshest critics and a fervent persecutor of the fledgling Christian church. His conversion came on the road to Damascus after Christ's crucifixion when, following a vision, he became convinced that Christ was alive. The resurrection confirmed his faith and Paul's life began anew. He quickly rationalized his experience into a firm, fixed belief, a particular character trait which also made him adept at organizing, evangelizing and settling disputes – the basic roles of a religious leader.

Soon after his conversion, he travelled to Jerusalem where, along with James, Peter and John, he would begin formalizing Christian theory into missionary policy. This new policy had two main aims: to make Christianity an active religion (Paul thought it was the duty of all converts to go out into the world and preach the word of God regardless of considerations of personal safety); and to make Christianity an all-inclusive religion. Paul had little time for the divisions and party differences that had already crept into the church. He insisted that there should be no distinction between Jewish and Gentile Christianity, despite the fact that Jewish law forbade Jews from eating with Gentiles.

Paul would spend the rest of his life travelling on evangelizing missions in and around the Near East, Asia Minor and the Mediterranean, and would be the first person to gain a toehold for Christianity in Europe. His chosen career was fraught with difficulty and danger. On his first missionary trip to Cyprus and Asia Minor he became ill, was stoned by an angry mob and left for dead in Lystra, and fell out with his travelling companion John Mark. The true zealot, however, is not easily dissuaded, and he continued on to Thessaloniki, where he started a riot and was accused of worshipping a rival emperor. All Roman subjects and citizens were expected to worship the ruling emperor and principal Roman gods – though beyond that they could worship pretty much whom they liked. Most of the people in the Empire, being polytheists, were quite happy with the arrangement. Christianity, on the other hand, a monotheism, posed the Roman authorities a problem. It was an exclusive religion; in order to convert to Christianity you had to reject all other gods, and that included the Emperor. A similar tension had existed between the Romans and the Jews in Israel and would culminate in the expulsion of the Jews from Jerusalem in AD 70.

On this occasion, Paul escaped prosecution and travelled on to Corinth in the Pelopnnese, where he established possibly his most famous and influential church. He was soon, however, in trouble again. The governor of Corinth, Gallia, accused him of practising an illicit religion. Paul's luck continued to hold; the case was dismissed and he was able to fulfil his most cherished ambition of travelling to Ephesus, the hub of Roman government and religion in Asia Minor. He would stay there three years, longer than any other city. Problems, of course, soon arose, although on this occasion they originated from an unexpected source. Paul's constant travelling did not allow him to monitor his religious outposts as closely as he would like. While in Ephesus, he received disturbing reports from Corinth. The church there was rife with quarrels and party differences. There was scandalous talk of of disorderly conduct at the Lord's Supper and even incest. Paul's response was to write a letter, 'I Corinthians', in which he not only chastised his followers for their behaviour but set out a strict code of conduct for future observance. At first, this approach had little effect. Newcomers to the church in Corinth had begun to question Paul's authority. The despatch of the letter 'II Corinthians', however, seemed to quieten things down. Paul would continue to instruct his churches in this epistolary fashion throughout the rest of his life, never allowing his converts to stray from the path he had marked out for them. When members of the church in Thessaloniki stopped work in order to prepare for the second coming, Paul fired off a quick missive, scolding them for truancy.

Paul's luck eventually ran out in Jerusalem when he was arrested by the Jewish authorities for taking a Gentile into the Temple. Again, his Roman citizenship meant that he was able to escape swift retribution – it is ironic to think that he was only able to spend his life travelling the Roman Empire, undermining its tenets and principles, because Roman law gave him the freedom to do so. Although he was kept in prison in Jerusalem for two years, he was able to exercise his right, as a Roman citizen, to be tried in Rome by the Emperor himself. It was during the journey to Rome that Paul is supposed to have been **shipwrecked** on Malta.

Unfortunately, the narrative in 'Acts' comes to an end upon Paul's arrival in Rome. It is known that he wrote his final letters, to the Philippians, the Colossians, Philemon and the Ephesians, during the two years he spent awaiting trial, and it is safe to assume that the verdict, when it eventually came, was not favourable. We are pretty certain that Paul paid the ultimate price for his faith. As far as the future history of the Christian church was concerned, however, the story could not have ended more happily. The cult of the martyr, beginning with Christ himself, was hugely important in bringing in new converts to the church.

Paul is meant to have spent just three months on Malta, during which time he is supposed have converted the entire population, including the Governor Publius, to Christianity. His legacy is everywhere. Most major towns on the islands have a St Paul's church of some kind. There are the St Paul's Islands, where the shipwreck is supposed to have occurred, and a St Paul's Grotto where the saint was apparently held captive during his stay. Unfortunately, for Malta's official naming committee at least, recent scholarship has raised doubts over whether Malta was really the site of the apostle's shipwreck. Until the late 1980s, it was taken as read that the Melita mentioned in the Bible was Malta. The counter-arguments are based on a mixture of textual analysis and meteorological observation. A ship sailing from Crete which ran into difficulties, so it has been argued, would be far more likely to pitch up in the western Greek islands than the southern Mediterranean. Furthermore, the island's people are described in the Bible as 'barbarous', yet the Maltese had been members of the Roman Empire for many years and had full Roman citizenship and so should have appeared, by the standards of the time, rather sophisticated. (It may, however, just have been the simple fact that they did not speak Greek or Latin that led to this sweeping conclusion of 'barbarity'.)

The Maltese, however, don't really care what the experts say. Religion exists because of faith not proof, and faith in the story of the shipwreck remains very strong indeed.

## The Eye of Osiris

On either side of the high prow of every Maltese fishing boat or *luzzu* you will see an inky oval blob, the reverentially painted open and ever-watchful Eye of Osiris, a simple superstition to ward off evil spirits. Catholic names and shrines also found on board show how the strands of the island's different cultures entwine.

Osiris (with his wife Isis and son Horus) is one of a trinity of ancient Egyptian gods. First deified as the god of fertility in the Nile delta regions of upper Egypt more than 4,000 years ago, Osiris developed a second role as god of the dead after his brother Seth murdered him and dumped his body in the Nile. His wife Isis recovered his body, but Seth found it and cut it up into 14 pieces and scattered them to the winds. Vigilant Isis searched for and found his phallus and thus enabled Osiris to become god of eternal life for the dead in the underworld, where he reigned as king and judge. Their son Horus, however, was a sky god, often depicted as a falcon, whose eyes were the moon and the sun. Wishing to avenge his father's death, Horus engaged his uncle Seth in a fierce fight and slew him. During the struggle Horus's left eye, his moon eye, was damaged (thereby explaining the phases of the moon). It is the all-seeing restored eye of Horus, combined with the knowledge of eternal life offered by his father Osiris, that has become the talisman from which evil spirits shy away.

# Food and
# Drink

*Eating Out, the Maltese Way 54*
*Maltese Tastes 54*
*Maltese Drinks 56*

04

Over 150 years of British colonial rule have left their mark – though thankfully its culinary influence is no longer omnipresent. Sometimes a menu will give you that stomach-tightening *déjà vu* of yesteryear school lunches, but the star turns of British cooking such as fish and chips are not hard to locate.

Maltese cooking is the product of many kitchens: southern Italy, Sicily, Greece and North Africa – the Italian influence is at present perhaps predominant. It has evolved as a simple culinary experience, made from produce that has been readily available, including hardy vegetables that thrive in the warm but harsh climate. Nothing goes to waste; the same ingredients are found in many different dishes.

## Eating Out, the Maltese Way

The Maltese traditionally take lunch at home and, until fairly recently, only a handful of restaurants, outside the hotels, opened at midday. The growth of the tourist trade, however, has begun to erode this tradition and it is now much easier to find somewhere to refuel in the middle of the day, especially in the big tourist hubs such as Valletta, Sliema, St Julian's and Buġibba. Nevertheless, eating out is still principally an evening pastime – the curtain does not even rise on the night's entertainment until at least 8pm, and, as in Italy, this follows on from the evening *passeggiata* (see p.154). The Maltese, like all Latins, abhor solitude or even dining *à deux* – to them, this is the preserve of honeymooning tourists. The curtain only falls when the last person has left, normally around 1am.

Traditionally Malta is known for fish, and often you will be shown the day's catch (check for clear eyes and red gills), though some fish is farmed. Local and imported meat is much better than it used to be. Vegetarians will survive: many establishments will run up special dishes, and pizzas are available everywhere. Standards of catering, decoration and service have risen markedly, along with the variety of kitchens – from Malay to Russian and everything in between – but so too have prices. Frankly, some establishments have slapped on major-city prices but don't deliver the goods.

Inevitably, the island has been infiltrated by American culinary imperialism. Try to avoid it – you did not travel to the Mediterranean to eat frozen fish. Addicts, however, will never be far from a McDonald's, Burger King, Kentucky Fried Chicken or Pizza Hut.

For price ranges used in this guide, and information on tipping, *see* p.79 and p.92.

## Maltese Tastes

The traditional diet in Malta varies with the season. In the past there was very little choice, and even now that there is a much wider variety of imported foods available, the high prices mean that the average Maltese household still lives mainly off fresh, local, seasonal products. **Vegetables** make up an important part of the Maltese diet, and in the winter a thick vegetable soup often appears on the table three times a week – with pulses and pasta as *minestra*, with a piece of pork as *kawlata*, or with fresh sheep's cheese and ricotta as *zoppa tal-armla* (widow's soup). The glorious spring and summer vegetables, including broad beans, aubergines, courgettes and tomatoes, provide a little more variety.

**Pasta** dishes are also part of traditional Maltese cooking, usually heavy stodgy baked affairs, such as *mqarrun fil-forn*, which is baked macaroni. **Pies**, such as ricotta and broad bean, spinach and tuna, or simply meat, are also commonly encountered lunch dishes.

As a strongly Catholic country, **fish** is traditionally eaten on Wednesday and Friday. Although fish can be bought every day from the fishmongers, the street vendors are out on Wednesday and Friday mornings. Grouper (*cerna*), amberjack (*acciola*), bream (*sargu*), swordfish (*pixxispad*) and a small dorado (*lampuka*), are all available. The most seasonal of all these are the *lampuki*, which make a superb pie. Towards the end of summer sit on the balcony at Gleneagles bar in Mġarr, Gozo, and watch the fishermen preparing for the *lampuki* season, their boats piled high with limestone blocks and palm fronds, to create anchored shades to attract the passing fish. At the height of the *lampuki* season you will often find fishermen on the street selling their fresh catch for unbelievably low prices.

**Meat**, especially home-reared lamb and pork, has always been popular with the Maltese, but the traditional recipes do not appear on many restaurant menus. An old and near-extinct tradition revolves around the Sunday roast. The lady of the household would prepare her meat on a bed of potatoes and onions, and season it with pepper, coarse sea salt and fennel seeds. Having covered it with a cloth, she would march the dish across the square to the baker who would tag it and put it in his cavernous oven with all the other villagers' food. Sadly, progress has curtailed this custom, but traditional Sunday aromas can occasionally be sniffed in more remote villages. Fresh vegetables from the courgette, aubergine and marrow family are always eaten with the meat.

A traditional Maltese meal might end with fresh **fruit** such as figs or peaches, or *gbejniet*, a delicious light goat's cheese sprinkled with ground peppercorns. On special occasions, a dessert may be bought from the local *dolceria*. Typical favourites include *kannoli*, deep-fried pastry tubes filled with sweetened ricotta, and *cassatella*, a ricotta cheesecake of Sicilian origin decorated with glacé fruit and marzipan.

Locally baked **bread** is a real treat. The traditional crusty loaf is the staple of the local diet. Buy one piping hot from any baker before 11.30am. *Ftira*, another local bread, is harder to find; it looks like a huge sun-tanned Polo mint – soaked in pungent olive oil and chopped tomatoes, it tastes delicious.

## Maltese Specialities

Cominotto (a tiny island off Comino) used to be overrun with rabbits (*fenek*), but not any more; they must have ended up in the national dish, **rabbit stew** (*see* recipe, p.56). *Hobż biz-żejt* is local bread which is rubbed with tomatoes until it turns pink, and then topped with tomatoes, capers, olive oil and seasoning. *Pastizzi* are oval pockets of flaky pastry – about three-bite-sized – stuffed with either a light ricotta cheese or a grim mushy pea concoction; both varieties are served warm. If you return home before sunrise, you will find a few bars open and men sipping glasses of sweet white tea while chomping *pastizzi*.

Other favourites include *minestra*, a thick soup eaten all year round made from eight or more vegetables, three or four pulses and a pasta, and allowed to cook for at least three hours. *Timpana*, a Sicilian dish by origin, is macaroni with minced meat, livers, tomatoes and eggs, baked under a topping of pastry – not for the weight-conscious. *Bragioli* is rolled beef stuffed with bacon, parsley, breadcrumbs and hard-boiled eggs.

## Maltese Drinks

### Wines and Spirits

Local commercially produced **wine** has not, in the past, had a good reputation. There is a story – probably apocryphal – that as the founder of one of the local wineries lay on his deathbed, he croaked to his two sons to approach. 'Listen well,' he whispered. 'I must tell you...' He paused to gather his last gasp. 'It is also possible to make wine from grapes.' Since 1999, however, locally produced wine has improved dramatically. It falls into three main price/quality groups. The cheapest category (**Masters, San Paolo**) cost under Lm1, but are best avoided – really more rough than ready. Winemakers **Delicata** and **Marsovin** produce a good range of wines. These are made from local and imported grapes and most are very drinkable. **Meridiana** vineyards produce a small quantity of high-quality wine made entirely from locally grown grapes, though with a relatively high price tag. You can also buy good imported wines at reasonable prices. All internationally known brands of **spirits** are widely available and are consumed in unbelievable quantities.

### Beers and Lagers

Simonds Farsons, the island's main brewer, produces **Cisk**, an excellent lager, an ale called **Hopleaf** and a stronger ale called **Blue Label** (a bottle of locally produced beer will usually cost 25–50c, compared with 55–85c for imports). The company also produces a popular fizzy drink, peculiar to Malta, which is called **Kinnie** – it looks like yesterday's cold tea, but tastes better. Marsovin brew **Löwenbräu** locally and the Coca-Cola company sells **Stella Artois**. Other leading brands of beer are imported, but tend to be more expensive.

**Rabbit Stew (*Fenkata*)**
*1 rabbit, cleaned and cut in pieces*
*½ bottle of red wine*
*2 carrots, diced*
*1 onion, finely chopped*
*1 or 2 cloves of garlic, according to taste*
*2 bay leaves*
*1 tin peeled tomatoes*
*3 tbs tomato paste*
Marinate the rabbit in the red wine overnight.
Fry the rabbit pieces in with the garlic until browned and remove from the pan. Fry the onions and carrots in oil until golden, then add the tomato paste and peeled tomatoes, bay leaves and the wine marinade. Add the rabbit pieces and simmer for 1½ hours. Serve with vegetables and fresh local bread, or with spaghetti.

# Planning
# Your Trip

When to Go 58
Tourist Information 60
Embassies and Consulates 61
Entry Formalities 61
Disabled Travellers 61
Insurance and EHICs 62
Money 62
Getting There 63
Getting Around 65
Tour Operators 72
Where to Stay 73

05

# When to Go

## Climate

At the height of **summer** do not be fooled by the sea breeze, the *majjistral*, which comes predominantly from the northwest; during **July** and **August** areas of high pressure sit over the central and southern Mediterranean basin and Malta bakes like a brick under cloudless skies.

In **May** and **September** the dry, hot sirocco blows in from North Africa, bringing with it the reddish Saharan sand and inducing a state of torpidity. They say in Sicily – the wind's next stop – that if it blows continuously for more than five days all crimes of passion should be forgiven.

The **winters** tend to be mild, but can sometimes be very wet. The first rains come in **October** or **November** and if they persist until **January** the islands can be as uncomfortable and damp as a cellar. The *gregale* is an aggressive winter wind that blows down from the northeast across the Adriatic into Malta, and is justly feared by fishermen and yachtsmen alike.

The *Times of Malta* publishes a very reliable land and sea forecast. Five-day forecasts for the Maltese islands are on *www. maltairport.com;* daily forecasts **t** 21 220310.

In the **spring** and **autumn**, it keeps pleasantly warm without rising to the stifling heat of summer, but it gets dark at about 6pm, so the evenings are quite long.

## Festas and Festivals

For National Holidays, *see* p.85.

Every village has at least one **feast** or *festa* in honour of its patron and favourite saint on a specific day each year. The majority of *festas* take place from May to September, the most popular being the Assumption on 15 August. The villagers (aided by their parish priest, church and band clubs) plot the celebrations, make the fireworks and petards, and gather in all their flamboyant finery for a weekend of noise, drinking and nougat. The day after is called *'xalata*, meaning 'a pleasure outing', and is for hangovers and picnics. Try to catch at least one *festa*. Each village's principal *festa* is listed in the text, and national *festas* and holidays are listed opposite. *See also* 'Topics', pp.45–6.

Village *festas* occur either on fixed dates – such as 15 August for the Assumption – or are held on the first or last Sunday in a specific month.

Please check dates for specific villages by calling the **Christian Centre for Tourists**, **t** 21 222644/240255.

The programme is usually as follows:

| | |
|---|---|
| **Eve of Feast** | 6pm Vespers and Mass |
| | 7pm Band Marches |
| **Feast Day** | 9am High Mass |
| | 7pm Procession and Band Marches |

There are also a few secular festivals. *See* the box opposite for further details.

## Rainfall and Temperatures in Malta

| Month | Sunshine (hrs) | Rainfall (mm) | Temperature (°C/F) (max) | (min) | Sea Temperature (°C/F) |
|---|---|---|---|---|---|
| January | 5.5 | 90.1 | 15/59 | 9.5/49 | 14.5/58 |
| February | 6.4 | 60.8 | 15/59 | 9.5/49 | 14.5/58 |
| March | 7.3 | 44.7 | 16.5/62 | 10/50 | 14.5/58 |
| April | 8.5 | 24 | 19/66 | 12/54 | 16/61 |
| May | 10 | 8.9 | 23/74 | 15/59 | 18.5/65 |
| June | 11.2 | 3.8 | 27/81 | 18.5/65 | 21/70 |
| July | 12.1 | 1 | 30/86 | 21/70 | 24.5/76 |
| August | 11.4 | 8.8 | 30.5/87 | 22/72 | 25.5/78 |
| September | 9 | 40.4 | 28/82 | 20.5/69 | 25/77 |
| October | 7.2 | 123.6 | 24/75 | 17/63 | 19.5/67 |
| November | 6.5 | 76.8 | 20/68 | 14/57 | 19.5/67 |
| December | 5.2 | 100.2 | 16.5/62 | 11/52 | 16.5/62 |

# Main Festivals

## March

**Mediterranean Food Festival**. A four-day festival usually held at the Mediterranean Conference Centre in Valletta. Maltese and foreign chefs present their own national dishes in a 'festive ambience'.

## April/Easter

**Valletta History and Elegance**. This Valletta festival is held during the week following Easter and features numerous concerts, recitals, folk music and theatrical performances in various venues around Valletta. Visit *www.vallettafest.com* for details.

## May

**Malta Fireworks Festival**. A recently conceived festival which offers a chance to appreciate the Maltese pyrotechnical talent long before the official religious season starts. It is held over two days at Valletta's Grand Harbour, Lascaris Wharf.

## July

**Malta Jazz Festival**. Malta's recreation of Jazz on a Summer Night has become a regular feature on its entertainment calendar. It features well-known international jazz musicians as well as home-grown talent. As is the law with jazz festivals, it is held outdoors, at Valletta's Grand Harbour Marina, with the bastions of the Order of St John providing a suitably spectacular backdrop. Call the Department for Culture and Broadcasting, **t** 21 220856, for details of tickets and participants.

**Farsons International Food and Beer Festival**. A Munich-style knees-up held in specially erected tents on the shores of the Lazzaretto Creek Marina. Contact the MTA, **t** 21 224444/5, for details.

## October

**Birgu Festival**. This features re-enactments of the ceremonies of the Knights of St John complete with full period costume, music, dancing and traditional Maltese food. Recommended if you like this sort of thing.

**Mdina Festival**. Another historical pageant with all the trimmings Including traditional folk music, dancing and crafts. The Birgu and Mdina Festivals are held on alternate years: in 2007, the Birgu Festival is taking place, while 2008 is the turn of the Mdina Festival. For details of these events contact the MTA, **t** 21 224444/5, or visit *www.visitmalta.com*.

## November

**Malta International Choir Festival**. International choirs compete for trophies and cash prizes at the Mediterranean Conference Centre in Valletta. For details, visit *www.maltachoirfestival.com*

# Village *Festas*

## February

**St Paul** Valletta

## March

**Jesus of Nazareth** Sliema
**St Gregory** Kerċem (Gozo)
**St Joseph** Rabat
**Our Lady of Sorrows** various parishes
**Palm Sunday** various parishes

## April/Easter

**Good Friday** Various parishes
**Easter** Various parishes
**St Joseph** Xagħra (Gozo)
**St Publius** Floriana
**St Augustine** Valletta
**Holy Cross** Birkirkara
**St Joseph** Ħamrun, Marsa

## May

**St Anthony of Padova** Birkirkara
**St Joseph** Kirkop
**Holy Trinity** Marsa
**St Paul** Munxar (Gozo)

## June

**Corpus Christi** Rabat, Għasri (Gozo)
**The Annunciation** Tarxien
**St Joseph** Għaxaq
**Our Lady of Fatima** Gwardamanġa
**Our Lady of Lourdes** Qrendi
**St Philip** Żebbuġ
**St Anthony** Mġarr (Gozo)
**St Catherine** Żejtun
**Sacred Heart of Jesus** Fontana (Gozo)
**St George** Qormi
**St Nicholas** Siġġiewi
**Our Lady of the Sacred Heart** Burr Marrad
**St John the Baptist** Xewkija (Gozo)
**Our Lady of Liesse** Valletta
**St Peter and St Paul** Mdina, Nadur (Gozo)

## July

**St Andrew** Luqa
**St Joseph the Worker** Birkirkara

**Our Lady of Mount Carmel** Fleur-de-Lys, Fgura, Gzira, Valletta, Mdina, Birkirkara, Żurrieq, Balluta
**St Paul** Rabat
**Immaculate Conception** Hamrun
**Our Lady of Sorrows** St Paul's Bay
**St Elizabeth** Għarb (Gozo)
**St Joseph** Kalkara, Msida, Żebbuġ
**Annunciation** Balzan
**Our Lady of Sokkors** Kerċem (Gozo)
**St George** Victoria (Gozo)
**St Sebastian** Qormi
**Our Lady of Doctrine** Tarxien
**Christ the King** Paola
**St Margaret** Sannat (Gozo)
**St Anna** Marsaskala
**St Venera** St Venera
**St Lawrence** St Lawrence (Gozo)
**Our Lady of Sorrows** St Paul's Bay
**St Dominic** Valletta

### August
**St Peter** Birżebbuga
**Our Lady of Pompeii** Marsaxlokk
**Our Lady of Lourdes** San Gwann, Paola
**St Joseph** Manikata, Qala (Gozo)
**St Gaetan** Hamrun
**Transfiguration of Our Lord** Lija
**St Lawrence** Vittoriosa
**The Assumption of Our Lady** Għaxaq, Gudja, Mosta, Mqabba, Qrendi, Attard, Dingli, Mġarr, Victoria (Gozo)

**St Helen** Birkirkara
**Stella Maris** Sliema
**The Assumption** Żebbuġ (Gozo)
**Maria Regina** Marsa
**St Paul** Safi
**St Bartholomew** Għarghur
**Our Lady of Loreto** Għajnsielem (Gozo)
**St Julian** St Julian's
**St Dominic** Vittoriosa

### September
**St Catherine** Żurrieq
**St Gregory** Sliema
**Our Lady of Cintura** Rabat, Gudja
**Our Lady of Mount Carmel** Xlendi (Gozo)
**The Nativity of Our Lady** Mellieħa, Senglea, Naxxar, Xagħra (Gozo)
**Our Lady of Grace** Żabbar, Victoria (Gozo)
**St Leonard** Kirkop
**St Francis** Rabat, Marsa

### October
**Our Lady of the Rosary** Gudja
**St Francis** Rabat
**Our Lady of Health** Rabat

### November
**San Koronato** Nadur (Gozo)
**San Fortunatu** Żebbuġ (Gozo)

### December
**Immaculate Conception** Cospicua, Qala (Gozo)

## Tourist Information

Government tourist offices are often ecologically unfriendly places: forests of brochures depicting impossibly attractive couples. The **Malta Tourism Authority** (MTA), *www.visitmalta.com*, is a welcome exception. Its information is useful and covers most aspirations without overloading you with paper.

### MTA Offices Abroad

**UK**: Malta House, 36–8 Piccadilly, London W1V 0PP, t (020) 7292 4900.
**USA**: 65 Broadway Suite 823, New York, t (212) 430 3799.
**France**: 9, Cité de Trévise, 75009 Paris, t (1) 48 00 03 79, *www.visitemalte.com*.

Your hotel will have maps, eating and activity suggestions. Should you wish to discover the whereabouts of the Malta Ornithological Society (PO Box 498, Valletta, t 21 230684), or simply where to find a cheap hotel in Gozo, the offices will help out.

### MTA Offices in Malta

**Valletta**: 280 Republic Street, t 21 224444/5; freephone t 800 72230 (*Mon–Fri 8–12.30pm, 1.15–5pm*). The MTA headquarters: 1 City Arcades, Valletta t 21 237747, 100 yards from the bus terminus inside the City Gate. This is the MTA's principal office for all tourist information.

In small villages where there is no tourist office, go to the police station, where they will be able to help out.

# Embassies and Consulates

Government representatives are there to help should you find yourself in trouble with the local police or even be in search of that elusive manufacturer of powder compacts. Definitely seek their assistance in the event of a lost passport or a serious illness.

**Australia** (High Commission): Ta'Xbiex Terrace, Ta'Xbiex, **t** 21 338201.

**Canada**: JM Demajo House, 103 Archbishop Street, Valletta, **t** 25 523233.

**European Union**: The Vines, 51 Seafront, Ta'Xbiex, **t** 21 345111.

**UK**: (High Commission), Whitehall Mansions, Seafront, Ta'Xbiex, **t** 23 230000, *www. britain.com.mt.*

**USA**: Development House, St Anne Street, Floriana, **t** 25 614000.

# Entry Formalities

## Passports and Visas

Malta is a EU country. EU passport holders sail through the formalities, which means much reduced queues for everyone.

Entry **visas** are not required by anyone holding a passport from the USA, Europe, Australia, Japan, or certain African and South American countries. People requiring visas should apply to the Maltese consul in their respective countries. Sojourns are limited to three months, but extensions are readily granted, if an application is made at Police Headquarters in Floriana before the three months are up. Employment is prohibited.

Non-EU passport holders must complete an **entry card**.

## Customs

Although the EU channel allows EU visitors to walk through largely unchallenged, customs officers remain vigilant. Malta is a small country and any imported 'nasty' such as food bacteria or rabies would have a devastating effect (certain foodstuffs are often banned). For non-EU visitors, the duty-free allowance per adult is 200 cigarettes or equivalent, one bottle of spirits, one bottle of wine and a 'reasonable quantity' of perfume.

If you arrive at the Pinto Wharf docks by car, you have 185 days' free movement before you must take the car out. While in Malta the car should be driven by its owner or owner's party rather than locals, as Maltese residents are not allowed foreign-registered cars and there are frequent checks.

Non-residents can bring as much **foreign currency** into the country as they wish, but any sum larger than €12,500 (Lm5000) should be declared on arrival to avoid problems on departure. There is no exchange control but taking anything more than €12,500 out of Malta should also be declared. In fact there is little point taking *liri* out of the country as trying to cash even modest amounts of *liri* overseas is an uphill struggle.

For residents of the EU, the usual regulations apply regarding what you can take home. Note that you are not allowed to bring fresh meat, vegetables or plants into the UK. If you need more information, call **HM Customs and Excise**, **t** (020) 8748 8010 and ask for the Customs Allowances section.

Travellers from the USA are allowed to take home duty-free goods to the value of $400, including 200 cigarettes or 100 cigarillos, 50 cigars or 250g tobacco, plus 1 litre of spirits (or 2 litres of fortified wine or other spirits under 22% alcohol); plus 2 litres of wine. Call the **US Customs Service**, **t** (202) 354 1000, or see the pamplet *Know Before You Go*, available from *www.customs.gov.*

# Disabled Travellers

*See* overleaf for a list of organizations that will provide general help and information for disabled travellers before leaving home. Some may also be able to give you up-to-date information about the situation in Malta.

Maltese **pavements**, where they exist, tend to be narrow and uneven, making life difficult if you are frail or in a wheelchair. Entrances to many **shops and hotels** can also be tricky, but the more modern ones have implemented the government's policy of improving access where possible.

**Bus transport** is nigh on impossible, but all other modes including the **Gozo ferry** are available. The principal **archaeological sites** (except the Hypogeum) can be seen with help, and **major churches** have wheelchair

## Disability Organizations

### In the UK and Ireland

**Holiday Care Service**, The Hawkins Suite, Enham Place, Enham Alamein, Andover, Hampshire SP11 6JS, t 0845 124 9971, *www. holidaycare.org.uk*. Gives information on destinations, transportation and tour operators.

**Irish Wheelchair Association**, Blackheath Drive, Clontarf, Dublin 3, t (01) 833 8241, *www.iwa.ie.*

**RADAR (Royal Association for Disability and Rehabilitation)**, 12 City Forum, 250 City Road, London EC1V 8AF, t (020) 7250 3222, *www.radar.org.uk*. Publishes several useful books as well as holiday fact-packs.

**Royal National Institute of the Blind (RNIB)**, 105 Judd Street, London WC1H 9NE, t (020) 7388 1266, *www.rnib.org.uk.*

**Royal National Institute for the Deaf (RNID)**, 19–23 Featherstone Street, London EC1Y 8SL, Infoline t 0808 808 0123, textphone t 0808 808 9000, *informationline@rnid.org.uk*, *www.rnid.org.uk.*

### In the USA

**Access America**, Washington DC, DC 20202, USA, *www.accessamerica.gov*. Provides information on facilities for disabled people at international airports. The US government website, *www.dot.gov/airconsumer/*

*disabled.htm*, also has useful information.

**American Foundation for the Blind**, 11 Penn Plaza, Suite 300, New York NY 10001, t (212) 502 7600, toll free t 800 232 5463, *www.afb.org*. The best source for information in the USA for visually impaired travellers.

**Federation of the Handicapped**, 211 West 14th Street, New York, NY 10011, t (212) 747 4262. Organizes summer tours for members; there is a nominal annual fee.

**Mobility International USA**, 132 East Broadway, Suite 343, Eugene OR 97401, t (541) 343 1284, *info@miusa.org*, *www.miusa.org*. Provides information and a range of publications for the disabled traveller. $35 annual membership fee.

**SATH (Society for Accessible Travel and Hospitality)**, 347 5th Avenue, Suite 610, New York NY 10016, t (212) 557 0027, *www.sath.org*. Advice on all aspects of travel for the disabled, for a small charge, or unlimited to members.

## Useful Websites

*www.access-able.com*. Information for aged and disabled travellers.

*www.access-ability.org/travel.htm*. Information on travel agencies.

**Disability World**, *www.disabilityworld.org*. Online network for disabled travellers, with links to other websites, archives and information on travel guides.

access; but the Museum of Fine Arts, the upper floors of the Grand Master's Palace and parts of St John's Co-Cathedral are inaccessible.

It is best to check with either the **MTA** or the **National Commission for the Disabled** in Santa Venera, t 21 487789/448521/441311, *www.knpd.org*. Both provide advice and a list of hotels. Many of the newer hotels, constructed while Malta's EU application was pending, elected not to incorporate rooms for the non-ambulant disabled. The **Westin Dragonara Resort** in St Julian's, the **Hotel Meridien Phoenicia** in Floriana and **The Victoria** and the all-inclusive **Fortina Hotel** in Sliema all have rooms specifically equipped for disabled visitors. The **Paola Rehabilitation Centre**, Corradino, Paola, Malta, t 21 693863/692221, *www.phrfmalta.com*, can organize wheelchair hire for a Lm10 a week and a Lm30 deposit, for up two weeks. It but does not have power wheelchairs.

## Insurance and EHICs

For emergency numbers, *see* 'Crime and the Police', pp.78–9.

Now Malta is in the EU all EU citizens have the right to free emergency treatment in government hospitals and clinics. They must obtain a **European Health Insurance Card (EHIC)** in advance in their home country. Visitors from elsewhere are advised to take out separate health insurance that covers repatriation. Check the small print in your **life insurance** or **health insurance policy** if you plan to go diving, parasailing, etc.

## Money

At time of writing, the unit of currency is the **Malta *lira* (Lm)** but the **euro** is due to be adopted in January 2008.

The **Malta *lira* (Lm)** is pegged to a basket of currencies that includes the US dollar and the euro, and is a soft currency not traded on any international exchange. In common with many economies dependent on tourism (about 35% GNP in Malta; it provides around 30,000 jobs), the *lira* is prisoner to strict exchange controls.

The currency is decimal and divided into *liri* and cents. Notes: Lm20, Lm10, Lm5, Lm2. Coins: Lm1, 50c, 25c, 10c, 5c, 2c, 1c. The euro is also divided into 100 cents. Inflation is tame.

At the time of writing, to buy one Malta *lira* (also known as the pound) you will have to give about £1.60, €2.35 or US$3.10. Try not to leave Malta – unless of course you intend to return – with any local currency at all. British provincial high-street banks will more than likely tell you to take it elsewhere – like back to Malta. There are no controls on the amount of money taken in and out of the country, but sums greater than Lm5,000 (€12,500) should be declared.

**Cash** and **traveller's cheques** can be exchanged at banks and hotels. Maltese hotels indulge in the worldwide custom of overcharging for this privilege, so the bank will be your best bet. Whenever you change money, keep the receipt: you will need it to get your hard currency back. Some local shops will take foreign currency at a marginally firmer rate than the banks when making purchases. **American Express**, **Diners**, **MasterCard** and **Visa** are accepted in most of the larger establishments. **American Express** has an office situated at High Street, Sliema, t 21 334051, which provides cashing and travel facilities for Amex card- and traveller's cheque-holders. **Thomas Cook** has branches in Malta – Valletta, Sliema, Paceville and Buġibba – and one in Victoria, Gozo. **Coppini**, an independent foreign-exchange dealer, has a head office at 58 Merchants Street, Valletta, and branches in Sliema, Qawra and St Julian's. **Western Union International** have a branch in San Gwann; contact FEXCO, t 21 378867.

There are four principal retail banks: **HSBC**, **Bank of Valletta**, **Lombard Bank** and the **Aps Bank**. You'll never be far from any one of them. All have installed 24-hour foreign-currency machines in the principal tourist areas. All the banks will provide you with cash against your MasterCard and/or Visa card. You need to show your passport for all transactions other than exchanging cash. Try

to avoid having money wired; 'unfortunate delays' in the labyrinthine central banking system are not uncommon. Queues can be tiresome and there aren't any specific times to avoid (*see* p.85 for opening hours).

## Getting There

### By Air from the UK

For such a small country Malta has a surprisingly large number of direct flights from most of the capital cities of Europe to **Malta International Airport** (MIA), *www.maltairport.com*, at Luqa, 4 miles (6.5km) from Valletta. The national airline, **Air Malta**, *www.airmalta.com*, has a modern fleet and an impeccable safety record.

Do not leave it until the last minute to check in for your return flight. All carriers are merciless about bumping you from planes they have overbooked; even on a full Business Class ticket your legal redress is almost non-existent. This problem is most pronounced in summer, so arrive 90 minutes prior to the scheduled departure time. The 10-minute Gozo helicopter airlink, *www.airgozo.com*, flies directly to MIA, but add a further 10 minutes for luggage.

### Scheduled Flights

**Air Malta** and **British Airways** franchise-holder **GB Airways** have been joined by a local discount operator, **Britishjet**, *www.britishjet.com*, in offering scheduled services from Heathrow and Gatwick. They have some 45 flights a week in summer between them. In addition, **Ryanair**, *www.ryanair.com*, flies from Luton and there are also direct services from Manchester, Glasgow, Birmingham, Bristol, Stansted, Newcastle, Dublin and Cork. The Heathrow–Malta flight time is approximately 3hrs 15mins. Contact **Air Malta**, 314–16 Upper Richmond Road, Putney, London SW15 6TU, t (020) 8785 3199; or Reservations/Ticketing Office, Malta House, 36–8 Piccadilly W1V 0PP, t (020) 7292 4900; or **British Airways** on t 0870 850 9850, *www.ba.com*, for reservations and information on fares – Super Pex, Apex, Eurobudget and Business Class. The only unrestricted return fare starts from around £300 (Business Class). Prices for

Apex start at around £100. It is worth asking about any 'World Offers' that might be running, when return tickets can be bought for as little as £80, although these must usually be booked well in advance.

## Charter Flights

Malta is principally a holiday destination and there is a smorgasbord of charter flights available: **Air Malta, Britannia, Caledonian, Monarch, Air 2000** and **Airtours International** fly round the clock from Heathrow, Gatwick, Manchester and 19 other airports in the UK and Ireland, depending on the time of year. Beware of trying to book seats only in high summer. Prices can be heavily discounted. Try the travel pages of the Sunday broadsheets or your local travel agent.

## By Air from Europe, North Africa and Beyond

**Air Malta** runs regular services to 45 cities in **Europe, North Africa**, the **Middle East** and the **Gulf**. These are reciprocated by some of the national carriers, including **Lufthansa** and **Alitalia**. In addition, **Air Malta** has services to **Catania** and **Palermo** in Sicily: four and two flights a week, respectively, in summer. **Air Malta** also flies twice a week to and from **Cairo** and has daily flights to **Tripoli** in Libya.

**Tuninter** has a twice-weekly service between **Tunis** and Malta, as does **Air Malta**. **Tuninter** also flies from Malta to **Monastir** in summer only.

### Flight Information in Malta

**Flight enquiries:** Malta International Airport (MIA) **t** 50 043333, *www.maltairport.com*.
**Air Malta:** Head Office, Luqa, **t** 22 999000, or Freedom Square, Valletta, **t** 21 240686/7/8. On Gozo: 13 Independence Square, Victoria **t** 22 999624/5.
**Alitalia:** 4th Floor, Airways House, High Street, Sliema, **t** 21 322992.
**Condor:** Worldwide Airline Representatives, Air Terminal Building, MIA, Luqa, **t** 21 693385.
**Corsair:** Robert Arrigo & Sons, 48 Main Street, St Julian's, **t** 21 317519.
**Lufthansa:** Departure Hall, MIA, Luqa, **t** 21 252020.
**Tuninter:** 161D Tower Mansions, lower Road, Sliema, **t** 21 320732.

## By Air from North America and Australia

London and Rome are used as hubs to Malta from both continents. The **Air Malta** offices listed below will recommend carriers and advise on fares.

### Air Malta Offices

A full list is on *www.airmalta.com*.
**Australia:** Breakaway Aviation Services P/L, Level 1, 123 Clarence Street, Sydney, NSW 2000, **t** (02) 9250 9444, *sydney@airmalta.com.au*. Melbourne office: *melbourne@airmalta.com.au*.
**USA:** There is no longer an Air Malta office in the US. See *www.airmalta.com*.

## By Sea From Europe

The route is via **Genoa, Salerno** or **Sicily**. **Grandi Navi Veloci** has once-weekly trips from **Genoa via Tunis** (local agents **Sullivan Maritime t** 21 226873 and **Grimaldi Ferries**, *www.grimaldi.it*, have a once-weekly service, temporarily suspended at time of writing). There is a weekly ferry from **Salerno** to Malta (local agents **Gollcher, t** 25 691550).

Alternatively, drive to the southern tip of Italy, to Reggio di Calabria, or to Naples, and take one of the many ferry services to Sicily. **Virtu Ferries** operate extremely efficient high-speed catamarans between Malta and two Sicilian ports, **Catania** and **Pozzallo**. One-way fares start from €65 (passengers) and €90 (car). The schedule varies over different times of the year, see *www.virtuferries.com* (**t** 21 318854).

## By Train and Coach from the UK

The lengthy **train** journey as far as Catania in Sicily encompasses many dubious treats: at least two changes (at Paris and Rome), the (inevitable) delays on Italian trains, a diet of railway food, and forced intimacies with complete strangers. For those travelling with an **Inter-Rail** or (for those from the US) **Eurail** card, see *www.interrail.com* or *www.eurail.com*, it makes more sense. These cards enable you to scoot around the whole of Europe for up to a month. For more comfort overnight, reserve a couchette. Fares are not cheap, and you also need to allow for an Italian supplement and the cost of the Catania–Malta ferry.

The websites *www.bahn.de* (the German railways website, which can give you journey times for most rail journeys in Europe – even those outside Germany) and *www.seat61.com* are useful for planning your railway journey. See also *www.railpass.com* if you are travelling from the US.

Strangely, **coach** travel is a feasible alternative. In summer **Eurolines/National Express** will take you as far as Rome, nonstop. There are departures from London on Wednesday and Friday at 10.30am, arriving in Rome early the next evening, in time for supper. The following morning, it is usually best to take a train or a plane for all points south. The train is very economical, but a tiring 10 hours. Air Malta and Alitalia have 20 flights a week from Rome to MIA between them in summer. The flight takes just over an hour. You could also continue by coach to Sicily and take the ferry from there; the Rome–Sicily ticket costs approximately £30, one way.

**Rail Europe Travel Centre**, 179 Piccadilly W1V 0BA, **t** 08705 848 848, *www.raileurope.co.uk*.

**National Express/Eurolines**, 52 Grosvenor Gardens, London, **t** 08705 143 219, *www.nationalexpress.com*.

## By Car from the UK

This is a more viable alternative to coach and rail, not least because you will not be at the mercy of Italian timetables. The journey is about 1,300 miles (2,150km) and can be done in two days, but it is more enjoyable to linger. Car ferries go from Salerno and Genoa on the Italian mainland or Catania and Pozzallo in Sicily (*see* above and p.308).

**Checklist**: car logbook (for Italy and Malta), Green Card (for Switzerland and Malta), full UK driving licence, basic spares (clutch cable, fan belt, radiator hose), first-aid kit. The best maps or atlases for France are Michelin, and for Italy Touring Club Italiano.

## Getting Around

For further information on getting to Gozo, *see* p.266. For Comino, *see* p.301.

## By Air

There is much talk of a fixed-wing service to be introduced between Malta and **Gozo**, but to date the only alternative to the ferry is the **Gozo helicopter service**, *www.airgozo.com*, **t** 21 561301, offering seven round trips daily. At the time of writing the service is planned to run year-round. Tickets can be booked through the website or by phone. Ask your hotel or agent in Gozo to arrange a taxi to meet you at the heliport, or you will have to take a short hike to the main road and catch a bus into Victoria.

The baggage allowance is 20kg per passenger in addition to one small item of hand luggage – excess baggage is charged at 35c per kilo. Fares: return Lm50; one-way Lm30; children (2–12) 50% fare and infants 10% fare.

The helicopter is also available for sight-seeing and photographic tours on a charter basis. Such a trip may cost anything from Lm20 to Lm60 per person.

## By Sea

### Malta–Gozo

The *Gozo Channel Co*, *www.gozochannel.com*, runs the principal shuttle route is from Ċirkewwa on the northwestern tip of Malta to Mġarr Harbour in Gozo. The 3-mile (5km) journey takes 25 minutes and operates approximately once every 90 minutes, day and night, in summer. At peak season most daytime crossings can be crowded, so, if you are planning to take a car, arrive half an hour before the scheduled sailing time. In winter the night service is infrequent.

Timetables change seasonally; copies are available free from most hotels, MTA offices and travel agents and from the website. Tickets cannot be booked in advance.

### Malta–Comino

Getting to Comino is more problematic; the only scheduled service is run by the Comino Hotel, when the hotel is open.

### Sliema–Valletta

The **Marsamxett Ferry**, **t** 23 463333, *www.captainmorgan.com.mt*, is the least aggravating way of getting to Valletta from Sliema. The 100-seater boat, her topsides painted blue to match the livery of a German beer company, beetles back and forth across the creek from the Ferries in Sliema to the Valletta bastions. The journey takes five minutes and runs approximately every 30 minutes Monday to Saturday from 7.30am to 6pm. Fares are 40c each way.

## Pleasure Cruises

The market is dominated by **Captain Morgan Cruises**, Dolphin Court, Tigne Seafront, Sliema, t 23 463333, *www. captainmorgan.com.mt*. During the summer months this well-respected fleet offers more variations on a theme than can be imagined: you can choose between **Malta** (*May–Oct daily except Sun; three times a week other months*), which includes transport from your hotel or apartment to Sliema marina, or **Comino and the Blue Lagoon**. Alternatively, you can opt for one of the company's theme cruises such as the **Pirates of the Mediterranean Cruise** (*Wed and Sat in summer*), where the crew stage sword fights, walking the plank and firing cannons. Or, perhaps, you might prefer the **Underwater Safari**, examining Malta's marine life from the vantage point of the glass-bottomed MV *Sea Below* (*four times daily except Sun*). The **Fernandes Sunset Cruise** runs in the evening with unlimited rum punch and a DJ. Captain Morgan not only provides its clientele with a range of destinations and activities but also offers a choice of ship types from the 65ft (20m) *Spirit of Malta* catamaran, through the 87ft (26m) schooner-rigged Turkish *gulet Fernandes*. All offer regular cruises around the waters and bays of Malta and Gozo, albeit at a slightly higher rate than a conventional pleasure cruise (the adult price for a full day's cruising on the *Spirit of Malta* is Lm26.75, including a meal and unlimited drinks). All excursions depart from the Ferries in Sliema except for the *Sea Below* (from Buġibba).

An alternative to Captain Morgan's omnipresence is provided by **Hera Cruises Ltd**, Abate Rigord Street, Ta'Xbiex, t 21 330583, *www.herayachtmalta.com*, whose 82ft (25m) twin-masted Turkish yacht (with mahogany interiors) the M/S *Hera* offers day cruises around the three islands, and a cruise round Comino.

On Gozo, **Xlendi Pleasure Cruises, t** 99 478819, organizes a trip beginning at Marsalforn, circling the island before heading off to Comino and the Blue Lagoon. In the evening **Frankie's Diving School, t** 21 563375, runs a *Sunset Cruise* from Mġarr which anchors off Comino for dinner.

## Boat Charters

The Maltese islands have many tucked-away coves and bays that are best reached by boat, and there is a handful of professional skippers who will take you swimming or fishing wherever you want to go. The principal official provider of yachts for charter purposes is (again) **Captain Morgan**. Would-be sea dogs can hire a 41ft (12.3m) yacht along with a skipper, fuel, sandwiches, soft drinks and snorkelling gear.

There are a few other companies offering a similar service for a similar sort of price. These include:

**AC Marine**, Pontoon F, Msida Seafront, t 99 495164.

**Nautica Ltd**, Nautica Marine, 21 Msida Road, Gzira, t 21 345138/9, *www.nautica.com.mt*.

**S and D Yachts Ltd**, Seabreeze, 10 Giuseppe Cali Street, Ta'Xbiex, t 21 331515, *www.sdyachts.com*.

**Sail Away Charters**, Pontoon G, Msida Seafront, t 79 708820.

**Fishermen** will also sometimes oblige if you can track one down. They will rarely go out for a full day and price is a matter of personal, and probably drawn-out, negotiation. Try **Marsaskala** and **Marsaxlokk** in Malta, and **Marsalforn** and **Mġarr** harbour in Gozo.

For **self-drive boats** try Oki-KO-Ki Boat Hire Co., near the Cavalieri Hotel in St Julian's, t 21 339831, which hires out craft from dinghies to speedboats. Age restrictions apply and a hefty deposit is required. The principal marine brokers and agents are listed under 'Yachting' (*see* pp.92–4).

## By Car

The Maltese are car-mad, although to witness the way many of them drive you would not know it. There are now an astonishing 240,000+ cars for a population of

400,000. When a significant percentage of this number is out in force (as on Sundays), the 800 miles (1,300km) of roads (an impressive statistic for an island only 16 miles/27km long) can appear all too meagre.

**Filling stations** are equipped with automatic dispensers. Most stations have attendants from 8am to 6pm. At all other times the automatic dispensers operate, taking Lm2 and Lm5 notes. No credit cards. **Unleaded petrol** costs about Lm0.42 per litre and **diesel** Lm0.39 per litre. Only 95RON petrol is available.

Malta has taken energetic steps to try to modernize its infrastructure, but the quality of the **roads** is still pretty terrible – they are an agglomeration of undulations, tyre-devouring potholes, malicious reverse camber and poor-quality tarmac that all conspire to make driving uncomfortable and potentially hazardous. None of the roads are numbered, few are properly lit, and after the rains all offer the grip of an ice rink. Nevertheless, improvements are underway. Watch out though: many of the good stretches of road have **speed cameras**, all confusingly set to different speeds. Look out for the camera signs and associated speed limits: **speeding fines** are Lm40. NB: All roads lead to Valletta, but the road network links nearly all the towns and villages, and, antiquated heaps notwithstanding, it should take no more than an hour to drive from one end of Malta to the other.

**Parking** used be a hassle of migraine-inducing proportions. However, a 1,000-space car park has opened 650ft (200m) from the Valletta bus terminus along with a slightly smaller one in Sliema. These private enterprises have eased the problem, but at a price; Lm0.65 for one hour. Try not to park illegally as the wardens have a quick-fire approach to violations: a Lm10 fine or towing. If your car is towed, go to the nearest police station, which should be indicated on the Tow Zone signs. If you do find a slot in a public car park, tip the attendant 20–30c (€1) when you leave. Also be warned that the revenue section of the police have been to Denver and discovered the 'Boot'; clamping and towing, with capricious justice, has begun in earnest. The fines are Lm15 and Lm45 respectively.

## Names and Signs

**Malti** is an unsophisticated language of connections and derivatives, and many place names are everyday words. For example: *ramla*=sandy bay, *marsa*=harbour, *qala*=small cove, *bahar*=sea or bay, *għar*=cave, blata=rock, *xaħra*=stony ground, *nadur*=lookout. *Triq* means street, *San* prefixes a saint's name and *Triq Il-Kbira* is the high or main street. *Misrah* means square, as does *piazza*.

As many of the major tourist roads have both **Malti and English names**, this guide uses the English spelling, although in the smaller villages the street names are invariably just in Malti. The Maltese have an infuriating habit of renaming their streets, especially after politicians; the late Nationalist prime minister, George Borg Olivier, heads the current crop. Again, ask if you get lost; local knowledge always supersedes the local honours system.

Road signs have improved markedly in recent years, but only a few display distances. All manner of natty new signs have sprouted, and navigating – by car or on foot in Valletta – is no longer a hit-and-miss affair. Conventional road signs are white on blue; signs directing you to a museum or site are white on brown, while Valletta has adopted a 'country stile' approach with strategically placed walking signs. Signs or graffiti bearing the legend RTO deal with the hunters' right to shoot birds during the *kaċċa*. It is not uncommon to see country road signs peppered with gunshot, having been used, presumably, for target practice.

## Hiring a Car

If the above has not put you off hiring a car (it should not, as Malta has some of the lowest car-hire rates in Europe), the major companies are represented at the airport and in the major tourist locations. The local car-hire companies, with tantalizing names like the Alcapone Car Hire Co., are just as good and often 10–20% cheaper.

Excellent vehicles from small family jeeps to Group A cars cost, from the major companies, Lm15 and Lm7 per day, respectively. The rates published are for seven days or more in peak season, and it sometimes pays to ignore

## Rules of the Road

- Be careful at **roundabouts**. Maltese drivers are very indecisive as to right of way – it is the code of the jungle rather than the highway code that counts.
- If you are involved in an **accident** do not, under any circumstance, move your car one millimetre until the police arrive to take measurements and adjudicate, even if the result is a noisy jam. If you do, your car-rental insurance may be made void. The only exception to this is a straight bumper-to-bumper collision. In this case, the cars can be moved to the side of the road without calling the police. Make sure the car you are driving has 'bumper-to-bumper' forms. One of these must be filled in, and signed by both drivers.
- Driving the wrong way down a **one-way street** is conventional practice and has its roots in the national love of gambling.
- No one ever indicates, uses a mirror or acknowledges a courtesy.
- Malta now has a veritable arsenal of **traffic lights**. In 1993 there was one set, and they were rarely switched on. Today, they are everywhere, comparatively speaking, and are only obeyed on the principal intersections. Always treat the lights with caution; don't be an amber gambler here.
- **Drive on the left** (as in the UK) and give way to the right.
- **Speed limits** are rarely policed or adhered to except by the speed cameras on the best roads, but they are: 80kph (48mph), and 40kph (24mph) in built-up areas.
- A familiar sight (and one to be avoided) is piles of scrap metal (in reality, 30-year-old Ford Populars) that belch blue smoke as they struggle to maintain 30kph (20mph) in the wrong lane. Occasionally, they may even career out of control as an ancient but vital component disintegrates.

these tariffs, especially with the smaller companies. A credit-card imprint will be taken as a deposit. If you have a specific requirement, it is advisable to request it in advance.

You will have to be over 25 and under 70 and to have held a full driving licence for 12 months; a few companies will hire to those outside these parameters. Insurances vary but all have mandatory third-party, fire and theft cover. Moving your car after an accident may invalidate your insurance.

Chauffeur-driven cars are expensive, and all are funereal Mercedes or Volvos; Wembley's has the largest fleet. You will often get better deals with the local firms than international giants, although these may be marginally easier to organize.

## Car Hire Companies

**Avis** (Msida), t 21 246640.

**Billy's Car Hire** (Mellieħa), t 21 523676.

**Gozo Garage** (Victoria), t 21 551866.

**Hertz** (Gzira), t 21 314636/7, *www.hertz.co.mt*.

**Mexico Garage** (Ħamrun), t 21 247888, *www.mexicogarage.com*.

**Percius** (Lija), t 21 442530.

**Rabat Garage** (Rabat), t 21 453975.

**Tony's Rentals** (Gzira), t 21 341695.

**Wembley's** (St Andrew's), t 21 389871.

## Breaking Down

Here are three breakdown companies:

**RMF**, t 21 225536, SOS 21 242222, *www.rmfmalta.com*.

**MTC**, t 21 433333/21 424326, *www.mtctouringmalta.com*.

**CAA**, t 21 23 316666/99 316666.

Only a few rental firms include breakdown cover; if yours does not, your thumb should get you back to the garage.

## By Bus

**Bus enquiries:** t 8007 2393, *www.maltatransport.com*.

*See* Bus Routes map, pp.70–71.

Buses have been the only means of public transport on Malta since the 6½ miles (11km) of railway shut in 1931. The yellow buses are for the most part rudimentary diesel antiquities with no air conditioning, meagre suspension, threadbare seating and sometimes grumpy drivers; in other words they are no different from most European transit systems. In one recent year, they carried an astonishing 32 million passengers. (There has been talk of new equipment, but so far only six characterless new buses are in service.) All vehicles have been christened with names as diverse as *Elvis Presley, King Of The Road* and *St Paul* on their shiny bonnets. Nearly all terminate in the village square or by the village church. If you want a bus to stop, wave frantically from the roadside bus stop; if you are inside, ring the bell.

The island is divided into three **bus zones** depending on the duration of the journey. Adult fares are 20–25c depending on zone, children are 15c and pensioners 10c no matter how long the journey. Passes for unlimited travel are available from one-day (Lm1.50) to seven day (Lm6). Details of fares and timetables are available from the Public Transport Association, Dun Gorg Preca Street, B'Bajda or from the main bus terminus in Valletta.

In **Malta**, the main terminus is outside **Valletta** at **City Gate**, where the buses orbit the large Triton fountain and from which tentacular routes spread across the island; just about every village is served, albeit infrequently. Do not be intimidated by the bustle of shoppers and hawkers at City Gate, and providing you know the number of the bus you wish to take there are tall signposts which will direct you to your bus. Nearly all buses originate in and return to Valletta, so cross-routing can be a problem; **Mosta** and **Msida** are the best bet. There is a helpful information booth at City Gate to help turn numbers into destinations. NB: destinations are not marked on any bus. If in doubt, ask – the Maltese have an encyclopaedic knowledge of the routes.

In **Gozo**, buses are grey with a red stripe. The terminus is in **Victoria** (Rabat). As all roads lead to Victoria, you have to change there when cross-routing. Buses meet most incoming ferries up to 8.30pm at **Mġarr** harbour. Don't expect a fluid bus service in Gozo; it is geared to the local working and school hours.

## By Motorcycle and Bicycle

People who think the Maltese islands are flat have never cycled them. The prevailing road and traffic conditions make on-road cycling a recommended pastime only for the very skilful or the very brave, and certainly not for children. Motorcycles and scooters are available for hire at approximately Lm10 for a single day, decreasing to Lm6 if hired for over three days. A crash helmet is obligatory, and apart from holding a driving licence you have to be over 21 and leave a deposit. *See also* Mountain Biking, p.90.

### Bike Hire Companies

**Magri Cycles**, Mosta, t 21 432890

**On Two Wheels**, Marsalforn, Gozo, t 21 561503.

**Albert's Motorbike Hire**, Gzira, t 21 340149.

**Med Sun Scooter Rental**, St Julian's, t 21 378711.

## By Taxi and *Karrozin*

Maltese cabs only really serve the visitor. Cabs are clean white chariots of varying vintages; a few are old Mercedes with huge ivory-coloured steering wheels belonging to the glory days of soft suspension. Most have shut-off meters (asking for them to be switched on is pointless). On the whole, drivers are not particularly interested in advancing Maltese tourist relations, and the well-intentioned government tariffs are merely laughed at.

For what it is worth, there is a fare structure operating from the airport which splits Malta into 11 zones with a published rate for each. In order for the scheme to work properly (i.e. in the customer's favour) clients need to buy a ticket from the arrivals desk kiosk and hand it to the driver before commencing their journey. Good luck.

Taxis are to be found on ranks in the larger towns. Ask, haggle, then agree the fare before getting in. Tipping is rarely offered or expected. The fares from the airport to Valletta, Sliema and St Paul's Bay are around Lm6, Lm8 and Lm10, respectively. Most taxis are private but the largest company, **Wembley's** in St Julian's, t 21 374141/374242, operates a very reliable 24-hour black cab service which has to be ordered or picked up from the Wembley garage in St Julian's. If you are staying in a hotel it is best to order yourself and ask the price on the phone, as rates from reception can sometimes be doubled.

*Karrozin* are horse-drawn carriages that have plied their trade since 1856. They are a good way to see the sights, especially in Valletta. The four-person canopied bench-seats are high up, and children enjoy the ride. *Karrozin* can be found outside most main tourist attractions. Haggle with all your skill before boarding – the Maltese who use the *karrozin* on Sundays do.

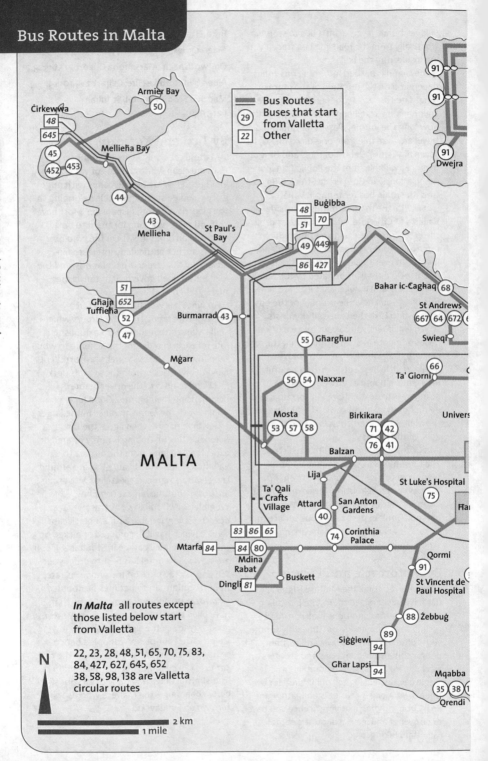

**Legend:**
- ▬▬ Bus Routes
- (29) Buses that start from Valletta
- [22] Other

Armier Bay
50

Ċirkewwa
48
645

45
452 453

Mellieħa Bay
44

43 Mellieħa

St Paul's Bay

Buġibba
48
51 70
49 449
86 427

Baħar ic-Ċagħaq 68

St Andrews
667 64 672

Swieqi

51
Għajn Tuffieħa 652
52
47

Burmarrad 43

Għargħur 55

Mġarr

56 54 Naxxar

Ta' Giorni

66

Mosta
53 57 58

Birkirkara
71 42
76 41

Balzan

University

**MALTA**

Lija

St Luke's Hospital
75

Ta' Qali Crafts Village

Attard
40

San Anton Gardens

Ha

83 86 65

Mtarfa 84

84 80
Mdina Rabat

74 Corinthia Palace

Qormi

91
St Vincent de Paul Hospital

Dingli 81

Buskett

88 Żebbuġ

Siġġiewi
89
94

Għar Lapsi
94

Mqabba
35 38

Qrendi

*In Malta* all routes except those listed below start from Valletta

22, 23, 28, 48, 51, 65, 70, 75, 83, 84, 427, 627, 645, 652
38, 58, 98, 138 are Valletta circular routes

N

91
91
91 Dwejra

▬▬ 2 km
▬▬ 1 mile

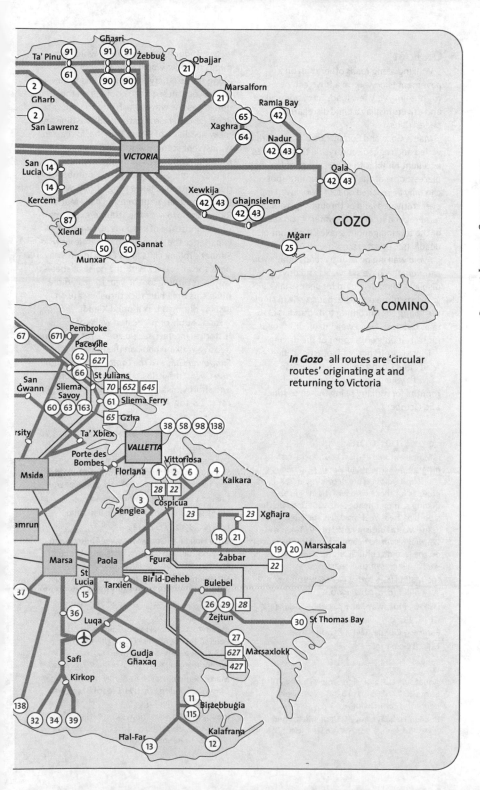

*In Gozo* all routes are 'circular routes' originating at and returning to Victoria

## On Foot

Walking along roads other than on a pavement (sidewalk) in a town can be frightening. Very few roads have sidewalks, and drivers display a blind disregard for pedestrians.

Malta, Gozo and Comino are blessed with a varied and rugged countryside that provides excellent **rambles** to peaceful out-of-the-way places. Some of the most rewarding spots can only be reached on foot. Avoid walking over cultivated land or through crops, and do remember a sunhat and water. If you see one of the few indigenous snakes, it will not be deadly (*see* pp.171–2).

Avoid walking on country roads where you can: very few have sidewalks and drivers display a blind disregard for pedestrians. If you do venture onto the roads, walk in single file facing the oncoming traffic and as close in as possible. Avoid walking on unlit roads at night, but only on account of the driving.

There is a plethora of fantastic scenery on Malta and Gozo and it is quite easy to come up with your own rambles, with the best months for walking being March to June and October.

Here, though, are a few areas which you might consider worth a meander or two: along the coast, try the **Dingli Cliffs** from where you can see Gozo bobbing on the horizon as the waves crash into the cliff face 850ft (260m) below or the wild coastline and rocky headland of **Għajn Tuffieħa**; for barren windswept scenery visit **Manikata** near **Mellieħa**, which is as barren and windswept as they come; **Selmun Bay** has a number of quiet countryside lanes fringed with wild flowers and hazelnut trees, as does **Marfa Ridge**; on **Gozo**: visit the strange, exotic man-made landscape of saltpans at **Xwieni** or experience the sweeping panoramic views of **Sannat**'s rolling cliffs at **Ta'Ċenċ**. In late May here, the air is thick with the noise of shearwaters returning for the year to nest; more birds, this time blue rock thrushes, are on display during a trek around **Xlendi**.

For a couple of suggested walks of historical interest, *see* pp.20–21. For a comprehensive walking book on the island try the *Sunflower Guide to the Landscapes of Malta and Gozo*. This little book packs in 70 long and short walks, 30 picnic suggestions and 7 car tours, together with maps and photos.

## Tour Operators

Malta features in most tour operators' programmes; the shoulder booking periods (April and October) are becoming increasingly popular for those who wish to avoid the glaring summer heat. Some variations on the standard 'two-week' package are listed here.

The **Malta Tourism Authority** (MTA), *www.visitmalta.com*, has comprehensive information on the island's cultural and sporting events, as well as listings of tour operators.

**UK:** Malta House, 36–8 Piccadilly, London W1V 0PP, **t** (020) 7292 4900.

**USA:** 65 Broadway Suite 823, New York, **t** (212) 430 3799.

**France:** 9 Cité de Trévise, 75009 Paris, **t** (1) 48 00 03 79.

### UK

**Aquatours Ltd**, 29a High Street, Thames Ditton, Surrey KT7 0SD, **t** (020) 8398 0505, *www.aquatours.com*. Diving.

**Belleair Holidays**, 314–16 Upper Richmond Road, Putney, London SW15 6TU, **t** (020) 8785 3266, *www.belleair.co.uk*. General, cultural, spa, weddings.

**Cadogan Travel**, 37 Commercial Road, Southampton, Hampshire SO15 1GG, **t** (02380) 828 300, *www.cadoganholidays.com*. General.

**Chevron Air Holidays**, Crownshield House, 143 St Leonard's Road, Windsor, Berkshire, **t** (01753) 851 267. General.

**Gozo Holidays** (Gozo), 151 Lower Church Road, Burgess Hill, West Sussex RH15 9AA, **t** (01444) 254 954, *www.gozoholidays.co.uk*.

**HF Holidays**, Imperial House, Edgware Road, Colindale, London NW9 5AL, **t** (020) 8905 9558, *www.hfholidays.co.uk*. A range of walking tours.

**Meon Villas**, Meon House, College Street, Petersfield, Hampshire GU32 3JN, **t** (01730) 268 411, *www.meonvillas.co.uk*. Gozo farmhouses, villas.

**Martin Randall Travel**, 10 Barley Mow Passage, Chiswick, London W4 4PH, **t** (020) 8742 3355. Architectural, heritage.

**Prestige Holidays**, 1 Fridays Court, High Street, Ringwood, Hampshire, **t** (01425) 480 400. Non-package, specialist tours.

**Ramblers Holidays**, Box 43, Welwyn Garden City, Hertfordshire AL8 6PQ, t (01707) 331 133, *www.ramblersholidays.co.uk*. Walking tours.

**Running and Sporting Tours**, PO Box 269 Brentwood, Essex CM15 8NR, t (01277) 264 444. For the energetic.

**Saga Holidays**, Saga Building, Middleburg Square, Folkestone, Kent CT20 1BL, t (01303) 71 1111, *www.saga.co.uk*. A range of holidays for the over-50s.

**St Peter's Pilgrims**, 87a Rushey Green, Catford, London SE6 4AF, t (020) 8244 8844, *www.stpeter.co.uk*. Religious.

**Sovereign**, First Choice House, London Road, Crawley, West Sussex, t (01293) 588 207, *www.sovereign.com*. General tours.

### Ireland

**747 Travel Ltd**, 81/2 Aungier Street, Dublin 2, t (1) 478 0829. General tours.

**Belleair Holidays**, c/o Dun Laoghaire Travel, 12 Pembroke Road, Ballsbridge, Dublin 4, t (1) 660 6321, *www.belleair.co.uk*. General tours.

### USA and Canada

**Academic Tours**, PO Box 370274, Brooklyn, NY 11237, t 800 875 9171, *www.academictours.com*.

A wide range of tours: follow in the historic footsteps of St Paul, the Knights of St John or British colonialists.

**Donna Franca Tours**, 470 Commonwealth Avenue, Boston, MA 02215, t 800 225 6290, *www.donnafranca.com*. Archaeology and history.

**Golden Escapes**, 75 The Donway West, Ste 710, Don Mills, Ontario M3C 2E9, t 800 668 9125, *www.goldenescapes.com*. Holidays for the over-50s.

**Pilgrim Tours**, PO Box 268, 3821 Main Street, Morgantown, PA 19543, t 800 322 0788, *www.pilgrimtours.com*. Offers a variety of religious tours.

**Reva Tours**, 1450 Rue City Councillors, Bur 520, Montreal, QCH 3A2E, t (514) 842 9016. General, cultural, archaeology, religious, etc.

**Scenic World**, 475 Sansome Street, Ste 850, San Francisco, CA 94111, t 800 952 0226, *www.scenicworldtour.com*. General tours, cultural, archaeology, religious tours, short breaks, etc.

**Ulysses Tours**, 645 5th Avenue, New York NY 10022, t (212) 371 7646, *www.ulyssestours.com*. General, cultural, archaeology, religious tours, short breaks, city tours, etc.

# Where to Stay

In a country which derives nearly 40% of its GNP from tourism there is, predictably, the full spectrum of accommodation available – from self-catering studios to 5-star hotel suites. Malta has adopted the World Tourism Organization (WTO) internationally recognized **'star' system**, which unfortunately does not tell the whole story, being based upon amenities and open to 'creative' interpretation by hotel operators, tourist organizations and managements. Tour operators have further confused the issue by doling out their own 'stars'. Furthermore, there is no recognition in the WTO's grading system for imaginative and sympathetic architecture, or lack thereof.

During the past couple of decades the government has worked at making the Maltese islands a more up-market tourist destination. To that end the only new building permits being issued are for 5-star hotels in Malta and Gozo, while existing hotels are being encouraged to upgrade.

# Hotels

There are nearly 200 registered hotels in Malta, Gozo and Comino. At the time of writing only a handful are 5-star; the majority have 3 and 2 stars.

It is generally safe to assume that a 5-star hotel will have hot and cold running everything and a 1-star will have clean respectable accommodation – there are no 'black holes' in Malta.

Only the independent traveller or the businessman will have to pay rack rates as 'bed stock' is invariably sold to package-holiday companies at substantial discounts. If you are staying for longer than a week outside the peak season, a friendly haggle with the proprietor will often be rewarding.

Tariffs are quoted per night in the high season and some include half-board.

For price ranges used in this book, *see* box on p.74. In this guide, official star ratings have been included, but accommodation is organized by price for B&B for a double room per night in high season.

## Hotel Price Ranges (see p.73)

| luxury | €€€€ | over Lm60 (€140) |
|---|---|---|
| expensive | €€€ | Lm35–60 (€80–140) |
| moderate | €€ | Lm20–34 (€47–79) |
| inexpensive | € | under Lm20 (€47) |

## Holiday Complexes, Aparthotels, Guest Houses and Self-Catering

Self-catering of any description sold through recognized tour operators and holiday companies has to be licensed by the government and is divided into four classes, with Class I having the most amenities. There is everything from studio rooms to three- and four-bedroom apartments. There is a wide selection in the brochures of the bigger tour operators and nearly all are along the northern coast in St Julian's, St Andrew's, Buġibba, Qawra and Mellieħa. A few properties are to be found inland in less conventional tourist locations. Facilities differ but most of the tatty operations are being cleaned up or denied licences.

## Villas and Farmhouses

The yen for privacy and the individual tastes of a fickle market have added to the number and quality of properties available, especially on Gozo. Again, those on offer through tour operators for short holiday periods have to be licensed.

**Farmhouses** are rural old stone houses that once housed families of goats, and tend to have character. **Villas** are likely to be more contemporary and made from yet-to-be-weathered local stone. Both usually have their own pools. You will find more villas in Malta; in Gozo there are more farmhouses. The leading operator in the UK is **Meon** (see 'Tour Operators', p.72), which represents Gozo Farmhouses Ltd, with over 25 farmhouses, modernized to an exceptional standard.

## Hostels

Malta is an affiliated member of the **Youth Hostels Association** (YHA) and an up-to-date list can be obtained from the YHA equivalent in your country or from the **YHA**, 17 Tal-Borg Street, Paola, t 21 693957. There are five hostels in Malta and one on Gozo. The MTA will furnish you with a further list of accommodation at affordable rates if the limited hostel space is taken up in the summer.

## Camping

The islands don't have a recognized camp site and 'wild' camping is officially prohibited, but a few hardy north European backpackers call **Ramla Bay** in Gozo home for the summer.

## Timeshare

Malta escaped the great timeshare scam, as perpetrated in the Canary Islands, but, if you hang around Bay Square in unappealing Buġibba or in Paceville for a nano-second, relentless touts with improbable lines in chat will swoop down like vultures and bite into your credit cards if given half the chance. For legitimate (and honourable) timeshare in Malta contact the **Malta Timeshare Association**, c/o Buġibba Holiday Complex, Tourist Street, Buġibba, t 21 580861.

# Practical A–Z

Conversion Tables 76
Children 77
Crime and the Police 78
Eating Out 79
Electricity 80
Entertainment and Nightlife 80
The Gay Scene 80
Health and Emergencies 81
Internet 82
Libraries 82
Living and Working in Malta 82
Markets and Shopping 82
Marrying in Malta 84
Media 84
Museums 85
Opening Hours 85
Packing 86
Postal Services 86
Religious Affairs 87
Sports and Activities 87
Telephones 91
Time 92
Tipping 92
Toilets 92
VAT 92
Women Travellers 92
Yachting Information 92

06

# Imperial–Metric Conversions

## Length (multiply by)
Inches to centimetres: 2.54
Centimetres to inches: 0.39
Feet to metres: 0.3
Metres to feet: 3.28
Yards to metres: 0.91
Metres to yards: 1.1
Miles to kilometres: 1.61
Kilometres to miles: 0.62

## Area (multiply by)
Inches square to centimetres square: 6.45
Centimetres square to inches square: 0.15
Feet square to metres square: 0.09
Metres square to feet square: 10.76
Miles square to kilometres square: 2.59
Kilometres square to miles square: 0.39
Acres to hectares: 0.40
Hectares to acres: 2.47

## Weight (multiply by)
Ounces to grams: 28.35
Grammes to ounces: 0.035
Pounds to kilograms: 0.45
Kilograms to pounds: 2.2
Stones to kilograms: 6.35
Kilograms to stones: 0.16
Tons (UK) to kilograms: 1,016
Kilograms to tons (UK): 0.0009
1 UK ton (2,240lbs) = 1.12 US tonnes (2,000lbs)

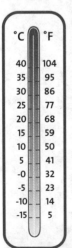

| °C | °F |
|----|-----|
| 40 | 104 |
| 35 | 95 |
| 30 | 86 |
| 25 | 77 |
| 20 | 68 |
| 15 | 59 |
| 10 | 50 |
| 5 | 41 |
| -0 | 32 |
| -5 | 23 |
| -10 | 14 |
| -15 | 5 |

## Volume (multiply by)
Pints (UK) to litres: 0.57
Litres to pints (UK): 1.76
Quarts (UK) to litres: 1.13
Litres to quarts (UK): 0.88
Gallons (UK) to litres: 4.55
Litres to gallons (UK): 0.22
1 UK pint/quart/gallon =
1.2 US pints/quarts/
gallons

## Temperature
Celsius to Fahrenheit:
multiply by 1.8 then
add 32
Fahrenheit to Celsius:
subtract 32 then multiply
by 0.55

# Malta Information

## Time Differences
Country: + 1hr GMT
Daylight saving late March to late September

## Dialling Codes
**Malta country code** 356

**To Malta from**: UK, Ireland, New Zealand 00 /
USA, Canada 011 / Australia 0011 then dial 356
and the full number including the initial zero

**From Malta to**: UK 00 44; Ireland 00 353; USA,
Canada 001; Australia 00 61; New Zealand 00
64 then the number without the initial zero

**Directory enquiries**: 1182
**International directory enquiries**: 1152

## Emergency Numbers
**Police**: 112
**Ambulance**: 112
**Fire**: 112
**Automobile Club** 24-hour breakdown service:
21 320349/333332.

## Embassy Numbers in Malta
**UK**: 23 230000; **Ireland** 21 824918;
**USA**: 25 614000; **Canada** 25 523233;
**Australia** 21 338201; **New Zealand** 21 435025

## Shoe Sizes

| Europe | UK | USA |
|--------|------|-------|
| 35 | 2½ / 3 | 4 |
| 36 | 3 / 3½ | 4½ / 5 |
| 37 | 4 | 5½ / 6 |
| 38 | 5 | 6½ |
| 39 | 5½ / 6 | 7 / 7½ |
| 40 | 6 / 6½ | 8 / 8½ |
| 41 | 7 | 9 / 9½ |
| 42 | 8 | 9½ / 10 |
| 43 | 9 | 10½ |
| 44 | 9½ / 10 | 11 |
| 45 | 10½ | 12 |
| 46 | 11 | 12½ / 13 |

## Women's Clothing

| Europe | UK | USA |
|--------|----|-----|
| 32 | 6 | 2 |
| 34 | 8 | 4 |
| 36 | 10 | 6 |
| 38 | 12 | 8 |
| 40 | 14 | 10 |
| 42 | 16 | 12 |
| 44 | 18 | 14 |

# Children

Disneyworld it is not; there are few sandy beaches – only four on Malta and one on Gozo that can properly be described as such – nevertheless, there are plenty of activities for the determined parent wishing to see their offspring amused by someone else for a time.

All the principal hotels have a decent pool and/or lido facilities and some have specialist children's pools. For committed water babies, a trip to the **Splash and Fun Park**, White Rocks, Baħar iċ-Ċagħaq, t 21 374283, *www.holiday-malta.com (open daily in summer, 9am–late)* between Sliema and Buġibba, might be an idea. This has two pools: one surrounded by mattresses and umbrellas and served by a snack bar; the other fed by a spaghetti junction of water chutes tipping people into the water at high speed. Parents and children should divide as appropriate on arrival. Buses 645 from Ċirkewwa, 68 from Valletta, 70 from Sliema or Buġibba.

Next door to Splash and Fun is Malta's latest tourist attraction: **Mediterraneo**, t 21 372218, *www.marineparkmalta.com (open winter Mon–Fri 10–5, closed Sat and Sun, summer open daily 10–5)*. Whether this thrills or horrifies will depend on which side of the animal liberation fence you stand. You can see reptiles, sea lions, parrots, pelicans, fish and invertebrates...before the star attraction, swimming with dolphins. To swim with dolphins (€108) you must be at least eight years old and an able swimmer – the pool is seven metres deep.

The more culturally minded may like to take the opportunity to visit **Ta'Qali Crafts Village**, t 21 412786 *(open Mon–Sat 9–12 and 4.30–7)*. Kids will probably enjoy the glass-blowing at **Mdina Glass**, t 21 415786 *(open June–Oct Mon–Fri 8–6, Sat 8–12; Nov–May, Mon–Fri 8.30–5, Sat 9–1)* or the **Phoenician Glassblowers**, t 21 437041, both also at the Crafts Village.

Also in Ta'Qali, near to the Crafts Village, is **Badger Karting**, t 21 421838, *www.badger.com. mt (winter Tues–Fri 5–11pm, Sat, Sun 12–11pm; summer Tues–Sun 7pm–1am; closed Mon all year round)*. They have 30 electric and 15 petrol-driven go-karts. The track is outdoors, so avoid going before the evening in August.

There is no minimum age, but in order to reach the pedals the driver must be at least 4ft 5in (135cm) tall. It is advisable to call beforehand to ensure availability.

The **Mdina Dungeons**, t 21 450267, *www.dungeonsmalta.com (open daily 10–4.30)*, will prove popular for those of a macabre disposition, i.e. all children. 'Discover horror, drama and mysteries from the dark past' invites the blurb – gruesomely rendered waxworks are the main attraction. On a more upbeat note, the **Playmobil Fun Park**, B36 Bulebel Industrial Estate, Żejtun, t 22 242445, *www.playmobilmalta.com (open July–Sept Mon–Sat 10–6, Sun 10–1; Oct–June 10–6 daily)* could provide a couple of hours' free entertainment. The German toy manufacturer has one of its largest factories on the island and has provided a shop, play area (with life-size replicas of their principal products) and water chutes to advertise the fact. Willy Wonka-esque tours of the factory are available on occasion. Telephone ahead to check times.

The **Razzett tal-Hbiberija** in Marsaskala, t 21 634412, *www.razzett.org (open Mon–Fri 9–3, Sat 11–3, Sun 10–4)*, has a collection of animals – monkeys, donkeys, ducks, goats etc. – and a little train which takes you around the enclosures. There is also a gym and large indoor swimming pool. The park is designed as a place where people with special needs can relax with their friends and families, and the whole centre (including pool) is fully accessible to the disabled. **St James's Cavalier Centre for Creativity** in Valletta, t 21 223216, has special theatre and cinema viewings aimed at children. Once or twice a week they also offer craft classes, such as glass painting and pottery for children. Call to find out the current programme.

There are also a couple of museums based on more conventional themes which may be of some interest. On Gozo, the **Pomskizillious Museum of Toys**, Xagħra, t 21 562489 *(open April Thurs–Sat only 10–1; May–mid- Oct Mon–Sat 10–12 and 3–6; winter Sat and public holidays only 10–1)*, has some exhibits which are over 200 years old. There is also an **Aviation Museum** at Ta'Qali, t 21 416095 *(open daily 9–5, including public holidays except Good Fri, Easter Sun, 15 Aug, 25 Dec and 1 Jan)* – two minutes' walk and signposted from the Crafts Village – where various aircraft and bits thereof are on display. Fans of more old-fashioned forms of transport might wish to visit **Birkirkara Station** where there are remnants of the steam railway that ran here until 1931. It also has a small playground.

Children are not generally great sightseers but there are a couple of options in this line that may appeal. One is the **helicopter sightseeing trip** around Malta; the other is an **Underwater Safari** examining the marine life of the islands in a glass-keeled boat. Both trips are operated by **Captain Morgan Cruises**, Dolphin Court, Tigne Seafront, Sliema, **t** 23 463333 (for further details and prices *see* p.66).

For a more conventional day, or even evening, out, you could try the **Eden Superbowl**, **t** 21 387398, in St George's Bay. The Eden Century Cinema complex (*see* below) is in the same road, and there are many places to eat in the new Bay Street shopping complex further down the hill. The top floor of Bay Street has an amusement arcade, with Quasar and a play area for small children. Teenagers, on the other hand, may appreciate a push towards one of Paceville's numerous **discos**. There are five main **cinemas** in Malta: **Eden Century Cinemas** in St George's Bay, **t** 21 377243, and Fgura, **t** 21 808000, the **Embassy** in Valletta, **t** 21 222225, the **Empire** in Buġibba, **t** 21 581787, and **Sun City Cine Palais** in Marsaskala, **t** 21 632857. Expect to see the same films as are showing in the UK, but a few months later.

If your children are particularly active, the island affords plenty of opportunities to indulge in pursuits such as **horse-riding** and **diving** – *see* pp.89 and 88–9 respectively.

For younger children, there are indoor playgrounds with climbing apparatus, balls etc.: **Playzone**, 211 Tower Road, Sliema, **t** 21 338741, and **Romp Around**, Swatar, Birkirkara, **t** 21 324351. Smaller versions can be found in the Gallarija Shopping Mall in Fgura and in the Bay Street shopping centre in St George's Bay.

When all else fails, try **Sweethaven Village**, the Popeye Film Set, Anchor Bay, **t** 21 524782, *www.popeyemalta.com* (*open June–Sept daily 9.30–7; Oct and Mar–May 9.30–5.30; Jan and Feb 9.30–4.30*). Although 'Sweethaven' has ruined one of the prettier northern bays (*see* p.183), children under 12 can enter free when

accompanied (they are vague as to adult-to-child ratio). The ticket includes a visit to the film set, four different animation shows, access to the splash and play pools, a boat trip round Anchor Bay (pools and boat trip summer only), glass-blowing and silver-smithing demonstrations, Santa's toy town and wine-tasting for the grown-ups. Next door is the children's Funpark with 10 or more rides. Entrance is free and the rides are paid for singly. Interests range from merry-go-rounds to a go-kart track (*open Nov and Jan–April Sat and Sun 9.30–6.30; May–Oct daily 9.30–5.30*).

Apart from getting bored, the other thing kids do is get hungry. A few restaurants in Malta have cottoned on to this. The **Black Pearl**, **t** 21 343970, is actually housed in a masted galleon docked at Ta'Xbiex Marina, giving kids (and adults if you like) the chance to pretend they are pirates up to no good on the high seas. The **Watercolours Family Café**, Islets Promenade, Buġibba **t** 21 572338, provides a separate play area for children, allowing their parents to eat in peace. If none of these takes your fancy, there is always the fast-food option. **McDonald's** is the current champion of the realm with six outlets, **Pizza Hut** and **Burger King** both have three, while **Kentucky Fried Chicken** has two.

If you are travelling with **babies or infants**, most English and Italian brand-named baby foods are available. Restaurants are relatively child-friendly, especially at lunchtime. A **babysitter** will cost Lm2–4 per hour; enquire at your hotel.

## Crime and the Police

Generally Malta is a safe place and time-share salesmen notwithstanding is fairly free from hassle. The Maltese look after their poor, elderly and infirm. The streets are safe day and night from dangers, and hooliganism and mugging are as rare as good drivers.

Since independence in 1964, tourism in Malta has developed at breakneck speed and has brought tremendous benefits, but there is no hiding from its side effects. Young men and women who even 15–20 years ago would have been content to remain in their towns and villages now want to be a part of the

## Emergency Telephone Numbers

**Ambulance, fire and police: t** 112
**The Armed Forces of Malta: t** 21 824212-4
**Malta Police Headquarters,** Floriana:
**t** 21 224001–9
**Gozo Police Headquarters,** Victoria: **t** 21 562044
**Emergency (air/sea) rescue: t** 21 809279 (day),
**t** 21 824220 (after 16.00 and weekends)
**Valletta Port Control: t** 21 241363
**Electricity (power failure): t** 21 223601;
on Gozo: **t** 21 556417
**Gas: t** 21 651661
**Water: t** 80 072222
**Traffic accident: t** 21 320202

new and changing Malta, and cracks have appeared in the hitherto granite-firm foundations of family life. This has resulted in a degree of envy and a sour tension; envy is manifested in an increasing number of burglaries, while tension is burnt off through violence in certain tourist areas such as Paceville. Hot-blooded stabbings and shootings, while uncommon, are no longer unheard of. Visitors are seldom, if ever, caught up in this petty violence, which is rooted in machismo, and is mostly over women.

Recently, Malta has developed a voracious appetite for **narcotics**, together with a tough judicial line on their use. Previously cannabis was treated as a harmless pastime, especially in Gozo, but now is policed as severely as heroin, cocaine and other chemicals, and possession will attract similar draconian penalties. In 1997 a female Swiss business executive was handed down a six-month gaol term – upheld on appeal – for possession of 2oz (6g) of cannabis; in most other countries, such a small quantity for personal use would be punished by a stiff warning. The police use random roadblocks and raid nightclubs. If you are stopped, do not try protesting about warrants or civil rights pertaining in your home country; your voice will fall on deaf ears and inflame the situation. You have been warned.

The *pulizija* (police) are for the most part unarmed, and wear a blue uniform almost identical to that in the UK. Every village has a station, even if it is staffed only by one man, open 24 hours a day – in the smaller villages it will sometimes be left unmanned.

Any crime you are involved in should be reported at once to the police and to your consulate. If you are involved in a motoring incident, do not move your car one inch until the police have arrived to take details, unless it is a minor bumper-to-bumper incident and you have the correct forms – *see* p.68 'Rules of the Road'.

The **Armed Forces of Malta** are responsible, among several other duties, for patrolling the seas with boats and helicopters, mainly to ensure that dope-dealers use Sicily and not Malta; they also rescue unfortunate yachtsmen.

## Eating Out

*See also* 'Food and Drink', pp.53–6.

Malta has a phenomenal number of licensed catering establishments, over 800 at the last count (excluding hotel restaurants). Those mentioned in the text are current, but in Malta chefs transfer their allegiances as quickly as footballers. Where possible, sound local establishments are featured (you probably won't have much trouble finding the more touristy ones), and many different palates are catered for.

Restaurant prices include VAT – 15% on all restaurant bills. It is not a service charge, which is normally left to your discretion: a 10% tip is about right.

This guide covers a broad selection of recommended places to eat, from top-class restaurants to basic eateries and simple cafés. They are listed alphabetically within each price range as shown in the box below. Note that these price ranges are intended as an approximate guide only.

### Restaurant Price Ranges

The price ranges below are based on a three-course dinner.

| | | |
|---|---|---|
| *expensive* | €€€€ | over Lm15 (€35) |
| *moderate* | €€€ | Lm8–15 (€18–35) |
| *inexpensive* | €€ | Lm5–8 (€12–18) |
| *budget* | € | under Lm5 (€12) |

# Electricity

Voltage is 220–240 AC, 50 cycles. Sockets are UK standard, with three square pins. Lights have both bayonet and screw fittings. Power surges and failures are rare, but bring a surge protector for computers, etc.

# Entertainment and Nightlife

**Bars** are divided into two distinct sorts: the village bar which is a microcosm of local life and intrigue, and bars aimed at the tourist market which tend to have a maximum three-year life span. In the second type you could be anywhere from Hong Kong to Gambia – with homogenized décor, copycat music and lager in a familiar bottle. They are a ritual meeting and courting ground for most age groups, tourists and Maltese alike. Friday and Saturday nights can be a real crush, and areas such as Paceville in St Julian's should be treated with a degree of caution. Parking can also be a nightmare around bars that are currently 'in'.

**Nightlife** in Malta is a mix between old-fashioned neon discos with rotating mirror balls and quite serious clubs playing the latest music and often featuring well-known international DJs. The most popular nightclubs are found in Paceville: **Places** and **Axis**. In the summer, open-air clubs are hard to beat – try **Amazonia** in Buġibba, **Gianpula** (in the middle of nowhere on the Rabat-Siġġiewi road) or **La Grotta** in Xlendi, Gozo.

The oldest **casino**, the **Dragonara Palace**, in St Julian's, was the summer residence of the Marquis Scicluna family until 1964, and is a beautifully proportioned classical villa on an attractive promontory. It is now part of the **Westin Dragonara resort**, *www.westinmalta. com*. In summer the dress code is 'smart-casual', otherwise a jacket and tie are required. The two other casinos are **The Oracle** in Buġibba and **Casino di Venezia** in Cottonera. Both have good restaurants. The **Manoel Theatre**, **t** 21 246389, originally built by the knights in 1731, is one of the oldest and smallest theatres in Europe. It is Malta's national theatre and the island's main venue for drama and concerts. The season runs from October to May. The **Eden Cinema**

**Complex** in St George's Bay has a multiscreen cinema complex and a tenpin bowling alley. There are also four cinema screens at the **Sun City entertainment complex** in Marsaskala, **t** 21 632422. Other cinemas can be found in Buġibba (**Empire**), Fgura and Valletta. The papers have listings for both films and plays.

# The Gay Scene

Malta is a strict Catholic country and has not always had the most tolerant of attitudes towards 'alternative' lifestyles. Even as recently as the early 1990s, it would have been very difficult to find any sort of recognizable gay scene. Thankfully, things are more open now and Malta has begun to tiptoe his/her way out of the closet. The age of consent, for both men and women, is 18.

Unsurprisingly, for a country with its own tradition of goddess-worship, and despite inherited Italian Catholic attitudes towards the sanctity of motherhood, it is lesbianism that flourishes most openly here.

### Gay Bars

**City of London**, Balluta Bay, **t** 21 331706. More popular with women than men, this is relatively cheap and quiet. It is also a nice suntrap on sunny winter days.

**Long Island**, Tower Road, Sliema (next to Europa Hotel). Nightclub with gay, lesbian and transvestite nights organized by 'Station to Station'; 70s, 80s and 90s music; *open Wed–Sun*.

**O Bar/Spa**, St Augustine Street, St Georges Bay, **t** 99 405861, *www.omalta.org*. Men only: a good place to meet the locals.

**The Oleander**, 10 Piazza Victoria, Xagħra (Gozo), **t** 21 557230. This is a famous eatery in its own right, but it is also very gay-friendly, especially on weekends.

**Pip's Bar**, Paceville.

**Saints Bar**, New Street, off Notabile Road, Mriehel. Bar popular with a transvestite crowd.

**Taverna del Ponte**, Marsalforn (Gozo). Very gay-friendly.

**The Tom Bar**, Crucifix Hill, Valletta, **t** 21 250780, *www.geocities.com/tombarmalta*; *open Tues–Sun 11.30–2pm, then 8.30pm–late*.

Malta's premier gay bar is very male and attracts sailors from around the world. It's open and packed all year round and reverberates to the sound of hardcore dance music.

## Gay-friendly Apartments

**Adonis Apartments, t** 21 250780, *www. geocities.com/adonismalta*. Four apartments in a converted farmhouse in Floriana, just outside Valletta.

## Gay Beaches

**Malta:** Ġnejna Bay, which can be reached via the footpath from Għajn Tuffieħa. In summer, you can also take the water taxi from Ġnejna Bay proper, and head for the rocky headlands.
**Gozo:** San Blas Bay, in the direction of Nadur. Ramla Bay, near Nadur, which according to aficionados is full of local talent.

## Gay Events

It's best to get information from websites such as *www.gaymalta.com* or *www. gaymaltatravel.com*.

Malta even has its own version of **Gay Pride**, although they have yet to organize any festivals or marches on the scale of London, Paris or New York. Contact **Pride of Malta Organization**, PO Box 420, Valletta, CMR 02, **t** 21 250780. There is also a bizarre **masked carnival** in Nadur three days before Ash Wednesday which many gay people attend.

# Health and Emergencies

If you are from an EU country make sure you have an EHIC card with you (*see* p.62).
**St Luke's Hospital** is Malta's principal hospital; Gozo has its own, the **General Hospital**. While neither is up to certain American or British technological standards, they do provide competent care. There are three private hospitals: **St Philip's** in Santa Venera, **St James Capua** in Sliema, and **St James' Hospital** in Żabbar. None of the private hospitals has accident or emergency facilities but always have a doctor in attendance for minor injuries and illnesses. Anything more serious should go to St Luke's.

Your hotel will be able to provide an **English-speaking doctor** at short notice. Larger towns, like Mosta, have **clinics/health centres** that deal with lesser emergencies. For

## Hospitals and Health Centres

### Public Hospitals
**Gozo General,** Victoria, **t** 21 556851.
**St Luke's,** Gwardamanġa, **t** 21 241251/247860.

### Private Hospitals
**Capua Palace,** Sliema, **t** 21 335235.
**St Philip's,** Santa Venera, **t** 21 442211.

### Health Centres
**Cospicua, t** 21 675492.
**Floriana, t** 21 243314.
**Gzira, t** 21 337244.
**Mosta, t** 21 433256.
**Paola, t** 21 691314.
**Qormi, t** 21 484450.
**Rabat, t** 21 459082.
**Victoria** (Gozo) **t** 21 561541.
**Centre for Holistic Therapies,** 125 St George's Road (above the Melita pharmacy), St Julian's, STJ 10, **t** 21 376360/381173. An excellent modern centre offering a range of treatments from acupuncture to physiotherapy.

minor complaints there is a rota of doctors who hold surgeries at the larger pharmacies. All **pharmacies** are flagged with green neon crosses and 12 are open on Sundays and public holidays; a list is published in *The Times of Malta* on Saturdays and Sundays. Most stock international medicines, including diabetic products and contraceptives. Should you fall foul of 'Mediterranean tummy' or 'Maltese-two-step', rest for 36 hours on a diet of bread and water – you might not need to gobble fistfuls of pills; diarrhoea is very dehydrating.

There are no inoculation requirements for Malta. There have been a few cases of AIDS.

## Water

The water is safe to drink but it does not taste very pleasant. Many brands of bottled 'table' water are available everywhere at a very reasonable cost.

## Things That Bite

Apart from the ubiquitous mosquito, there is nothing on land that will do you any harm; snakes are uncommon and, like spiders, are not poisonous. Some of the local wild dogs are unsavoury, but rabies is not a problem.

In recent years there have been many jellyfish sighted. The larger ones are less poisonous, but the common small transparent ones can give a very nasty sting. The best advice is to look around and see if others are swimming. You can buy 'Sunsafe', a combined sunblock and jellyfish repellent, from pharmacists, and it's good to have some antihistamine cream with you especially if swimming with children.

## Internet

For sending and receiving e-mails, there are numerous **Internet cafés**. Here is a selection:

**Cyber Café**, Merchants Street, Valletta, **t** 21 240680.

**Cyber Street**, Baystreet Complex, St Georges Bay, **t** 21 384422.

**Gozo Business Systems**, Borg Olivier Street, Victoria, **t** 21 565565.

## Libraries

The national library, the **Bibliotheca**, Republic Square, Valletta, **t** 21 224338 (*open to the public daily except Sun*), the last public building completed by the Knights (in 1796), houses a plethora of source material, including the archives of the Order of St John. The **public lending library** is in **Beltissebh**, next door to the police headquarters in Floriana, **t** 21 224044. Gozo has its own **reference and lending libraries** in **Victoria**: Vajringa Street and St Francis Square, **t** 21 556200 (*open Oct–June Mon–Fri 8.45–5.15, Sat 8.15–1.15; July–Sept Mon–Sat 8.30–1.15*).

## Living/Working in Malta

Since EU membership all EU nationals can stay and work in Malta, but they first need a **work permit** – contact your own embassy for details.

There are various conditions imposed for **permanent residency**. Immigrants who become permanent residents are charged a flat rate of 15% income tax. There are no death duties in Malta. For further information, contact the **Ministry of Finance**, Floriana, **t** 21 236306.

Business and offshore tax and company registration questions should be addressed to **Malta International Business Authority (MIBA)**, Palazzo Spinola, St Julian's, **t** 21 344230/3, or any of the major international accountancy partnerships.

The following cultural centres may also prove useful:

**The British Council**, c/o The British High Commission, Whitehall Mansions, Ta'Xbiex, **t** 23 230000.

**Alliance Française**, 108 St Thomas Street, Floriana, **t** 21 238456.

**The American Center**, Development House, St Anne Street, Floriana, **t** 21 241240.

**The German-Maltese Circle**, Messina Palace, 141 St Christopher Street, Valletta, **t** 21 246967.

**The Italian Cultural Institute**, 'Vecchia Cancelleria', Piazza San Giorgio, Valletta, **t** 21 221462.

## Markets and Shopping

There will always be a siege mentality in Malta. Nothing is wasted, stocks are normally high, and if you can't find what you want, someone somewhere will make it for you.

### Food

Vans of fruit and veg are the travelling **greengrocers**, each with their own 'patch'. The freshest produce is on Monday and Thursday afternoons, after the twice-weekly wholesale fruit and veg market at Ta'Qali. Measurements are metric, and you should expect a few cents' mark-up in price for the privilege of being a tourist.

**Butchers** normally follow shop hours and are tucked away in side streets. Surprisingly, **fish** is harder to track down. Go to Azzopardi on the Mosta Road, St Paul's Bay or in Gzira, or to the covered market in Valletta. In Gozo try the fishermen in Mġarr harbour who will sometimes oblige. **Valletta Fish Market**, Barriera Wharf, is a wholesale market, open from 4.30 to 6am. Each town and village has its own **supermarket** varying in size from 10-product hole-in-the-wall establishments to Tower Stores in Sliema and Smart in Birkirkara where you will be able to find anything from garden furniture to Marmite (but still buy your fresh produce from the vans).

## Shopping Malls/Centres

Like the rest of the world, Malta has come to appreciate the benefit of putting lots of shops together in large air-conditioned halls – the mall has come to Malta. Several have appeared in recent years. The characteristics of malls are the same the world over: cleanliness, convenience, comfort and blandness – and Maltese malls are as comfortable and faceless as any other; once inside there is very little to remind you what country you're in. The range of goods and services, however, soon overcomes any aesthetic qualms.

**The Plaza Commercial Centre**, Bisazza Street, Sliema, t 21 343832. Has everything from designer clothes, leather goods and jewellery to restaurants, banking facilities and a Maltacom office. Favoured retailers include Benetton, Lacoste, Body Shop, McDonald's and a good Chinese restaurant.

**Bay Street**, St George's Bay, t 21 380600. More restaurants and shops, including a Marks and Spencer food shop selling wines, teas, etc., but no fresh food or ready meals.

**Arkadia Commercial Centre**, Victoria, Gozo, t 21 558333. The brightest and newest of the shopping centres in Gozo, Arkadia sells everything from cars to hair baubles, via Balinese furniture and clothes. It also houses Gozo's best supermarket.

Other shopping centres can be found in Valletta – **Embassy Shopping Complex**, t 21 227436 – and in Fgura – **Galleria**, t 21 807070.

## Markets

Markets thrive all week. Apart from food (including fish sometimes, but not meat) there will be clothes, fabric, extraordinary china figures, a plethora of household items and hundreds of punk-coloured buckets. Do not expect orderly queues – eye-contact with the vendor is what counts. **Valletta**'s main market takes place on Sunday in **St James's Ditch**, but there is a daily market in **Merchants Street**. Behind the Grand Master's Palace is an **indoor market** that affords a full choice of fresh fish, meat, poultry and vegetables (*open Mon–Sat 5am–7pm, except Wednesdays when it closes at 2pm*). There is a fish market on Sunday morning in

**Marsaxlokk. Victoria**, Gozo, has its own open-air market beneath the citadel, in the **Piazza It-Tokk**. The usual stalls of T-shirts, bolts of cloth and brooms are to be found as well as good cheap straw hats; in the maze of streets running off the square you will find the fresh produce.

## Clothes

While the shopping is not Via Condotti, an Italian influence does prevail, through what is imported. All the usual chains (both UK and Italian) are represented but at prices higher than you would expect. Gozo is famed for its **lace** and is still the best place to buy it. Sometimes it is difficult to tell the difference between hand- and machine-made work, so ask and be convinced before you hand over your cash; inevitably, proper handmade lace will be more expensive. The small village of Sannat has long been the centre of this intricate and ancient craft, where you will still find women (the elderly and the very young) sitting in the shade of the doorways working with their bobbins (*see pp.288–9*).

## Crafts and Souvenirs

There is a Crafts Centre and a Crafts Village in Malta, and a Crafts Village in Gozo. **Ta'Qali**, a disused Second World War airfield in the centre of Malta, is the largest of the three. Here in the original RAF Nissen huts there is an exhaustive array of local handicrafts and craftsmen displaying their skills – potters, lacemakers, wrought-iron forgers and glass-blowers, who will make you a vase or a doorstop while you watch. Chunky knitwear and jewellery are also for sale. Aspiring knights or fancy-dress fanatics can even buy a full suit of armour. Entrance is free: quality and prices are generally okay.

The **Empire Arts and Crafts** centre in Rabat (near St Paul's Catacombs) also sells lacework, paintings, glass and ceramics and, again, you have the opportunity to watch the artefacts being created. The place has the look and feel of a shopping mall to it.

**Ta'Qali Crafts Village**, Ta'Qali, Malta, t 21 412786.

**Malta Crafts Centre**, St John's Square, Valletta.

Ta'Dbiegi Crafts Village, between Għarb and San Lawrenz, Gozo.

Empire Arts and Crafts Centre, 20A/B St Agatha Street, Rabat, t 21 450837.

## Antiques

Malta has a thriving antiques business mostly situated in and around the towns of Attard, Birkirkara, Balzan and Lija. The Maltese love to wrangle so expect to haggle, although don't expect to win.

Mizzi Antiques, 240 Zabbar Road, Fgura, t 23 676100.

Antiquaria, 180 Rudolph Street, Sliema, t 21 341998.

Gozo Antiques, 35 Enrico Mizzi Street, Victoria, Gozo, t 21 562422.

Paul Borg Antiques, Birkirkara, t 21 484592.

Touch Wood Antiques, Birkirkara, t 21 487587.

## Art Galleries

Malta's artistic heritage is strong, and it is home to several very good art galleries which mainly specialize in locally produced art.

Galleria Cremona, 5 Misrah Mesquita, Mdina, t 21 451280. Dedicated to the Maltese impressionist Marco Cremona, whose work often sells for as much as Lm500.

Gallery G, 4 Ugo Mifsud Street, Lija, t 21 421984. Showcases local and visiting artists.

Joe Xuereb, Bahhara Street, Għajnsielem (Gozo), t 21 553559.

St James's Cavalier, Valletta, t 21 223216. Houses exhibitions of local and foreign artists in a beautiful setting.

## Marrying in Malta

The construction of a range of new 5-star hotels will no doubt help Malta's image as a potential honeymoon destination. For couples who can't wait that long, however, it is quite possible to get married on the islands. The procedure is relatively straightforward: both parties need to lodge their application (form RZ11), birth certificates and a sworn statement proving that neither party is married (form RZ21) with the Maltese authorities at least six weeks and not more than three months before the wedding. If these criteria are met, you need not spend more than a day on Malta.

The choice of venue is up to you – from register office to hotel lobby, but, because Malta is a Catholic country, you cannot get married in a Catholic church unless at least one party is Catholic. The application forms can be obtained from, and the relevant papers should be sent to: Marriage Registry Division, 197 Merchants Street, Valletta, t 21 225291/2. For details of Catholic marriage procedure, write to Curia Marriage Office, PO Box 29, Valletta, t 21 245332.

## Media

### Television

Forests of aerials give you more than a hint of the role television plays in Maltese life. The broadcasting authority has been independent of government control since it first went on the air in 1962. There are four local television stations. Television Malta (TVM) broadcasts news, soccer and Anglo-US imports. Net TV and Superone are owned by the Nationalist and Labour parties respectively, and these also have imported programmes, sports and wonderfully biased news. Smash TV seems to have become chiefly a religious channel. On all these channels, all programmes except imports are in Malti.

There is also a cable franchise, Melita Cable TV. Malta has had satellite TV for around a decade and most of the better hotels provide it as standard in their rooms. Nonetheless, it is the deregulated Italian TV stations that remain the undisputed champions of the airwaves. As well as football, their blue-tinged late-night quiz shows are immensely popular.

### Radio

There are many local radio stations – political, religious, music old and new, and university. Classic FM with BBC News is broadcast by Campus FM, the university channel, on 103.7FM, while they are not broadcasting their own programmes.

## Newspapers

Newspapers are prolific, with four dailies, three weeklies and four Sundays. The principal English-language papers are *The Times* and *The Independent*. In all the local papers politics are invariably centre stage. UK and European newspapers are available late in the afternoon on the day of publication; UK Sunday papers are available on Sunday mornings. The only US papers available are the *International Herald Tribune* and, rather more spasmodically, *USA Today*. *Time* and *Newsweek* are punctual. In Gozo all foreign papers, except the UK Sundays, are a day late.

## Museums

The **national museums** (as distinct from those associated with individual churches, like St John's Co-Cathedral), cover archaeology, fine arts, the megalithic sites, the Second World War, maritime history, the State Rooms and Palace Armoury. Admission is free for those under 19 or over 65.

All national museums are closed on public holidays. For up-to-date information call **Heritage Malta, t** 22 954000, *www. heritagemalta.org* or the MTA, *www. visitmalta.com*.

Remember that tickets for the Hypogeum at Hal Saflieni must be bought at least one week in advance, and that visitor numbers are restricted. *See* p.226 for opening hours.

## Opening Hours

**Winter**: 1 Oct–15 June

**Summer**: 16 June–30 Sept

Malta follows the great Mediterranean tradition of the siesta, a three-hour midday break that has cemented family life for generations. Lunch is taken at home, rarely at restaurants, and in summer white-collar employees work shorter hours. Very few shops are open on a Sunday and everything is shut fast on national holidays (*see* below).

## Shops

Food shops 7am–1pm and 4–7pm. Some larger supermarkets stay open 9am–7pm.

## Banks

**Winter** Mon–Fri 8.30–12.45; 2.30–4 Tues and Fri only; Sat 8.30–12. **Summer** Mon–Fri 8–12.45; 2.30–4 Fri only; Sat 8–11.30. There is a 24-hour foreign-exchange facility at Malta International Airport (closed Christmas and New Year's Day). In larger towns, foreign

### National Holidays

Almost everything shuts down on national holidays. A few restaurants and bars stay open, buses run reduced services, taxis and ferries run as normal and a pharmacy will be open somewhere. Be warned, roads and beaches are crowded.

**1 January** New Year's Day.

**February** The Valletta Carnival, three days before the beginning of Lent, hails the end of winter and the coming of spring; adults and children run amok in fancy dress among carnival floats. Gozo Carnival takes place a few days later.

**10 February** St Paul's Shipwreck, Valletta.

**19 March** St Joseph's Day.

**31 March** Freedom Day.

**March–April** Nearly all the larger towns have their own Good Friday and Easter Sunday processions and celebrations.

**1 May** Workers' Day.

**7 June** Sette Giugno.

**29 June** The L-Imnarja *festa* celebrates the end of the harvests and quickly turns into a jamboree of picnics, wine, music and dance in the gardens of Buskett. Donkey- and horse-races are also held the next day in nearby Rabat.

**24 June** St John's Bonfires. A fiery celebration of the knights' patron saint at Fort St Elmo and St John's Square, Valletta.

**15 August** Seven villages and Victoria celebrate the Assumption, also referred to as Santa Marija.

**8 September** Victory Day signals the end of the Great Sieges both of 1565 and 1940–3 with, among other forms of celebration, traditional boat races and a regatta in the Grand Harbour.

**21 September** Independence Day.

**8 December** *Festa* of the Immaculate Conception.

**13 December** Republic Day.

**25 December** Christmas Day.

exchange departments remain open outside these hours, normally 4–7 in summer and 3–6 in winter.

## Pharmacies

Mon–Fri 9–1 and 4–7; Sat 8.30–12. Special weekend opening times are posted in the local papers.

## Government Offices

**Winter** Mon–Fri 7.45–12.30 and 1.15–5.15. **Summer** Mon–Fri 7.30–1.30.

## Commercial Offices

8.30–12.30 and 3.30–5.30. In the summer months many offices are either closed from 12.45 or have a skeleton staff.

## Museums

Opening hours vary, but all the **Heritage Malta museums** are open daily 9–5, closed 24, 25 and 31 Dec, 1 Jan and Good Fri.

## Cathedrals and Churches

The two cathedrals in Valletta and Mdina, Mosta church, the cathedral in Victoria and the church in Xewkija in Gozo all have similar hours to the museums. As a general rule, the larger parish churches open every morning from 6 to 10.30 and again in the afternoon from about 4.30 to 7. Each village keeps its own idiosyncratic hours.

## Post Offices

Mon–Sat 8–12.45. The main post office in Valletta remains open Mon–Sat 8–6.30 in winter, and 7.30–6 in summer.

## Maltacom

8.30am–11pm. The office in Valletta closes at 10am. The St Julian's and MIA branches are open 24 hours a day including public holidays.

## Markets and Vans

Markets run from dawn to 12 noon. Fruit vans keep shop hours but are not around in smaller towns on Wednesday or Saturday afternoons. They are best stocked on Monday and Thursday afternoons.

## Packing

Take as little as possible in the summer months. Simple **cotton clothes** are ideal for the heat. Malta is not a 'jacket and tie' country unless you are attending a function or Mass on Sundays. Some churches such as Ta'Pinu require long-sleeved shirts and long trousers; for the majority, common sense and respect is all that is required.

If you go outside the peak season, a **cotton sweater** or **jacket** will suffice for the evenings. For the winter, depending upon your constitution, you should take one **woollen sweater** or a range of **thermals**. Women should take note that Malta is a very Catholic country and skimpy clothes are not only frowned upon but considered disrespectful.

It is a sensible idea to take with you all necessary **prescription medicines**, **high-factor sun creams**, **mosquito repellent**, a **hat**, **sunglasses** and **driving licence**. In addition, photocopy the relevant pages of your **passport**, and note down all relevant **traveller's cheque and credit card numbers**.

A stout pair of **walking shoes** is a good idea if you are planning to do any country walking. A **torch** for some of the gloomier church paintings is also worth considering. For anyone who is attached to the clipped intonations of the World Service, taking a **short-wave radio** with you is another good bet.

## Postal Services

In **Malta** the General Post Office is in the Auberge d'Italie, Merchants Street, Valletta, **t** 21 224422. In addition to normal services it provides a philatelic service and an expedited datapost service. In **Gozo** the post office at 129 Republic Street, Victoria, **t** 21 556435, offers the same services. *See* 'Opening Hours', left. Poste restante is available at the main post offices if written application is made in advance to the postmaster-general at the main post office in Valletta. There is a poste restante for pleasure yachts (*see* 'Yachting Information', p.93).

The local post Is reliable. Letters in Malta cost 7c; stamps are available from most newsagents. A letter posted to the UK or USA should take five or eight days respectively, and cost 16c to the EU (cards and letters up to 20g) and 22c to the USA. Reminders of the British colonial influence are the red postboxes; one or two wall-mounted boxes in the villages bear Queen Victoria's insignia, VR.

### International Couriers

**DHL International**, DHL Building, Ganni Vassallo St, Luqa, t 21 800148. It is worth noting that Thomas Cook and DHL have come to a working arrangement whereby the **Thomas Cook** offices in Valletta, Sliema and Victoria can be used as DHL drops.

**FedEx**, Seasped House, Triq Ninu Cremona, Paola, t 21 807807.

**TNT**, Courier House, Youth Gardens, Luqa, t 25 584600.

## Religious Affairs

Malta is a devoutly Roman Catholic country with over 357 churches. Nearly all services are held in Malti, although there are 19 churches in which Mass may be celebrated in English, three of which are on Gozo. Places of worship for other denominations:

**Church of Scotland, Methodist and Free Churches**: St Andrew's Scots Church on the corner of South Street and Old Bakery Street, Valletta, t 21 222643.

**Anglican**: St Paul's Anglican Pro-Cathedral, Independence Square, Valletta, t 21 225714. After Sunday service there is a coffee morning and a book exchange in the vaults. In Sliema there is the Holy Trinity Church, Rudolph Street. On Gozo, the Anglican Mass can be heard in the Seminary in Victoria.

**Synagogue**: Spur Street, Valletta.

**Greek Orthodox**: St George's, 83 Merchants Street, Valletta.

**Evangelical Church of Germany**: South Street, Valletta, 21 454145.

**Mosque**: Corradino Hill, Paola.

At St Barbara's in Republic Street services are in French and German and at St Catherine of Italy in Victory Square, Valletta, Mass is said in Italian. For archtraditionalists there is always St John's Co-Cathedral in St John's Square, Valletta, where Mass is said in Latin. For further information, contact either the church directly or your consular official. Times of services are advertised in the *Malta Sunday Times*.

## Sports and Activities

### Beaches

The mean sea temperature in July, August and September is 73°F (23°C). The coastline of the islands is not pitted with long stretches of sandy beach, but the waters are exceptionally clear; it is the water itself that has always been important to the Maltese, not how you enter it. A 'beach', therefore, can be sand, rock, a concrete lido, even a boat-ladder or a diving-board. The only thing it can't be is steps into a freshwater swimming pool; 'sweet water', as they call it, has none of the properties of sea water, only a lot of chemicals.

### A Few Words of Caution

People will tell you that the **currents and undertow** around the islands are minimal; it is not true, especially of the northwest coast and the Malta–Gozo channel. Gozo may look close from Comino, but don't even think of trying to swim it.

The Maltese possess a prolific arsenal of **speedboats**, and it is a rare season when a bather is not struck, so keep a lookout. If snorkelling, swim with a marker buoy. Do not swim off rocks when it is rough: a wave will probably splatter you against them.

All beaches in Malta are prone to **pollution**, ranging from sewage outflow and rubbish to the rank-smelling food fed to the fish in the tuna pens. Contact the local MTA office to find out which beaches they are currently advising people not to swim from, or have a look in the local papers for the same information.

**Nude bathing**, and that includes topless bathing, is **illegal** on Malta, However, if the urge to disrobe is just too strong then it is easy to hire a boat and sail to an isolated cove, inaccessible by foot, where you can display as much or as little as you like, entirely unnoticed by anyone else. If you think going unnoticed by other people is not exactly the point, then there are a couple of spots, at **Fomm ir-Riħ** and **Għadira Bay**, where a form of **unoffical nudism** is practised. However, tread carefully and respect Maltese standards of decency. If in doubt, cover up.

There are 12 **sandy beaches** on Malta, two on Gozo and two (just) on Comino. Nearly all have been corralled by hotels but they are open to the public. The only private beach in Malta belongs to the Comino Hotel in San Nicklaw Bay. Conventional sandy beaches offer safety, ease of access, facilities for those with families, but not necessarily the best swimming. They also attract the biggest crowds, especially at weekends.

The sandiest beach in Malta is **Għadira** or **Mellieħa Bay** on the northeast coast. The island's shores to the **north** and **northeast** are calmer and less steep than those to the south or west. Along these coasts from Sliema to Ramla are countless **beach clubs** or **lidos**, all of which offer access to the sea, bars and shelter. They charge an entrance fee (Lm1.50–5) and are often allied to a hotel. Should your idea of exercise be the creak of a right elbow-joint, the occasional opening of an eyelid and inhaling the aroma of coconut oil, look no further. On the **northwest** coast as far as **Ġnejna** and **Fomm ir-Riħ Bay** is a hotchpotch of sandy beaches, smooth cream-coloured rocks and little coves. The only method of entering the water on the **southwest** coast up to **Għar Lapsi** is by boat-ladder. The sea under the sheer cliffs of **Dingli** is deep and sometimes rough. To the **south**, **Island Bay**, **Peter's Pool** and **St Thomas Bay** are well-known spots – access can be tricky, and Peter's Pool is best reached by boat.

In **Gozo** the sandiest beach is **Ir-Ramla** (if you count red sand as sand). Other good places to swim in Gozo are **Mġarr ix-Xini**, **San Blas**, **Qala Point** and the tiny **Għasri Valley**. **Comino** has a 30ft (10m) handkerchief of sand in the **Blue Lagoon**. This can hardly be called a beach, but if you swim there before or after the pleasure cruises invade, it can fairly be described as sublime. The public beach in **Santa Marija Bay**, with its few trees, is pleasant and less populous.

## Diving and Snorkelling

**Emergencies: t** 21 809279 (day), 21 824220 after 4pm and weekends.

**Diving** off the coast of Malta is superb – with clear warm waters, nothing to devour you, and highly competent instructors and guides. The coastal waters of Malta are well known among the diving fraternity. This has resulted in an infrastructure in which the novice can easily be trained. Every school has to be licensed and has equipment for hire. If you already have an internationally accepted diving certificate you still need to obtain a **Malta Dive Permit** from the Department of Health, 15 Merchants Street, Valletta, **t** 21 224071, in order to be allowed to dive. To do this you need to complete an application form, which can be found at any dive centre, and, most importantly, provide a valid medical certificate (a medical check-up can easily be arranged through any dive centre and will cost around Lm3). To be able to lead a dive you need a medical certificate as well as a logbook, two photos and Lm1, in return for which you will be issued with a C Card Instructor's permit. If you would like to learn, the school will arrange everything; the open-water courses (BSAC or PADI) last for a minimum of five days and cost from Lm110, including equipment hire.

There are **dive sites** suitable for all abilities: beginners might, perhaps, like to start their watery escapades among Comino's reefs between **Għar Għana** and the **Blue Lagoon** or

## Diving Centres and Schools

### Malta
**Dive Systems**, under the Tower, Tower Road, Sliema, **t** 21 319123.

**Maltaqua**, Mosta Road, St Paul's, **t** 21 571873.

**Meldives**, Tunny Net Lido Complex, Mellieħa, **t** 21 522595.

**Scubatech Diving Centre**, Alka Street, St Paul's Bay, **t** 21 580617.

**Strand Diving Services**, Ramon Perellos Street, St Paul's Bay, **t** 21 574502.

**Sub-Way Scuba Diving School**, Pioneer Road, St Paul's Bay, **t** 21 570354, *www.subwayscuba.com*.

### Gozo
**Atlantis Diving Centre**, Qolla Street, Marsalforn, **t** 21 561826.

**Frankie's Diving Centre**, Mġarr Road, Xewkija, **t** 21 563375.

**Gozo Aqua Sports**, Green Valley, Rabat Road, Marsalforn, **t** 21 563037.

### Comino
**Tony's Diving**, Comino Hotel, **t** 21 573051/2.

the shallow waters of the **Santa Marija Caves** off **Comino**. Skilled cave and night-divers could try any of: **Anchor Bay, Ahrax Point, Ċirkewwa** or **Qawra Point** in Malta; **Dwejra Point** in Gozo or the **Santa Marija Caves** and **Irqieqa Point** around **Comino**. The ultimate dive sites are probably the **Blue Hole** off **Fungus Rock** and the 115ft (35m) tunnel drop at the nearby inland sea at **Dwejra, Gozo**. These are recommended for experienced team divers only. For flora and fauna, **Għar Lapsi** and **Qawra Point** are the favoured sites during the day with dentex, groupers and sponges on display. At night, you can watch the nocturnal meanderings of octopuses and crabs at the **Blue Lagoon**.

Snorkellers will enjoy the waters' clarity, but it is mandatory for all divers to fly the **Code A flag** or an **inflatable red marker buoy** to warn off the lunatic fringe of speedboat owners. Equipment is for sale in any tourist location. *The Diving Guide to the Maltese Islands* by Ned Middleton (Swan Hill Press, £16.99) has as much information as you could ever need on diving and dive sites in Malta.

The **MTA** has a list of schools and recommended dive sites (*see* box opposite). Spear-fishing is forbidden, as is removing any ancient booty you may unearth. St Luke's Hospital has a **decompression chamber**, t 21 234765, and the Armed Forces of Malta have a **rescue helicopter** and patrol boats.

For more information contact the **British Subaqua Club** at 16 Upper Woburn Place, London WC1H 0QU, **t** (020) 7387 9302, or the **Association of Professional Diving Schools**, Msida Court, 61/2 Msida Sea Front, **t** 21 336441.

## Fishing

In Malta fishing is neither sport nor recreation, but a way of life. You don't need a licence to fish in Maltese waters but spear-fishing is prohibited. Wherever you see a sea wall you will find a man with an impossibly long rod, bait and very few fish, if any, at his side. Onshore fishing is an end-of-the-day therapy – most of the fish are found in the deeper waters of the Malta–Sicily channel. To fish for swordfish, *dentici* or even *lampuki*, seek the help of a fisherman who will know where to look. Try **Marsaxlokk Bay** or **St Paul's Bay** on Malta, or **Mġarr** and **Marsalforn** on

Gozo (*see* 'Boat Charters', p.66). You won't find the great ocean sailfish in the saline Mediterranean, but occasionally **shark** sightings occur way out to sea. This encourages glory-seeking Italians to depart **Mġarr** laden with buckets of offal in vain pursuit.

## Football

The premier national league comprises 10 teams and competes from August to June. Matches are generally played on weekends and in the afternoons. The impressive **National Stadium** (17,000 seats) at Ta'Qali hosts the international matches as well as premier league matches. The teams all have evocative throwback second names like Tigers, Hotspurs and Rovers.

Football is akin to a religion and is treated with reverence, albeit raucous; it has none of the mindless violence that has plagued English football. If the team near where you are staying wins a match, however inconsequential, expect parades of cars bearing team colours and blaring horns. Postpone any notion of sleep. **Malta Football Association**, 280 St Paul's Street, Valletta, t 21 222697, provides information.

## Horse-riding

Riding is available, unaccompanied or accompanied, near the Marsa and throughout Malta and Gozo. Fees are around Lm5 per hour, and Lm8 for a two-hour ride. Schools include:

**Bidnija Riding School, t** 21 414010.

**Golden Bay Horse Riding, t** 21 573360.

**Star Horse Riding, t** 9985 7491.

## The Marsa Sports Club

The Marsa is where the Turks made their encampment during the Great Siege of 1565. Since 1901 it has been home to the majority of Malta's land-based recreations. The club is open Mon–Fri 9am–9pm, weekends 9–5. Temporary membership is available to visitors on a daily, weekly or monthly basis (Lm2, Lm10 and Lm30 respectively) which includes use of the bar and restaurant. Initial contact should be made through your hotel or directly to the **Marsa Sports Club** (MSC), t 21 232842.

## Horse-racing

**The Marsa Racing Club**, Racecourse Street, Marsa, t 21 224800. Holds a meeting every Sunday afternoon from October to May. Trotting races are the more thrilling and outnumber the flat by seven to one. There can be as many as nine races on the card. In Malta, racing ranks a close second to football, and the theatre of a trotting race has to be seen to be believed – remember the Maltese are passionate gamblers.

## Golf

Oscar Wilde described golf as 'a good walk ruined', which is a little unfair to the flat 18-hole, par-68 course situated within the racetrack of the Marsa. The shortish fairways are green, and so presumably are the greens when you reach them – there are over 50 sand bunkers. The sixth and only named tee is called 'the maid's bedroom' and no one will say why. Clubs are available for hire at Lm3, and green fees are Lm15 for 18 holes and Lm10 for nine holes. Annual overseas membership costs Lm160. Tee reservation in essential. Open on Mon, Wed and Fri from 7.30 and in the afternoons only on Tues, Thurs, Sat and Sun. It can get crowded; days to avoid are Tuesday afternoons, Thursdays and Saturday mornings.

The Marsa Club may, however, soon lose its golfing monopoly. The government is looking at proposals for the development of 18-hole golf courses in Malta and Gozo.

## Tennis and Squash

The club has 17 all-weather tennis courts that cost Lm3.50 for a hard court, Lm4 for clay per 90 minutes and Lm5.20 for the three floodlit courts which can be hired until 10pm in summer. It is advisable to book if you wish to play in the late afternoon or at weekends. There are also five squash courts. Lm2.40 for 45 minutes; again, book if you want to play after 4.30pm.

## Polo

The game has regained some of its colonial cachet with those who can afford it. It is fun to spectate, even if the horsemanship does ape that of the Marx Brothers in *A Day at the Races*. Free for spectators.

## Archery

The national sport of Bhutan has a strong following in Malta. Matches are played at the Marsa. Contact the **Archery Association of Malta**, t 21 240460.

## Snooker

Snooker is rapidly growing in popularity, principally due to the efforts of local professional Tony Drago, who has achieved some success on the international circuit. In 1997, the inaugural **Malta Rothman's Grand Prix** event was staged at the new SAS Radisson Bay Point Resort and attracted a host of top-class professionals. The Marsa Club has two full-size tables; games are 50c each.

## Other Activities

The Marsa also has a **cricket pitch** (spectating at the twice-weekly matches is free), a large **swimming pool** (free with daily membership), an 18-hole **mini-golf course** (a round is 50c for children and 75c for adults) and **table tennis**.

# Mountain Biking

Cycling on Malta's fearsome roads is not advisable; there are no official road cycle paths. The off-road terrain and scenery, however, cries out to be mountain-biked (according to some people, anyway), particularly on Gozo. Potential bike trails include **Wied Qirda Valley** in Żebbuġ and **Chadwick Lakes** near Dingli; on Gozo: the valleys just inland from **Ramla Bay**, **San Blas** and **Daħlet Qorrot**. You can hire bikes from:

**Lilly Whites**, St George's Road, Paceville, t 21 375921.

**Magri Cycles**, Eucharistic Congress Street, Mosta, t 21 432890.

**On Two Wheels**, Rabat Road, Marsalforn, Gozo, t 21 561503.

The **All Terrain Club**, 106 Islets Promenade, Buġibba, will be able to provide you with all the relevant information.

# Parasailing

Adapted boats lift you 115ft (35m) into the air, and you cruise around for 8 minutes praying the cable won't break. Try St Julian's, St Paul's and Mellieħa Bay.

## Rock Climbing

There are no mountains proper but plenty of sheer seaside cliffs to test the nerve and ability of even the most experienced rock climber. There is also no formal climbing organization, but **Andrew Warrington**, **t** 21 372396, 994 90377, runs a small group of local climbing enthusiasts. Before embarking on a climb, remember to pack a mobile phone so that you can call the rescue unit, **t** 21 809279 (*day*), 21 824220 (*after 4pm and weekends*) should you get into difficulties.

## Shooting

The *kaċċa* is a very unsavoury part of Maltese sporting life. *Kaċċatur*, or hunters, are responsible for the deaths (by shooting, netting, caging or trapping) of nearly 4 million birds a year. The great Mediterranean sea eagle and the peregrine falcon are among the many species which are now extinct in the islands (*see* Topics, pp.46–7). The true sporting side of shooting can be found at **Malta Shooting Federation**, PO Box 340, Valletta, **t** 21 412506, where trap, skeet etc. are harmlessly shot at.

## Running

The **Malta Marathon** is run from Mdina to Sliema over the statutory 26 miles (42km) in February/March. For questions regarding entry contact **Marathon Challenge**, **t** 21 344378.

## Water-polo

The sport is the summer's football – an exciting and, in Malta, noisy game. Matches are played, out of the anger of the sun, in the late afternoon. Contact the **Aquatic Sports Association**, National Swimming Pool, Gzira, **t** 21 322884.

## Water-skiing

Skiing is nearly as easy as it looks, but monoskiing is not. The ideal time is very early in the morning or an hour or two before sunset when the sea is usually oily calm and empty. Facilities are available from any hotel that has a beach, or from the larger sandy beaches. A current fad with children aged 10 upwards is being towed on a massive inflatable 'sausage' that is ridden like a horse (but seats five or six) until it overturns and tips them into the sea amid yelps of delight. Rides cost approximately Lm5–7 for 10mins.

## Windsurfing

This would become the national summer sport if someone could dream up a team angle to it. The Maltese possess all the right ingredients: the sea, nautical skills, a reckless attitude to speed, and verve. Tuition and boards can be found on the larger beaches and at some hotels. National Championships are held in September and October. Try **Zammit and Cachia Ltd**, Cachia Buildings, Triq il-Kanun, Qormi, **t** 21 484572.

## Skydiving

The **Maltese Falcon Skydiving Association**, **t** 21 572799, has courses and can provide tandem jumps for the truly foolish.

## Other Sports

For information on other sports and sporting events, including the **International Air Rally**, motor-racing, **martial arts**, **badminton**, **hockey** and **basketball**, contact the MTA in Valletta (*see* p.60).

## Telephones

**International country code: t** 356.

**Directory Enquiries: t** 1182.

**Go Mobile enquiries: t** 1187.

**Overseas Operator: t** 1152.

**Vodafone enquiries: t** 1189.

**Maltacom** has offices in **Malta** at MIA Airport, Ħamrun, Mdina, Qawra, Sliema and St Paul's Bay, Valletta. The main office in St Julian's (Mercury House, St George's Road) is open 24 hours a day. In **Gozo**, the only Maltacom office is in Republic Street, Victoria, but, as in Malta, there are plenty of **Telecard** booths. Making an overseas call from any of the Maltacom offices or booths is appreciably cheaper than from your hotel. Cheap rate is Mon–Fri 6pm–midnight and Sat–Sun 8am–midnight. Supercheap night rates are every night from midnight to 8am – for five minutes to the UK or Italy the cost is 95c, and to the rest of Europe it is Lm1.70. Telecards are available in three denominations: Lm5, Lm3 and Lm2, from any Maltacom office and from many other stores and bureaux de change.

In most cases your hotel will help out with international **fax** requests. Public facilities are only available from the Valletta, St Julian's and Malta International Airport offices and from the Victoria office, Gozo. Note that the t 0800 **freephone access system** does not function here when dialling 0800 abroad.

**Local calls** are easier. There are two principal methods: the first is to use the phone booths which now proliferate across the islands; the majority are either red or see-through, and work only with the ubiquitous Telecard; there is also a rarer breed of coin-operated booth which is usually yellow, and costs 10c for a call to a land phone and 25c to a mobile. The more traditional method is to simply ask the local barman or shopkeeper. Local calls to a land line anywhere within the islands of any duration are charged at a flat rate of 10c; in a shop you will be charged about 15c (or 25c to a mobile). Just walk in and ask.

Most **mobile phones** now work on the islands. If yours does not, you can buy a 'pay-as-you-go' SIM card for Lm10, which gives you a credit with a six-month time window.

## Time

Malta is one hour ahead of GMT apart from late March to late September when the clocks are put forward and become two hours ahead of GMT.

## Tipping

Generally, tip 10% in restaurants when service is not included, and for taxi fares.

## Toilets

Invariably the public toilets are spotlessly clean; nearly all have a legacy of sound-swooshing British plumbing in vitreous china bowls. Almost every village has a matched pair and quite a few underground, often in the square. There's sometimes an attendant – it is considered polite to leave a few cents.

## VAT

VAT was reintroduced to Malta in 1999. There are two rates of tax: accommodation is charged at 5%, otherwise the rate is 18%. Food (not restaurants), medicine, education, maritime services and air, sea and public transport are exempt from VAT.

## Women Travellers

You will need both parts of your bikini. Nude and topless bathing in public or in private lidos is against the law. Laws do not exist to dictate what clothes you may go walking or shopping in, but anything less than shorts and shirt may mean that you are politely asked to dress by the police.

Maltese men have been flattered all their lives by mothers, aunts and grandmothers, so expect them to have an inflated idea of their own attributes. In keeping with most Latin races they tend to behave in a playful but harmless manner. If this offends you, one or two tough verbal rebukes should send them scurrying; otherwise invent a nearby husband.

Pharmaceutical products for women and cosmetics are available in pharmacies and some supermarkets.

## Yachting Information

**Position**: the European Datum for the Grand Harbour Breakwater: 35° 54'.18 N – 14° 31'.5 E; for Marsamxett Harbour: 35° 54'.35 N – 14° 30'.6 E.

For thousands of years mariners have sought refuge in Malta's greatest asset, her natural deep-water harbours; the **Grand Harbour**, for commercial shipping (except for Kalkara Creek), lies to the southeast of the Valletta peninsula, and the **Marsamxett Harbour**, for pleasure yachts, lies to the northwest of it.

Marsamxett Harbour comprises three creeks; Lazzaretto, Msida and Sliema. The first two have been adapted into modern marinas. The present capacity in **Msida Creek** is for 672 yachts up to 60ft (18m) in length on 15 serviced pontoons. The smaller stern-to quay in **Lazzaretto** is reserved for yachts longer than 60ft (18m). In addition there are

151 berths in the **Mġarr Marina** in Gozo for boats up to 52ft (16m) in length and 214 berths and 33 superyacht berths in the new Grand Harbour Marina in Cotomera. All the services come under the **Malta Maritime Authority** whose administrative office is: Msida Marina, Ta'Xbiex, t 21 332800, *www.mma.gov.mt.*

## Arrival and Departure Procedures

Before arriving, fly the 'Yellow Duster' ('Q' flag) and a courtesy flag. The customs berths are in Lazzaretto Creek; if they are occupied, drop anchor in the creek and take all the ship's papers, crew list and passports to Customs and Immigration. Then contact the Harbour Master on VHF channel 9 or go to the Yacht Centre office in Ta'Xbiex. Anchoring within the confines of the creek is only permitted until a berth has been allocated. If in doubt, contact **Valletta Port Control** or **Malta Radio**, which monitor VHF channels 9, 12 and 16.

## Customs and Immigration

The customs and immigration office is in Ta'Xbiex and is open 8am–7pm daily in summer and 7.45–5.15 Mon–Fri in winter. The ship's master will need to report there immediately after berthing and 24 hours before departure with all ship's and crew papers. If you are accompanied by a **pet**, tie up on the customs berths as usual but do not take the animal ashore. If the animal has correct paperwork and vaccinations, it may be allowed ashore: Malta is part of the 'Passports for Pets' scheme, but entry will depend on your animal's point of origin. The authorities are very helpful here and usually visit and clear arriving vessels expeditiously.

## Berthing Fees

A 46–52ft (14–16m) vessel on a serviced pontoon (including water and electricity) in summer is Lm53 plus VAT per week. The comparable rate for a 60ft (18m) vessel in Lazzaretto Creek is Lm.57–60 plus VAT per week, with water and electricity extra. If you wish to stay for a longer period it is advisable to write (or e-mail *info@mma.gov.mt*) and request a berth for the specific period that you wish to stay.

## Yacht Centre Facilities

There is one main centre, in Ta'Xbiex. International telephones, showers and public conveniences, and a poste restante for ships' mail, are all available.

## Weather Forecasts

Broadcast daily by **Valletta Port Control** (Valletta Radio) on VHF channel 12. On MW, the frequencies are 2182 kHz and 2625 kHz; also on **Malta Radio** on Channel 4. Forecasts are four times a day at 9.03, 13.03, 19.03 and midnight, one hour earlier in winter. The forecasts are valid for 50 nautical miles around Malta and are usually reliable. The **Department of Civil Aviation** publishes an excellent land and sea forecast daily in *The Times of Malta.*

## Winds

The prevailing wind is the northwesterly *majjistral* (mistral). The southerly and torpid *xlokk* (sirocco) blows mostly in late September and sometimes in late spring. The *tramuntana* from the north hardly blows at all. The most feared is the northeasterly winter wind, the *gregale*. It blows down through the Adriatic from the cold mountains above; a blow usually lasts at least three days and brings with it terrible seas and high winds. Avoid.

## Bunkering, Gas and Duty-free

Duty-free stores will be sealed on board a foreign-registered vessel until departure; a charge is made for the attendance and services of the Customs Officer. For bunkering fuels contact **Falzon Service Station**, t 21 491026, or a broker/agent. Gas bottles can be refilled (about Lm3 for a 3kg bottle and Lm5 for a 10kg bottle) at any of the principal chandleries (*see* below).

## The Royal Malta Yacht Club

The club is situated at Couvre Port, Manoel Island, t 21 333109. The Secretary will have information on its racing calendar and the Comino Regatta in June. Members of recognized yacht clubs around the world can avail themselves of the club's facilities; check with the Secretary. The Yacht Club will be moving to an alternative location on Manoel Island at some point in the next few years. They should be keeping the same telephone number, so call the Secretary to verify location.

## Repairs, and Services

**Malta Superyacht Services**, Bormla, t 23 996019.

**Manoel Island Yacht Yard**, t 21 334453/4, in Manoel Island is the largest and most reputable in the central Mediterranean. The **Kalkara Boatyard Co.**, Kalkara Wharf, Kalkara, t 21 661306, has a 55-ton haul-out crane on its wharf in the eponymous creek in the Grand Harbour. **Bezzina Ship Yard**, 1–3 Church Wharf, Marsa, t 21 829091, can accommodate yachts up to 212ft (65m) in its docking facilities, also in the Grand Harbour.

## A Few Regulations

• The maximum speed in any creek and both harbours, or within 300 yards of a sandy beach or 200 yards of any other foreshore, is 10 knots.

• No vessel is to be moved from one position to another without prior permission.

• Oil or garbage is not to be disposed of in harbour.

• Fees are to be paid 24 hours before intended departure.

• A vessel can anchor for the night in any of the bays and inlets in the archipelago.

• Filfla island is out of bounds.

## Divers

For underwater repairs contact **Commercial Divers**, 'Seabreeze', Giuseppe Cali Street, Ta'Xbiex, t 21 331515, or **Strand Diving Services**, t 21 574502.

## Mechanics

A number of firms offer a marine engineering service. Try **Marine Engineers**, Cardona Engineering Works, Żebbuġ, t 21 462014, or **Willis Brothers**, Qormi, t 21 496991.

## Laundry and Dry Cleaning

The closest is **Diamond Wash**, Testaferrata Street, Gzira, t 21 311655, *www.diamondwash.eu*.

## Electrical Appliances

**Delta Homecentres** have six branches. Head office, t 21 331071. **Forestals Ltd** are on the Strand between Gzira and Sliema, t 23 436000.

## Chandlers

**RLR**, **Gauci Borda**, **Nautica**, **International Marine** and **Medcomms** are all to be found in Ta'Xbiex and Msida, and have just about everything you need.

## Principal Agents and Brokers

**Roland Darmanin**, S & D Yachts, 8 Marina Court, Giuseppe Cali Street, Ta'Xbiex, t 21 339908.

**Christian Ripard**, RLR, 156 Ta'Xbiex Seafront, t 21 331192.

# Valletta and
# the Three Cities

*Malta's capital, Valletta, is
immediately impressive: somewhere
you can be truly subjective and get
away with it. It can become what
you want it to be: a historically
seductive fortress built by crusading
knights in shining armour,
a commercial centre that looks like
a miniature Manhattan with its
skyscrapers cheese-wired off, or
simply a city with an incredible
cathedral, fascinating Baroque
architecture, and museums and
cafés to linger in.*

# 07

## Don't miss

⭐ **A walk through
the old streets**
Central Valletta **p.100**

② **Cathedral
treasures**
A Caravaggio master-
piece in St John's
Co-Cathedral, Valletta
**p.104**

③ **Past peoples**
Museum of Archaeology,
Valletta **p.121**

④ **A lush flora**
Argotti Botanical
Gardens, Floriana **p.126**

⑤ **Sea tales**
Maritime Museum,
Vittoriosa **p.140**

*See map overleaf*

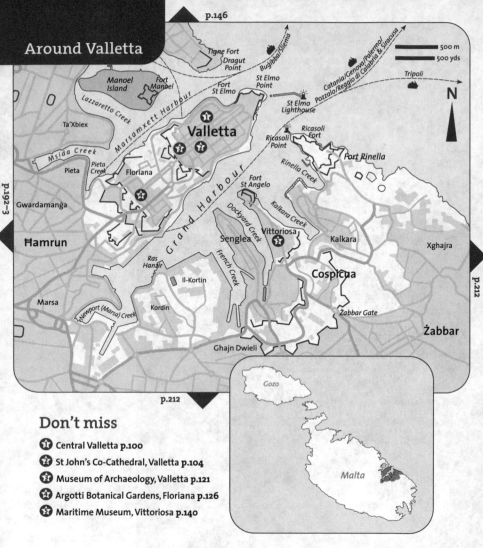

p.146

## Don't miss

1. Central Valletta p.100
2. St John's Co-Cathedral, Valletta p.104
3. Museum of Archaeology, Valletta p.121
4. Argotti Botanical Gardens, Floriana p.126
5. Maritime Museum, Vittoriosa p.140

As European capitals go, **Valletta** is a rarity – it is only just 420 years old. The city is not therefore a place of impacted civilizations that bears the trace of its country's history in its architecture. On the contrary, it was actually a planned city.

Valletta was named after Grand Master de la Valette. The city was devised, in the wake of his victory against the Turks in the Great Siege of 1565, with two aims: to be a formidable Christian fortress able to withstand the forces of Islam, and to be a congenial home for the aristocratic flower of Europe, the chivalrous Order of the Knights of St John. Consequently, within its bastion walls it acquired all the trappings of a capital city, most of which remain – parliament, the judiciary and government; plus offices of the larger private enterprises. Its charms are readily apparent. Yet for all its

*Grand Harbour, Valletta, Senglea, and Vittoriosa have all the ingredients of the picturesque – ancient buildings, fortifications, narrow and precipitous streets, national costume, local religious festivals, and an unconscionably romantic history.*

Evelyn Waugh,
*Labels*, 1930

fine architecture and noble birth Valletta lacks character and soul. Neither has it avoided 21st-century phenomena such as unemployment, drugs-related problems and a diminishing population. To most Maltese it is just Il Belt, literally 'the city'; a place to work or somewhere to find something unobtainable elsewhere. The city empties at sunset and many even go home during the long lunch hours.

Across the Grand Harbour from the Valletta promontory is the area known as the **Three Cities**, variously called Senglea, Cospicua and Vittoriosa, the original home of the Order. Until they built Valletta, the Three Cities were the island's de facto capital, and the area bore the brunt of the Great Sieges of both 1565 and 1941–3. A tightly knit working-class community lives in the narrow streets, and they have remained largely untouched by touristic development. All this is in the process of change. In recent years a new marina has opened in Dockyard Creek, and the Casino di Venezia has been installed in the superbly renovated Vittoriosa Wharf. But at present there is still much here to attract anyone who is not particularly interested in the history of the Order.

## Valletta

Valletta itself may now be an UNESCO World Heritage City, but it is also a schizophrenic one. By day it is a thriving and bustling capital: idle dissenters loiter outside the law courts, lawyers and businessmen lean on the bar of the Café Cordina having their morning fix of espresso, housewives rummage around **Merchants Street market** for bargains, and tourists meander up and down Republic Street. The splendours of **St John's Co-Cathedral**, the displays in the **Museum of Archaeology**, the **Grand Master's Palace** and the **Armoury** ensure that an enduring stream of visitors tramp the city's streets.

By night, however, it wears a sombre mask. Venture into Valletta after the sunset *passeggiata*, when all the shops are shut and the businessmen have returned home, and you wonder if it is the same place. Everywhere is closed save for a few bars, and the littered streets can offer up a foreboding impression (this is deceptive; the streets are safe). Life does go on in the residential *quartiers* past **Palace Square** – here the Maltese gossip on doorsteps, shout across the narrow streets, or tinker with their cars – but this is not a tourist town by night. There are, however, a few good restaurants open in the evening, and the easy parking and quiet streets can make a pleasant change from the frenetic activity of other areas.

Until recently, Valletta was a city without much civic self-respect. People, especially tourists, would arrive, see or do what they had to

## Getting to and around Valletta

### By Bus

Just outside City Gate and revolving around the Triton Fountain, like horses on a fairground carousel, are the island's fleet of buses. If you hop on any bus from anywhere in Malta that is heading away from the sea, eventually you will end up here.

### By Boat

If you are in the Sliema/St Julian's area, the least aggravating and quickest way to get to Valletta is by travelling on the Marsamxett Ferry, which leaves approximately every 30 minutes from the Ferries in Sliema; the crossing takes just five minutes and you disembark by the water-polo pitch.

### By Car

Arriving by car is trickier than it appears on the map – Valletta is flagged from most places – owing to the city's convoluted one-way system and to the near-impossible task of finding a legitimate place to park in the city itself. Make sure the car you are driving is licensed to enter Valletta (only cars with a V on the tax disc are allowed).

Within the city walls, gamblers can try to find a hole outside the Auberge de Castile et Leon, in Pope Pius V Street, by the bombed-out shell of the Opera House or in the car park in front of the Grand Master's Palace. The best spot is outside Giannini's Restaurant in Windmill Street by St Michael's Bastion; not only will the helpful attendant look after the hub caps, but for a decent tip he will wash your car as well. If you are planning to park on the streets, make sure you are within the designated boxes; many cars are towed every day in Valletta. Towed cars are taken to the MCP car park and are fined Lm45. One of the easier parking options is to use the underground MCP car park opposite Hotel Le Meridien Phoenicia.

You can avoid all this hassle by following the signs for the Park and Ride opposite Mizzi House in Blata l-Bajda on National Road. Another park-and-ride service operates from 9am to 1pm daily (excluding Sun) between the car park entrance and St John's Co-Cathedral.

**Taxis** and *karrozin* can be found near the Auberge de Castile et Leon, in Great Siege Square and by City Gate. For most of the day Republic Street is pedestrianized from City Gate to Palace Square.

---

and leave, mildly shocked at the unkempt state of the place. Now it is once again becoming somewhere to linger – try any of the outdoor cafés surrounding Queen Victoria's statue in **Republic Square** – as well as to explore.

Keep an eye out also for interesting exhibitions, plays or shows on at **St James's Cavalier**, **Manoel Theatre** and the **Mediterranean Conference Centre**.

## The Planned City: the Building and the Architecture of Valletta

One month after the Great Siege was raised in September 1565, Grand Master de la Valette was confronted with vociferous disquiet in his ranks. To the older knights, 'the Turk always returns' was axiomatic, and in reality they had not won – the Turk had lost. Fort St Elmo was devastated, as were parts of St Angelo; the knights had neither the manpower nor the fortifications to withstand another onslaught, which was expected some time in the following spring. The Order simply had to remain somehow: they were the cork which kept the infidel Turk in his eastern Mediterranean bottle. Malta was as far west as the European monarchies and powers were prepared to let him venture.

Before the end of 1565, and at the grand master's request, Pope Pius V sent Francesco Laparelli to Malta; 44 years of age, an ex-pupil of Michelangelo and a leading proponent of military engineering, his brief was to advise on the wisdom of creating a wholly fortified virgin city – a planned city.

The chosen site, **Mount Sceberras**, was an undulating peninsula of limestone rock. It jabbed out into the Mediterranean like an aggressive finger in between the Grand and the Marsamxett Harbours and was, save for Fort St Elmo, undefended and uninhabited. Within just six days of his arrival, Laparelli proposed his plan: a girdle of fortifications built around Mount Sceberras. The fortifications would stretch up to the highest landward point on the peninsula, some 500 Sicilian *cannes* (1 *canne* = 6ft 9in/ 2.065m) inland from the pile of rubble that was Fort St Elmo's gate. Inside this massive fortress enceinte, a grid-pattern city would be hewn mostly out of the living rock, the details of which could be improvised as they progressed. One of the most persuasive arguments Laparelli used to sway the vacillating septuagenarian de la Valette and his council was that it would be cheaper to erect a whole new city than to demolish the old fortifications and evacuate Malta. Like most architects he was wildly optimistic, but the Order's council believed him. The foundation stone of the new city was laid on 28 March 1566 amid much pomp, three months after Laparelli's arrival.

Work was initially slow due to a shortage of slaves, labourers and masons; up to 4,000 were needed. By 1568, the year the magistracy had passed to the Italian del Monte, the streets had been laid and Laparelli felt able to return to Italy leaving his Maltese assistant, the parochial Gerolamo Cassar, temporarily in charge. (The quixotic Laparelli was to return only briefly the following year before succumbing to the plague in Crete while serving in the papal fleet.) Earlier, Cassar was dispatched to Italy to absorb as many aesthetic influences as possible. Architecturally at this time, Mannerism and the beautiful Renaissance marriage of the straight line and the circle, were ready to give way and accept a new discipline, the curve of Baroque. Cassar must have returned home in a quandary, for his paymasters were nigh on bankrupt after the enormous expense of the fortifications, and were after all monastic warriors of Christ with tastes to match. But Valletta was to be a truly joint effort between Laparelli, the Italian motivator with a grasp for the grand scheme, and Cassar, the skilled Maltese architect and details man. That said, with Laparelli's final departure Cassar's achievement was one stop short of totalitarian architecture. Before he died in 1581 he was responsible in Valletta alone for the Grand Master's Palace, St John's Co-Cathedral, the seven original *auberges*, and many private houses and churches.

The complex project was executed following practices remarkably similar to those of the late 20th century. The Council of the Order set about purchasing all the required land and issuing stringent planning guidelines. There were approximately 1,125 private plots, none of which could be bought for speculative purposes, and to avoid undesirables nominee purchases were outlawed. A successful purchaser had to commence construction within six months, and complete the building by the end of the following year. No structure was allowed to be set back from, or extend on to, the street, and courtyards had to be contained within the plot. There was to be adequate provision for the storage of water, and connection to a central sewage system was mandatory. Laparelli's street plan was wide and designed to take advantage of the cleansing sea breezes. Anyone buying a corner property had to embellish the corners for the benefit of all. Unlike their accommodation in Rhodes, where the knights were ghettoed in a *collacchio*, there was no intention of segregating the Maltese; Valletta was 3½ times larger than Birgu (Vittoriosa) and could accommodate everyone.

Grand Master del Monte formally moved the Order to the unfinished city on 18 March 1571 and by 1610 all the plots were sold. Valletta was a resounding success, and the population rose to approximately 4,000 (today it is approximately 9,000). Later on in the 17th and 18th centuries, with the Turkish threat diminishing and the evolution of Baroque, the Order grew to revel in the symbiosis of art, architecture and wealth. Its additions and embellishments subtly changed Valletta from principally a Renaissance to a Baroque city – and, despite even the gimlet-eyed attentions of the Axis bombers, it is still Laparelli's and Cassar's city.

## Valletta City Sights

### Orientation

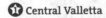 **Central Valletta**

*Adieu, ye cursed streets of stairs! (How surely he who mounts you swears!)*

Lord Byron, 'Farewell to Malta', 16 May 1811

**Republic Street** is the main thoroughfare, the island's principal shopping street and the axis for a walking tour of the main sights. Before it became Republic Street in 1974, its different names flagged the city's history – as Strada San Giorgio, Rue de la République, Strada Reale and Kingsway.

The city is laid out on a neat grid approximately half a mile (1km) long by 650 yards (600m) wide. The diminutive dimensions belie its roller-coaster topography. Apart from Republic Street there are two other main arteries: **Merchants Street** and **Old Bakery Street**, and both spine down the Sceberras peninsula from **City Gate** towards **Fort St Elmo** on the point. The cross streets fall off these streets in steps and/or alleys to the **Grand** and **Marsamxett Harbours** and a further road rings the entire city.

In the following descriptions, the numbers in square brackets refer to numbered sights on the city map (*see* p.102).

## From City Gate to the Castellania

**[1] City Gate.** Known originally as the Gate of St George, this was the main entrance through the bastions into the city. It later became Porta Reale, and then King's Gate. The present dull City Gate was erected to provide a wider passage in 1964. Outside, the **Triton Fountain** is another contemporary Maltese work from the 1950s.

**[2] Palazzo Ferreria and the Old Opera House** give an untidy first impression of Valletta. The **Opera House** was designed by EM Barry, architect of the Royal Opera House in Covent Garden, London, and completed in 1866. Its unpopular design was intended to reflect the imperial bearing of the British Empire. It was gutted by fire in 1873 and reopened four years later. The contentious structure was destroyed by the Luftwaffe in 1942 and has languished as an eyesore ever since. The 60-year polemic over its future design and use will run and run. The **Palazzo Ferreria**, on the left opposite the remains of the Opera House, was built in the late 19th century on the site of the Order's arsenal or *ferreria*, as the private residence for a wealthy wheat-importer.

**[3] St James's Cavalier.** The two cavaliers of St James and St John were designed to defend Valletta against land-based attacks. The original function of St James's was to provide a raised platform on which to place landward facing guns. Most of the internal space was filled with compressed earth, surrounding a series of chambers and a ramp through which cannons were rolled onto the roof. During the British period, St James's was used as an officers' mess, a water store and finally a food store. Today it is the **Centre for Creativity**, which holds art exhibitions, plays, concerts and children's activities. The building has been sympathetically restored to reveal both its original 16th-century structure and the subsequent British changes.

**[4] Our Lady of Victory.** This rather sorry-looking church was the first the knights built in their new city to commemorate their victory in the Great Siege of 1565. De la Valette laid the foundation stone and was initially buried here before being interred in St John's Co-Cathedral. Grand Master Perellos altered the façade in 1690 and placed the bust of Pope Innocent XI above the door.

**[5] Church of St Catherine of Italy.** Designed by Cassar for the Italian knights and abutting their *auberge*, St Catherine's church is also looking weary. The façade and porch were added in 1713 and the octagonal church is still used today by the Italian community.

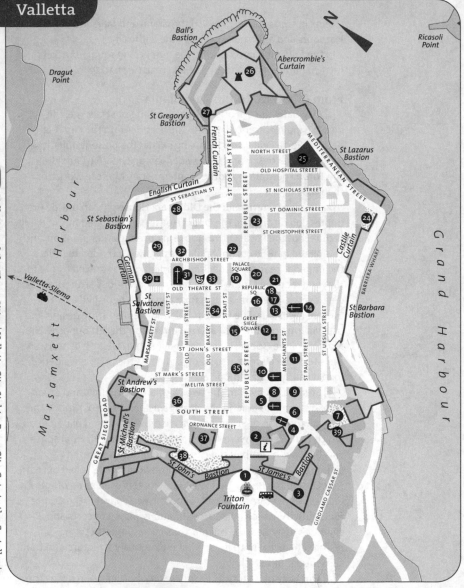

The main altarpiece of the *Martyrdom of St Catherine* is one of Mattia Preti's favourite subjects.

**[6] Auberge de Castile et Leon**. The *auberge* of the knights of Spain and Portugal is the capital's finest example of 18th-century mature Maltese Baroque and has a rare and grand symmetry. Situated at the highest point of the peninsula, on a site originally designated for the Grand Master's Palace and partially shadowed by St James's Cavalier, it was remodelled in 1741 around Cassar's far more austere original of 1574. The effervescent façade with its precise detail was handled by either Domenico Cachia or Andrea Belli.

Grand Master Pinto, who commissioned the building for his Iberian countrymen, was a showy, luxurious man, who revelled in the competitiveness of European monarchies. There is a wonderful portrait of him by de Favray in the Sacristy of St John's. Here, above the portal and set amidst flags, weapons and accoutrements, is a bust of Pinto, and over the central window is his escutcheon. The crowning decoration on top of the cornice is the arms of Castile et Leon. The two cannons date from 1756.

Historically, the grand chancellor of the Order was a knight of Castile et Leon, and the knights were to defend St Barbara bastion facing the Grand Harbour. The *auberge* was once the British forces' headquarters and now houses the office of the prime minister. With a touch of irony, the statue facing the *auberge* from the roundabout is of Manwel Dimech, one of the founders of Malta's socialist movement.

**[7] Upper Barracca Gardens**. The colonnaded public garden, **Il Belvedere d'Italia**, on top of St Peter and St Paul's demibastion, was once a covered play area for the boisterous Italian knights. A plot to overthrow Grand Master Ximenes, known as the Priests' Revolt, was hatched in the building in 1775, and the roof was removed after the plot had been rumbled. Overlooking the Three Cities and the harbour, the public gardens offer the best **panorama** in Valletta; this has long been a favourite spot for many, not just for pigeon-chasing children. Among the statues are Sir Thomas Maitland (governor 1813–24 and known as 'King Tom') in a rare contemplative pose, *Les Gavroches* by Maltese sculptor Antonio Sciortino, and a bust of Winston Churchill.

**[8] Auberge d'Italie/General Post Office**. The duty of the knights of the Italian *langue* was to defend the immediate bastions of St Peter and St Paul, and the post of admiral of the fleet was traditionally the sinecure of their *pilier*. The ubiquitous Cassar designed this *auberge* as a single-storey edifice and it displays a typical example of his one major architectural hallmark, the use of massive and rusticated quoins – the external corners of walls. The Italian Grand Master Carafa added the top floor in 1683 at the same time as his deliciously theatrical, very Italian piece of Baroque nonsense above the main door; trumpets, Roman armour, flags, escutcheons, weapons and ornamental drapes are all thrown together around his nonchalant-looking bust. The building once housed the law courts and a museum.

**[9] Palazzo Parisio**. Opposite the post office is the Palazzo Parisio, another government building. This gloomy late 18th-century structure is notable only because Napoleon made it his headquarters for five days during his brief plundering stay en route to the Egyptian campaign in June 1798.

**[10] St James's Church**. Built in 1612 to serve the knights of Castile et Leon, the church was to all intents and purposes rebuilt by Giovanni Barbara in 1710. The oval plan, rich detail on its narrow façade and ornate carvings above the central window, are redolent of Roman Baroque. In 1663 the church was the focus of a religious scandal when the silver pyx of consecrated Hosts was stolen.

**[11] Castellania**. On the corner of Merchants and St John's Streets, the Castellania housed the law courts. It was completed in 1760 during Grand Master Pinto's reign (hence the florid stonework and his ever-present crescent emblem). The figures either side of the first-floor balcony represent Justice and Truth. After the Priests' Revolt of 1775, three of the conspirators were tried, strangled and decapitated, and their heads were placed on spikes by St James's Cavalier. At the apex of the building's corner is a pillory stone for lesser miscreants. For the hook above it, there are two explanations: one says it was used to hoist up the bells of St John's, the other more plausibly states it was used to suspend convicts sentenced to imprisonment in a cage.

The building has been put to somewhat less gruesome uses since then, having even been a girls' school. In 1896 it became the office of the Health Department, and it was here that the physician and prominent archaeologist Sir Themistocles Zammit discovered the Mediterranean strain of brucellosis in 1905.

## [12] St John's Co-Cathedral and Museum

**⚫ St John's Co-Cathedral and Museum**
*t 21 220536, www. stjohnscocathedral.org; open Mon–Fri 9.30—4, Sat 9.30–12; closed Sun and public holidays; adm (includes museum); free for worshippers, members of the clergy and ICOM card-holders; mass is heard daily and High Mass, said in Latin, at 9.15 on Sun*

This extraordinary edifice houses Malta's finest art treasures and its splendour tests the limits of the lexicon; words like 'lavish' and 'opulent' fall far short of the mark.

### History and Exterior

After the knights left Birgu (Vittoriosa) in 1571, the need to replace St Lawrence's Church with a new Conventual church – one for the brotherhood of the entire Order – was of paramount concern. Yet the new building, dedicated to their patron saint St John the Baptist, had to be more than a place of collective worship: it had in time to be a place which could embody the wealth, glory and power of the Order itself. With tact, Cassar designed a clean but heavy façade in homage to the then austere military attitudes of his paymasters. For the next 80 years, the interior remained as stark as the exterior.

Work commenced in the autumn of 1573 on a simple but somewhat heavy Renaissance-influenced plan: a wide screen façade, an entrance between two Doric columns with twin bell towers either side (the spires of which were removed during the

*Magnificent church, the most striking interior I have ever seen.*

Sir Walter Scott, 1831

Second World War). The interior was also to be conventional – a single rectangular nave below a great barrel vault with an apse at the northeast end and eight side chapels, one for each of the *langues*, between the huge reinforcing buttresses.

The church was consecrated on 20 February 1578 and was built and paid for by the French Grand Master de la Cassière. Other parts of this calmly severe building were added later; the sacristy in 1598, the oratory in 1603, and the loggia annexes in 1736. The two cannons date from 1600 and 1726; the former, with lion handles, bears the Battenburg coat of arms, and the latter the arms of Grand Master de Vilhena.

## The Interior

*Inside there is no single spot where the eye can rest for one moment that is not ablaze with decoration.*

Evelyn Waugh,
*Labels*, 1930

As your eyes adjust from the harsh sunlight to the muted, even gloomy interior(*see* interior plan, p.106), they are drawn down the 190ft (58m) length of the nave to the altar, trying, and failing, to take in the opulence and the fields of frescoes en route. Nothing quite prepares you for the engulfing effect of such affluence; not even Napoleon's wholesale depredations have dimmed it. With every election to the magistracy, or even a promotion, a knight had, by statute, to provide a *gioia* (gift) to the Order's church. St John's and the neighbouring chapels of each *langue* were lavished with gifts in expensive rounds of knightly one-upmanship. As the threat of Infidel wars diminished, the Order grew wealthier (and softer) and its tastes became more flamboyant.

**The nave.** The Order's inherent ostentation was given further rein upon the death of a knight, for only a knight, and then only one of distinction, could be interred in St John's. The entire pavement of the nave is made up of 364 tessellated tombs; the earliest, in the Chapel of Aragon, dates from 1602. Some of the symbols are garish and some simple, but each is individual. One of the memorial slabs by the Republic Street entrance belongs to a French knight, Anselmo de Caijs. His inscription translates: 'You who tread on me, you will be trodden upon; reflect on that and pray for me.' Annoyed at not being promoted, he apparently took his grievance to the grave.

The bronze and marble Baroque **mausoleum** remembers Italian Grand Master Zondadari, nephew of Pope Alexander VII who was once an inquisitor in Malta.

**The vault.** Nikolaus Pevsner, the architectural historian, states that Mattia Preti's work depicting the life of St John the Baptist in the vault of St John's is 'the first realized example of high Baroque art anywhere'. The work was commissioned in 1661 by the Cotoner brothers, Rafael and Nicolas, grand masters from 1660 to 1680. The vault is illuminated by six oval windows and divided into six bays, which in turn are sub-divided into three, thereby creating one

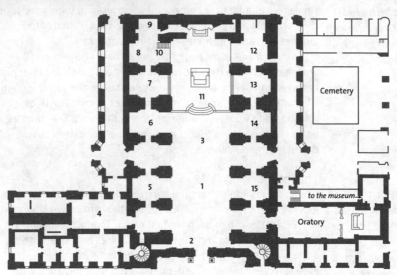

*St John's Square*

1 Nave
2 Zondadari Mausoleum
3 Vault
4 Sacristy
5 Chapel of Germany
6 Chapel of Italy
7 Chapel of France
8 Chapel of Provence

9 Chapel of Anglo-Bavarian Langue
10 To the Grand Masters' Crypt
11 The Sanctuary
12 Chapel of Our Lady of Philermos
13 Chapel of Auvergne
14 Chapel of Aragon
15 Chapel of Castile

stone canvas for 18 episodes in the Baptist's life. Not strictly frescoes – Preti painted in oils directly onto the barely primed and porous stone – they took five years to complete. The cycle commences on the left of the first bay by the main door and ends with the beheading, on the right above the altar. The figures on either side of the windows are of individual knights, and saints revered by the Order.

In the **sacristy**, Antoine de Favray's terrific portrait of Grand Master Pinto, one of the island's best paintings, is poorly served by the lighting. Painted in 1747, it tells chromatically and stylistically how far the Order and its magistracy had departed from its crusading Hospitaller origins. Dressed in flowing ermine robes, Pinto almost sweats vanity and decadence as he points at the jewelled crown symbolically placed in front of his redundant steel helmet. Other works include the late 16th-century *Baptism of Christ* by Matteo Perez d'Aleccio (once St John's titular painting), the old Aragonese altarpiece of *St George* by Frederico Potenzano from 1585, a portrait of Grand Master Nicolas Cotoner by Mattia Preti and a portrait of Preti himself. In what is now the entrance to the sacristy there was once a chapel for the remainder of the English *langue*, which ceased to exist after 1540, following Henry VIII's break with Rome. Note Preti's lunette of the *Birth of the Virgin*. At the foot of the pillar is his tombstone; a grateful Order had made him a Knight of Grace.

## The Chapels and Sanctuary

*Walk clockwise beginning to the left of the main door.*

In Cassar's original layout each of the chapels was gated and compartmentalized; the narrow ambulatory that now exists was cut through the walls on Preti's instigation in the 17th century. The **chapel of Germany** is dedicated to the Epiphany. Towards the end of the 17th century Stefano Erardi painted the altarpiece, the *Adoration of the Magi* and the two lunettes. The white marble altar is the only remaining 17th-century Baroque altar in St John's. The **chapel of Italy** houses the painting of St Jerome, the second of Caravaggio's works in Malta. It was stolen from St John's Museum in December 1984 and recovered in August 1987 after which it was restored and returned to its original setting. Caravaggio's startling, almost photographically precise, style manages to convey both the physical and metaphysical compassion in St Jerome even though the study shows only his face and torso (somehow even St Jerome's ever-present talisman, the skull, appears benign). By comparison, Preti's refined altarpiece of the Italian knights' patron saint, St Catherine, and the black marble mausoleum of Grand Master Carafa, pale into undeserved insignificance.

The **chapel of France**, dedicated to St Paul, was 'restored' in the 1840s by those who wished to purify Christian art and eradicate the Baroque legacies. The walls and altar were changed and the only principal work to survive is Preti's altarpiece. The mausoleums are a languidly reclining Vicomte de Beaujolais, brother of the future King Louis Philippe, Grand Masters de Rohan and Adrien de Wignacourt, and his brother Marquis Giochim de Wignacourt. All except for the Vicomte's (and possibly the Marquis's) were badly 'altered' during the anti-Baroque purges. The **chapel of Provence** is dedicated to St Michael; Provence was the most senior of the *langues*. The imperial eagle, from Grand Master Lascaris's arms, is on the wall and he and his predecessor, Grand Master de Paule, are both interred here. Their inlaid mausoleums are typically ornate. Stairs down to the crypt are to the right as you face the **Anglo-Bavarian Chapel**, also known as the Chapel of the Relics. Essentially a large niche, it was given to the *langue* in 1784 and held the principal collection of the knights' reliquaries until Napoleon stole them. The bronze gates are from the next chapel, on the other side of the Sanctuary, to Philermos. The old wooden figurehead of St John is said to have come from the *Grand Carrack* in which the knights sailed from Rhodes, and this piece evidently had no cash value to Napoleon.

The **Grand Masters' Crypt** is not always open and it houses the mausoleums of the grand masters who reigned from 1522 to 1623, including de la Valette and de L'Isle Adam. The only memorial here to a knight below the rank of grand master is dedicated to Sir Oliver Starkey, de la Valette's loyal English secretary – a great honour. At the east end of the south aisle is the **chapel of Our Lady of Philermos**, also known as the Blessed Sacrament, and a much-venerated chapel. The most important remaining work is the Renaissance Cross dating from 1532. Tradition says the silver gates – a gift in 1752 from two knights – were painted black to resemble coarse iron when Napoleon was looting St John's for his war chest. If true, the ruse worked. In the **chapel of Auvergne** the only mausoleum belongs to Grand Master Gessan, whose distinction comes from having had the briefest reign of any grand master, less than four months in 1660. The altarpiece between exaggerated barley-twist columns is of *The Martyrdom of St Sebastian*, to whom the chapel is dedicated.

The **chapel of Aragon** is the finest of the chapels and dedicated to St George. Preti's altarpiece of *St George* was the artist's calling card (from Naples) to Grand Master de Redin in 1658, which won him the coveted commission of decorating the vault of St John's (*see* pp.105–6). All the paintings in the chapel, including the lunette of poor *St Lawrence* about to be griddled to death, are by Preti and encapsulate a decade of his work. The four grand masters' mausoleums are ranged chronologically: de Redin, Nicolas Cotoner, his brother Rafael and Perellos. Note the exuberant Florentine sculpture on Nicolas Cotoner's, where the whole mass of military paraphernalia is supported by two buckling slaves – predictably North African and Levantine. A sombre bust of *Perellos* sits above Mazzuoli's figures of *Charity and Justice* on his monument.

The chapel of **Castile et Leon** is dedicated to St James, and the altarpiece is one of Preti's last works. De Vilhena's splendid bronze mausoleum (note him inspecting plans of Fort Manoel in relief on the front) is in contrast to the surprisingly classical and restrained monument to Grand Master Pinto. The oval mosaic of Pinto was taken from one of de Favray's works.

Following liturgical changes in the mid-17th century the sanctuary was balustraded off and the layout altered. The high altar is made of lapis lazuli and other semiprecious stones. The fine 16th-century Flemish bronze lecterns were a gift from the Duke of Lorraine, and Grand Master Garzes contributed the walnut choir stalls. The huge Baroque sculpture of the *Baptism of Christ* dates from the end of the 17th century. Above, in the apse, Preti painted *St John in Heaven*.

## St John's Oratory and Museum

**St John's Oratory and Museum**
*open same times as church*

The oratory was built at the request of Grand Master Alof de Wignacourt in 1603, as a place of worship and for adult novices waiting to be admitted to the Order. Until Preti took charge of the decoration in the 1680s it remained, like St John's itself, clinically functional; the gilding, the painted soffits, Grand Master Carafa's marble altar were all added at Preti's instigation. His Baroque updating was designed around Caravaggio's huge canvas *The Beheading of St John the Baptist*, which until then had been illuminated by a window on the western flank.

### The Beheading of St John the Baptist

As a painter, Caravaggio was defined by his unique ability to transform religious subjects into almost three-dimensional life. His inspired use of shadow, halftones and subtle light gives powerful physical presence to his subjects – and nowhere more effectively than in this composition. *The Beheading* is a magnificent picture that captures the tortured emotions of each individual present at the chilling scene and is set in the deep shadows of a prison. The old lady gripping her head knows the wrong that has been done; the executioner's discarded sword and St John's sheepskin fall out together from underneath the red cape; the jug-eared gaoler with outsize keys points to Salome's salver which she clutches with dread. But the most haunting image to emerge out of the chiaroscuro is not the pitifully trussed-up St John but the executioner himself. From behind his back he stealthily removes a knife from its sheath in order to finish the work his sword started. His brow is deeply furrowed and his body taut – this is one execution he would rather not have had to perform. He alone tips the painting from being violent into a vilification of violence. The expressions of the two onlookers dramatize the pornographic nature of public brutality.

### Caravaggio

Michelangelo Merisi da Caravaggio (1571–1610) was born in the town of Caravaggio in the north of Italy. He trained in Milan and is regarded as the greatest of Italy's 17th-century painters. By the time he journeyed to Malta from Naples in July 1607, he was already a celebrated artist in Rome, having attracted both public acclaim and personal notoriety. Soon after his arrival he commenced *The Beheading* for the Oratory of St John's. During the ensuing year he painted prodigiously and trained as a novice in the Order; in July 1608, after a papal dispensation, Grand Master Alof de Wignacourt admitted him into the Order with the rank of Knight of Grace. His Maltese *œuvre* includes paintings of de Wignacourt in different poses (the only one known to survive hangs in the Louvre), *St Jerome* which hangs in the chapel of Italy, and at least two other works that are either 'lost' or destroyed.

As a master of realism, and light and shade, his skills were a revelation to Maltese artists and their patrons in the Order. Yet, despite his success, Caravaggio's fiery character was destined to cause trouble. Fourteen months after his arrival and just two months after he had received his Insignia of St John and Belt of Knighthood (and gifts of two slaves and gold from a grateful de Wignacourt) he was arrested for an unknown crime. The undocumented story states that he was imprisoned in the dungeons of Fort St Angelo from which he somehow escaped and fled to Sicily. It has been cynically, but probably accurately, suggested that his escape was orchestrated with de Wignacourt's blessing. Either way, he was tried *in absentia*, defrocked and expelled from the Order on 1 December 1608 as a 'putrid and fetid limb'. From Sicily he travelled back to Naples. Following a near-fatal fight, he sailed north to Porto Ercole, then a simple Spanish outpost, to await a papal pardon. After another violent altercation and a few days' imprisonment, he died of malaria, alone on the beach of Porto Ercole, in 1610, only days before his pardon arrived. He was only 38.

07 | Valletta and the Three Cities | Valletta City Sights: St John's Co-Cathedral and Museum

## Cathedral Museum

From outside the oratory, and from some of the museum's upstairs windows, you can see the **cemetery** where many of the knights killed during the siege of 1565 are buried. The highlight of the museum is 29 finely crafted tableaux of Flemish tapestries found in its three principal rooms. The three cycles of tapestries were commissioned by Grand Master Perellos, upon his election to the magistracy in 1697, from Jodicos de Vos in Belgium for the incredible sum of 40,000 *scudi* (approximately double the cost of a major fort). The 14 square panels (20ft/6m by 20ft/6m) are divided into two seven-piece cycles and all are modelled on drawings by Rubens, with the exception of the *Last Supper* which was from a Poussin. One cycle tells the *Story of Christ* from the *Annunciation*, through his *Entry into Jerusalem* to the *Resurrection*; the other portrays different allegories including the *Triumph of Charity*, the *Destruction of Idolatry* and the *Four Evangelists*. An additional 14 oblong panels (6ft/1.8m by 22ft/6.6m) are hung as fillers in between the principal square panels and majestically depict the *Disciples*, the *Virgin Mary*, *Christ* and, rather immodestly, the *Gracious Donor*. The tapestries used to be hung in St John's each year on 24 June, the feast of St John the Baptist, but now are on permanent exhibition in the Cathedral Museum.

Among the other exhibits and vestments is a collection of antiphonies (illuminated choral books) donated by the Order's first ruler in Malta, Grand Master de L'Isle Adam. There is also a sparse collection of church silverware. The blame for the sorry state of what must have been one of the most valuable collections of silver in Europe can again be laid at Napoleon's door. He stole almost all of it in 1798, together with the silver plates from the Sacra Infermeria (*see* p.117), and melted his plunder into bullion. Ironically, it went down with his flagship *L'Orient* in Aboukir Bay during the Egyptian campaign. One surviving piece of interest is a 17th-century silver-gilt monstrance (it looks like a very ornate mantelpiece clock with an oblong face), which held the Order's most treasured possession – part of the forearm, ostensibly, of St John the Baptist. Grand Master von Hompesch took the forearm when he fled Malta in 1798 and it ended up in the Imperial Russian collections. Somehow, the monstrance slipped through Napoleon's greedy fingers.

## From the Palazzo di Città to Palace Square

**[13] Palazzo di Città.** The Municipal Palace or Banca Giuratale (1720) are grand names for what was and still is the Public Records Office. The building gave many style hints for the splendid Auberge de Castile et Leon put up 10 years later. Built during the brief reign of strait-laced Grand Master Zondadari, it is somewhat out of character with its paymaster. It is a handsome squared-off building of accessible proportions, but with a leaden cornice that is lightened only by the Baroque centrepiece which overflows like a fountain.

**St Paul's Shipwreck**
*hours can vary but tend to be Mon–Fri 11–12.45 and 4–6 and Sat 11–12 and 4–6; multilingual leaflets and/or a sacristan are on hand; NB the main door is often shut or looks shut; try the smaller side entrance just around the corner; adm free, but leave a donation*

**[14]**St Paul's Shipwreck. Cassar originally built this church but it has been remodelled and redecorated twice since. As befits a building dedicated to one of Malta's patron saints, it is lavish (though not always tastefully so), and it houses some venerated possessions. The plan is a Latin cross, the dome elliptical and the floor tessellated. The wooden gilded statue of St Paul is by Melchiorre Gafa and is solemnly carried through the streets on 10 February each year, the day St Paul's shipwreck is commemorated. Gafa's brother Lorenzo designed the chapel of the Blessed Sacrament in 1680 (left aisle), and de Favray painted the altarpiece. The ceiling frescoes depict St Paul's brief sojourn in Malta and were painted at the turn of the 20th century, while the main altarpiece of St Paul and St Luke is from the late 16th century and by the Florentine, Filippo Paladini. Donated to the church by Pope Pius VII in 1818, and most treasured of all, is part of the block upon which St Paul was said to have been beheaded, as well as what is believed to be a part of his right wristbone.

**[15] Great Siege Square and the Law Courts.** The Law Courts were erected after the Second World War on the site of the Auberge de Auvergne, which suffered extensive bomb damage. The bronze Great Siege monument facing it is by the Maltese artist Antonio Sciortino.

**[16] Republic Square.** Cafés have expanded into the square and it is an excellent place to pause for refreshments. During the Order's reign the square was known as Piazza Tesoreria after its treasury building, and in 1891 the British cleared its orange grove and renamed it Queen's Square. In the same year, Valenti's statue of a diminutive Queen Victoria enveloped in Malta lace replaced the statue of Grand Master de Vilhena on the occasion of her Diamond Jubilee (de Vilhena, having originally stood at Fort Manoel, now stands in Floriana).

**Bibliotheca**
*open winter Mon–Fri 8.15–5.45, Sat 8.15–1.15; summer Mon–Sat 8.15–1.15; adm free, but note visiting time is limited to 30 minutes; it is possible to photocopy certain items for a small charge*

**[17]**Bibliotheca (1786–96). Behind Queen Victoria is the Bibliotheca or National Library. The library, designed by the Italian Stefano Ittar, was a gift from the French knight de Tencin during Grand Master de Rohan's reign and the last major civil building project the Order was to undertake. With its four Venetian-style arches, this neoclassical building was completed in 1796. The Order first established a library in 1555, soon after its arrival. In 1612 a law was enacted which forbade a knight's own volumes from being disposed of after his death and the library steadily grew from these and other bequests. Today the Bibliotheca houses all the written records of the Order from 1107 to 1798 including the *Processi*

07 Valletta and the Three Cities | Valletta City Sights: From the Palazzo di Città to Palace Square

*Nobilari,* a knight's proof of his maternal and paternal lines of nobility, which was required to ensure his acceptance into the Order. Also stored here – the main hall is 140ft (42m) long – are the documents of Baldwin I of Jerusalem, the papal bull of Paschal II sanctioning the Order in 1113 and Charles V's 1530 donation of the islands to the Order. In total there are approximately 400,000 works including the records and minutes of the *Università* and 46 incunabula – books printed before 1500. In what can only be assumed a monstrous fit of Gallic pique, Napoleon ordered all the records to be destroyed but fortunately knightly shuffling of feet saved the priceless collection.

There is a changing display of documents and books, and the statue on the main stairs is of Dun Karm, the national poet.

**The Great Siege of Malta and the Knights of St John**
*open every day 9–4; headsets available in 13 languages; adm*

**[18] The Great Siege of Malta and the Knights of St John.** This 'walk-through attraction' is situated in the basement of the Bibliotheca building, and the entrance is next door to Café Premier at the back of Republic Square. Wearing headphones and carrying a Walkman-sized box, you walk from room to room following the history of the Knights of St John – from the Crusaders through the Great Siege to the modern day. Well worth seeing, though not for the ultra-claustrophobic.

**[19] Palace Square.** This historic square is relegated to the status of car park, predominantly for the use of the Maltese parliament which sits in the Grand Master's Palace. From such an egregious end, its beginning was thankfully befitting a 'Palace Square'. Two of the many extraordinary events to have taken place in Malta happened on this spot: the presentation of the George Cross to the Maltese people here during the Second World War by King George VI (*see* pp.35–7), and the 1799 execution of Father Michael Xerri and 33 others by the French after a failed plot to overthrow the besieged French garrison.

## [20] The Grand Master's Palace (1571)

**The Grand Master's Palace**
*open daily exc Fri, 10–4; closed 24, 25, 31 Dec, 1 Jan and when Parliament is in session; adm; contact local tourist office for day-to-day information*

The Grand Master's Palace is an almost square building occupying an entire block and housing Malta's House of Representatives, the Palace Armoury, the president's office and notable state rooms (the Armoury and the state rooms are open to the public). In days past, it was the official residence of the grand master, and until 1928 the British governor's residence. The main entrance is from Palace Square, but visitors should enter through the Palace armoury (follow signs from the main door). On the Palace Square façade are tablet citations from George VI and President Roosevelt.

The first site chosen for the Grand Master's Palace was the highest point of the new city, where the Auberge de Castile et Leon stands, but Grand Master del Monte preferred life in the more level centre of Valletta. Incorporating one of the very first of the new city's houses – which conveniently belonged to the grand master's nephew – Cassar began work on the Palace in 1571. As a whole, the design is rather unsatisfying and grand. It has suffered the usual tinkering (at the second entrance, for example), and the squat elevation framed by heavy quoins needs to breathe within an empty square as Cassar had intended. By contrast, the two inner courtyards lend it grace.

## The Courtyards

Originally planted with aromatic orange trees, **Prince Alfred's Courtyard** was rearranged by Governor le Marchand in 1858 and named after Queen Victoria's second son, who visited Malta that year as a humble midshipman. Recently restored, the palace clock was a gift from Grand Master Pinto in 1745 (needless to say, the menial figures who strike the bells are Moors). In 1861 the statue of Neptune was moved to Neptune's Courtyard from the fish market in the south of the city by Governor le Marchand (Grand Master Alof de Wignacourt had placed the statue in the market to celebrate the completion of his Rabat–Valletta aqueduct, in 1615). The wall fountain behind Neptune bears the Perellos escutcheon.

## The Interior and State Rooms

**The Interior and State Rooms** *on the piano nobile, the first-floor living quarters, are security men-cum-guides who will escort you through the state rooms; the House of Representatives is closed to the public*

The **corridors** (Armoury, Entrance and Prince of Wales) were undertaken by the Sienese Niccolò Nasini in the 1720s and paved by Governor le Marchand in the 1860s. Nearly all the lunettes tell of victorious seafaring engagements against the Turks and the pictures are of grand masters and European aristocrats. The **Armoury Corridor** leads to the **House of Representatives**, or Parliament. Off it is the **Council Chamber of the Order** or the Tapestry Chamber, where the old legislative assembly sat. Grand Master Perellos, who donated the magnificent tapestries in St John's Museum, also made a gift of the exquisite Gobelin Tapestries, *Les Tentures des Indes*, upon his election to the magistracy in 1697, and like those at St John's they all bear Perellos's arms. The 10 panels are of paradisaical scenes from the Caribbean and South America. Among the most colourful are 'The Animal Fight' and 'The Fisherman', but all overflow with fine descriptions of what must have been, for many contemporary viewers, alien creatures from an unrecognizably verdant land. They were woven in France based on paintings given to Louis XIV in 1679 by the German explorer Prince Johann Moritz of Nassau. It is said that during the sea voyage from Marseilles to Malta in 1702 they were seized by a privateer who forced the captain to ransom them back for their original price. Below the chamber's richly decorated ceiling are frieze panels depicting the victories and voyages of the

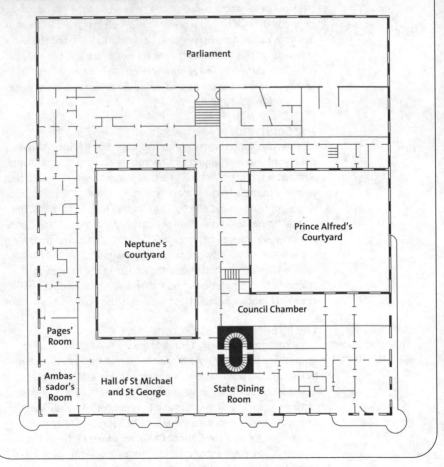

Order's navy. In between are 10 figures symbolizing human virtues and a painted crucifix to which grand masters and council members would raise their hand when swearing oaths.

The **State Dining Room** was badly damaged during the Second World War. It holds some unflattering and self-important portraits of British royalty from George III (Malta became part of the British Empire during his reign) to a youthful Queen Elizabeth II. The Chapter Hall of the Order became the **Hall of St Michael and St George** after the inception of the British chivalric Order of the same name in 1818. The frieze is a contemporary and vivid account of 12 salient events from the Great Siege of 1565, painted by Matteo Perez d'Aleccio not long after the siege was raised; it commences to the left of the throne with the arrival of the Turkish fleet in May of that year. The minstrels' gallery opposite depicts six scenes from the Book of Genesis. It was once part of the grand master's private chapel and is said also to have come from the poop deck of the *Grand Carrack* in which the knights sailed from Rhodes.

The Ambassador's Room (or Red Room) and the Pages' Room (or Yellow Room) are the only other state rooms open to the public. The grand master would receive foreign dignitaries and hold private audiences in the **Ambassador's Room**. The frieze, also by d'Aleccio, illustrates episodes from the 200 years of the Order's history before its arrival in Malta. Of the many paintings in the Red Room, the most striking is of the dandified German knight, Frederik Langreve von Hessen. This feminine and languid young man with long hair, lace and velvet clothing, and outrageous shoe buckles, was the gallant captain general of the Order's galleys in the mid-17th century. He died a cardinal and is buried in the cathedral at Breslau in Poland. The de Favray painting is of *Grand Master de L'Isle Adam receiving the keys to Mdina* after the Order was given the islands in 1530. The luckless and vain Louis XVI gave the portrait of himself to his compatriot and friend Grand Master de Rohan in 1784, seven years before his luck finally ran out on the guillotine. The suit of armour worn by Grand Master Alof de Wignacourt in his portrait is on display in the Palace Armoury. The **Pages' Room** was the waiting room for the 16 boys who were enrolled in the Order as pages by their noble European parents before they were 12 years of age. When they were 18 they could apply to become a knight. The frieze, more of d'Aleccio's handiwork, depicts various noteworthy events of the Order's 13th-century history prior to its departure from the Holy Land. Note the four 16th-century Urbino majolica vases, and de Favray's stirring portrait of de la Valette.

## [21] Palace Armoury

**Palace Armoury**
*open daily 9–5; closed Good Fri, 24, 25, 31 Dec, 1 Jan; adm*

The original armoury was on the first floor, but since 1976 it has been Malta's House of Representatives; the present armoury is housed in the stables off the courtyards.

A knight's armour became the property of the Order after his death; only swords and daggers could be disposed of as part of his quint (*see* p.29). The British jettisoned a large part of the collection to clear space, but the armoury still contains 5,000-plus pieces in its comprehensive collection of 16th- to 18th-century military hardware. Just about every piece of **armour** (pauldrons, rerebraces, vambraces, coudres, gorgets) of the 15-piece jigsaw that was needed to envelop a crusading knight is displayed. So too are many of the **instruments** (swords, arquebuses, forks, halberts) designed to penetrate it. Notable pieces include: a full damascened suit, said to weigh 110lb (50kg), made in Milan for Grand Master Alof de Wignacourt (in Caravaggio's portrait of 1608 hanging in the Louvre, de Wignacourt wears this suit), a wonderful Italian suit of armour made for the French Grand Commander de Verdelin, the Italian half-suit worn by de la Valette and, close by, is a photograph of the ceremonial sword and dagger given to him by King Philip II of Spain after the Great Siege of 1565. Needless to say, Napoleon's magpie tendencies account for their absence: having stolen the dagger, he always carried it in his luggage for good luck, and both weapons are in the Louvre today. Other items include a devilishly clever Italian combined sword and pistol, uncomfortable-looking helmets, cannon, mortar, pistols, arquebuses and a grand master's carriage from the late 18th century. The standards are those of the different *langues*. The vanquished are also represented, with cases of Turkish weapons and what is claimed to be part of Dragut Rais's clothing.

## From the Wartime Experience to the Malta Experience

**The Wartime Experience**
*Embassy Shopping Complex, St Lucia Street; t 21 222225, www.embassycomplex. com.mt shows daily, 10, 11, 12 and 1pm on the hour; adm*

**[22] The Wartime Experience**. Crumbling and tired, the Hostel de Verdelin (1662) is nevertheless a welcome ornate intrusion in bleak Palace Square. It was designed by Francesco Buonamici, the Order's resident engineer, who established the Baroque style in Malta. Note the almost eroded bird motifs on the right façade: they were a part of the arms of Grand Commander de Verdelin; he once owned the house. Upstairs is a small theatre showing a lump-in-the-throat 45-minute archive film composition of the second siege of Malta during the Second World War. It is worth seeing. There is also a small static exhibition. In addition there is a similar audiovisual show, the Valletta Experience. There is a decent café/restaurant, The Bistro, inside.

**Casa Rocca Piccola**
*t 21 231796, www. casaroccapiccola.com; open Mon–Sat 10–4, closed Sun and public holidays; tours on the hour; adm*

**[23] Casa Rocca Piccola**. Past Palace Square at 74 Republic Street is an elegant private *palazzo* open to the public; it dates from the late 16th century. The Marquis Nicholas de Piro, whose family home it still is, gives an erudite tour through the principal rooms. It provides, together with the numerous heirlooms, a socio-historical record hitherto not found in Malta. Artefacts arranged on the enfilade first floor include children's toys, a knight's sedan chair, a fine piece of 16th-century furniture, a fascinating 'portable' chapel, a mid-17th-century marquetry bureau, numerous portraits, a Venetian chandelier and a rare set of late 18th-century medical instruments from the Sacra Infermeria.

**[24] Lower Barracca Gardens and the Second World War Memorial**. The gardens are part of St Christopher's Bastion and have a view of the harbour mouth. At their centre is a small Greek-style folly built in memory of Governor Sir Alexander Ball, who led the siege against the French in 1800 and subsequently became Britain's first civil commissioner of Malta. The French, during the 1798–1800 siege, when a rat was a treat and a feast, cultivated these gardens along with many of Valletta's open spaces.

Below and next to St Lazarus's Curtain, on what was an old gun emplacement, is the Second World War Memorial and Siege Bell Monument. They commemorate both the 50th anniversary of the presentation of the George Cross and those who died during the conflict. The monument was unveiled in May 1992 by Queen Elizabeth II.

**[25] Mediterranean Conference Centre/Sacra Infermeria and the Malta Experience.** Surrounded as they were by the trappings of wealth and privilege, it is easy to forget that first and foremost the knights belonged to an Order of Hospitallers, formed to heal the sick who made pilgrimages to the Holy Land. Maintaining a hospital was one of the very first of the treasury's priorities; each knight, from the grand master down, had to serve and nurse in the hospital. A knight from the French *langue* was the Grand Hospitaller, each *langue* was allocated a day in the hospital during the week and their duties rotated; the grand master attended every Friday. Patients were addressed as *seigneurs malades*, irrespective of rank, race, creed (although non-Catholics had to receive instruction after three days in the Great Ward), and were attended to in the same manner. The finest medicines were dispensed. Pastoral care was undertaken and a 12th-century prayer was said every evening. Food was the best available, all the plates and cups were made of solid silver. Needless to say Napoleon's avaricious hands turned the lot into 3,500lb (1,600kg) of bullion and the booty was lost for ever when his flagship sank in Aboukir Bay; all marine salvage attempts have hitherto failed.

The **Sacra Infermeria** was one of the first buildings in the new city, commenced in 1574 during the reign of pious old Grand Master de la Cassière, who also built St John's. The Great Ward, 500ft (150m) long, and one of the longest unsupported roofed expanses in Europe, was designed to hold 300 iron cots (with canopies of wool in winter, cotton gauze in summer), and could accommodate up to 900. In 1800 the British imaginatively renamed the infirmary 'Station Hospital' and used it as such until 1919, whence it became the principal police station. Like most of Valletta, it was virtually destroyed by Axis bombs during the Second World War. It was finally renovated and in 1979 it reopened as the immense Mediterranean Conference Centre. Part of the same large complex is the static **display of the Knights Hospitallers**, complete with full-size models. It traces the history of their original role.

The **Malta Experience**, set in the centre in an air-conditioned purpose-built auditorium, is a 50-minute infomercial on Malta in 10 languages. It romanticizes and telescopes history with the help of thousands of slides and a sound-bite script – yet does manage to entertain.

**Knights Hospitallers display**
*open Mon–Fri 9.30–4.30, Sat, Sun and public holidays 9.30–1.30; adm*

**The Malta Experience**
*t 21 243776, www. themaltaexperience. com; six shows daily on the hour, Mon–Fri 11–4; Sat, Sun and public holidays 11, 12 and 1pm, with an extra 2pm show Oct–June; adm; facilities for disabled visitors*

07 Valletta and the Three Cities | Valletta City Sights: From the Wartime Experience to the Malta Experience

## [26] Fort St Elmo

**Fort St Elmo**
*open Sat 1–5 and Sun
9–5 only; non-
obligatory guided tours
every hour on the hour;
on two or three
Sundays a month (not
Aug) 'In Guardia' is
enacted; military
parades in period
costume – check with
the MTA for exact dates
and times; adm on 'In
Guardia' days,
otherwise free*

Historic and battle-scarred Fort St Elmo houses the police academy (or, as the oxymoronic sign would have it, 'The Academy for Criminal Justice'), on the upper level – the lower levels were used in the prison scenes in the film *Midnight Express*. Parts of the fort have been reopened to the public, and it houses a War Museum. The MTA has produced an excellent keyed free map.

### History

When the Order first sailed into the Grand Harbour in the autumn of 1530 all that stood on the barren promontory of the Sceberras peninsula was a 15th-century fortified watchtower. In 1552 the star-shaped Fort St Elmo was hastily built by the knights on solid rock to provide protection to both the Marsamxett and Grand Harbours. There was a flaw in its siting, however: the fort was exposed to the heights of the peninsula (part way down Republic Street).

When on 18 May 1565 the **Turkish** armada hove into view, the first decision made by the Turkish command – one that proved to be catastrophic – was to lay siege to St Elmo. To that end they established a battery of cannons on the heights of Sceberras; the small fort was expected to fall within 10 days.

Dragut Rais arrived on 2 June and immediately recognized Admiral Piali's and Mustapha Pasha's gross error, but too many Turkish lives had already been lost to alter tactics. So, he swiftly established a further position on what is now Dragut Point and set about cutting off St Elmo's lines of reinforcement across the Grand Harbour to Fort St Angelo. On 18 June Dragut Rais was mortally wounded, but by the 20th the fort was effectively surrounded. The survivors of the beleaguered garrison knew that defeat was imminent. A parley was sought, but Mustapha Pasha would give no quarter. The fort was finally stormed and taken on 23 June 1565, the eve of the feast of St John, the Order's patron saint.

It had taken 31 days of remorseless bombardment during which 1,500 Christian lives were lost, nine knights were captured, 89 were killed and 27 wounded, while only five Maltese soldiers swam to Fort St Angelo and safety. For the Muslims, it was a Pyrrhic victory; their losses totalled over 8,000, including the octogenarian warrior Dragut Rais, nearly 25 per cent of their entire army. The battle was the turning point in the Turkish campaign.

St Elmo was rebuilt, enlarged and improved during the Order's reign, and was briefly captured during the 'Priests' Revolt' in 1775. The British reinforced the bastions in the late 19th century and added further gun emplacements in the 20th century. The St Elmo breakwater, jutting out to sea in a contortion of rusted steel, was destroyed in a daring Italian E-boat raid on 25 July 1941, before St Elmo's guns picked them off.

## [27] The National War Museum

The National War Museum
*open daily exc Fri, 9–5; closed 24, 25, 31 Dec, 1 Jan; adm*

The National War Museum opened in 1975 and occupies the western fraction of the fort's enlarged compound. The entrance is at the eastern end of the **French Curtain** in Lower St Elmo. The museum is not large: nonetheless it houses a small and poignant collection with exhibits from 1798 to 1945. Principally, its displays deal with the **Second World War**. The most treasured item is the original George Cross awarded to the entire population on 15 April 1942 by King George VI. Among the larger exhibits are: a wingless *Faith*, one of the three Gloucester Gladiator biplanes that were the sum total of the Allies' air-preparedness in the first weeks of the war; an E-boat or *barchino esplosivo*, a tame-sounding Italian name for a speedboat full of explosives; and General Eisenhower's Willis Jeep used in 'Operation Husky', the invasion of Sicily in 1943. Do not miss the two milestones at the entrance, one of which is defaced. The Allied command naïvely believed that such a ruse would induce an invading Axis force to wander the island helplessly lost and confused.

## From the Auberge de Bavaria to the Archbishop's Palace

[28] **Auberge de Bavaria** (1629). This *auberge* was built as a private house, the Palazzo Carnerio, and subsequently purchased for the newly instituted Anglo-Bavarian *langue* in 1784 (the commander of the cavalry was usually drawn from its ranks). It has been an army officers' mess and a school, and is now the government housing ministry, but it is not worth a detour.

[29] **Auberge d'Aragon** (1571). Cassar built this, the first and the smallest of the *auberges*. The 'fat' Melitan mouldings around each of the three windows are typical, as are Cassar's chunky quoins. Through the 19th-century portico the intercommunicating rooms encircle a peristyle courtyard. Further down West Street is the Aragonese church, Our Lady of Pilar, built in 1670.

The head of the *langue* was usually the grand conservator in charge of all supplies for both soldiers and hospitals. The building was the prime minister's office in the 1960s and is now the Ministry for Economic Services. Like many of the government organizations here, they don't mind visitors.

[30] **St Paul's Anglican Cathedral** (1839). The Auberge d'Allemagne was demolished to provide space for this cathedral, the only major non-military edifice erected by the British during their occupation, paid for by Queen Adelaide – Queen Victoria's aunt and King William IV's widow – while she was convalescing in Malta. From

out at sea, its 206ft (63m) spire blends in with the Carmelite's dome, and together they are something mariners aim for in inclement weather. The monument in front is to Dun Michael Xerri who was executed in 1799, together with 33 others, by the French in Palace Square.

**[31] Carmelite Church.** The present church with its landmark dome that dominates Valletta's skyline bears no resemblance to Cassar's original 16th-century work, which suffered irreparable bomb damage during the Second World War. It is not by chance that the dome just eclipses its Anglican neighbour.

**[32] Archbishop's Palace** (1622). Designed by Tommaso Dingli, this dark and forbidding building is still used by the church. The second storey was added in the 1950s.

## [33] Manoel Theatre (1731)

**Manoel Theatre**
*open Mon–Sat; tours at 10.30, 11.30 and 4.30 on weekdays and 11.30 and 12.30 on Sat; adm for theatre and museum; a comprehensive list of drama, dance and musical performances is available at MTA offices, or call t 21 246389 for box office, or visit the website*

Inconspicuously located in Old Theatre Street next to a wine bar called Il Buko, this fascinating little purpose-built Baroque building is said to be the third-oldest European theatre still in use. It was built by the benign autocrat Grand Master de Vilhena 'for the honest recreation of the people', according to the Latin inscription above the doorway. Before its restoration it served as a dosshouse, a dance hall and a cinema.

The 650-seat auditorium is quite unlike a conventional modern theatre, oval in shape with a tiny stage and orchestra pit. The stalls seat only 272, but above them and beneath the gilded ceiling and chandelier are three full tiers of boxes, including one very discreet grand master's box. All the delicate frescoes are of Mediterranean scenes and in 22-carat gold leaf.

The first performance on 19 January 1732 was of the tragic opera *Merope* performed by the Italian *langue*. The novices took the female parts, and the set was designed by de Mondion in a style less forbidding than his Fort Manoel. Today there is a resident orchestra for what is now Malta's national theatre. Sir Yehudi Menuhin, Dame Kiri Te Kanawa and Vladimir Ashkenazy are among those who have performed here.

### Palazzo Bonici and Strait Street

The Palazzo Bonici a few doors away from the Manoel Theatre is now a compact museum with various artefacts, music scores and costumes, etc. from the theatre's archives and vaults.

**[34] Strait Street.** There is nothing to see here, but the narrow and grubby street is notorious. During the Order's reign it was a venue for illegal duelling, a 'sport' which grew in popularity among the young knights as the prospects of earnest warfare diminished. (Often, in order to facilitate a duel, two knights would 'accidentally' bump into one another in the narrow street.) The punishment, if they were caught, varied from expulsion to solitary confinement in St Angelo's oubliette (*see* p.141). During the British occupation Strait Street acquired the unattractive sobriquet 'the Gut' – brothels, tacky bars, music-hall dives and streetwalkers, all under crude flashing lights. It was end-to-end sleaze, the Mediterranean fleet's peacetime Saigon. Fortunately, not much of the inglorious history remains.

## [35] Auberge de Provence/Museum of Archaeology (1571–5)

**Auberge de Provence/Museum of Archaeology**
*open Sat–Thurs 9–5; closed Fri and 24, 25, 31 Dec, 1 Jan; adm*

The Auberge de Provence in Republic Street was the third of the French *auberges* (the Auberge de France was totally destroyed in 1942), and was designed by Cassar. The size of the building is deceptive, subtly hidden in the decoration of the façade; it actually spans from the heavy rusticated quoins, through four shops on either side of the portico, beneath the alternating triangular and segmental pediments. The knights of Provence were the most senior of the *langues*, and their head was the *grand commandeur*, president of the treasury and governor of the arsenal. From the mid-1820s to 1954 the *auberge* housed the Union Club of the British armed forces.

The Museum of Archaeology is in the process of being refurbished. The ground floor, which houses the prehistory exhibition, is the only part open at time of writing. Exhibitions of other periods, including Punic, Roman, Byzantine, Medieval and Arab, will open over the next few years. Once fully refurbished, the museum should be more thematic and chronological, with bilingual storyboards and audiovisual shows. Although the part that is open now is but a small fraction of the whole, the museum is still well worth visiting, especially in conjunction with an excursion to any of the prehistoric sites in Malta or Gozo (the oldest freestanding monuments in the world).

When complete, the new layout will be as follows. In the basement, there will be a courtyard and museum café, and four rooms of temporary exhibits. The ground floor houses the central information desk, and permanent rooms displaying prehistoric artefacts from the early, mid- and late Neolithic phases. Included in these displays are 'the sleeping lady' from the Hypogeum and, from Tarxien, the megaliths, the altar from the South temple and an immense frieze block carved with ocular spirals. There will also soon be a small museum shop. The small mezzanine floor will accommodate study and conservation laboratories. The upper, and largest, floor will feature diverse displays from the Punic and Roman periods through to the arrival of the Arabs in AD 870 and the reign of the Knights of the Order of St John. There will also be a Valletta room and a numismatic room.

## [36] Admiralty House/Museum of Fine Arts

**Admiralty House/Museum of Fine Arts**
*open daily exc Fri, 9–5; closed 24, 25, 31 Dec, 1 Jan; adm*

In the late 1590s the museum was one of the first of Valletta's buildings to be erected when a knight, Jean de Soubiran, built himself a modest *palazzo*. In the early 1760s, the architect Andrea Belli remodelled it into a more sumptuous *palazzo*, giving free rein to some of the lavish excesses of 18th-century Baroque – of de Soubiran's home only the basement loggia and courtyard remain. From 1821 to 1961 it became Admiralty House, the home of the British naval commander-in-chief of the Mediterranean fleet. Naval luminaries like Admiral Codrington and Lord Mountbatten were based here. Since 1972 it has housed the Museum of Fine Arts.

Allow at least 45 minutes for a look around the 30 rooms of exhibits, predominantly paintings, from the 14th century to the present day. The curator's staff office is next to Room 24 on the ground floor; in certain instances they will be more helpful than some of the gloomy lighting. Begin on the first floor, Rooms 1–13. **Room 1**. 14th-century religious icons. **Room 2**. 15th century. Note the direct and bright *Madonna with Saints* by Domenico di Michelino and the *Nativity* scene by Maestro Alberto. **Room 3**. 16th-century north Italian paintings, including work by the Tuscan, Filippo Paladini. He arrived in Malta as a man condemned to life in the galleys but Grand Master de Verdalle had more purposeful employment in mind: Paladini was to decorate the chapel at the Grand Master's Palace, and rooms in Verdala Palace. Note the dark rendition of *St Lawrence's Martyrdom* over hot coals and griddle. **Rooms 4 and 6** have paintings from the Venetian school, notably the *Raising of Lazarus* by Andrea Vicentino and *A Man in Armour* by Domenico Tintoretto. **Room 5**. Dutch school. The painting by the Renaissance artist Jan van Scorel, *Portrait of a Lady*, is one of the museum's most treasured works and has in the past been attributed to Hans Holbein; note how tautly she clasps her hands. **Rooms 7 and 7a**. Apart from the 17th-century paintings the terrace room contains sculptures by the Maltese Antonio Sciortino, including the *Great Siege Monument* and *Les Gavroches*. **Rooms 8–10** contain mainly large canvases from the 17th century. Note *Christ the Redeemer* by Guido Reni which used to hang in the grand master's bedchamber, the truly horrific *Martyrdom of St Agatha* by Giovanni Baglione, the *Portrait of Grand Master Alof de Wignacourt* in his armour (itself on display in the Palace Armoury), another interpretation of *St John's Beheading* (the young girl with the platter awaiting his head is almost too eager) by Mathias Stomer and an unmerciful painting by the French Caravaggist, le Valentin, in which Judith dispassionately beheads a slumbering Holofernes. **Rooms 12 and 13** are dedicated to the 17th-century Calabrian artist Mattia Preti, whose work adorns many of the island's churches but who is most famous for his vault frescoes at St John's Co-Cathedral.

The forceful *Martyrdom of St Catherine*, a theme to which Preti liked to return, is matched with the temperate *Baptism of Christ* and the very human depiction of *The Incredulity of St Thomas*.

On the ground floor in **Room 14** the 18th-century French painter Antoine de Favray successfully captures the pomp of knights he portrayed: the femininity of de Chambrey belies his seafaring skills, and the grandiose Grand Master Pinto is tempered only by the studiousness of the penultimate of Malta's grand masters, de Rohan. In **Room 15** note Claude Joseph Vernet's *Fire on the Tiber*, a searing image of the destructive forces of fire.

**Rooms 16 and 17** contain 18th-century Italian works. **Room 19** displays Italian paintings from the 19th century that feature Malta, and **Rooms 20–23** have Maltese works from the 17th to the 20th centuries. Note the striking 1966 *Benedizione* by Willie Apap.

**Room 24** and the basement courtyard and loggia are devoted to contemporary exhibitions. In the **basement** are artefacts relating to the Order: paintings, armour, coins, religious objects and a paltry collection of some of the Sacra Infermeria's silver which somehow slipped through Napoleon's grasp. There is a crude, but effective, model of the Valletta fortifications. In the **loggia** are to be found changing exhibitions of contemporary art by Maltese artists.

## From St John's Cavalier to the Lascaris War Rooms

**[37] St John's Cavalier, the Embassy of the Sovereign Order of St John** (1582). Built either side of what was St George's Gate (now City Gate), St John's and St James's Cavaliers were vital landward defences for artillery inside the main enceinte of the fortifications, set above the bastions and counterguards in order to fire deeper into the enemy lines. The **Sovereign Military Hospitaller Order of St John of Jerusalem, of Rhodes and of Malta** has maintained its embassy in the splendidly restored Cavalier since 1968. The Order is today based in Rome, in effect a state within a state, and the present grand master is a Scot, Andrew Bertie. The Order continues to do charitable works within developing countries around the world, while on a local scale they help to maintain services such as a blood bank and the Maltese Cross Corps, a body similar to the St John's Ambulance.

**[38] Hastings Gardens**. When General the Marquis of Hastings, governor of Malta, died at sea in 1826, his family built a neoclassical monument in which to inter him. The public space that evolved around the monument became the Hastings Gardens. The sheer magnitude of Valletta's fortifications is very impressive from here. Walk carefully along the glacis (the open slope in front of the fortifications); the stone and earthworks are over 20ft (6m) thick.

**[39] Lascaris War Rooms**. This is a good place to visit at the end of a sightseeing tour; it has its own clear signposting and can be found beneath the Upper Barraca Gardens. This began as a complex of 17th-century tunnels cut deep into the limestone of the Lascaris bastion. During the Second World War it was used as Malta's command centre to track the movements of Axis and Allied ships and aircraft. Various Allied commanders, including Eisenhower, Montgomery, Alexander and Cunningham, used it at some time as a base to direct operations.

# Floriana

Floriana, Valletta's immediate suburb a shortish walk from City Gate, offers the interesting **Argotti Botanical Gardens** and **St Philip's Gardens**, laid out in what was the most landward of Mount Sceberras's fortifications and the **Floriana Lines**. The town itself was planned by the compulsive builder Grand Master de Vilhena soon after he assumed the magistracy in 1722. The land was to be sandwiched between the fortifications of the Floriana Lines (which span the girth of Mount Sceberras from Pieta Creek to the Grand Harbour) and Valletta's bastions in a grid pattern with wide-open spaces. In spite of Axis bomb damage during the Second World War, much of the original scheme remains; furthermore it is the site of the Air Force and Royal Malta Artillery War memorials.

## The Floriana Lines: Defences for Fortress Valletta

Canny Grand Master de Paule feared a major Ottoman offensive in 1634 and, as often in times of crisis, turned to Rome for help. Pope Urban VIII heeded his request and sent the engineer Pietro Paolo Floriani, a celebrated military engineer and sometime critic of Laparelli, the engineer of Valletta.

Due to the longer ranges and increased destructive powers of 17th-century weaponry, Floriani proposed enclosing the high ground beyond Valletta itself with a massive rectangular enceinte. He planned further to add a complex of bastions, ravelins, counterguards, deep ditches and a neck-like hornwork protruding down the Grand Harbour. The stupendous cost of the proposals – they were larger than the entire fortifications of Valletta – met with loud criticism, but commenced in 1636. Two years later, and exasperated with the constant sniping, Floriani returned to Italy where he died later in the year. His replacement, Vincenzo da Firenzuola, began work on the Margherita Lines around the Three Cities instead and it was not until 1640 that work recommenced on the late Floriani's designs. The work on the massive defence system continued falteringly for many years.

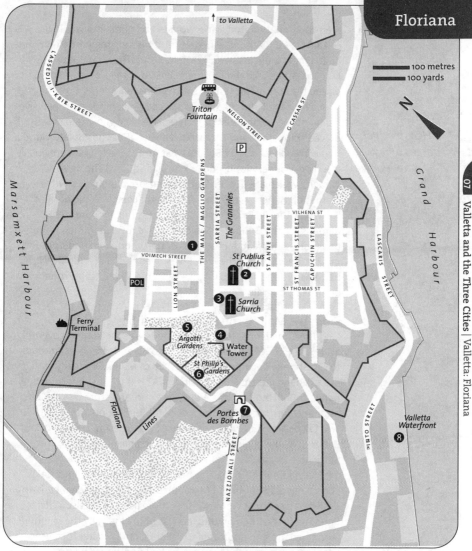

100 metres
100 yards

## Floriana Sights

Floriana's best sights are described below; numbers refer to the map above.

### [1] The Mall and Maglio Gardens

The French knight Jean Lascaris was an ugly and stern authoritarian who succeeded the opulent de Paule. He was a killjoy who became grand master in his 75th year and died in 1657 a wizened 97; today he is remembered in a Maltese slang insult, *wicc Laskari*, meaning 'a really sour face'. Lascaris was convinced that his youthful knights needed physical exercises to keep at bay the

*Here perish sloth,
here perish
Cupid's arts,
Knights, where
on you this strip
I now bestow,
Here play your
games and steel
your warlike
hearts,
Not let wine,
women, dicing
bring you low.*

eternal damnation that wine, women and gambling would be certain to bring. So, in the first years of his long reign (1636–57), he built a narrow enclosure (since demolished) in what is now the Maglio Gardens, for the ball game *palla a maglio*, or pall-mall, and placed the stanza (*see* left) in Latin on its wall.

Today the Mall and Maglio Gardens begin behind the impressive **Independence Monument** which replaced the grand and much-moved statue of Grand Master de Vilhena. (That has finally found a home in Pope John XXIII Square by St Anne Street; it had previously stood on Manoel Island, and in Republic Square.) The narrow gardens, which are 1,300ft (400m) long, are punctuated with statues of Maltese luminaries. The football pitch to the right of them was the old British military parade ground. Close to the gardens are the **Granaries**, which look like rows of immense piggy-bank corks but are in fact the lids of the wood-lined underground grain stores in which the Order preserved two years' supply. With a banker's eye, the knights maintained a highly profitable monopoly on the sale of grain.

## From the Mall to the Porte des Bombes

**[2] The Church of St Publius**. St Publius was the Roman governor at the time of St Paul's shipwreck in AD 60 and after his conversion to Christianity became the first bishop of Malta. Originally designed by Giuseppe Bonnici in 1733, this is the last important parish church built by the Order. The entire structure was rebuilt after near destruction by the Axis bombing. The portico and its two tall bell-towers were added in 1882 to a design by Dr Nicola Zammit, who was also responsible for the new façade at St Nicholas Siġġiewi.

**[3] Sarria Church** (1676). This bizarre-looking small cylindrical church has a disputed but undoubtedly elegant provenance, being designed by either Lorenzo Gafa or more likely the artist Mattia Preti. The first church on this site was built in 1585 by the knight de Sarria Navarro and dedicated to sailors. Grand Master Nicolas Cotoner commissioned the present building, hence his cotton-flower motif, following the virulent nine-month plague of 1675 when over 8,000 people died. The lunettes and the paintings are by Preti. The church is maintained by the Jesuits.

**[4] Wignacourt Water Tower.** The rocket-like tower opposite was a staging post and fountain with fresh water that flowed along the Mdina–Valletta aqueduct built by Grand Master Alof de Wignacourt in 1615; it is his escutcheon above the door.

**[5] Argotti Botanical Gardens**. In 1805 a Carmelite friar with the deliciously implausible name of Carolus Hyacinthus was appointed Malta's first professor of natural history by the British governor, Sir Alexander Ball. Hyacinthus assembled the plants in Floriana's

⭐ **Argotti Botanical Gardens**
*public gardens open daylight hours, private gardens open summer 7.30–12.30; winter 8–11.30 and 1–3.45*

Mall and 50 years later they were moved to the site of the present Argotti Gardens, then the preserve of a deceased knight with the equally improbable name of Ignatius de Argote De Gusman.

The gardens are divided into two, the public and the private, and both are open to the public. There are many hundreds of cacti, succulents and other plants, indigenous and foreign.

**[6] St Philip's Gardens** are below the Argotti Gardens on the saint's eponymous bastion. This point is almost the very end of Valletta's landward fortifications; beyond lie the counterguards and the Porte des Bombes.

**[7] Porte des Bombes**. On any trip into Valletta you will pass through or by the Porte des Bombes, one of two gates built between 1697 and 1720 that once pierced the curtain-wall defences of the Floriana Lines (the northern gate, the Gate of Our Lady, has been destroyed). Originally a simple single-arched structure with a drawbridge, the archway was doubled in 1868 when the curtain wall either side of it was dismantled to allow traffic to flow. Its escutcheon and emblems are those of Grand Master Perellos in whose reign it was constructed.

**[8] Valletta Waterfront**. The recently revamped area within the former old grain stores next to the ferry terminal has shops, cafés and restaurants. So long as you don't get here when cruise liners are moored directly in front and blocking the view, it can be a very pleasant spot to while away a summer evening or sunny winter's day.

*07 Valletta and the Three Cities | Valletta: Floriana*

## Tourist Information in Valletta

(i) **Valletta >**
*1 Freedom Square
(just inside City Gate),*
*t 21 237747*

MTA's free **city map** is short on cartographic information, but the staff are helpful. In keeping with the improved **signposting** across the island, Valletta now sports a couple of dozen blue signposts that aid navigation of the streets tremendously.

There are four **national museums**: the **Archaeology Museum**, the **Fine Arts Museum**, the **War Museum** and the **Palace Armoury**.

**Disabled visitors** should note that many of Valletta's pavements are cracked and none of the principal sights such as the Grand Master's Palace and St John's Co-Cathedral have facilities which provide access above ground-floor level. **The Malta Experience**, the refurbished **Museum of Archaeology** and the **Maritime Museum** in Vittoriosa all have disabled access.

## Services in Valletta

**Bank of Valletta's** main branch is on the corner of Republic Street and St John's Square. Mid Med and Thomas Cook both have **foreign-exchange offices** in Republic Street. Coppini Foreign Exchange Bureau is to be found at 58 Merchants Street.

The **police station** is situated in the Law Courts.

The **post office** is at the top of Merchants Street and **Maltacom** has an office in Nofs in-Nhar Street that is open for international calls seven days a week.

**Air Malta** has offices in Freedom Square and **British Airways** can be found at 20/2 Republic Street.

## *Festa* in Valletta

**Floriana** remembers **St Publius** on the third Sunday after Easter.

## Shopping in Valletta

A big **market** is held every Sunday in St James's Ditch, beginning at the Triton Fountain from approximately 6.30am to 1pm. You can find everything: puppies, plants, Sunday papers, stereos, watches, impossibly long 30ft (9m) fishing rods and tackle, antiques, *brocante* (which here means anything with rust on it), lace, confectionery, clothes, Tiger Balm. If you are ochlophobic avoid it. Valletta has a **daily market**, a scaled-down version of the Sunday one, beginning at St John's Square in Merchants Street; its stalls are full of bolts of cloth, religious pictures, tapes and useless but riveting cheap imports from the Far East.

You will only find food in the newly refurbished **covered market** a little further on in Merchants Street. The **fish market** beneath Lower Barracca Gardens on the wharf deals wholesale. This is where to come if you don't mind getting up at 4am – it is shut by 6.30am – and want to buy a box of a fresh catch.

Republic Street, the main thoroughfare, is for the most part pedestrianized, and stores are to be found off it in most of the side streets before Palace Square. **Jewellery and clothes shops** predominate. Beginning inside City Gate at the would-be bazaar, Freedom Square, is the Artisans' Centre with a comprehensive choice of good **Maltese souvenirs**. Beyond the mess that was the Opera House just before the Post Office in Merchants Street is an excellent **newsstand** for English, American and European media. South Street has a few good shops: on the corner is Wembley's, a decent little food store; further down is Edwards, the best in the city for **handbags** and **shoes**; ABC is a comprehensive **stationers**; Galea's Art Gallery has watercolours from Lm25 and Mothercare has opened a branch. Around the corner in Strait Street is La Valette Art Gallery. Back in Republic Street is Charles Grech for **spirits** and **cigars**, the Economic British Dispensary which serves '**toilet preparations**', and Sapienza's with the best selection of **English books** in Malta – together with a comprehensive Melitensia section. Further along Republic Street, Square Deal sells **clothes** for the sartorially brave and Tip Top has **audio and electronic goods**. In St John's Square is the Crafts Centre while not far away in Zachary Street is Micallef with **antique and reproduction furniture** and **prints**. The charming, and much photographed, old **flower kiosk** of F Zammit is on the corner of Republic Street and St John's Square. For the unstructured look in **men's clothing** try Pop 84 at the Merchants Street corner of the square. BHS is in Merchants Street along with the other **tailors**. For **cakes** go to C Camilleri which has been in operation since 1843; nearby L Psaila still sells **confectionery** by weight from glass jars. Marks and Spencer has a branch in Old Theatre Street next to the Café Cordina, and on the other side of Cordina's is Ascot House for **classical men's clothes**. Republic Street continues past Palace Square and there is a small **antique shop** and a couple of small **silversmith workshops**: the Silversmiths' Shop, and Ardnael near to Casa Rocca Piccola.

## Where to Stay in Valletta

In keeping with its quiet night-time bearing, Valletta has only a few hotels. **\*\*\*\*\*Hotel Le Meridien Phoenicia**, The Mall, Floriana, **t** 21 225241, *www. starwoodhotels.com* (€€€€). Built in a 1920s colonial style – now owned by Granada of (former) motorway service station fame – the Phoenicia always was the grandest of the island's hotels. Just outside City Gate, it was modernized and extended in 1992. The layout provides 136 rooms and suites and two rooms designed for the disabled, two restaurants, two bars, a business centre and a pool set in private 7-acre (3ha) gardens. They also offer an impressive afternoon tea and high tea. For the expense account businessman in need of proximity to Valletta it is the only call.

**\*\*\*Castille Hotel**, Castille Square, **t** 21 243677–9, *www.hotelcastillemalta. com* (€€). An excellent, reasonable and centrally located – facing the Auberge de Castile et Leon – establishment. It was converted around 35 years ago from an imposing old *palazzo*. There are only 38 rooms; those on the first or second floors are more generous. The second of its two restaurants, the simple Italian **La Cave**, is in the cellars – the other is atop the roof – and is frequented by the cognoscenti.

***The Osborne**, 50 South Street, t 21 232127, *www.osbornehotel.com* (€€). Spurned by Evelyn Waugh in 1930 but patronized by HSH Prince Louis of Battenburg and the Duke of Bronte. It provides 60 efficient rooms 150 yards from Republic Street. Said to be 'gay-friendly'.

**British Hotel**, 40 Battery Street, t 21 224730, *www.multahotel.com* (€€). This old stalwart can be tricky to find, perched above the bastions, but has a Royal Circle view of the Grand Harbour and the Three Cities. Quiet and family-run for nearly 75 years, it has 44 simple rooms (nos.105–6 have huge balconies), most now refurbished with air-con; the ubiquitous sun-trap roof and a **restaurant**. Good value as a place to stay, especially for long periods.

**Grand Harbour Hotel**, 47 Battery Street, t 21 246003, *www.grand harbourhotel.com* (€€) Almost next door to the British Hotel, the Grand Harbour has 25 rooms and is similar to its neighbour, but a little smaller and lacking its quirky charm.

## Eating Out in Valletta

The dining scene in Valletta is mostly the province of business and expense-account holders, and then only at lunchtime; except at weekends, hardly anyone comes into the city to eat in the evening. Note though that various tracts of the culinary wasteland have taken root in Valletta: detouring Freedom Square, Republic Street and South Street will avoid Burger King, McDonald's and Pizza Hut respectively.

**Giannini's**, 23 Windmill Street, by St Michael's demibastion, t 21 237121 (€€€€). For dramatic views of Manoel Island and hearty portions try Giannini's. This converted town house

is a good business venue. The small bar is downstairs and the restaurant upstairs. Offers three gourmet menus including a 'journey through the Maltese islands'. Afterwards nibble *Helwa tal-tork*, literally 'Turkish sweet', over a coffee and muse over why the Maltese have permitted the magnificent Fort Manoel to disintegrate. *Book in advance. Mon–Fri lunch, Mon–Sat dinner.*

**Blue Room**, 59 Republic Street, t 21 238014 (€€€). Chinese restaurant serving good-quality standard fare in pleasant relaxed surroundings. Just a few doors past the Grand Master's Palace.

**Rubino**, 53 Old Bakery Street, t 21 224656 (€€€). One of the only restaurants to serve genuine traditional Maltese dishes. Excellent food and extensive wine list. Charming, helpful proprietor always in attendance. Booking essential. *Lunch Mon–Fri; dinner Tues and Fri; closed August.*

**Ambrosia**, 137 Archbishop Street, t 21 225923 (€€). Presently 'the best' restaurant in Valetta, small bistro with frequently changing menu and a good wine list. *Booking essential. Lunch Mon–Fri, dinner Fri–Sun.*

**Bar Sicilia**, 1a St John's Street, t 21 240569 (€). Can be tricky to find. It is on a platform terrace above the Victoria Gate overlooking the Grand Harbour and Three Cities. Inside it is minute but everyone congregates on the terrace in summer. From the small menu pick *spaghetti alle cozze* and the *lampuki* when in season, or a simple omelette. *Lunch only.*

**La Cave**, Castile Square, t 21 243677 (€). In the cellars of the old *palazzo* that now houses the Castile Hotel. On a blustery winter or spring day try a large crusty pizza, a salad and a bottle of heady Barolo from their full wine list; together they will ensure the afternoon is a complete write-off. On Tuesday evenings there is live Latin American music.

**Da Pippo**, 136 Melita Street, t 21 248029 (€). The most popular restaurant in Valletta. You could be in a Roman side street – there are cool rough-hewn stone walls, green-and-white checked tablecloths and wooden furniture. There is no written menu; what is served is what is freshest at the time. The choices are extensive and ever-changing, however – principally pasta, risotto, fish and meat specials. If it is on, try *falda* – shank of beef stuffed with minced pork and beef. *Booking essential. Lunch Mon–Sat.*

## Cafés and Bars in Valletta

The Italian influence prevails in the city's cafés. The most famous is the Café Cordina facing Republic Square; a two-sip espresso chased by an *averna* is the day-long medicament of the lawyers and businessmen who frequent the long chrome bar. The frescoes in the vaulted ceiling are by Giuseppe Cali and the chandelier is Murano crystal. Outside, and shaded by large umbrellas, in the square itself are **Cordina's**, **Eddies** and the **Café Premier**, all of which serve basic, and for the most part unappetizing, snacks and beverages all day – Cordina's *pastizzi* however, while not traditional, are excellent. These are places to meet up and write cards. On Lascaris Wharf is **Café Jubilee**, **t** 21 240920, a convivial bar specializing in Mediterranean cuisine.

At the City Gate end of town and opposite the remains of the Opera House in South Street is the popular indoor **Café Prego**. It serves a good cappuccino and has been in the same family for 60 years.

**Café Ranieri**, halfway down Republic Street, is a narrow marble and mirror establishment that bustles at lunchtime. **Café Teatro**, 115 Old Theatre Street, **t** 21 232574, in the superbly ornate Manoel Theatre, provides a trendily cultural backdrop for a coffee and a chat.

If you ever want to get away from the bustle of Republic Street for a little quiet and shade try **Café Marquee** in small St John's Square – it is opposite the main entrance of St John's Co-Cathedral. If you are in Melita Street, there is **Café la Veneziana**. The smart **Café Cadena** is in Merchants Street. Sit here and watch burly men with improbable bulges in their heavy coats visit the Russian Cultural Centre and Language School next door.

The best on-the-hoof snacks come from **Aguis**, opposite St Paul's Shipwreck in St Paul's Street; it is no bigger than a broom cupboard but the *pastizzi*, *piselli* and flaky *timpana* are very tasty. If you queue with the Maltese, you might improve your grasp of the language.

# The Three Cities

Today tourism may be Malta's single-largest money-earner, but the nation remains a maritime one. From the 7th century BC, when Phoenician traders first anchored their vessels laden with precious eastern cargoes, the harbour has been the island's most valuable asset. Almost every seafaring power throughout history has at one time coveted the protection that the Grand Harbour could afford a fleet. The towns of **Senglea**, **Vittoriosa** and **Cospicua**, and their sheltered creeks, continue to be defined by their proximity to it.

The Three Cities (christened by Napoleon in the somewhat benighted hope that a shared identity would impose civic order on the Maltese who lived there) are still also confusingly referred to by different names: either collectively as 'the Cottonera' after the surrounding fortification lines, or individually by their pre-Great Siege names of L'Isla (Senglea), Birgu (Vittoriosa) and Bormla

# Getting to and around the Three Cities

## By Car

The Three Cities can be frustrating places to find and negotiate by car, but the plethora of new road signs do help to get you in the general direction. (Certain sights such as Forts St Angelo and Rinella – well worth visiting – and the Mediterranean Film Studios at Fort St Rocco – a total waste of fuel – post their own signs). From Valletta follow signs for Marsa where, at the main roundabout, you should follow the sign marked 'Airport'. Pertinent signs should reappear but this time but they will be marked 'Bormla' and/or 'Maritime Museum'; stick to the trail of the Maritime Museum like a bloodhound and keep the mosque's minaret on your right. At the next T-junction Senglea is to the left and Vittoriosa (unhelpfully flagged Birgu) and Kalkara are to the right. Upon arriving at Vittoriosa, go straight on if you do actually intend to visit the Maritime Museum. If you wish to explore Vittoriosa, enter via the main gate at the Poste de Provence. Just before the 'No Entry' sign at the beginning of Main Gate Street turn right into St John's Tower Street where you should be able to park.

## By Bus

**Vittoriosa bus terminus** is located opposite the Poste de Provence and, if you are going to Senglea and Cospicua, the relevant buses stop adjacent to the main square.

---

(Cospicua). Together, though, they cohere into one large industrious (not industrial) town, strongly aligned to the Malta Labour Party; almost the entire workforce is dependent for a living on the dockyards and their ancillary businesses. Despite the island's common heritage, the inhabitants of the Three Cities tend to distance themselves from the other towns and villages. Yet, perversely, they maintain a fierce pride and competitive spirit between each other. Even the people of Valletta used to refer to them as '*min naha l'ohra*' (those from the other side). The new **yacht marina** that has been constructed here has happily not shattered the tranquillity.

Anyone whose appetite has been whetted by the history of the knights should walk around the narrow little streets of Vittoriosa, where the Order first established itself; the restored **Fort St Angelo** and the excellent **Maritime Museum** are here. Senglea and Cospicua have very little of conventional interest, owing for the most part to catastrophic bomb damage during the Second World War. (In April 1942 alone, 3,156 tons of bombs fell in the dockyard area.) Don't expect genteel cafés or leafy piazzas in which to repose – they are for the most part unaffordable and unwanted commodities. The street life here is different and noisier. The housewives' high-pitched scream, '*aeya!*', used to attract the attention of children, friends, husbands or dogs, is an ear-denting and constant refrain. Idleness is not a common pastime and even on hot afternoons and Sundays you catch people fabricating furniture, rebuilding a wall or tinkering with an old marine engine. The first time you hear a frightening screech rend the hot mid-afternoon air, don't duck – it is just the old air-raid sirens signalling the end of the day's labours in the dockyards.

## History

Phoenicians, Romans, Arabs and Normans all found shelter here, settled and fortified, however modestly, the site of Fort St Angelo. In addition (save for the 9th-century Arabs), they supposedly built temples to their gods – the Phoenicians to Astarte, their goddess of fertility, and the Romans to Juno, wife of Jupiter. Count Roger the Norman erected a church where the church of St Lawrence now stands. Alas, none of their heritage remains.

There were only two principal towns in Malta when the Order, weary and despondent from wandering the Mediterranean for seven years, first camped under the leadership of Grand Master de L'Isle Adam in the autumn of 1530: the capital, Città Notabile (Mdina) and **Birgu**. As a hardened body of seafaring knights, the Order chose not to move in with a soft Maltese aristocracy in Mdina. Instead, they moored their fleet between the two peninsulas of the Grand Harbour in Porto delle Galere or Galley Creek (now **Dockyard Creek**). Immediately thereafter, and only half-heartedly, they began to change the cramped settlement of ramshackle houses at the water's edge that was Birgu into a congenial convent of *auberges*, a church and a hospital.

De L'Isle Adam found a ruinously poor fort at the tip of Birgu called **St Angelo**, where armaments consisted of 'two guns, two falcons, and a few old mortars'. Nevertheless he set about reinforcing it, but it was not until 11 years later under Grand Master de Homedes that substantial works commenced. Initially, the Emperor of Spain's Italian military engineer, Ferramolino, advised abandoning Birgu altogether and starting afresh on Mount Sceberras, advice de Homedes rejected and that the Order was later to regret. The preliminary works in 1541 entailed the fortification of the northern flank of Birgu, the reinforcement of St Angelo and its separation from Birgu itself by a wide ditch. After Ferramolino was killed in 1550, his replacement Pietro Pardo advised on further defensive works to **L'Isla**, the parallel and uninhabited peninsula. Despite the unwelcome attentions of the Turks and Dragut in 1551, construction of **Fort St Michael** on L'Isla was completed within three years. However inventive and wily these new and hastily built defences were, they were anything but comprehensive.

Twelve years later during the **Great Siege of 1565** the towns of Birgu and L'Isla and their forts of St Angelo and St Michael were bombarded constantly for nearly four months. As a single fighting and defensive unit the two peninsulas were somehow able to withstand the Turkish might. Vittoriosa (Birgu) was fortified to the east and south, Senglea (L'Isla) to the west and south, and to the north the **Great Chain** stretched across the mouth of Galley Creek (Dockyard Creek) protecting the Order's fleet. After the Turks' defeat, the knights, instead of immediately repairing the damage, husbanded their resources and concentrated on their new project – the fortified city of Valletta.

During the middle of the 17th century, when the Floriana Lines (*see* p.124) were under construction, focus returned to the Three Cities with the creation of the **Margherita Lines** (1638) to protect Cospicua (and to a lesser degree Vittoriosa and Senglea) from the vulnerable east and south. In a similar but more grandiose vein, the Margherita Lines were to be incorporated into yet another new defensive scheme, the **Cottonera Lines**. Work began on Grand Master Nicolas Cotoner's Cottonera Lines in 1670 to a design by the Duke of Savoy's engineer, Maurizio Valperga. The defences were to provide fortified shelter for 40,000 people, with eight formidable bastions, two semibastions and connected curtains that would stretch in a vast semicircle for 15,000ft (4,572m) from French Creek to Kalkara Creek. Grand Master Nicolas Cotoner nearly bankrupted himself with the project, and work came to an abrupt halt upon his death in 1680. (Much still stands, most impressively the **Żabbar Gate**.)

In the early 19th century, after Malta became a **Crown Colony**, the British continued to exploit the Order's established naval tradition. The Three Cities and the Grand Harbour became the home of the Mediterranean fleet; even Fort St Angelo was renamed HMS *St Angelo*. This era was to be the heyday of the Three Cities, when the magnificent warships of the 19th and 20th centuries provided employment and prosperity in a time of comparative peace in the central Mediterranean. Then the outbreak of hostilities in 1939 and the hitherto unknown (in Malta's terms) dimension of aerial warfare brought about in 27 months what the Turks had failed to do in 268 years – the near-total destruction of the area.

The skill of the Luftwaffe and the Regia Aeronautica meant a sizable proportion of the £30 million post-war grant from a grateful Britain was spent on the reparation of the piles of rubble the Three Cities had in effect become. Unfortunately, the rebuilding was hurried and lacked any semblance of a plan; but the communities did return and the dockyards began to function once again.

In the 1970s and early 1980s the dry docks expanded considerably. Diverse commercial concerns were courted by the entrenched socialist prime minister, Dom Mintoff; the Chinese built a massive dry dock, and parts of Fort St Rocco were converted into the **Mediterranean Film Studios**. It was here that, among many other 'epics', the dire *Raise the Titanic* was filmed, almost entirely in its huge water tank. The producer, Lew, Lord Grade, wryly commented on the financial black hole that his movie was to become: 'Raise the Titanic – it would have been cheaper to drain the Atlantic.' More recent productions filmed here have been more successful (*Gladiator, Count of Monte Cristo, U571* and *Troy*).

## Senglea (L'Isla)

This barren and stubby finger of land pointing into the Grand Harbour separates two strategic waterways, **Dockyard Creek** and **French Creek**. The town, along with its immediate neighbour Cospicua, was almost totally destroyed during the Second World War, and there is little to see here except some early fortifications on the west and the photogenic vedette, or lookout post.

The peninsula was totally uninhabited until Grand Master de Homedes (1536–53) turned it into his lush private park. His successor, Grand Master de la Sengle, had more altruistic ideas; in 1554 he settled the land and distributed free plots to anyone prepared to build a house. After Fort St Elmo fell on 23 June 1565 during the Great Siege, the Turkish commanders turned their fire onto Fort St Michael at the landward end of the peninsula. On the morning of 7 August 1565, the Turks simultaneously stormed both peninsulas (8,000 Muslim soldiers attacked Fort St Michael alone),

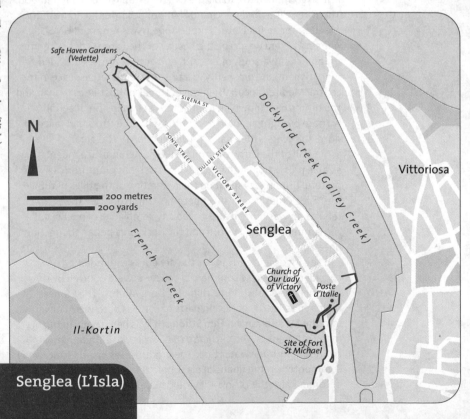

but this proved to be another disaster for the Turks, who lost 2,000 men, with a similar number of wounded; the knights escaped with comparatively light casualties. The historic old fort survived, only to be dismantled by the British early in the 20th century to make way for two dry docks for the Royal Navy.

The post-war plan has one principal street, **Victory Street**, that runs from the rebuilt church of Our Lady of Victory at the landward end to diminutive **Safe Haven Gardens** at the harbour end. The view of Valletta, Vittoriosa and the whole of the Grand Harbour from the gardens provide a stirring panorama. Located here is Senglea's totem – a hexagonal vedette with an intricately carved relief of two eyes and two ears representing constant vigilance for an enemy fleet. Under the vedette and just below the surface of the water, the Great Chain, forged in Venice, spanned the mouth of Galley Creek (Dockyard Creek) to Fort St Angelo and prevented the Turkish ships entering the creek during the Great Siege. After the Turks' defeat, Senglea (known originally as L'Isla, then Senglea after its founder), was dubbed Città Invitta, 'the unconquered city', but it never caught on.

## Vittoriosa (Birgu)

Historically, whoever commanded the thin promontory of Vittoriosa effectively controlled the creeks of the Grand Harbour, and over the centuries all invaders, hostile or peaceful, have established themselves here. Sadly, nothing apart from two Siculo-Norman windows survives from the pre-1530 settlers. Yet there is more to see here than anywhere else in the Three Cities: an excellent **Maritime Museum**, the unceremonious and seemingly humble first *auberges* of the Order, fortifications that date back to the Great Siege, the sombre **Inquisitor's Palace**, the stirring **church of St Lawrence** and, amazingly, many ancient little streets that survived horrific bombardments during both Great Sieges of 1565 and of 1940–3. The knights only fortified the northeast flank of Vittoriosa; the recently restored **Fort St Angelo** has been given to the Knights of St John and is once more closed to the public. Vittoriosa ('Victorious') replaced the old name of Birgu after the Great Siege of 1565. Both names are commonly used. Further afield in Kalkara the late 19th-century **Fort Rinella** is now open; if you have travelled here by car, it is worth visiting (*see* pp.143–4).

### Orientation and Historical Sights

Begin in St John's Tower Street just in from the main gate, the Poste de Provence. Victory Square is a good orientation point if you get temporarily lost in the narrow little streets, but you can't go far wrong – Vittoriosa is only 850 yards long by 400 yards at its widest.

None of the old *auberges* is open to the public. The row of structures, Nos.19–26 (except Fort St Angelo) along the **Vittoriosa Wharf** past the old Naval Bakery (now the Maritime Museum), has been sympathetically renovated. The Captain's House now houses the Casino di Venezia, while further along, an undistinguished apartment block has replaced one of the knights' grain stores. All seven original *auberges* (Auvergne and Provence shared quarters) were built around 1535 and were occupied until 1571 when the Order moved to Valletta. Four still stand, to the northeast of Victory Square in Hilda Tabone Street (formerly and often marked Britannic Street). All of the various *postes* were named after the *langues* whose duty it was to defend them, with the exception, that is, of the **Poste de Genoa** – a Genoese ship happened to be in port in May 1565 at the start of the Great Siege, and its luckless crew was conscripted by de la Valette into battle.

In the following descriptions, numbers refer to the map (*see* opposite).

**[1] The Gate of Provence**. The simple main gate into town was restored by Grand Master de Vilhena in the early 18th century. The two other entrances into the city, the elaborately carved **Advanced Gate** and the **Couvre Porte Gate**, are to the left and behind the **Poste d'Aragon**.

**[2] St John's Cavalier**. From 1928 to 1948 the roof was the home of the Maltese Meteorological Office.

**[3] The Bishop's Palace**. Built in 1542 and enlarged during the 17th century.

**[4] Knights Hall**. Derelict.

**[5] Armoury and St James's Cavalier**. Situated behind the cavalier (now partly a training school) was the old store for the Order's ordnance. In the early 18th century the British converted it into their first naval hospital on Malta.

**[6] Poste de Castile**. On the morning of 7 August during the 1565 Great Siege, 4,000 Turkish soldiers attacked the Poste de Castile (simultaneously a force of 8,000 Turks stormed Fort St Michael in L'Isla), and came close to breaching the defences here, at the time one of Birgu's most formidable. Grand Master de la Valette successfully led a tiny relief force from Fort St Angelo, and the casualties, for such a bloody battle, were small: the Turks lost 200 men, and the knights only 60.

It is possible to continue to walk along all the old northeast defences as far as the Fort St Angelo ditch, taking in the **Poste d'Allemagne** and the **Poste d'Angleterre** and leaving the **Sacra Infermeria** on your left. Midway between the two *postes* is a gap down to the water's edge known as the **Infermeria Sally Port**; here wounded soldiers from the besieged Fort St Elmo were brought ashore at night during the Great Siege.

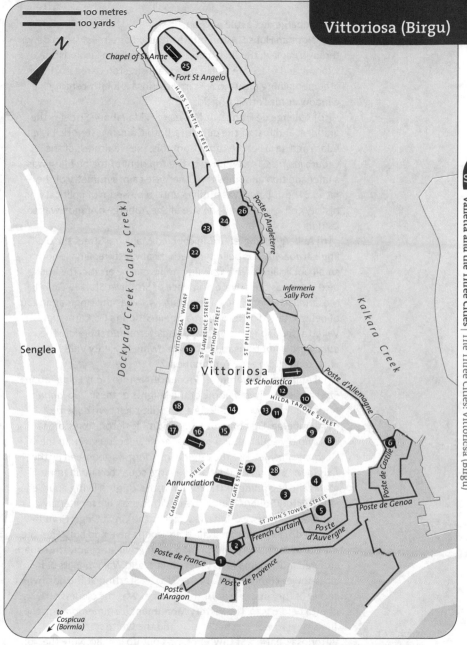

Vittoriosa (Birgu)

Senglea

Vittoriosa

St Scholastica

Chapel of St Anne
Fort St Angelo

**[7] Sacra Infermeria**. The large building almost at the edge of Victory Square was one of the first de L'Isle Adam constructed in 1531. In the mid-1600s, and after the new Sacra Infermeria in Valletta became operational, the hospital was transferred to its present site in Valletta.

**[8] Auberge de Castile et Leon.**

**[9] Norman House.** Although the house has almost fallen down through neglect, the first-floor 15th-century twin Siculo-Norman window and frieze are still in reasonable (restored) repair. The only other remaining pre-1530 relic in Vittoriosa is a 14th-century window inside Fort St Angelo.

**[10] Auberge de France.** At Nos.24–7 Hilda Tabone Street is the grandest and first of the *auberges*. Both Grand Masters de L'Isle Adam and de la Sengle came from this, the wealthiest of the Order's *langues*. The window to the top right of the building was a later addition and ruins the otherwise calm symmetry of the façade. The *auberge* was until recently a museum of political history and it is believed the site of the Auberge d'Aragon was to its right.

**[11] Auberge d'Angleterre.** In cobbled Majjistral Street the old English *auberge* has been sympathetically restored and is now a small public library – its opening hours can be erratic. The house next door was the private residence of Sir Oliver Starkey, Grand Master de la Valette's loyal secretary (who has the singular honour of being interred next to his master in St John's Co-Cathedral, Valletta (*see* p.108). The *langue* d'Angleterre, and therefore the *auberge*, did not transfer to Valletta owing to Henry VIII's break with Rome during the Reformation.

**[12] Auberge d'Auvergne et Provence.** Near to No.17 Hilda Tabone Street was the shared home of the knights of these two *langues*. After the 1571 move to Valletta each built their own *auberge*.

**[13] Auberge d'Allemagne.** Now a humble decorating store facing onto Victory Square, it is a part of the new façade given to the German *auberge* after the original building was bombed by the Axis in the Second World War. The large squat bollard in front marks the beginning of the *collachio*, the knights' living quartier.

**[14] Victory Square.** The centre of Vittoriosa's life for literally hundreds of years. During the worst of the Great Siege, Grand Master de la Valette marshalled his troops here and bolstered the morale of the hungry and cannon-weary civilians. Sadly the square suffered much damage in the Second World War when its old clock-tower-cum-vedette was destroyed. Starting at the northwest corner of the square in St Anthony Street was the old Jewish ghetto before 1530. The **Victory Monument** (commemorating the Turks' defeat) was erected in 1705 and the white statue of Vittoriosa's patron, **St Lawrence**, was put up in 1880. Note the iron railing on the former – the sword and cross pin down the Turkish crescent.

**[15] St Joseph's Chapel.** The 18th-century chapel is now a fascinating and comprehensive little museum full of social, ecclesiastical and military paraphernalia. Its most treasured

**St Joseph's Chapel**
*open daily 9.30–12 and 3–4: all times approximate; the friendly curator is invariably on hand; adm free but leave a donation*

possessions are the hat and sword of Grand Master de la Valette. Among the other exhibits are the last white ensign from HMS *St Angelo*, eight pennant flags from each of the different *langues*, a well-thumbed pack of cards from 1609, an 18th-century sedan chair, a Latin Vulgate bible printed in 1598 in Venice, and a 16th-century Venetian atlas. Note the very long scissors with flat ends; they were devised by a crafty and cautious priesthood to administer the Host during outbreaks of the plague.

**[16] Collegiate Church of St Lawrence.** St Lawrence's church is one of the most historically venerated churches in Malta. A church is said to have been built on this site in 1090 by Count Roger the Norman when Birgu was the island's second parish. At the beginning of the 16th century Roger's church was enlarged and on their arrival in 1530 the Order adopted it as their first conventual church. Two years later it was severely damaged by fire, destroying many of the treasures the Order had brought from Rhodes. The church was restored and it was here that Grand Master de la Valette assembled his knights and townsfolk on the eve of the Great Siege to say Mass. He and the other survivors returned to give thanks after the Turks' ignominious defeat in the September of 1565. After the Order moved to Valletta it became the inquisitors' church for over 200 years. In 1820 it was elevated to a collegiate church. During the Second World War much of it was damaged but it has since been faithfully restored. To celebrate its 900th anniversary, Pope John Paul II visited it in 1990.

St Lawrence is a powerful Baroque church, designed by **Lorenzo Gafa** in his birthplace. The west-facing setting is almost too ideal: 25 yards away from the water's edge on a high plinth, it accentuates the Order's brand of militant seafaring Catholicism. Work began in 1681 and it took 16 years to complete. Gafa's plan provided for a wide three-bay façade with a two-storey centrepiece, not unlike his later cathedral in Victoria, Gozo. Only the left-hand tower was added in the early 18th century and the church remained very lopsided for over 200 years; the right-hand one was built around the outbreak of the First World War (neither tower was to Gafa's design). The explosive depredations of the Second World War ravaged much of the outer church and, sadly, Gafa's original dome. The two statues in the niches either side of the main west door are of *St Paul* and *St Lawrence*.

Much of the rich marble Latin-cross interior is often being tinkered with; accordingly some of the paintings may be swathed in protective dust sheets. Also, when works are being carried out on the dome, the interior can be very gloomy, but the altarpiece of poor St Lawrence being griddled to death will still shine out.

**[17] Freedom Monument.** In front of the church the monument poignantly, if naively, shows the end of a not- always-happy

179-year Anglo-Maltese relationship. Unveiled on 31 March 1979, the day HMS *London* and the Royal Navy weighed anchor in the Grand Harbour for the last time, it depicts a naval rating bidding adieu to a Maltese citizen.

## [18] Maritime Museum/Naval Bakery

**✪ Maritime Museum/Naval Bakery**
*open daily 9–5; closed Good Fri, 24, 25, 31 Dec, 1 Jan; adm; NB disabled facilities are only available weekdays*

In 1841 the Admiralty architect William Scamp designed and built the impressive Naval Bakery on the site of the Order's principal arsenal and slipway, where the galleys were hauled out for repairs. The bakery turned out bread and biscuits for the entire Mediterranean fleet for over a hundred years. After the Second World War it became stores and offices, principally the Admiralty's Constabulary. In July 1992 the first phase of its conversion into the Maritime Museum was inaugurated.

Planned to expand over all three floors, the exhibits are slowly increasing; there are now nine different areas of exhibits (mainly on the first floor). They encompass diverse aspects of maritime history from marine archaeology, to the instruments used by Customs and local boat-building techniques. Unlike some museums in Malta the lighting is excellent and the paintings, models and ephemera are shown to good effect. Among the exhibits of note are: a fine painting of the Order's galley squadron engaging Muslim ships off Alexandria in 1644, two rare French cannons, a massive reconstructed Roman anchor and a restored figurehead from HMS *Hibernia* – originally the Celtic god Dagda, 10ft (3m) tall, was outside Fort St Angelo. The many models of note include Grand Master Adrien de Wignacourt's sumptuous ceremonial barge, an oared 17th-century galley, a huge 8ft (2.5m) training model of one of the Order's 18th-century ships of the line and a model of the first lateen-rigged Gozo ferry boats.

**[19–23]** This stretch of the Vittoriosa Wharf is currently used for berthing large private yachts and is undergoing restoration and development.

**[24] Auberge d'Italie** is a site only. The Emperor Charles V's Act of Donation settling the islands on the Order stipulated that the Admiral of the Fleet was to be the *pilier* or head of the *langue* of Italy. To be near to their fleet and Fort St Angelo, the Italian knights built their *auberge* away from their brothers-in-arms.

## [25] Fort St Angelo

'If so small a son [Fort St Elmo] has cost us so dear, what price must we have to pay for so large a father [St Angelo]', remarked Mustapha Pasha, the Turkish general, while gazing out to Fort St Angelo from the ruins of Fort St Elmo which he had just taken at a cost of over 8,000 of his men during the Great Siege of 1565.

After nearly a 200-year wait, the Order of St John has finally been granted the right to utilize, and is therefore now responsible for, the upper floors of Fort St Angelo; restoration works are proceeding on areas such as **St Anne's Chapel** and the **Majjistral Palace**. The scale of the fort just cannot be grasped from outside its walls, and unfortunately it is no longer open to the public. Ultimately, even a Fort St Angelo eroded by time, neglect and the elements will stand as a monument to Malta's strategic role in the conflicts – military and religious – that have bedevilled the central Mediterranean theatre for more than a thousand years.

Primitive fortifications on the site are believed to have pre-dated the 9th-century Arab occupation. After Count Roger the Norman sacked the Arabs in 1090 he strengthened what existed on this important position at the head of the Grand Harbour. A keep within a fortified enceinte subsequently served the feudal overlords until the arrival of the Order in 1530. Grand Master de L'Isle Adam found a crumbling fort unable to withstand modern artillery. Immediately, he began a programme of modifications which took 30 years to complete: the Italian engineer Antonio Ferramolino built a landward cavalier and excavated a deep wet ditch to separate St Angelo from Birgu (which also served as a harbour for the Order's flagship); the seat of the ousted governing de Nava family was converted into the magisterial palace, and the 15th-century Chapel of St Anne was restored. (It was in this chapel that Grand Master de la Valette prayed during the Great Siege and here, ironically, that he died of heat exhaustion aged 75 in August 1568 while praying after a good day's hunting in Buskett.)

## The Oubliette

In 1906 the British War Department turned Fort St Angelo over to the Royal Navy, and it became Malta's naval barracks. Just before the handover to the Navy, however, a loose stone slab was uncovered, under which, 13ft (4m) down in the living rock, was a hollowed-out pit, the feared oubliette.

It was here in pitch darkness – freezing in winter, sweltering in summer – that miscreant knights were imprisoned indefinitely; sentences were arbitrary and without a time limit, but usually knights were kept there until they were either expelled from the Order, as 'putrid and fetid limbs', or executed. Those awaiting execution – by deliciously indelicate methods that only blue-blooded aristocrats could dream up: being strangled to death and left in the gutter to be eaten by stray dogs, or trussed up like chickens in weighted sacks and tossed into the Grand Harbour – were said to regard death as a merciful release from the dank living hell of the oubliette.

After Malta became a part of the British Empire, the Royal Navy added and subtracted fortifications, and in 1912 the Navy reclassified the fort as a land-based ship known as HMS *Egmont*: the fort's governor became the flag captain, the different storeys became 'decks' and the rooms 'cabins'. After a further and final name-change in 1933 the fort became HMS *St Angelo*. During the Second World War it took 69 direct hits from the Axis bombers and until the British forces' withdrawal in 1979 it remained the headquarters of the commander in chief of the Mediterranean fleet.

In the 1970s, an amusing, if surely apocryphal, story was told of a NATO Joint Command gathering in Fort St Angelo. The Turkish representative, upon entering the reception, was said to have remarked: 'Good evening, I believe I am the first Turk to have penetrated thus far.'

07 Valletta and the Three Cities | The Three Cities: Vittoriosa (Birgu)

As the Great Siege wore on in the hot summer of 1565, St Angelo was the vital keystone in Grand Master de la Valette's brilliantly run campaign. From within the fort he kept St Elmo reinforced and victualled, provided supporting fire, and sent out relief troops to the *postes* in Birgu. Ultimately, it was here that he planned that the Order would make its final stand with a handful of brave knights in the event that Birgu fell to the Turks. After the Order's victory, and with the knights ensconced in Valletta, repairs were undertaken and it became the Order's dreaded prison.

Fort St Angelo remained largely unaltered until the end of the 17th century when Carlos de Grünenberg, the Emperor of Spain's engineer, advised that works to the northeast flank at the entrance to the harbours were necessary. The then financially embarrassed Order subtly and successfully suggested he might like to pay for the four batteries himself; this he did and placed his own escutcheon above the fort's main gate. The best examples of his efforts (the last to be undertaken in the Order's reign and which basically define the fort as it stands today) can be seen facing Kalkara Creek. When Napoleon sailed into the Grand Harbour in 1798 the fort's 80 guns remained embarrassingly silent.

**[26] Site of Slaves' Prison**.

**Inquisitor's Palace**
*open daily 9–5; closed Good Fri, 24, 25, 31 Dec, 1 Jan; adm*

**[27] Inquisitor's Palace.** In Malta the Inquisition rarely spent time painfully extracting heretic confessions – by hanging a weighted accused from his/her bound wrists while they were tied behind his back – and the palace is a dullish experience despite the added items of furniture and improved signs. Basically, this was where the pope's envoy resided, and the courtroom and cells are disappointingly tame.

The palace is built around three small courtyards, and rooms sprout from them and the main staircase like a maze. Note the

## The Only Coup

**Grand Master Jean l'Evêque de la Cassière** (1572–81) was the only grand master ever to be deposed by a *coup d'état* and imprisoned.

A monastic, tough-talking soldier with an unforgiving streak of Christian zeal burning through him, he was already in his 70s when elected in 1572. The liberalism of the Reformation and his somewhat debauched, lawless young knights were a cause of great anxiety to his orthodoxy: what had happened to the Order's crusading morals? In vain, he tried to stop the womanizing, gambling and duelling, and having failed he summoned papal intervention in a fit of pique – the Order was henceforth saddled with an inquisitor. The knights' patience was by now exhausted, and they staged a bloodless coup to remove the now-deaf octogenarian on 5 July 1581. He was escorted to St Angelo, where his imprisonment caused little hardship: he was allowed four knights, four priests and more than 20 other domestics. However, Pope Gregory XIII again intervened and summoned both him and his detractors to Rome. De la Cassière was found innocent of all the 46 charges brought against him, but he died before he could return to Malta. He was given a triumphal funeral in December 1581 and his body was returned to St John's Co-Cathedral (which he had built and paid for), but his heart was removed and buried under a black marble slab in San Luigi dei Francesi in Rome.

ceiling above the main stair on which the inquisitor's emblem – four linked black and white crosses chillingly resembling a swastika in reverse – is painted. The principal room at the top of the stairs gloomily displays the coat of arms of each inquisitor (the black hats denote the rank of inquisitor while the red denotes that of cardinal). The only fun to be had is in the courtroom, two rooms to the left. Sit in the inquisitor's chair and try to imagine the poor wretches forced through the low door (designed to make even the most heathen bow) to await their trial.

The history of the Inquisition in Malta began during the reign of Grand Master de la Cassière (1572–81, see 'The Only Coup', opposite). At his behest the pope sent an inquisitor to try to ensure that only unsullied Catholic souls wore the cross of the Order. In reality this important post just caused political strife – the inquisitor answered to Rome and held certain authority over the sovereign grand master, while the appointment of the bishop of Malta was the responsibility of the Emperor of Spain. Of the 63 inquisitors who served in Malta, 25 became cardinals and two became popes. Needless to say Napoleon abolished the position in 1798.

**[28] Residence of Conventual Chaplains.**

## Fort Rinella (Kalkara)

**Fort Rinella (Kalkara)**
*call the Fort's Keeper, t 21 640131, to confirm display times; adm free but leave a generous donation; information and souvenirs are also available; well signposted from the Valletta area*

The planet's oceans were, to the thinking of the Victorian British military, the exclusive domains of the Royal Navy. So when a 'Club Med' nation such as Italy trifled with the RN's de facto superiority by building a fleet of well-armed iron ships, it was too much of an impertinence. Despite the cordial relations between the two powers, the Admiralty acted with haste. The coastal defences of Malta and Gibraltar – the hinges of the Royal Navy's authority in the Mediterranean – were to be improved by the addition of four Armstrong 100-ton guns. In 1878 work began on two new batteries in Malta at Rinella and Tigne. It was not until the mid-1880s, however, that the gun, whose 1-ton shells took six minutes to load and had a range of more than 3 miles (5km) while being able to pierce 21in (53cm) of wrought iron, was operational. Alas, technology marched on. By the beginning of the 20th century breech-loading armaments had replaced slow-burning powder, and by 1906 the Armstrong guns were obsolete and decommissioned without ever having been fired in anger.

Since 1991, volunteers have restored Fort Rinella and a tour – accompanied and unaccompanied – of the entire emplacement is now possible; it is well worth visiting. A snapshot view of life within a Victorian military battery has been faithfully reproduced with original artefacts – right down to the barrack rooms and cast-iron latrines. From the 'viewing platform' you can see what you're

## Tourist Information in the Three Cities

The **MTA** in **Valletta** (*see* p.127) gives away a useful **walking map** of Senglea and Vittoriosa, but street names may have changed. Don't be alarmed by stares or sideways glances. The people who live in these tight-knit communities are merely curious; they are among the friendliest and most open in Malta.

## *Festas* in the Three Cities

**Senglea** remembers the Birth of the Virgin Mary on 8 September, **Vittoriosa** favours St Lawrence's feast on 10 August, and in **Cospicua** the Immaculate Conception is celebrated on 10 December.

## Eating Out in the Three Cities

There is a handful of cafés where you will find a reviving cold drink. In **Senglea** the **Equinox Café** is by the church. In **Vittoriosa** try the **Café du Brazil** or **Old City Pub** beyond the Freedom Monument. In Victory Square you'll often find a fruit vendor, while 50 yards away in St Anthony Street there is a good baker; buy some tomatoes, fruit and bread and then sit by the water's edge and muse on the vicissitudes of the Grand Harbour.

not missing at Fort St Rocco (the Mediterranean Film Studios) and Fort Ricasoli. Every third Sunday of the month there is living history display of Victorian garrison life.

# Cospicua (Bormla)

Dom Mintoff may have been born here, but there is still nothing to see in the narrow and stepped streets of the largest and last of the Three Cities to be founded, except a forest of TV aerials and parts of the Margherita Lines. The city's original name of Bormla was replaced by Cospicua, meaning 'conspicuous', on account of its valour during the Great Siege.

# The Northeast Coast

*This stretch of coast is the island's most intensely built-up and touristy area, and construction continues at a steady pace. Yet, inexplicably, buzz and tranquillity coexist in the summer-parched streets: in the lunacy of Paceville after dark, the eerie splendour of Valletta's illuminated bastions that form a dramatic backdrop across the harbour, or the spectacular fireworks of the festa reflected in the inky waters of St Julian's Bay.*

# 08

## Don't miss

**1 Spending spree**
Shopping at Sliema
p.154

**2 Illuminations across the water**
Night view of Valletta's fortifications from Sliema Creek p.154

**3 To the islands**
Cruises from Sliema Creek p.154

**4 *Festa* time**
St Julian's p.159

**5 Party through the night**
Paceville nightlife p.164

*See map overleaf*

1 km
1 mile

N

Ghallis Rocks

Qualet Marku

De Redin Tower

Baħar iċ-Ċagħaq Bay

Buġibba/Sliema

Baħar iċ-Ċagħaq

White Rocks
Splash and Fun Park

Magħab

Ras I-Irqieqa

Fort Madliena
Pembroke

Madliena

Il-Misraħ

Għargħur

Pembroke Fort

St George's Bay
Casino
Dragonara Point

Paceville

Il-Qaliet

Ix Xgħarjriet

Ta'Ċokenou

St Julian's

Spinola Palace

Tal-France

Spinola Point

St Julian's Bay

Tal-Għoqod

Spinola Point

St Julian's Point

Tal-Mejda

Balluta Bay

Sliema Point
Għar id-Dud

Ix-Xieki

Sliema

Is-Simblija

Iklin

Gżira

Tigne Fort
Dragut Point

San Gwann

Sliema Creek

Il-Qasbija

Manoel Island

Fort Manoel

Fort St Elmo

Il-Bwieraq

Lazzaretto Creek

Balzan

Birkirkara

Ta'Xbiex

Marsamxett Harbour

Valletta

Msida Creek

Msida

Pietà

Pietà Creek

Floriana

Grand Harbour

Gwardamanġa

Santa Venera

Senglea

Hamrun

Newport (Marsa) Creek

p.168

p.234

p.96

Gozo

Malta

## Don't miss

⭐ **Sliema shopping p.154**

⭐ **Sliema Creek promenade p.154**

⭐ **Sliema Creek cruises p.154**

⭐ **St Julian's *festa* p.159**

⭐ **Paceville nightlife p.164**

*The industry of the Maltese in cultivating their little island is inconceivable. There is not an inch of ground lost in any part of it; and where there was not soil enough, they have brought over ships and boats loaded with it from Sicily, where there is plenty and to spare.*

Patrick Brydone, *A Tour through Sicily and Malta*, 1773

Along the northeast coast, the two biggest towns, **Sliema** and neighbouring **St Julian's**, have the highest population on the archipelago (albeit with just 30,000 inhabitants), and together they constitute Malta's most popular destination – each year around 950,000 visit this area at some time during their stay. There are more than a hundred places to stay – hotels, guesthouses and holiday complexes – and that figure does not include rental apartments. You will also find excellent shopping and nightlife; restaurants, bars and cafés; beaches and all the waterborne antics that money and human inventiveness can come up with.

But the overbuilding has resulted in a straining infrastructure. There were no Ozymandian visions here, and instead of a harmonious skyline parts of the area simply resemble the gap-toothed grin of a none-too-successful prizefighter. The northeast coast has many good points, but aestheticism is not one of them.

# From Ta'Xbiex to Gwardamanġa

Apart from the **yacht marinas** at Ta'Xbiex and Msida, there is little to detain you here. The yachts themselves are the star turn in the continuous suburb that encircles Marsamxett Harbour. The place has a transitory feel; boats and their crews sail in and out from all corners of the globe, and the small hotels of Pieta and Msida are layover establishments for US and Middle Eastern oil workers.

## Msida and Ta'Xbiex

**Msida** is known for its new yacht marinas and sometimes treacherous roundabout with attendant traffic jams. The warren of streets nearby is full of panel beaters, an industry that will always enjoy full employment in Malta.

**Msida Creek** is the most sheltered part of Marsamxett Harbour and was once a natural fishing settlement. It takes its name from *mysada*, the Arabic word for a fisherman's hut, a further corruption of which is *sajd*, meaning fish. Until the Second World War the creek extended 80 yards back to the old 18th-century wash house in the Birkirkara Road, built by a German knight and fed by an underground spring. During the war, rock and rubble were purposely dumped in the creek's shallows and much land was reclaimed. The huge **yacht marina** was developed in 1989 and has proved a success with yachtsmen and tourists alike. The **parish church of St Joseph** (1893) has two altarpieces painted by Giuseppe Cali.

## Getting to and around Msida, Ta'Xbiex and Gwardamanġa

**Buses** with two-digit numbers that start with a 4 or a 5 will go to Mosta via Pieta and Msida; a 6 via Pieta and Msida to Ta'Xbiex and Sliema. The 75 is a 'special' from Valletta to St Luke's Hospital. Ta'Xbiex Marina is not clearly flagged, so follow the one-way system for Gzira and then head for the masts. Msida can get snarled up with traffic in the rush hour.
The Ghawdex **ferry** sails daily for Gozo from the Sa Maison quay in Pieta.

Ta'Xbiex is a quieter, more genteel area of villas and embassies. A stroll along the quays of the second and smaller yacht marina is – apart from the chandleries and a good little park – the main reason for lingering here.

The second marina is in **Lazzaretto Creek** and got its peculiar name from Italian *lazzaretto*, for an isolation hospital. The bed of the creek was the safest place for the submarines of the Royal Navy 10th Flotilla during the air raids of the Second World War (the Ministry of Defence and the War Ministry had foolishly decided against cutting submarine pens into the rock) and it remains the best of the many refuges in the archipelago. Malta imported most commodities including plagues (*see* p.150) and facing the creek is the old **Lazzaretto quarantine hospital** with its nearby scaffold from which transgressors of the quarantine were hanged. The scaffold was dismantled in 1839, but a vestige of the old precautions remains; these days a yacht arriving in Malta with a pet on board is required to lie at anchor in the creek.

# Pieta and Gwardamanġa

There is not much to see or do here. Gwardamanġa is mainly residential and Pieta is one of the main arteries leading to the west of the island. **Gwardamanġa** used to be one of the more pleasant areas around Marsamxett Harbour. However, since the war it has become heavily urbanized and is now known for housing Malta's principal hospital, **St Luke's** (1938), which occupies almost the entire peninsula that divides the Pieta and Msida Creeks. Lord and Lady Mountbatten resided at **Villa Gwardamanġa**, and Queen Elizabeth II stayed at her uncle's villa during her numerous visits, first as princess and then as queen.

Before the outbreak of the Second World War, HMS *Terror*, a rusting survivor of the First World War, awaited her scrapyard fate in **Pieta Creek**. Her feeble guns and the four Gladiator biplanes were the sum total of the Allied defence on Malta when Italy declared war on 10 June 1940. The first air-raid victims of the war, two children and their mother, were killed here at 6.50 the following morning.

## Services between Msida and Gwardamanġa

**St Luke's Hospital** in Gwardamanġa (sometimes abbreviated to G'manġa) is signposted off the roundabout.

### *Festas* between Msida and Gwardamanġa

**Msida**'s *festa* to St Joseph is on the first Sunday after 16 July.

**Gwardamanġa** and **Ta'Xbiex** celebrate Our Lady of Fatima on 4 June, and St John of the Cross on the 33rd Sunday of the year.

## Yachting between Msida and Gwardamanġa

This part of Malta has two principal marinas, at **Msida** and **Lazzaretto**. Each of these is divided into two quays: Msida Creek is made up of **Msida Marina** on the southeast side of Msida Creek and **Whitehall Quay** on the north. Together they can accommodate around 700 yachts up to 60ft (18m) on 15 fully serviced pontoons. Lazzaretto Creek has two smaller quays, **Lazzaretto** and **Ta'Xbiex**, which are reserved for yachts longer than 60ft (18m).

The harbour master has an office at the **Yacht Centre**, in the same building as the local police force and customs and immigration in Ta'Xbiex at the entrance to the Msida Marina. A **secondary Yacht Centre office** with the same facilities is in Marina Street, Pieta. For more comprehensive information, arrival procedures, berthing fees, forecasts, and other

anchorages in Maltese waters *see* 'Yachting Information', pp.92–4.

## Where to Stay between Msida and Gwardamanġa

The Msida, Pieta and Gwardamanġa area has many new developments. Smaller hotels have sold up to become apartment blocks.

**\*\*Hotel Helena,** 192 Marina Street, Pieta, t 21 336417, *info@englishplus malta* (€). Close to the marina, with a minute pool and 26 rooms in a narrow building.

## Eating Out between Msida and Gwardamanġa

**Black Pearl,** Ta'Xbiex Marina, t 21 343970 (€€€). Impossible to miss on the Ta'Xbiex and Msida headland is this schooner, which lies like a whale on the quay after a chequered life which began in Sweden in 1909, and ended ignominiously at the bottom of the sea during the filming of *Popeye*. Good basic Italian food; the old-ship décor and position lend an authentic note. *Closed Sat and Sun lunchtime in summer, Mon in winter and last 2 weeks Jan.*

**Busy Bee,** Ta'Xbiex Seafront, t 21 331738 (€). Good for tea or a quick snack of local pastries. Give the *kannoli* a try – these are deep-fried pastry tubes filled with sweetened ricotta cheese.

**Mama Mia,** Msida Yacht Marina, Ta'Xbiex Seafront, t 21 337248 (€). Formerly the Manhattan; in a spectacularly ugly modern building, this relaxed restaurant has a wide enough menu to satisfy the fussiest.

# Gzira and Manoel Island

**Gzira seafront** is not an ideal holiday destination but nor is it as grim as *Holiday Which?* magazine once implied when it singled out nine of the world's holiday black spots that 'should be avoided like the plague'; Gzira ranked sixth on the list. Some of its easily avoided offerings include sleazy prostitutes, uncollected garbage

## Getting to and around Gzira and Manoel Island

By **car**, follow the signs for Ta'Xbiex and Sliema. There is a **taxi** stand adjacent to the Valletta-bound bus stop in Gzira.

and fetid water. Yet life in the quiet streets off **Gzira Circus** behind the seafront is totally different: immaculate terraced houses, clean pavements, excellent local shops and pharmacies – all the hallmarks of community pride – are in evidence.

**Manoel Island** is joined to the mainland by a short 40-yard bridge. Steeped in history, Fort Manoel and Lazzaretto are finally being restored after years of neglect. They form part of a new commercial/residential development on Manoel island which should be completed over the next few years. All that currently stands are the **Manoel Island Shipyard**, a good shipping facility in the central Mediterranean, and the **Royal Malta Yacht Club** at Couvre Porte, the old Baroque entrance to Fort Manoel. The Yacht Club is scheduled to be moved to a new location as part of the new development.

### History: Plagues, Wars and a Fort

*Adieu, thou damned'st quarantine, that gave me fever, and the spleen*

Lord Byron, 1811

In 1643, more than 100 years and two serious plagues after the Order came to Malta, Grand Master Lascaris constructed the *lazzaretto*, or **quarantine station**, on the south shore of what was then called Bishop Island, now Manoel Island. The Order had already instituted a quarantine system in Rinella Creek and Corradino in the 17th century.

With their usual determination the Order managed to keep the worst bubonic plagues out of Malta; even letters were slit open, soaked in vinegar and fumigated. Sleeping on the job by the yellow-uniformed health guards (today the internationally recognized quarantine flag flown by all arriving ships is yellow) was punishable with a three-year term as a galley slave, and the noose awaited those who broke the quarantine. Irrespective of rank, all visitors were incarcerated for a period of 18–80 days, depending on their point of embarkation. Lord Byron, already not over-enamoured with Malta, which he referred to as 'this infernal oven', spent 18 days in the *lazzaretto* on his homeward journey from Greece in 1811. In Greece he had carnally overindulged on women and boys, and gorged himself on food and wine. According to his companion John Galt, he had acquired an interesting concoction of ailments: 'an ague, and a clap, and the piles all at once'. Somewhere in the remains of the *lazzaretto* is a stone upon which he carved his name. Other well-known *lazzaretto* alumni were Disraeli, Coleridge, Thackeray and Sir Walter Scott. Scott remarked in 1831: 'It is unpleasant to be thought so very unclean and capable of poisoning a whole city.'

Outbreaks of the plague vanished from Europe in 1841 but the *lazzaretto* remained in use for many years. It was converted into a quasi-hospital during the First World War, when at Churchill's instigation Malta reverted to its Hospitaller origins and became 'the nurse of the Mediterranean'. At the begining of hostilities in the Second World War all the buildings were requisitioned by Allied Command for the 10th Submarine Flotilla; the isolation units were converted into dormitories and stores. To supplement their rations, the submarine crews established a private pig farm. The Axis bombed the base, and no one knows who got to the pigs first.

## Fort Manoel

Fort Manoel represents the zenith of fort design and construction. It was once described as 'the classic example of a Baroque fortress, bold yet precise, elegant yet a hard functional machine'. The complex challenge for military engineers was to protect the besieged as well as to satisfy their paymasters aesthetically. It is now undergoing much-needed restoration.

**Grand Master de Vilhena** commissioned the French military engineer de Tigné to protect the Marsamxett Harbour. His initial plans, modelled on the technical mastery of Vauban, were altered by the Order's resident engineer, de Mondion. In 1723, a year into de Vilhena's reign, ground was first broken on the fort he personally was to pay for and which was to bear his name. The huge building took three years to complete and is low, almost squat, with four fierce corner bastions; the imposing curtain walls are protected by ravelins under which lurked a cobweb of mines. The raised centre parade ground housed a fine little Baroque chapel to St Anthony of Padua, de Vilhena's patron saint, a governor's house and barrack blocks. The fort was designed to accommodate a 500-strong garrison and even what remains of it shows off a powerful mathematical and geometric form. The **Couvre Porte**, the southern gateway and now the Royal Malta Yacht Club, is a grand Baroque gesture to the exuberant tastes of the paymaster.

When the French invaded in 1798, Fort Manoel fell after just a couple of hours. Ironically, after their own defeat in 1800, many French soldiers were imprisoned here before being shipped back home. The Second World War saw terrible punishment inflicted on the fort from Axis bombs meant for the neighbouring submarine pens. Fifty years' decay and the indifference of both the British and Maltese governments have taken an almost equal toll. Yet Fort Manoel's massive but elegant outline can still be appreciated from Valletta's higher bastions. The rest of Manoel Island, including the *lazzaretto* buildings, is part of a huge redevelopment project.

## *Festa* in Gzira

On the second Sunday in July, **Gzira** celebrates its *festa*, in honour of Our Lady of Mount Carmel.

## Where to Stay in Gzira and Manoel Island

**\*\*\*\*Kennedy Nova**, 166 The Strand, **t** 21 345480, *www.kennedynova.com* (€€€). It has the big advantage of a rooftop pool and bar, but neither the bedrooms nor the public rooms are as good as those at the Waterfront.

**\*\*\*\*The Waterfront Hotel**, The Strand, **t** 21 333434, *www.waterfronthotelmalta. com* (€€€). The newest and best hotel in this area, the Waterfront Hotel has 116 rooms all with balconies, and a rooftop pool with views of Manoel Island and Valletta. There is full wheelchair access throughout the hotel and one room is equipped for special needs. The hotel has a pizzeria, as well as its main restaurant **Regatta**.

**\*\*\*Milano Due Hotel**, 113 The Strand, **t** 21 345040, *www.milanoduehotel.com* (€€€). There are 108 generous rooms (some with facilities for the disabled), a sun terrace and a decent restaurant.

## Eating Out in Gzira and Manoel Island

### Gzira

This stretch of seafront is upgrading itself with shops and eateries. The very popular **Café Jubilee** is on The Strand opposite the bridge to Manoel Island. **Maxim's** sell good traditionally made *pastizzi*, and the **Britannia Bar** is an expats' haunt which serves sandwiches. Further down The Strand and past the two hotels is **Black Gold**, the sort of bar that appeals to serious drinkers.

**Chez Philippe**, 181 The Strand, **t** 21 330755 (€€). Two doors down from Maxim's, this restaurant was formerly Bon Pain, and this sign remains above the door. Chez Philippe has a relaxed, friendly atmosphere, good food and a decent, well-priced wine list; Internet access. The salads and imported French cheeses are possibly the best in town, and other dishes range from pasta to specialities such as duck with banana. *Lunch Mon–Sat, dinner Wed, Fri and Sat; closed first week Jan and month of Aug.*

**Waterfront Pizzeria**, The Waterfront Hotel, The Strand, **t** 21 335048 (€). Similar high standards as other Pizza Express restaurants around the world. Very light and airy, with smiling, efficient service.

### Manoel Island

The new development on Manoel Island will provide many new bars and restaurants.

**Jonathan's**, Royal Malta Yacht Club, Couvre Porte, **t** 21 313291 (€€). Pleasant place to eat outside in summer. When *lampuki* is on, order it. Membership is not required. Due to move, so check location. *Closed Mon.*

# Sliema, St Julian's, Paceville and Around

The suburbs of **Sliema** and **St Julian's** have grown in limestone leaps and concrete bounds. The majority of tourists and Maltese gravitate towards this area. An oil and water mix of staunchly middle-class Maltese and a youth intent on heading into the social stratosphere (via an apartment on Tower Road) co-exist with many good hotels, restaurants and bars, busy nightlife and shops. Thirty thousand Maltese – that is 7 per cent of the island's population – are spread among seven parishes, and from April to October the continuous coastal development of Sliema to St Julian's is wall-to-

500 metres
500 yards

N

*Mediterranean*

*Sea*

wall holiday town. Be prepared to leave with a smouldering wallet and molten credit cards; like everywhere in the Mediterranean, Malta can be expensive.

## Sliema

*Sliem*, meaning 'hail', is the first word of a fisherman's prayer to the Virgin Mary. Beginning as a fishing settlement, by the end of the 19th century Sliema had grown into a summer retreat from the claustrophobic heat of Valletta. Wandering in the quiet backstreets

# Getting to and around Sliema

The **Marsamxett Ferry** is the quickest and by far the least aggravating way of getting to Sliema from Valletta. The journey is only five minutes in duration, and the ferry plies the route every 35–40 minutes, arriving and departing from the Ferries at the bottom of Tower Road on the waterfront. Day cruise boats also leave from here.

By **car**, the capital Valletta is only 3 miles (5km) away, but the traffic is usually extremely tiresome. Finding a car-parking space on the street is well nigh impossible in this area. The open car park at the Ferries (opposite Magic Kiosk) is worth a try – the attendant will sometimes double-park your car if you leave him the keys (25–50c). It is probably easier, however, to follow signs to the multistorey car park up the hill of Tower Road.

The **bus terminus** is just by the Ferries.

**Taxis** are plentiful and there is a seemingly inert rank by the Magic Kiosk café.

you will see a handful of the graceful early 20th-century villas that once made up the town. Those which remain are destined to be replaced by rivetingly dull blocks of flats; even the last elegant and detached villa in Balluta Bay has been sold for redevelopment. Today, a Sliema address is the aspiration of many Maltese, and the town is a place for **shopping**. If you cannot find what you require within the approximate boundaries of Mrabat Street, the head of Balluta Bay, Tower Road and Dragut Point, you probably don't need it anyway; there are all manner of shops in the main streets and tucked up blind alleys. Amid all this modern affluence, one of Italy's more gratifying pleasures has long been adopted – the *passeggiata*. Before dusk closes in, circuses of Maltese families with their sleeping babies, and marauding children, gravitate along the coastal promenade between the Għar id-Dud and St Julian's, making pit stops for nuts, seeds, nougat and ice cream.

**☆ Shopping in Sliema**

## Around the Town

The awesome bastions and curtain walls of Valletta, one of the most spectacular sights in Malta, can only really be appreciated from the **Sliema Creek promenade** at night. The orange glow of the illuminations casts spectral shadows and dazzling highlights, and conjures up dreamy images of the knights and their armies of sturdy workmen toiling night and day to erect the Christian fortress city. At night, and from a distance across the water, the city is a somnolent yet dazzling feat of architecture. Sliema Creek is also the starting point for **cruises** around the Grand Harbour and to the Islands (*see* p.157).

There is not much to see on the headland region around Dragut Point and Tigne as they are currently being redeveloped as a mixture of residential and commercial space, but they are rich in history. The Turks established an artillery battery on the Tigne headland and pounded away at Fort St Elmo during the Great Siege of 1565. It was on this tip of land, at the mouth of Marsamxett Harbour and Sliema Creek known as **Dragut Point**,

**❷ Sliema Creek promenade**

**❸ Sliema Creek cruises**

that the besieging corsair and mercenary Dragut Rais was mortally wounded by a splinter of rock from a cannon ball, three days before Fort St Elmo fell (*see* pp.47–9).

Long after the Christian victory, the knights' military engineers inexplicably continued to ignore the strategically important promontory. **Tigne Fort** (1792) was the last of the Valletta defences to be commissioned, and was paid for by Grand Master de Rohan and Chevalier Tigne, who intended it to be a secondary foil to the might of Fort St Elmo. The 15 cannons of the diamond-shaped fort, when fired in concert with those of Fort St Elmo, would slam the door on an enemy attempt to occupy Marsamxett Harbour. Tigne's cannons gave spirited covering fire in support of the brave knight de Soubiran who put to sea in his lone galley to defend what was left of the Order's honour during the French invasion of 1798. He attacked and sank a French warship after it had landed men in St Julian's but two hours later his own guns were silenced by Napoleon's General Vaubois. A year later, while the Royal Navy blockaded the French in Valletta, the cannons of Forts Tigne and Manoel bombarded the city. The British steadily enlarged the fort until it bore little resemblance to the original and by the Second World War it positively bristled with guns and searchlights.

On the Għar id-Dud is yet another coastal defence converted into a pizzeria, **Il-Fortizza**, which was the old Sliema Point Battery, built by the British in 1872. The drastic change of use has been well executed: the Gothic-style doors and vaulting remain, and it is easy to appreciate the vantage point it enjoyed. The tower was added in 1905 when the battery became an observation station.

The architecturally unadventurous **church of the Sacred Heart** houses an evocative altarpiece of the emaciated *St Jerome* in his cave, with only death's head, a Bible and a cross for company. Generally acknowledged to be Giuseppe Cali's masterpiece, it is a powerful and indoctrinating image.

## Beaches around Sliema

The word 'beach' liberally translates in Malta to 'seaward entry point' and can therefore be anything from sand to rock; precious little of the former exists in this area but there is an abundance of the latter. All the public beaches are free and don't become uncomfortably crowded, even in the height of summer, but getting in and out can be tricky for young children and the elderly. There are many private lidos along the coast which incorporate other facilities, such as restaurants and sports equipment hire.

Heading east from the Balluta side of St Julian's Tower to the end of Tigne Beach is more than 2 miles (3km) of mostly smooth rock beach all invisibly named and divided up. From inside Balluta Bay to the Tower is the **Torri and Exiles Beach** named after the water-polo team who have their pitch, café and public gardens there. Next is a long stretch extending past the Surfside Lido known as **Font Għadir**, meaning 'deep pool', for the cobalt-blue water falls away deeply off the rocks here. Along this stretch are uniform squares hewn out of the rock which used to be the private summer 'pools' for the ladies of Sliema. Not only were the rock pools lined with canvas, but a three-sided screen was erected to ensure that the bashful ladies were safe from inquisitive eyes. On very rare occasions you still see this practice in Malta or Gozo when nuns go swimming. The next port of call for the beachcomber is the **Għar id-Dud**, literally translated as 'cave of worms'. The rocks are not so smooth here and if there has been a swell the waves can crash around viciously. Left towards Tigne on the northeast peninsula is **Qui Si Sana** meaning 'here is health', and the final stretch of beach is called **Tigne Beach**. At the far end is the Union Club Lido where young boys are initiated into the ethos of Latin machismo by diving from the tops of the rocks into the sea. Occasionally a complete hash is made of a dive and you are left wondering what psychological damage has been done.

**Private lidos** have anything from parasols to three-course lunches. Beginning at St Julian's Tower, the best are the **Surfside**, the **Preluna**, the **Jumbo**, the **Plevna**, the **Tigne Court** and the **Union Club**. Entrance is usually around Lm1.50–4.50.

## Services in Sliema

There is a large **post office** in Manwel Dimech Street (which is also known as Prince of Wales Drive). Right at the top of this street both HSBC and the Bank of Valletta have **cash machines**.

## Festas in Sliema

Sliema's four parishes celebrate no fewer than four *festas*: **Our Lady of the Sea**, or Stella Maris, on the Sunday after 18 August; **Our Lady of the Sacred Heart** or Sacro Cuor on the first Sunday in July; **St Gregory the Great** on the first Sunday in September; and **St Frances** on the first Sunday in October.

## Shopping in Sliema

Retail activity is centred around **Tower Road** and **Bisazza Street**, up from the Ferries, and nearby in the long uphill slog of Manwel Dimech Street. The hub is the **Plaza Shopping Complex**, which, despite causing a few parking problems, has provided the area with everything from Benetton to Body Shop, as well as a number of shops with a more local flavour.

### Clothes

Most international brand names and chain stores are here, but prices are often higher than they are in the UK. There is a **Marks and Spencer** on The Strand, which does not sell fresh food. There are also branches of **British Home Stores** and **Miss Selfridge** on Tower Road, and **Monsoon** and **Next** on Bisazza Street.

### Food

There is a good local **baker** 200 yards up St Vincent Street behind the Ferries. Three **vegetable and fruit vans** operate the lucrative pitch by the Ferries; the very freshest is sold Monday and Thursday afternoons after the twice-weekly Pit Kali (wholesale vegetable market). At the beginning of Tower Road is a local confectioner, the **Chocolate Box**, cool and full of Italian cakes and sweetmeats. The largest supermarket in Sliema, **Tower Stores** is housed in the multistorey car park. You will get free parking for purchases over Lm5, but remember to take your parking ticket into the shop with you.

### Miscellaneous

A short distance further along towards the Għar id-Dud Promenade **Kodak** print digital pictures from a memory stick and have a one-hour-developing shop, charging nearly double UK prices for processing. In the Piazzetta Centre, at the beginning of the Għar id-Dud Promenade, is a large chemist, **Chemimart**, which stocks European brands.

### Gifts

Tacky resort apparel, baseball caps, T-shirts, rucksacks and cigarette lighters, all garishly emblazoned 'Malta', are available everywhere. On the other hand, there is always a silver-filigree cross of the Order of St John (a **Maltese cross**) from **Victor's Jewellery** in Tower Road, or one of the expanding collection of excellent miniature **Heritage Homes** from **Jomar** at 4 High Street.

Malta produces a prolific and well-printed selection of **books** that make perfect souvenirs. **Agenda Bookshop** in the Plaza is the best.Tucked up Tigne Street, off Tower Road, is **Charles Palmier's** tiny **art gallery**, with reasonably priced souvenir prints.

## Sports and Activities in Sliema

The **Fortina Spa Resort** (*see* right) towards Tigne Point has **spa therapies**, **exercise classes** and a **gym**.
**Captain Morgan cruise fleet**, in Sliema Creek, **t** 23 463333, *www. captainmorgan.com.mt*. Of various companies of this kind, none come close to matching Captain Morgan's standards of food or service. The longest cruise takes in all the islands from 9.15–5 (*Lm21, children Lm12; includes buffet*); day trips to Comino

and around the Grand Harbour are also popular. Other excursions include a jeep safari, an underwater safari in a glass-bottomed boat and a 20-minute helicopter sightseeing tour, as well as a combination of all three. They also run a historical bus tour of the Three Cities. Very popular with younger people is the Spirit of Malta Cruise (*10–6, no fixed programme; Lm26.75; children Lm16.50; includes lunch*).

## Where to Stay in Sliema

### Luxury (€€€€)

In the next few years the completion of the Tigne and Manoel Island developments will doubtless add a few more hotels to this vicinity. In the short term, however, the Tigne development especially will mean that the two hotels bordering the area will be right next to a huge building site.
****Fortina Spa Resort**, Tigne Seafront, **t** 23 460000, *www. hotelfortina.com*. The gloomy and cramped lobby area does not do justice to the cheerful rooms upstairs. The Fortina offers a wide range of spa therapies and has an attractive pool area built out into the harbour.
****Preluna**, Tower Road, **t** 21 334001, *www.preluna-hotel.com*. Faces Għar id-Dud Promenade and the sea but can be a little noisy. The lobby is a bit gloomy, the rooms brighter. It too has a lido and pool at the water's edge.

### Expensive (€€€)

****Diplomat**, Tower Road, **t** 21 345361, *www.diplomat.com.mt*. Opened in 1992, the Diplomat is a walk from the centre, midway between Sliema and Balluta Bay, facing the sea. The pleasantly decorated rooms are small but comfortable; only the side rooms have balconies. The rooftop pool is a pleasant suntrap. There is also a cocktail bar with piano.
****Victoria Hotel**, George Borg Olivier Street, **t** 21 334711. Next to the Capua Palace Hospital, this opened in 1997 and has a sun terrace, a rather small pool and satellite TV in each of its 120 rooms as well as a pleasant, cosy bar called the 'Penny Black'. It

also has rooms with extra facilities for disabled people.

***Metropole**, 50 Sir Adrian Dingli Street, **t** 21 339700. Towards Balluta, the largest of the three-star establishments, with 160 none-too-sharp-looking rooms, a ground floor and rooftop bars with 'poolette'.

***New Tower Palace Hotel**, Tower Road, **t** 21 337271, *www.newtower palacehotel.com*. Faces the sea, and has access to rocky beaches. Each room has a generous balcony and there is a sun deck on the 7th-floor terrace. Right next door is the wonderful Gelateria Lungomare (*see* below).

Moderate (€€)

The majority of hotels in Sliema carry three stars. The most notable are listed below.

***Europa**, 138 Tower Road, **t** 21 330080. Just past the Preluna, with basic amenities but a central position – a place for those who want to be in the thick of things.

***Imperial**, Rudolph Street, **t** 21 344762. Was once an old hunting lodge; the sweeping staircase, high ceilings and old-world charm remain. There is a secluded pool. Slightly tired and can be noisy.

***Hotel Roma**, Għar il-Lenbi Street, **t** 21 318587, *margie@hotelroma. com.mt*. On the other side of the Preluna from the Europa is the Roma, small and modern with useful café-cum-meeting place on the ground floor, no pool but a sun deck. Not for those with limited mobility.

Inexpensive (€)

**Berkely Hotel**, 102 Howard Street, **t** 21 313764, *berkely@mol.net.mt*. The best of the two-star hotels in Sliema. Located only 250 yards away from the seafront, it can sometimes be monopolized by Scandinavians, whose exacting standards the hotel matches. It was taken under new management a few years ago and has since been fully refurbished. All the rooms have air conditioning, fitted fridges and satellite TV. There is also a small roof garden. Lift.

**Tudor Hotel**, 52 Sir Arturo Mercieca Street, **t** 21 330332. Formerly the Hotel Elba; close to the sea and a comfortable and reasonable place to stay. Lift.

## Eating Out in Sliema

There are countless **cafés** in Sliema behind the Ferries and along the Għar id-Dud, offering a cappuccino, a beer or simple freshly prepared snacks. **Anni Venti**, the **Magic Kiosk**, **City of London**, **Giorgio**, **Café Roma** and **La Columba** are all reliable.

**Il Galeone**, 35 Tigne Seafront, **t** 21 316420 (€€€€) This small restaurant is a long-time favourite for both lunch and dinner, serving mainly Italian dishes, but with a few home-spun inventions thrown in.

**Il-Merill**, St Vincent Street, **t** 21 332172 (€€). Good old-fashioned British colonial food with some local dishes as well.

**Portopalo**, Tigne Seafront, **t** 21 331915 (€€). Next door to Il Galeone, this serves good pasta dishes, although the service can be somewhat tardy.

**TGI Fridays**, Il-Fortizza, Tower Road, **t** 21 346897/8 (€€). Set in an old British watchtower overlooking the sea, this restaurant has become part of the American chain, and serves very large portions of 'American-style' food. It is great for families with children.

**The Army and Navy**, The Strand (no telephone; €). The old Forces stalwart; they will fry up anything and everything better than anyone else.

**La Cuccagna**, Amery Street, **t** 21 346703 (€). Cosy, tiny restaurant serving excellent crispy pizzas and a few tasty pasta dishes. *Open Tues–Sun eves, and Sun lunch.*

**The Surfside**, Tower Road, **t** 21 345384 (€). Bar and restaurant with pizza and pasta, served on the terrace in summer. Very nicely placed right on the Font Għadir beach, 10 yards away from the sea, opposite the Tower Palace Hotel.

For the best in ice cream, two establishments stand out: **Offshore** by the Ferries and, right next door to the New Tower Palace Hotel, the **Gelateria Lungomare**, where they offer more than 30 different, absolutely delicious flavours to choose from.

# St Julian's Bay, Balluta, Paceville and St George's Bay

**St Julian's Bay** takes its name from a chapel dedicated to St Julian, where during the Order's reign the fishermen would congregate; now it is the island's year-round mecca for eating, drinking and nightlife. The curving bay (sometimes referred to as Spinola Bay) is trying to return to its fishing origins, and many of the buildings at the water's edge have benefited from skilled and sympathetic restoration. For details of the *festa see* p.161.

⚓ **St Julian's Bay**
*festa*

When Sliema gently nods off after the evening *passeggiata*, St Julian's and the sometimes raucous and younger neighbouring *quartier* of **Paceville** begin to stir for what will be playtime well into the early hours.

## History

After the Great Siege had begun in May 1565 the scourge of Malta, **Dragut Rais**, landed in St Julian's Bay with a small armada of 15 ships and 1,500 men. At the age of 80 this old warrior was again enlisted by his old paymaster, Suleyman the Magnificent, to join in what the forces of Islam hoped would be the final annihilation of their old foe, the **Order of St John**. It was to prove one campaign too many for the man known as 'The Drawn Sword of Islam'. He was killed by a stone splinter on what is now called Dragut Point, in Sliema.

By June 1798, when **Napoleon** invaded Malta, enough time had passed for the knights to acquire dissolute and high-handed habits. His arrival literally and metaphorically obliterated their horizons with a forest of masts; 472 French ships were anchored along this coast. **General Vaubois**, Napoleon's governor designate of Malta, had an almost unopposed landing with his troops in St Julian's Bay before marching to Mdina to dine with the bishop. The fact that it took as long as 48 hours for Napoleon to extract Grand Master von Hompesch's ignominious capitulation was the only surprise. The tide turned when **Nelson** arrived to blockade the island and St Julian's became a victualling and repair base for his fleet.

## What to See

On arrival in Malta a knight was not automatically entitled to a residence in an *auberge* of his *langue* and some preferred to 'live out'. In 1688 the Italian knight Admiral Raffael Spinola built the **Palazzo Spinola** on the then-deserted hill sloping down to the bay. His great-nephew, Giovanni Spinola, a bailiff of the Order, reconstructed the Palazzo Spinola in 1733 in its present form – an

## Getting to and around St Julian's Bay and St George's Bay

St Julian's is 5 miles (8km) by **car** from Valletta via the regional road, and more than 2½ miles (4.5km) from Sliema on the coastal road; both are signposted. **Parking** can be a major problem, especially in Paceville. The Maltese exchequer receives a healthy boost from parking fines, so do not think you are safe just because the sun has set. There are car parks at **Pender Place** (just after you turn off the regional road to Paceville/St Julian's) and at the **Hilton Hotel**. Both are signposted from the regional road. The **Hotel Intercontinental** in the centre of Paceville can provide further parking.

**Bus no.62** terminates at the head of the bay, **nos.67 and 68** carry on to St Andrew's. **No.70** runs between Sliema and Buġibba along the coast road in summer.

If you get stranded, **Wembley's, t** 21 374141/ 374242, on St Andrew's Road, operates a reliable 24-hour **taxi** service.

imposing confection with a confused but elegant façade. Dwarfed by the neighbouring Hilton Portomaso Development, it now houses the offices of the **Malta International Business Association** and a Tourist Information Office. The small church of the Immaculate Conception, 250 yards away, was built in 1688 by Raffael Spinola to ease the burden of his pastoral care (Valletta was then a tiresomely long horse-ride away).

Another and much later confection is the **Dragonara Palace**, now the **casino**, on the very tip of Dragonara Point. Folklore tells that a dragon lived in the caves and hollows hereabouts, but the noises were no more than howling wind traps and the scurrilous tales of the dragon were spread by canny smugglers.

The palace was built as a summer residence for Emanuele Scicluna, a shrewd banker who was made a Marquis in 1875 on the strength of a loan to Pope Pius IX. The new Marquis, not a shy, retiring man, lived up to the motto engraved over the large stone entrance gate of his carriageway: *Deus Nobis Haec Otia Fecit* ('God made these leisures for us'). The central courtyard, now the gaming rooms, contained lush gardens, around which the interconnecting rooms of the colonnaded villa were built. A humanitarian and a hedonist, he would surely have approved of the subsequent uses of his villa as a hospital in the First World War, a home for bomb refugees in the Second World War and a casino from 1964. He would undoubtedly have disapproved of its grim ochre paintwork, the neon signs and a bizarre bottle-green statue of himself in the forecourt.

### Beaches

All along the coast from Balluta Bay to St George's Bay are **lidos**, most with concessions such as water-skiing, windsurfing, etc. Club Neptune's heated water-polo team pool in Balluta Bay is open for matches and swimming. There is a bar and restaurant. Just past the lido of the Cavalieri Hotel (presently closed) there is a small stretch of rocks to swim off. The next piece of seafront is taken up by the entrance to the Portomaso (Hilton) Marina, so to reach the next piece of public beach you have to detour inland around the Hilton. The beach club of the Westin Dragonara Resort, the **Reef Club**, is a very comfortable and popular beach, with bars, cafés and pools for children. At the head of the next bay, St George's Bay, is an 80-yard stretch of sand which should also be perfect for children. Nearer the open water is the **lido of the Corinthia Marina Hotel**, which has a great terrace on which to enjoy long cocktails.

## Festas around St Julian's Bay and St George's Bay

(i) St Julian's >
*Spinola Palace,
St George's Road,
t 23 160420*

St Julian's *festa* is on the last Sunday in August. **Our Lady of Mount Carmel** has a feast day on the last Sunday in July.

## Sports and Activities around St Julian's Bay and St George's Bay

The most popular non-water activities are in St George's Bay and are owned by the Eden Leisure Group. A sophisticated 20-lane air-conditioned **bowling alley** and huge **multiplex cinema** are the main attractions. The bowling alley can get booked up; call **t** 21 387398 to reserve a lane. For people who don't want to risk twisting an ankle or dislocating an arm, the bowling alley has a bar.

Water polo is played at the Sliema pitch beneath Il-Fortizza on the Għar id-Dud, but the neighbouring Neptunes team in Balluta Bay is the team to watch. **Oki-KO-Ki Boat Hire Co.**, Spinola Bay, St Julian's, **t** 21 375874, *tonybanis@onvol.net*. Gives water-skiing lessons and hires out small put-put boats, more powerful speedboats and rowing boats for those of a more nervous disposition.

## Where to Stay around St Julian's Bay and St George's Bay

There are already over 20 **hotels** in this area, excluding the massive **St George's Park** complex with its 965 apartments – and more have been planned. This has become 'the' area for hotel construction in recent years – and now has the highest concentration of 5-star hotels on the island. For apartments and houses to rent (or buy) recommended agencies are **Dhaha**, **t** 21 354825, *www.dhaha.com*, and Frank Salt, **t** 21 377373, *www.franksalt.com.mt*; both are in front of the Hilton Hotel on St George's Road.

**St Julian's**
**\*\*\*\*\*Hilton Hotel**, St George's Road, **t** 21 383383, *www.hilton.com.mt* (€€€€). The Hilton is part of a residential/commercial development which includes Malta's first tower and a man-made marina. The hotel has a beautiful pool area and extensive water-sports facilities, including a sailing club for children, and the excellent **Blue Elephant** Thai restaurant.

**\*\*\*\*\*Westin Dragonara Resort**, Dragonara Road, **t** 21 381000, *www.westinmalta.com* (€€€€). Built on the site of the old Dragonara Palace, the Westin Dragonara has 300 large rooms, including a highly commendable 14 with disabled facilities, and each with cable TV. There is also a health and leisure centre, a conference centre, a sunken garden, two tennis courts, three pools and a shopping promenade. Of its restaurants, **Palio's** offers decent Mediterranean fare while **Quadro** is more formal and specializes in fish. The resort also owns the **Reef Club**, a favoured old haunt for both locals and tourists alike; the **Bedouin Bar** there is a great place for meze or cocktails. The Westin Dragonara Resort also encompasses the **Dragonara Casino**. **\*\*\*\*Cavalieri Hotel**, Spinola Road, **t** 21 336255, *www.saga.co.uk* (€€€). On the spit where the bay opens to the sea, the Cavalieri can be seen from anywhere along Tower Road. Recently revamped and in a great position, it has a nice sheltered sea-swimming area. Exclusively for customers of Saga Holidays.

### Balluta

*****Le Meridien, Balluta, t 23 110000 (€€€€). Swish new hotel dwarfing the Balluta Bay, with four restaurants, four bars and a pleasant terrace.

### Paceville

You either love it or hate it here, but wherever you stay the parking will be a nightmare. If you are a light sleeper, pack earplugs, sleeping pills and a bottle of Scotch.

****Golden Tulip Vivaldi, Dragonara Road, t 21 378100, www. goldentulipvivaldi.com (€€€). On the periphery of the mess that is Paceville, opposite the entrance to the Westin Dragonara; some rooms have great sea views. Rooftop pool; parking.

***Hotel Rokna, Church Street, t 21 384060, www.roknahotel.com (€€). If you want tranquillity you should not come to Paceville, but the Rokna is a compromise with 21 rooms and a pizzeria. It is opposite an eye-poppingly hideous modern church and the car park of the Portomaso/ Hilton development (so handy, if costly, parking is easily available).

***St George's Park Complex, t 21 351147, tggroup@maltanet.net (€€). This is huge and comprises four principal buildings designed in a post-modern pastiche of cream and pastel colours. They house over 1,000 beds in different configurations, studios to penthouses; two pools, a games room, a mini-market, a hall-sized restaurant and a pub within its soulless confines.

### St George's Bay

The area is dominated by the Corinthia Beach Resort which is divided into two hotels.

*****Corinthia Marina Hotel, t 21 381719 (€€€€). This is a slightly smaller ( with a mere 200 rooms), less glamorous version of its sister hotel, the San Gorg – it feels better, though. There is a tapas bar Tapa Tapa, a wine bar Vinotheque and a café. A comprehensive kids' club operates at the Marina for children staying at the San Gorg and Marina Hotels.

*****Corinthia San Gorg Hotel, t 21 374114 (€€€€). The main part of the Corinthia. All 250 rooms have a sea view and several have facilities for disabled people. The rooms are, however, slightly on the small side. There are four restaurants, Fra Martino, Henry J Beans, Corsairs and Frejgatina (specializing in fish), all with alfresco terraces (Corsairs and Frejgatina only open in summer). There are two tennis courts, a gym and a private lido.

*****Inter-Continental, St George's Bay, t 21 377600 (€€€€). Opened in 2003, the Inter-Continental has the best conference facilities in Malta and houses another four restaurants. Although it is very grand, and has a rooftop pool garden, visitors should note that it is not directly on the seafront, and is in the middle of the noisy nightclub neighbourhood.

*****Radisson SAS Bay Point Hotel, t 21 374894 (€€€€). On a grand scale, yet the décor is surprisingly plain. All 253 rooms have large balconies but are themselves somewhat small; the junior suites don't even have sofas. Nonetheless, it provides good, slick service guided by a 'Yes, I can' mission statement. In truth, this hotel is probably more suited to businessmen than couples or families – the huge 400-seater restaurant is not the most intimate of environments and there are no dedicated disabled rooms. There is a 24-hour bistro, a compact pool and a gym.

## Eating Out around St Julian's Bay and St George's Bay

No one eats around here much before 9pm; the bars (see below) are the first port of call. Some restaurants here charge big-city prices for food which is inconsistently prepared by volatile chefs, but a smorgasbord of kitchens prove that there is life beyond pasta. In recent years, there has been an attempt to smarten up the St Julian's eating experience. The terraces of some of the principal restaurants, including San Giuliano, Caffé Raffael, Bouzouki and Dolce Vita, have been amalgamated into a rather pleasant waterfront promenade.

## St Julian's

St Julian's hosts the current crop of fashionable restaurants.

**Zest**, Hotel Juliania, **t** 21 387600 (€€€€). Stylish, Asian fusion food: expensive but worth it. In summer the tables on the terrace are lovely. *Dinner only; closed Sun.*

**Dolce Vita**, St Joseph's Street, **t** 21 337806 (€€€). It has been serving reliable Italian food for years, but stay with the fresh fish and pasta in summer, and soups and meat in winter. The bamboo-covered terrace is popular in summer, so book in advance.

**Mezè**, St George's Road (next to Labour Party Club), **t** 21 387600 (€€€). Serves food from different Mediterranean countries (Maltese, Greek, Spanish, Italian). This place has as close to a 'London' feel as you will find in Malta. *Closed lunchtime, and Mon in winter.*

**Peppino's**, St Joseph's Street, **t** 21 373200 (€€€). Opposite Dolce Vita and next to the old church is one of the perennially 'in' places for a rendezvous. On the ground floor is a wine bar with a good selection of foreign wines and a small selection of often overcooked pasta dishes; the main restaurant is upstairs. The quality of the cooking depends on how busy it is but the atmosphere never flags. Popular with the over-40s.

**San Giuliano**, 3 St Joseph's Street, St Julian's Bay, **t** 21 332000 (€€€). The proprietors were responsible for the revival of the old fishing area, and consequently the restaurant has an enviable position overlooking the bay. The standard of the Italian dishes varies according to the chef's moods and the service can be dilatory. Fish, veal and home-made *tiramisù* are good choices. Dining here during the St Julian's *festa* firework display is worth twice the bill even if the chef is crabby; access is via a spiral staircase

only. *Book weekends. Closed Sun lunch and 7–31 Jan.*

**Bouzouki**, 135 Spinola Road, **t** 21 387127 (€€). A serious Greek restaurant with spartan décor but sensible prices, and the service is efficient. The wine list, however, is disappointing and expensive. The terrace beside the new promenade is a good spot for a lingering summer lunch or dinner. Begin with mixed starters, meze, and then have properly cooked kebabs or garlicky grilled prawns. You can't smash plates to the hackneyed strains of Zorba the Greek in this establishment. There are 10 alfresco tables. *Dinner only; closed Sun.*

**Caffé Raffael**, Spinola Bay, **t** 21 352000 (€). The sister restaurant to the San Giuliano, this is close to the water's edge, and enjoying a superb position, Caffé Raffael serves pasta and pizza outside under large canvas umbrellas. The service can lag here, too, even when it is not busy, but the atmosphere in the evenings is as buzzy as the Pizza Diavola is hot.

**Papparazzi**, St George's Road, **t** 21 374966 (€). A busy ground-floor pizzeria next door to the Raffael. It serves stuffed baked potatoes and pasta as well as pizzas.

**Piccolo Padre**, Main Street, **t** 21 344875 (€). Opens onto the sea and serves crusty pizza and spicy pasta. It also has a cosy basement where you can hear the waves breaking. *Dinner only, and Sun lunchtime in winter.*

## Paceville

**Marco Polo**, Dragonara Road, **t** 21 331995 (€€€€). Oriental plate-grazing here is not a bargain, but it serves a patois of Chinese and Malay food in elegant, if characterless, surroundings.

**Tana del Lupo**, Wilga Street **t** 21 353294 (€€€). Excellent family-run Sicilian restaurant importing most of its food direct from Sicily. Sometimes accepts more customers than it can handle. *Closed Mon eve.*

**La Maltija**, Church Street, **t** 21 339602 (€€). Offers a wide range of traditional Maltese cooking at reasonable prices.

**The Avenue**, Gort Street, **t** 21 351753 (€). Popular with locals, child-friendly and excellent value but often full and can get noisy. *Closed Sun eve.*

**The Emperor of India**, Elia Zammit Street, t 21 374595 (€). On the site of the old Cossack Russian restaurant. A good Indian takeaway, with vegetable dishes and free home delivery.

**Ir-Rokna**, Church Street, t 21 384060 (€). Offers good thin-crust pizzas with quick-fire service in somewhat uninspiring surroundings. If you eat there at night, the hideous church is tastefully unlit.

# Entertainment and Nightlife around St Julian's Bay and St George's Bay

Saturday night is lemming night and Paceville is the cliff's edge off which the young population, tourists and locals, throw themselves; it is traditional in Malta to let your hair down at weekends. Bars, discos and a shoulder-rubbing vibrancy are all squeezed into this small steaming area. The social order of the island is changing and Paceville can and does explode, but on the whole the police are able to manage Latin tempers when 'boys get upset over girls'. If age is a sensitive issue, it is easy to feel like a pensioner from another planet; you don't have to be young to enjoy the activity, but it does help.

Malta has three **casinos**, one on Dragonara Point. The gaming rooms are open Mon–Thurs 10am–6am and Fri–Sun 24 hours. Entrance is Lm2 and free if you are dining in the restaurant, the Marquis Room, and for guests at the Westin Dragonara Resort. In July and August the dress code is 'smart-casual' and for the rest of the year a tie is required. The 'slots', where no dress code applies, are at the rear and the casino has a *salon privé* for the high-rolling Italians. Even for non-gamblers, the casino can seem a million miles from Paceville as it catches what little evening summer breeze there is.

 **Paceville nightlife**

## St Julian's Bay

Bars are the evening's first course, where people congregate in the balmy nights of summer to spill out on to the pavements.

**Peppino's** wine bar, for the next generation up.

**Ryan's**, above the bus terminus, an Irish pub with Guinness on tap.

**Saddles**, George Borg Olivier Street, t 21 339993. Long established, and attracts a teenage crowd to the internet wine bar on the first floor.

**The St Julian's Band Club**. Well located, with a sleepytime porch from which an older generation looks on with bemusement.

## Balluta Bay

**The Bar, Balluta Buildings**. Funky new bar open 8am till late. Serves breakfast, lunch and dinner (salads, sandwiches and daily specials). It transforms into a trendy nightspot after dark.

**Muddy Waters**, 56 Main Street. Another drinking venue popular with local 20s and 30s; it can get extremely tight and sweaty. This is a real 'guys' place with its long narrow drinking bar and CD Wurlitzer. In summer, when the place really jumps, the music lovers and drinkers often spill out onto the surrounding pavements.

## Paceville Bars

As the hours wind on, the pastel and neon décor of Paceville comes alive. A ghetto of graphically designed and evocatively named bars offer fuel for the night. The names sometimes change but the places remain the same.

**BJ's** in Ball Street is for an older crowd and has weekly jazz bands in summer.

**Fuego Salsa Bar** and **Sabor de Mexico** – popular bars with a Latin theme.

**Hacienda Bar** at Bay Street – very popular with the young university crowd.

**Qube** – very cool vodka bar.

The list of bars goes on and on, with different ones opening and closing constantly. There are also plenty of pubs, such as **O'Casseys** (bottom of the steps opposite Axis nightclub) and **Black Bull Pub**. In the summer, the **Reef Club** at the Westin Dragonara is open a few nights of the week, providing good music and bars on the beach (usually Wed and Fri), and the **Bedouin Bar** at the Reef Club is a great place for cocktails at sunset.

### Paceville Nightclubs

As with the bars, nightclubs in Paceville take turns in attracting the 'in' crowd, complete with girls dancing on the bar and sweaty crowds. Hot spots include **Places** (always heaving with people; a neon feel to it), **Eyecon** and **Axis Discotheque**, whose 'Matrix' on a Saturday night is usually packed.

# Madliena, Għargħur and Baħar iċ-Ċagħaq

On the Coast Road going towards St Paul's Bay, **Madliena** occupies the hills and valleys that form the wild sprawl of high ground in between the sea and the start of the Great Fault and the Victoria Lines. Primarily a residential community of villas for the well-heeled, neither Sliema nor Valletta are far away.

Hidden behind it is **Għargħur**, the old village of the Madliena area. The medieval village would always have been safe; the **Great Fault** is at its most impressive and impenetrable nestled between the Falka Gap and the valley, Wied id-Dis. It is another place to walk or cycle. The village keeps very much to itself, aloof in its ancestry and sealed off from outside influences. Bubbling under the seeming tranquillity is a spooky air of trespassing into the unknown. Even the name Għargħur offers a little hint: *għar* means cave and *għur* means ogre.

## Madliena and Għargħur

**Fort Madliena**, at 433ft (132m) above sea level, is an inconspicuous fort constructed by the British in 1878 to beef up the northeast flank of the Victoria Lines. Radar played a vital role in Malta's survival during the Second World War and the fort housed the main radar station. After the war NATO operated it until the British forces left in 1979. St John's Medical Corps – the last recognizable vestige of the Order – now uses the fort as its training school.

Coming from Madliena Hill, the road to **Għargħur** snakes over a defunct viaduct and up through the village's back door past an old 17th-century church. The road winds around the old fly-tipping favourites of fridges and car wrecks towards the **Great Fault**. From this belvedere the whole of the north of Malta stretches out below and it is easy to see how the landmass formed; it simply shattered in two and the hard coralline limestone falls away vertiginously beneath. The **church** is at the centre of this picturesque village, where despite numerous access roads there is a pervading sense of being cut off in time. Horse-drawn carts plod slowly through the square; trapped finches hop dementedly in minuscule cages hung from the doors of the *kaċċatur*. Old women swelter in black clothes

08

The Northeast Coast | Madliena and Għargħur

## Getting to and around Madliena, Għargħur and Baħar iċ-Ċagħaq

**Madliena** can be reached off the main Sliema–Mosta road, but the easiest route is either through St Andrew's or off the Coast Road. The main signposted turning before White Rocks is best for both Madliena and **Għargħur**. The signpost to the Madliena Cottage restaurant leads to a road – Caf Caf Lane – of suspension-destroying quality.

No **bus** would make it up Madliena Hill so the **Baħar iċ-Ċagħaq** bus 68 stops at the bottom. Nos.64, 667 and 671 terminate beforehand in St Andrew's. **Għargħur's** bus service, Nos.55 and 56, plies a tortuous route via Naxxar infrequently. The **Great Fault**, the scenery and relatively few cars have meant that fit cyclists and walkers are commonplace. There is a striking short walk along the Great Fault from the **Naxxar Gap** to Għargħur.

while they scrub the stone steps of their houses a short distance away from the **Playboy Bar**. Behind the church, in perennial shade, is the **King George VI Bar** with its classical and proud sign contrasting with the crumbling stone. The parish church of St Bartholomew has been credited to Tommaso Dingli. Work commenced in 1638 and from stylistic evidence it took 20 or more years to complete. Parish churches, apart from being the centre of their villages, are symbols of ostentation and wealth, but this church with its gloomy interior and more contemporary façade (reconstructed in 1740) is, like the village, subdued.

## Baħar iċ-Ċagħaq

**Mediteraneo Marine Park**
*t 21 372 218, www.marineparkmalta. com; open 10–5; closed Sat and Sun in winter; adm*

By the small bay of Baħar iċ-Ċagħaq, and clearly visible from the road, is the **Mediteraneo Marine Park**, where the attractions feature sea lions, reptiles, pelicans, fish and invertebrates, and offers swimming with dolphins.

During the Second World War, to be posted here as a lookout was considered a plum job: outside of the main target areas and by the cool waters. On **Qrejten Point** is another of the 13 coastal towers Grand Master de Redin constructed in 1658–9.

### *Festa* at Għargħur

Għargħur's *festa* to St Bartholomew is on 24 August or the first Sunday thereafter.

### Activities at Baħar iċ-Ċagħaq

The **beach** at Baħar iċ-Ċagħaq is not ideal, due to its proximity to the road, and the sea hereabouts is tested regularly for contamination from rubbish (so look for signs on the beach before venturing into the

water). The rock bathing is safe and the refreshment caravans attest to its popularity with the Maltese.

**Splash and Fun Park, t** 21 375021/ 374283, *www.holiday-malta.com*. Next to the Mediteraneo Marine Park Lost or damaged swimwear can be replaced at the small kiosk, and there are a café and changing rooms. A mass of chutes empty hordes of shrieking children into a deep pool. At a safe distance is a large circular swimming pool for those more interested in doing nothing. *Open from 9am.*

# The North Coast

For many thousands of visitors each year the northern coasts are much more than just another holiday destination — it is one of the Christian world's great tenets that the Apostles St Paul and St Luke were shipwrecked here, at St Paul's Bay in AD 60. There is no proof, but for the visitors and Maltese the belief remains unshakeable.

This region of inland ridges and fertile valleys was until the 18th century the island's poorest. Cut off from three-quarters of Malta by bad communications across the Great Fault, it was not really called home by anybody until around 150 years ago. The rugged open bays lay prey to any invader, from opportunistic Barbary corsairs to Napoleon. Now the shores have become Malta's costa and the armada continues, but in Boeings rather than galleys.

# 09

## Don't miss

⭐ **British bastion**
The Victoria Lines **p.169**

⭐ **Angling pursuits**
Fishing off St Paul's Islands **p.176**

⭐ **Into the depths**
Diving off Ras il-Qammieħ **p.183**

⭐ **Step back in time**
Skorba Temples **p.187**

⭐ **Lying on the ocean**
Swimming at Fomm ir-Riħ Bay **p.187**

*See map overleaf*

pp.264–5

Ahrax Point
Mġarr/Buġibba
White Tower Beach
Little Armier
Ramla Bay
Marfa Point
Ċirkewwa (Paradise Bay)
Marfa
Dahlet ix-Xilep
Il-Parsott
*M e d i t e r r a n e a n   S e a*

Ras Il-Qammieħ
Red Tower
Il-Ghadira
Mellieħa Bay
Ras il-Griebeg
Blata il-Bajda
Buġibba/Sliema

Rdum il Qammieħ
Bisqra
Il-Kortin ta' Għajn Żejtuna
Tal-Blata
St Paul's Islands
Fra Ben Tower
Qawra Point

Qammieħ Point
Popeye Village
Mellieħa
Selmun Palace
Paul's Statue
Ras il-Mignuna

Ras in-Niexfa
Anchor Bay
St Paul's Bay
Qawra
Ghallis Point
Ghallis Rocks

Ras il-Waħx
Xemxija
Rxawm Point
Rdum I-Abjad
Buġibba
Il-Ħamra
Salina Bay
Ghallis Tower

Ix-Xagħra l-Ħamra
Manikata
Pwales Beach
San Pawl Il-Baħar (St Paul's Bay)
Salt Pans
Il-Hotba I-Bajda

Ramla tal-Mixquqa (Golden Bay)
Għajn Tuffieħa
Pwales Valley
Gћejn Razul
Kennedy Memorial Grove

Il-Karraba
Il-Hotba ta'S.Martin
San Pawl Milaghi
Bur Marrad
Il-Ghadira

Ras il-Pellegrin
Gћejna Bay
Gebel Għawżàra
San Pawl Milqi

Roman Baths
Mġarr
Skorba Temples
Żebbieħ
Tal-Milord
Hal-Dragu
Fort Mosta
Naxxar Gap
San Pawl tat-Tarġa

Castello Zammitello
Ta'Hagrat Temples
Targa Gap
Tal-Wej
Il-Gwejdia

Fomm ir-Riħ Bay
L-Iskorvit
Ta'l-Abatija
Besbesija
Falka
Il-Hotba Ta'Żakkrija
Naxxar

Ras ir-Raħeb
Fomm ir-Riħ
*V i c t o r i a   L i n e s*
*Dwejra Lines*
Ta'Mlit
Mosta

Gozo
Malta

pp.192–3

## Don't miss

1. The Victoria Lines p.169
2. St Paul's Islands p.176
3. Ras il-Qammieħ p.183
4. Skorba Temples p.187
5. Fomm ir-Riħ p.187

There are few surprises or illusions along this coastline today. The *sine qua non* of the package holiday has conquered: big hotels, unedifying blocks of flats and half-built sites muscle in amid the ever-so-plausible patter of the timeshare touts. To obliterate the worst horrors you will need dark glasses and a sense of nostalgia (after all, the northern coasts always were difficult to defend). But many of the beaches have their good points, with gentle sands and coves – such as Paradise Bay and Little Armier.

# The Great Fault and the Victoria Lines

*Then cried the
soul of the stout
Apostle Paul
to God:*

*'Once we frapped
a ship, and she
laboured
woundily.*

*There were
fourteen score
of these,*

*And they blessed
Thee on
their knees,*

*When they
learned Thy
Grace and Glory
under Malta by
the sea!'*
Rudyard Kipling

🔟 Victoria Lines

Millions of years ago the Maltese islands split from Europe so that they no longer formed the final brick in the marshy landmass south of Sicily. The landmass shattered, producing a series of faults and rift valleys which tilted downhill in an easterly direction and formed the landscape much as it is today. The most serious of these is the **Great Fault** which almost bisects the island and runs from Fomm ir-Riħ in the west until it peters out in Baħar iċ-Ċagħaq, 9 miles (15km) away on the east coast. Its near-vertical face – 784ft (239m) at its highest point – means the valleys and settlements below and to the north of it have always been indefensible and expendable. Smaller faults such as Wardija, Bajda, Mellieħa and Marfa Ridges bump along less dramatically northward towards Comino.

With the arrival of the Order in 1530, warfare left the era of 'rape, pillage and enslave' and entered a more sophisticated period. The natural defence afforded by the Great Fault to the harbours, Malta's prize asset, became apparent. In the 17th century the knights began to construct entrenchments in the gaps at Bingemma, Falka and Naxxar, and a fort at Nadur ('lookout').

During the 1870s, when Malta was under British colonial rule and the rumbles between the British, French and Russian Empires continued, the defences along the Great Fault were reinforced even further. A late 19th-century engagement would involve an enemy out of sight of land armed with massive guns capable of firing shells 4 miles (7km) or more. In 1875 the construction of the three great gun-emplaced forts began at Bingemma, Madliena and Mosta. Further defences and batteries were built at Għargħur and Targa and a continuous line of coralline limestone entrenchments linked them, along practically the entire fault line. None of these defences was meant to defeat a northern invasion, simply to delay a naval assault on the harbours. In 1897 the then complete and impressive defences were officially called the **Victoria Lines**, in honour of the monarch's Diamond Jubilee.

What remains of the Victoria Lines can best be appreciated on foot, especially at the western end by Bingemma Gap. For the more slothful, any of the corkscrew hairpins that twist down the four main gaps of Bingemma, Falka, Targa and Naxxar indicate what the escarpment must have been like to an invader.

## Salina Bay

A cake-shaped sliver of that rarest of sights, an undeveloped section of the north coast, separates Salina from the *costa* that begins in Qawra and ends in Xemxija. The Sol Suncrest Hotel in

## Getting to Salina Bay

By **car**, if you are driving east towards Valletta, treat the Salina Bay corner by the Għallis Tower with caution. Although new road markings and a crash barrier have made this corner safer, lack of street lighting and high speeds result in the crash barrier being used far too often.

There are direct **buses** from Sliema, nos.652 and 645, and no.449 from Valletta.

Qawra (*see* p.178) is built on the northwest shore of the bay. The salt-making industry that had survived intermittently since Roman times switched to Salina, meaning 'saltpan', after Mellieħa was depopulated in the 16th century. Malta has always had very little exportable local produce and, in order to make such a precious commodity in quantity, Grand Master de la Valette had the original salt pans dug at the head of the bay. After the Order was sacked by Napoleon in 1798 the pans fell into disuse; in the middle of the 19th century the British reworked them.

### What to See

The **Għallis Tower** on the eastern headland, one of the 13 towers built by Grand Master de Redin between 1658 and 1659, has recently been restored. Its opposite number on Qawra Point, the **Fra Ben Tower**, now a restaurant, was built by Grand Master Lascaris some 20 years earlier; both were designed to be defended rather than being simple signalling relay stations.

The knights further improved their fortifications in the bay with the *fougasse*, a wickedly clever early mortar-cum-landmine which the British kept loaded and primed during the Second World War. It consisted of a hole, 6ft (2m) deep, dug into the living rock, at the bottom of which was placed a fused keg of dynamite. On top of this were packed sufficient rocks, bits of metal and hurtful debris to maim an entire enemy platoon. The gaping hole is still to be seen in the rocks by the entrance to the Coastline Hotel.

The inauspicious **Kennedy Memorial Grove**, an understated and simple structure, is at the head of the bay behind the saltpans. The shady grove of trees was planted in 1966 as a living memorial to JFK. The three principal species reflected the prevailing view of the man at the time: the olive represented peace, the oak strength, and the flowering oleander his love of beauty and life. On the plaque are inscribed the words 'Ask not what your country can do for you – ask what you can do for your country'.

## Where to Stay and Eat in Salina Bay

****Coastline Hotel, t** 21 573781 (€€). As its name suggests, by the coast; 211 rooms, pools and a gym.

**Fiorini D'Oro**, Naxxar Road, **t** 21 570999 (€€€). Italian restaurant serving excellent fish and pasta dishes. Just off the coast road: turn off next to the ladies selling vegetables on the roadside. *Closed Mon.*

# St Paul's Bay and Around

At the beginning of the 20th century, St Paul's Bay was a listless, peaceful fishing village with 180 inhabitants. In the few decades it has grown like a giant, unhindered, on a diet of foreign currency, to become unashamedly Malta's *costa*. It is Marbella without the crooks and Blackpool without the illuminations, where the Bognor Regis Restaurant exists happily with bumper cars, saucy postcards, pale ale and timeshares; it is basically a mass-market destination (trying ever-so-hard to be something else). Yet it does provide what is required to work off 50 weeks' tension in two – sun, sea and sex. Break out the sunscreen, shut your eyes and slab out like a seal on the rocks – the wonderful waters have escaped almost unscathed.

## History

*Then Festus, when he had conferred with the council, answered, 'Hast thou appealed unto Caesar? Unto Caesar shalt thou go.'*
Acts of the Apostles 25:12

In AD 60 the governor of Palestine, Porcius Festus, allowed Paul of Tarsus passage from Caesarea to Rome to stand trial for heresy before the Emperor Nero, and in so doing set Malta's religious destiny in motion.

In the autumn, under armed guard, the **Apostles St Paul and St Luke** sailed from Palestine for Crete, their intended refuge for the winter months. Rome, wise in the vicious winter habits of the Mediterranean, prohibited all voyages between 11 November and 5 March. But Julius, St Paul's centurion guard, wanted to press on as far eastward as possible. He was ill advised: the *gregale*, an infamous and violent northeast winter wind, struck soon after they left Crete. The storm overtook their ship and, after 14 days and nights of lashing seas and tempestuous winds, all 276 passengers and crew were shipwrecked on the northern coast of Malta.

St Luke wrote: 'And when they were escaped, then they knew that the island was called Melita. And the barbarous people shewed us no little kindness: for they kindled a fire, and received us every one, because of the present rain and because of the cold' (Acts of the Apostles, 28:1–2). The local inhabitants – St Luke uncharitably referred to them as 'barbarians' as they spoke neither Greek nor Latin – were a little bemused by their unexpected visitors; but in the chilly winter dawn they hospitably gathered wood for a large fire near the head of the bay. While building the fire, on what is today the site of the **church of St Paul's Shipwreck**, a deadly snake bit St Paul's hand. He shook it off into the flames as if swiping at an insect. Within moments this bedraggled Jew (St Paul was a short bow-legged man with thinning hair, an incongruously straggly beard and a beaked nose that lunged out from under wide bushy eyebrows) had not only survived certain death but secured himself a place in Malta's history and folklore. Local people believe that it is thanks to St Paul that there are no poisonous snakes in the

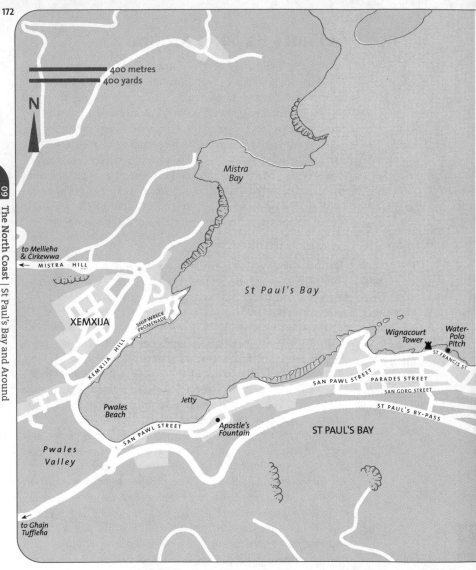

archipelago, and that the poison he took from the viper he threw into the tongues of the women, notorious for their gossiping.

**Publius**, the Roman governor of the islands, heard of St Paul's bizarre survival and welcomed him at his country villa, where today the remains of the **church of San Pawl Milqi** ('St Paul Welcomed') stand. St Paul then cured Publius's sick father at the governor's main residence, said to be the site of **Mdina Cathedral**, and converted the grateful Publius to Christianity. (Publius was subsequently to become the first bishop of Malta and then Athens; he was later martyred and canonized.) Although they were

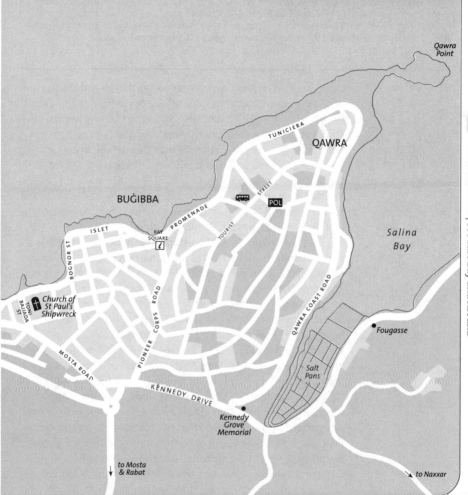

Rome's valuable prisoners, Publius allowed St Paul and St Luke three months at liberty preaching on the island. When the seas had calmed and another vessel was found, crowds of newly converted Maltese gathered to witness their departure for Syracuse and Rome, and whatever grisly fate Emperor Nero had in mind for the prisoners.

## A Catalogue of Invasions: AD 61 Onwards

Thanks to its inviting topography, St Paul's Bay was always going to be near the top of any prospective invader's list. In 1090 the Norman, **Count Roger I**, used St Paul's Bay to end 220 years of Arab

## Getting around St Paul's Bay

A **car** is a necessity, especially out of season. Valletta is about 9½ miles (16km) away. St Paul's Bay is the hub for what little cross-routing can be achieved. *See* route map, p.168. **Taxis** can be found in Bay Square, Buġibba, and in Qawra along the Coast Road fronting onto Salina Bay.

St Paul's Bay is well served by **buses**: nos.43, 44, 45, 49 and 50 from Valletta, and no.48 from Ċirkewwa. Eight buses stop in Bur Marrad, but you will need a car to get up to Wardija; no bus would make it up the hill.

occupation. A tiny Norman force landed at the head of the bay and duped the entire Arab army into rushing down from Mdina onto the plain while Roger's main army landed further westward. The **Moors** plagued the island with invasions in the early 15th century, but it was not until the mid-1400s that they arrived in earnest. Eighteen thousand of the King of Tunis's mercenaries landed along the north coasts, laying siege to Mdina. St Paul is celebrated as intervening from the heavens on a ferocious white charger. He and his horse repelled the Muslim arrows and saved the day. There is a Preti painting of this scene in Mdina Cathedral.

In 1565 the Turkish **General Mustapha Pasha** attempted a final and desperate re-invasion, after the initial evacuation of his troops following the Turks' defeat in the Great Siege. He must have pondered the grim end to an otherwise illustrious career that awaited him in Constantinople. With a demoralized force of 9,000 he marched towards Naxxar and Mdina while Admiral Piali's ships headed for St Paul's Bay. Their plan was as badly executed as the earlier siege. Mustapha Pasha's men were stopped in their tracks and retreated to St Paul's Bay. On the summer-parched Pwales Valley and the beach at St Paul's, a bloody hand-to-hand battle took place. While trying to board their ships, and survive a rearguard action in the bay's shallows, the Turks were mercilessly slaughtered by the Christian knights. Mustapha Pasha and Admiral Piali sailed off for the Levant at sunset, leaving more than 3,000 bodies to putrefy in the blood-red waters of St Paul's Bay.

The invasions paused during the Order's reign, but **Napoleon** disembarked troops here and at Mellieħa in the dead of night in June 1798. During the ensuing and ultimately successful **British naval blockade** of 1798–1800 the bay's wide mouth was, with Marsaxlokk, one of Nelson's victualling ports.

During the **Second World War**, when St Paul's was still no more than a fishing village, the RAF built a rest camp for pilots and mechanics. A few bombs from Axis bombers landed on the village, one of which obliterated the original church of St Paul's Shipwreck. After the Italian surrender in September 1943, St Paul's Bay (again with Marsaxlokk Bay) was home to the 76 warships of the defeated Italian Navy.

# Qawra, Buġibba, St Paul's Bay, Xemxija and Mistra Bay

Grand Master Alof de Wignacourt (1601–22) was a prolific builder, aided by the engineering skills of Gerolamo Cassar's son Vittorio. The **Wignacourt Tower** (1609) overlooks the northern approaches to the bay and was a prototype for the subsequent and much larger forts of St Lucien, St Thomas and St Mary's on Comino. The tower has been restored twice (the last time in 1997) and now houses a tiny local museum.

**Wignacourt Tower museum**
*check locally for times*

In the fisherman's cove of La Scaletta, 500 yards away, opposite the Il-Gillieru Restaurant at the end of Toni Bajada Street, is the chapel-like **church of St Paul's Shipwreck**. According to tradition it was on this site that St Paul and St Luke first kindled the physical and spiritual fire of 'the barbarous [Maltese] people'. A place of worship has been known to exist here since the early 14th century. Grand Master Alof de Wignacourt enlarged the church with a portico arcade on a podium. His addition of the three arches on either side, together with a tiny bell cote, give the building more gravitas, without detracting from its intimacy. A stray bomb almost levelled it during the Second World War, but it has been sympathetically restored.

What can look like just another of the many roadside shrines on the St Paul's Road near the head of the bay is in fact **Għajn Razul** (the Apostle's Fountain). Two stories are told about this shrine to St Paul: one is that he and his fellow survivors were thirsty after the shipwreck, so he struck a stone and water miraculously gushed out; the other says that he baptized the first Christians from the spring. Either way, the water is not drinkable.

Heading north out of St Paul's Bay through Xemxija is an easily missed turning for **Mistra Bay**, a secluded inlet in St Paul's Bay. Just before the turning is a weathered archway that was once the sumptuous mid-18th-century entrance to the Monte di Redenzione estates of Selmun fame. The little narrow **beach** of coarse sand and seaweed is approached through a corridor of rampant bamboo. This is not speedboat territory, and the bathing and snorkelling are good.

On the small headland in 1658, Grand Master de Redin built the **Pinto Redoubt** and in the 18th century Grand Master Pinto added a stable block for the cavalry stationed in Mdina. Today it is the home of a **fish farm**. Since its arrival in 1991 the number of hopeful fishermen sitting peacefully on their tiny stools with their 23ft (7m) bamboo rods has increased dramatically.

## Sports and Activities

The obvious aquatic variations proliferate along this coastline. A patch of smooth rocks, a bit of shade, a few cold drinks and a ladder into the water constitutes a **lido**; add somewhere to eat and you are on the way to an empire. The **Luzzu** and the **Club** in Qawra and the **New Dolmen** in Buġibba have many facilities to choose from, and are among the more popular. The best **diving** is off **Qawra Point** and around the islets of St Paul's. Many Roman anchors have been discovered in the sands off Qawra Point, the largest being over 13ft (4m) long and weighing 3½ tons. Three licensed establishments for beginners and experts are **Strand Diving** underneath the Il-Gillieru restaurant and **Maltaqua** in Mosta Road (both in St Paul's Bay) and **Subway** in Xemxija. Fishermen can cheat in Mistra Bay – escapees from the fish farm are easy prey – but fishing off **St Paul's Islands** at dusk is idyllic. **Water polo**, the summer's football, is played at the **Sirens**' team pitch, 100 yards from the Wignacourt Tower in St Gerald Street, St Paul's Bay.

 St Paul's Islands

The **Captain Morgan Underwater Safari** (*see* p.78) offers a one-hour cruise four times a day during July–August from the quay in **Buġibba** next to Bognor Beach. The glass-bottomed boat shows off what marine life there is, the remains of HMS *Kingston*, sunk during the Second World War, and the statue of the 'Seafarers' Christ', plonked on the sea bed after Pope John Paul II's visit in 1990.

# Bur Marrad and the Wardija Ridge

**Bur Marrad** is an amorphous sprawl of truck garages and houses either side of the main road that runs from St Paul's Bay to Mosta. With a couple more filling stations it would resemble a continental rest stop. **Wardija**, with no distinct village to call its own, is the limestone ridge nearest to the Great Fault and rises to 469ft (143m), lower by 6ft (2m) than the highest ridge, Mellieħa. The Wardija Ridge spans from Għajn Tuffieħa to St Paul's Bay and is the residential preserve of very-well-to-do Maltese. It is sparsely populated and a good place to amble or ramble, for more than anywhere else in Malta the air has a wild aroma all year round. The scenery is panoramic, especially when viewed from the old British gun emplacements overlooking St Paul's Bay (even Buġibba looks pleasant). Standing here, it is easy to understand how the area got its name: *wardija* means 'guard'.

## San Pawl Milqi

On the slopes of the Ġebel Għawżara hill is the partially restored church of San Pawl Milqi, *milqi* meaning received or welcomed. It is badly signposted, and then only from the Mosta direction.

Tradition states – and there is some scanty evidence to support this – that in AD 60 Publius, the island's Roman governor, had a sprawling country villa here, where he fed the two Apostles and fellow survivors of the shipwreck (see pp.49–52 and 171). A community was known to exist here from 2 BC until it was destroyed by fire early in AD 1, a date that conflicts with the tradition. The site was resettled again midway through the 4th century and the first record of a church dates back to 1488. The present structure was built around 1620.

During the First World War, British troops discovered evidence of a large stone wall but the site was not properly excavated until the 1960s. The Italian Archaeological Mission unearthed a substantial Roman settlement primarily involved in producing olive oil: stones and basins used for removing the olive stones still exist. One set of engraved symbols translated to PAULUS, another was of a man and two ships. Even so, it remains unclear whether the two saints spent their first three days here or near Tal-Ħereb in Wardija, where other scant traces were found.

The church was a vandal's playground and is now walled in; the key is available from the Museum of Archaeology or the sprightly can clamber over the east wall. Evidence of Roman ingenuity is clearly visible but expect to be a little disappointed at the poor maintenance of this important site.

## Services in and around St Paul's Bay

In Bay Square, there is an HSBC bank with a multi-currency 24-hour foreign exchange machine. **Maltacom** has two offices, in St Paul's Bay and in Qawra. The nearest **24-hour clinic** is in Mosta above the **police station**. Local **doctors** have open surgeries for minor complaints; your hotel will advise you which is the nearest.

## Festas in and around St Paul's Bay

The parish church of **Buġibba** is dedicated to **Our Lady of Sorrows**; her festa is celebrated on the last Sunday in July. The **Shipwreck of St Paul** is celebrated on the Sunday closest to 10 February with an evening procession to the church of St Paul's Shipwreck, where a bonfire is lit. On 29 June an open-air Mass is said at 6pm underneath the statue of St Paul

on **Selmunett**, the largest of St Paul's Islands.

## Where to Stay in and around St Paul's Bay

Without exception, the accommodation in this area is block-booked by major tour operators, making hotel rack-rates meaningless.

### Qawra

Driving along the Qawra Coast Road fronting onto Salina Bay, the impressive façades of the immense hotels and apartment blocks are reminiscent of old Hollywood sets.

****Canifor Hotel**, Triq in-Nakkri, t 21 582780, www.canifor.com (€€€). With just 150 rooms. Situated near Qawra's shops, bars and restaurants, it also has a restaurant and bar of its own as well as a games room, sauna, gym and heated pool.

****Hotel San Mark**, Il-Konz Street, t 21 571329 (€€€). Nearly lost in the no-man's-land that divides Qawra and Buġibba is this well-run place with 75 cosy refurbished rooms. The pool is also on the small side but is secluded behind dry-stone walls and a couple of hardy trees.

****Qawra Palace, Qawra Coast Road, t 21 580131 (€€€). A little further down from the Sol Suncrest (see below), the Qawra is not as big, a mere 389 rooms, but has the same views, pleasant rooms, two pools and a lido onto Salina Bay. The drawback is a massive restaurant which can get very busy.

****Hotel Santana, Gozo Road, t 21 583451 (€€). On the outskirts of Qawra, with 203 rooms, three restaurants and a 120-seat theatre-style conference centre. A reliable eatery, Hannibal's Restaurant, is opposite.

****Sol Suncrest, Qawra Coast Road, t 21 577101, www.suncresthotel.com (€€). One of the largest hotels in Malta and the best in the St Paul's area, with 413 rooms. It is marble-clad and swanky, but the staff have a professional and genuinely caring manner. Amenities include six restaurants, squash courts and a small gym, three pools and two lidos with their own diving school.

## Buġibba

****Dolmen Resort Hotel, Qawra Road, t 23 552355, www.dolmen.com.mt (€€€). Block after block of self-catering apartments, guesthouses and hotels are to be found here, all sub-Dallas flash with mirrored glass curves. The impressive facilities include four pools, a private lido and a huge conference hall. Nearly all of the 387 air-conditioned bedrooms enjoy excellent views, but unlike the Sol Suncrest there is an antiseptic and self-important air to the place. Looking very out of place in the garden by the pool are the remains of a prehistoric fisherman's temple. Having inadvertently damaged it (one of the blocks with a fish motif made it to the Museum of Archaeology), the hotel then took its name and logo from the trilithon entrance. The Dolmen Resort also houses a casino, the Oracle.

***Buġibba Holiday Complex, Tourist Street, t 21 580861, www.islandhotels.com (€€). This is the biggest local complex, but away from the seafront. The rooms are comfortable, the pools adequate and the shelves of the mini-market well stocked.

Buccaneers, St Anthony's Street, t 21 585324 (€). For those who loathe missing out on anything, including noise, this is the place to stay.

## St Paul's Bay, Xemxija and Mistra Bay

The accommodation here is mostly holiday apartments. Walk around and look for landlords' signs in windows or ask at a newsagent or supermarket: someone's brother-in-law will have a second cousin who knows of a cheap, clean apartment to rent.

****Gillieru Harbour Hotel, Church Square, t 21 572723, www.gillieru.com (€€€€). Quiet and modern, family-owned and built in 1994 with only 50 generous rooms on the water's edge, this has the facilities you would expect: large balconies, a roof pool, two restaurants and a very personal air. Make sure you ask for a room facing the bay; the ones that don't front onto Church Square and its restaurants.

Xemxija, meaning 'sunny place', is on the north side of the bay and has limited hotel accommodation.

***Ambassador, Shipwreck Promenade, t 21 573870, www.ambassadormalta.com (€€). On the waterfront is this peaceful hotel with soporific views, which is contracted out exclusively to Thomson's Holidays.

# Eating Out in and around St Paul's Bay

## Qawra

Qawra has a couple of good restaurants.

Gran Laguna, Qala Street, t 21 571146 (€€€). This tiny restaurant, above the briny saltpans of Salina, looks as if it has been created out of the Sicilian owner's sitting room. Far more attention has been paid to the predominantly Sicilian menu than the décor, and the fish is invariably well cooked. *Open for lunch and Sun eve; closed Wed and 23 Dec–10 Jan.*

**Savini**, Qawra Road, **t** 21 576927 (€€€). Overlooks the Kennedy Grove. The décor is Laura Ashley twee, and the food is good but can be fussy – their speciality a surf 'n' turf of steak covered in a lobster sauce. Food is always prepared to order. Be patient. *Open for dinner only.*

## Buġibba

One of the few restaurant foods that has more profit in it than pizza is ice cream, and Buġibba is overflowing with both.

Needless to say, fast food and 'with chips' eateries abound, as well as numerous bars including **Caesars** and the **Miracles Bar** in Bay Square and the intriguingly named **Big Bum** in Tourist Street.

**The Grapevine**, Pioneer Road, **t** 21 580625 (€€€). Trattoria-style restaurant serving good Mediterranean food at fairly reasonable prices.

**Peking**, Tourist Street, **t** 21 573114 (€). Decorated in a pseudo-Cantonese style, the Peking offers a welcome gastronomic break. It is large and buzzy, and the food can be erratic, but it is worth a visit.

## St Paul's Bay, Xemxija and Mistra Bay

**The Admiral**, Main Street, St Paul's Bay, **t** 21 571360 (€€€). Small family-run restaurant serving French/Italian food.

**Nostalgia**, Mosta Road, St Paul's Bay, **t** 21 576887 (€€€). On the main road going into St Paul's Bay, this is a large and rather gloomy restaurant, but it serves good fish and meat dishes.

**Palazzo Santa Rosa**, Mistra Bay, **t** 21 582736 (€€€). This is huge and on the beach, but in no way dominates this sometimes tranquil bay. Sympathetically built in local stone, it boasts two different dining areas under a tall palm and a couple of old squat olive trees. The food is the usual Italo-Maltese but with lighter grub at lunchtime. The more formal restaurant is only open in the evening, except for the ubiquitous

Sunday lunch. *Book in high summer. Closed Mon.*

Down by the sea and clustered around the church of St Paul's Shipwreck are three good and very different eateries worth seeking out. (however, do note that parking can be a problem here.)

**Il-Gillieru**, **t** 21 573480 (€€€). The oldest, built over the water and with its own jetty to which boats can be tied in summer. Not surprisingly, this restaurant specializes in fish; it is huge, and can take itself a little too seriously. Don't expect the throb of a continental atmosphere, but the lapping sea and the views are hard to beat; come here on business, or a special occasion.

**Da Rosi**, **t** 21 571411 (€€€). Opposite, a small, narrow restaurant that attracts a younger set who crowd it out in summer. The pasta is good and the plain grilled meats are well prepared. This is a place for a date. *Dinner only, Mon–Sat.*

**Macedonia**, **t** 21 573391 (€). Next door, very popular with the locals for its good crusty pizza, but the pasta is invariably overcooked. It can hop late in the evenings and at weekends, and there is a bar where you can wait for your table.

# Nightlife in and around St Paul's Bay

In the summer this part of the island has a nightlife to equal that in Paceville. Most of the later bars and clubs are located in Buġibba.

**Flamingo Bar** is owned by a keen skydiver, so anyone with interests in that direction should head here for a drink.

The **Heritage Pub** has great live music, while the **Oceanic Bar and Grill** has 'Coyote Ugly'-style dancers.

Other popular bars are **Rookies** (sports events and live music), **Fuego Salsa Bar** and **Miracles Bar** (in the main square).

The two main nightclubs are **Caesars** and **Amazonia** (on the beach opposite the Dolmen Resort Hotel, *summer only*).

# West of St Paul's Bay

## Mellieħa and Mellieħa Bay (Il-Għadira)

*Qisu mill-ayrax tal-Mellieħa. (He comes from the wilds of Mellieħa.)*

Maltese insult said of an uncouth man

Mellieħa is a craggy and picturesque hilltop town with bewitching cave dwellings and houses that cling like limpets to the rock face. It has a comparatively modern street plan, with none of the haphazard charm of the southwest, but Mellieħa has its own different and more affluent appeal.

The village was built on top of the Mellieħa ridge as one of the 10 original parishes of 1436, and was entirely depopulated within 100 years, because of the indefensibility of the northern shores against the itinerant corsair slave-traders. The mainstay salt industry collapsed – the word *mellieħa* roughly translates as someone who makes or deals in salt – and was not finally resettled until the 1840s under the safety of the British umbrella. Today, with a total of around 4,750 people, the population is equal to that of St Paul's Bay.

**Mellieħa Bay** is the largest sandy beach in the Maltese islands, and is located a mile (1.5km) down the ridge and out of town. The gently shelving approach to the water makes it ideal for children, and unlike some of the northwest beaches there are no dangerous undercurrents to contend with. Unfortunately there are the inevitable crowds in peak season and at weekends, and a busy road which runs parallel to the beach. In all weathers, the bay is very popular with windsurfers. It is also known as Il-Għadira, meaning 'the swamp', as it once was. The marshy land behind the road is now a much-needed wildlife preserve.

### History

Mellieħa Bay, with its wide mouth and shallow sea, has always been a natural place to land, and not just for invading corsairs. A theory put forward in 1952 by the precise-minded Professor Burridge states convincingly that **St Paul** fetched up here, and not on the rocks of St Paul's Bay. The many Roman wrecks discovered in Mellieħa Bay seem to add weight to his contention.

On 7 September 1565, in the very last hours of the **Great Siege**, Don Garcia of Toledo, the Spanish viceroy of Sicily, disembarked his long overdue 8,000-strong relief force. After a bloody battle in the shallows of neighbouring St Paul's Bay, the battered remains of the Turkish army fled back to Constantinople to face the Sultan's wrath.

**Napoleon** chose Mellieħa Bay as one of his seven points of invasion in June 1798, when General d'Hilliers and his troops marched up the beach. Over a century later, and almost as an

## Getting around Mellieħa

Since the bypass around Mellieħa to Ċirkewwa (signposted at the main roundabout) was opened in the 1980s, much less traffic has ploughed up and down Mellieħa's snaking roads. The road to Mellieħa itself is well signposted from St Paul's Bay, 3 miles (4.5km) away; allow 25–30 minutes if travelling from Valletta by **car** and much longer by **bus**. In this split-level village, none of the public services is grouped together.

The **bus terminus** is in the shady 26 May 1990 Square next to the Sanctuary of Our Lady of Mellieħa, and a snoozing **taxi**-driver is never far away. Buses nos.43, 45, 48 and 645 serve both Mellieħa and the beach.

afterthought, the **British** built 150ft (45m) of slit trenches below the western ridge of the town overlooking the bay. During the **Second World War** the limestone caves in the ridge's face were used as bomb shelters.

### Sights Around Mellieħa

**Selmun Palace**
*usually open weekends*

**Selmun Palace** is an eye-catching castle perched at the top of Mellieħa ridge, and clearly visible along most of the northeast coastline. The land upon which it was built was given to Monte di Redenzione degli Schiavi, a charitable organization established in 1607 under the patronage of Grand Master Alof de Wignacourt to ransom enslaved Christians. The palace itself was constructed in the mid-18th century by Domenico Cachia to imitate, but not mock, the Verdala Palace; despite its Baroque features, such as the elaborate balcony, it still has a castle's robustness. The escutcheon above the entrance is that of the Redenzione and nearby is the aptly named chapel of **Our Lady of Ransom**.

**Our Lady of Ransom**
*usually open weekends*

In Mellieħa the parish church of **Our Lady of Victory** is a gloomy, cumbersome early 20th-century edifice with a beacon-like position in a benchless corridor of a square. Inside is a stirring painting by Giuseppe Cali of *The Shipwreck of St Paul.*

**Shrine of Our Lady of Mellieħa**
*open daily*

Of much more interest is the chapel of the **Shrine of Our Lady of Mellieħa**, situated near the parish church off the main street in 26 May 1990 Square (renamed after the day Pope John Paul II visited the sanctuary). This domed little building, the oldest Marian shrine in Malta, was once the original parish church. Legend says it was built on the site of a cave-church visited by St Paul and St Luke and that the faded icon of the Madonna above the altar was painted by St Luke, an unlikely supposition. Everything about it is friendly and uplifting. Inside is a tiny museum with hundreds of votive offerings. These range from the frankly absurd – a signed picture from Norwich City Football Club thanking the church for its Second Division championship in 1972 – to heart-rending prayers of thanks. A display of memorabilia from Pope John Paul II's visit is behind a screen; you can even buy souvenirs with his Holiness stamped on them. For an example of the simple power of faith, visit the **Grotto**, a cave-shrine dedicated to the Madonna. The entrance is on the road opposite the steps that lead down from the square. You descend about 70 steps to reach an underground spring at the heart of the cave. The waters are said to have miraculous powers to heal the diseases of children, and the rock walls are covered with votive gifts.

# The Marfa Peninsula: Paradise Bay, Ċirkewwa, Ramla and Armier

This is an isolated part of the island, and unless you are staying at one of the two hotels, the main reason for coming here is to catch the Gozo ferry. It gets extremely crowded at weekends, but on the plus side there is excellent diving and the mini-cliffs at Aġmar are usually pleasantly peaceful.

### Marfa and the Red Tower

Marfa, meaning 'landing place', is a 4-mile (7km) stretch of hard coralline limestone and maquis. Permanently uninhabited, it has mainly been used as a signalling outpost. Some of the redoubts, entrenchments and towers that deterred a catalogue of prospective invaders still exist.

**St Agatha's Tower** or the **Red Tower** commands the high ground on Marfa ridge. The huge, forbidding and somewhat faded terracotta-coloured fort was built by Grand Master Lascaris and became operational in 1649. The tower's size and position gave it a dual role: not only a defence but also a signalling link between the towers on Gozo and St Mary's on Comino which ultimately led to Valletta. A brief but spirited defence was put up by the 49-strong garrison when the French landed in 1798 and the British employed it as a signalling station during the last war. Today two men monitor local shipping from it, and visits are at their discretion.

### Beaches

The beaches are sandy coves, and sometimes seaweed traps. The best two are **Little Armier** – signposted Ray's – and **Paradise Bay**, accessed via a steep flight of steps. White Tower beach is crowded and unclean while the tower itself is private and guarded by a pack of savage dogs. Ramla is reasonable, although it does seem to catch a swell, and Armier Bay is simply untidy. In midweek the current through the Comino Channel keeps the sea clean and makes the coast ideal for snorkelling, diving and rock fishing.

Avoid all the beaches here at weekends and public holidays, when the Maltese invade. On the northwest coast, undercurrents can become strong after bad weather.

# Getting to and around Ċirkewwa

By **car** the journey time to Ċirkewwa should be 35 minutes from the Sliema area, and 45 from Valletta; follow the signs for Mellieħa and then Ċirkewwa. On a hot August day the **bus** journey can be a sweltering hour-long trip. **Taxis** are always at the landing, but be prepared to be held to ransom; here there really are two different prices. It is a tourist rip-off at Lm10–Lm12 from the Valletta area. At the **Marfa** landing, 'Gozo Charlie' operates a regular and reliable service to **Comino's Blue Lagoon** on the unregal *Royal 1*. A placard next to the fruit vans in Xemxija will alert you to any delays on the **Gozo ferry**. Arrive at Ċirkewwa 30 minutes before the scheduled departure time in summer, the system is first come first on.

You are not allowed to miss the **Popeye Village**, so the signposting is good from both Mellieħa and Għajn Tuffieħa. The nearest **bus** stop is at Mellieħa Bay from which it is a 1-mile (1.5km) walk west.

## Activities

The shape of the promontory means that whichever way the wind and sea are going you can **dive** here. Ċirkewwa has a cliff-dive down to 100ft (30m) off the point and is popular with photographers. The caves beneath the cliff are home to groupers and other fish. A good beginner's dive is **Ahrax Point**, the northern tip of Malta. The water goes down to 33ft (10m), below which is a reef full of marine life and a cave. Not-so-ace speedboat drivers like to cut this point very fine, so take a marker buoy. The boulder-strewn shoreline of **Ras il-Qammieħ** round the Ċirkewwa headland is accessible only by boat and has an exposed cave dive.

**✪ Ras il-Qammieħ**

## Anchor Bay, or Popeye Village

**Popeye Village**
*t 21 524782,*
*www.popeyemalta.com;*
*adm, children*
*under 12 free*

This was the prettiest and the smallest bay in Malta until 1979 when the director Robert Altman recreated Sweethaven here and scarred it indelibly with Hollywood's leaden boot. Neither Robin Williams as Popeye nor the world's cinema-going public liked *Popeye, the Movie*; the film sank quicker and deeper than the Roman anchors from which the bay takes its name. Sadly, it will be known as Popeye Village until Hollywood makes a sequel in which Bluto wins the hand of Olive Oyl and destroys Sweethaven in a genuinely heroic act of revenge.

The whole place is too ghastly for words. Faceless amusement-arcade bodies of Popeye, the Oyl Family (Olive, Castor et al.) and the rest of the cast accompany a shed full of tacky souvenirs, but sadly no spinach stall.

In the old cartoons, Sweethaven looked like a gaggle of clapboard houses built in a topsy-turvy and lean-to manner by a team of short-sighted, drunk or incompetent carpenters. It does in reality too. The village was built in seven months and was designed to stand for a further eight months. That was nearly 30 years ago. To depress matters further, an awful rudimentary Soviet-era-style 'fun park' has been added. To be fair, though, they have spent a lot of effort of late on improving the entertainment (*see* p.78).

Fortunately, the tissue-sized beach of coarse sand has been left alone. Lie there and try to imagine what the Romans would say if they travelled forward in time to collect their lost anchors.

## Għajn Tuffieħa and Golden Bay

A headland separates the two popular sandy beaches of **Għajn Tuffieħa** ('the spring of the apples', so named after an underground spring) and **Ramla tal-Mixquqa** (unimaginatively called 'Military Bay' under the British and now, with an equal disregard for reality, referred to as Golden Bay). Both beaches lie at the northwestern end of the Pwales Valley, 3½ miles (6km) from St Paul's Bay and in between the Wardija and Bajda ridges. Thousands of years ago the greater part of the valley was under water, but today it is the most fertile valley in Malta and is cropped all year round.

On the eve of the Great Siege in May 1565, the Turkish fleet anchored and watered its ships in Għajn Tuffieħa prior to their invasion at Marsaxlokk. Grand Marshal Copier, in command of the Order's cavalry squadron, must have wondered how long it was for this world as he helplessly watched the armada of 181 vessels, packed with Muslim soldiers, approaching.

During the Second World War, Għajn Tuffieħa Bay was used as a training ground for the naval canoeists who would eventually provide vital information for the Allied invasion of Sicily. In **Golden Bay** the British built an unattractive military camp (which is now the greatly improved Ħal Ferħ Holiday Village) and a naval rifle range.

### Note

When the weather is, or has been, rough, there can be a dangerous undertow on both of these beaches, which has been known to exhaust even strong swimmers. In the high summer, bouts of sea pollution have been known to occur here (as they do elsewhere in Malta; see 'A Few Words of Caution', p.87).

### Activities

The bays along this coast are sheltered from the prevailing northeast summer wind so at weekends and public holidays the commonest sight is flesh in shades varying from lobster-pink to coconut-brown. All water sports from a sedate pedalo to the irksome jet-ski are available on both beaches, but Golden Bay beach offers more variety. If you are getting fed up with sandcastles, there is horse-riding at **Golden Bay Horse Riding**.

Off-road **walking** is a popular recreation and to the north the tracks will ultimately feed you into Mellieħa via the hamlet of

**Golden Bay Horse Riding**
**t** 21 573360

## Getting to Għajn Tuffieħa and Golden Bay

The easiest route is along the valley floor from St Paul's Bay. For **Golden Bay** turn right after about 3 miles (5km) and for **Għajn Tuffieħa** continue straight on for another 500 yards. Golden Bay has a large car park with a **taxi rank** and easy access to the beach. The **buses** run frequently in summer, less so in winter, and the service ends before dusk. Għajn Tuffieħa has a much smaller rough patch of rock that doubles as a **car park** in front of the shell of the Lascaris watchtower (1637). The Għajn Tuffieħa **bus terminus** is in the Golden Bay car park. You can reach the beach by boat or a long swim round the headland. From the land, it is only accessible via a couple of hundred steps cut into the rock.

---

**Roman Baths**
*someone can show you around, usually Mon–Sat 10.30–4, Sun 12–2, but dependent on the weather; leave a tip*

Manikata. The modern church was designed by Richard England after the style of 1930s architecture as an imaginative complement to the low-built local farmsteads. The red and white fairy lights that adorn its edges are the villagers' experiment. The southern and rougher cliff track leads on to the Ġnejna Bay area (*see* below).

On the road to Mġarr, about 1 mile (1.5km) away, are the **Roman Baths**. Having been discovered in 1929 by farmers, and excavated in the same year, the baths were restored again in 1961 by UNESCO. The setting, with its tangled prickly pears and vegetation, is particularly striking.

Bathing was an integral part of Roman culture and the 'spring of the apples' would have been the nearest plentiful water supply to Mdina/Rabat. The sparse remains demonstrate how sophisticated the Romans and their engineering were; with changing rooms, U-shaped communal lavatories, a small swimming pool, a *caldarium* built above a small furnace, a *tepidarium*, and the final and inevitable *frigidarium*. The best-preserved of the mosaics are to be found in the changing rooms and in the *tepidarium*, and the whole complex is flash with ingenious design.

# Mġarr and Ġnejna Bay

The village of **Mġarr** at the top of the **Ġnejna Valley**, in between the Victoria Lines and the Wardija Ridge, is not to be confused with the harbour of the same name in Gozo. Settled only in the 1850s, it is an undecided little place of 2,400 people, known for its agriculture and for being the Land-Rover capital of Malta. The villagers are to be seen either dismantling trashed gearboxes and engines or lugging crates of tomatoes to market (*mġarr* can also mean 'marketplace').

Mġarr and the sandy beach at Ġnejna Bay were loved by Admiral Sir William Wordsworth Fisher (the poet's grandson) and Sir Harry Luke (lieutenant governor of Malta from 1930 to 1938). Their affection for the place was reciprocated: both had a street named after them.

## Getting to and around Mġarr and Ġnejna Bay

From St Paul's Bay the **road** is signposted to Għajn Tuffieħa and forks left for Mġarr; alternatively the route is west from Mosta and Rabat. The no.47 **bus** does not go on to Ġnejna Bay. The bus stop is to be found next door to the police station.

The **Skorba Temples** are located down a path on the left on the Għajn Tuffieħa road, and are poorly signposted.

### Mġarr

You cannot miss the **Egg Church**, as it has always and will always be known. The nickname for the Church of the Assumption was earned in a true tale that illustrates the devoutness of Maltese Christian faith.

In the 1930s Father Salmone, Mġarr's charismatic parish priest, whipped up support from the impoverished villagers for a new church to be built out of the produce of the land. Every week each villager delivered eggs or vegetables for him to sell, the proceeds going into the building fund. The church took many years to build and the large dome and the tiny cupola, resembling an egg in a cup, serve as a permanent reminder of its origins. The last detail, made when both funds and farmers were exhausted, was the painted second clock, its hands steadfastly fixed at 15 minutes before the devil's hour of midnight – in such a devout village, this is surely an unnecessary superstition.

**Ta'Hagrat Temples**
*keys at the Museum of Archaeology in Valletta*

The Ta'Hagrat Temples, 100 yards from the police station, are historically significant but not much to look at, and are only of interest to the very archaeologically minded. The fenced-in site was first excavated in 1925. The remains hint at two temples, one large and one small on either side of a small courtyard, dating back to the Ġgantija and Saflieni phases respectively.

**Castello Zammitello** on the Ġnejna road was built in the early 19th century as the delightful honeymoon lodge of the noble Sant Cassia family. After the unsolved and mysterious murder of the Count Sant Cassia on the Castello's doorstep in 1989, the family not surprisingly sold up. Ironically, the Castello has now been converted into a wedding hall.

### Ġnejna Bay

Ġnejna Bay is known as Mġarr's beach and is signposted 2 miles (3km) west out of Mġarr past Castello Zammitello. The road plunges into a 20° gradient, which is murder on foot, especially on the way back up. There is a car park of sorts at beach level but no bus service. The **sandy beach** is ideal for children, and the arc of boathouses hollowed into the soft limestone cliff face adds to the charm of this naturally pretty but sometimes crowded bay. Above are the remains of the **Lippia Tower**, one of four similar watchtowers built by Grand Master Lascaris in 1637. Out of season, on warm, calm days, it is a tranquil and often empty spot.

Beyond the refreshment caravan and around the rocks to the right towards the bulbous flat-topped headland of **Il-Karraba** is a secluded area of smooth rocks which serves as one of the island's few overtly gay bathing areas.

## Żebbieħ and the Skorba Temples

Żebbieħ is a nondescript place whose couple of hundred inhabitants would surely have slunk into Mġarr, less than half a mile (1km) away, were it not for tradition and the important **Skorba Temples**.

🖈 Skorba Temples

The fabric of the ancient Skorba Temples has fragmented badly, but their history remains intact. Skorba's importance lies in filling in hitherto well-kept secrets in the calendar of Malta's prehistory, specifically the pre-Copper Age. Together with Ġgantija they are believed to be the oldest freestanding structures in the world.

The complex was uncovered by the archaeologist David Trump during his excavations in 1966. Evidence in the shape of a wall told of a prehistoric village on the site. Further evidence of human habitation, livestock and crops were found and carbon-dated back to the earliest prehistoric phase, the Għar Dalam.

In the middle of the site are the flattened stones of a three-apse temple from the Ġgantija phase. The floors made of *torba* – a crushed compound of limestone and water and still in use today – can be seen, as can one eroded megalith approximately 11ft 6in (3.5m) tall.

**Red Skorba** and **Grey Skorba** are the names given to Neolithic periods and corresponding pottery, fragments of which are on display in the Museum of Archaeology, where the keys to the site are available.

## Fomm ir-Riħ

🖈 Fomm ir-Riħ

Fomm ir-Riħ is basically an almost inaccessible bay, one of the most beautiful and the last remaining undeveloped bay in Malta. Clear azure waters, good snorkelling (and a dive for skilled divers off the point of Ras ir-Raħeb), deserted rocks and stunning sunsets are all on offer. The cliffs and the headland of Ras Il-Pellegrin are praised by walkers, picnickers and doe-eyed lovers.

The only approach to the gravelly foreshore, other than by boat, is by means of a very tricky footpath that was cut into the rock face by the ex-prime minister, Dom Mintoff. He obviously liked to flirt with his own mortality, because he used to ride his horses along this extremely narrow path at the weekends. He survived the experience – therefore his equestrian skills must have equalled his political nous.

The point of **Ras ir-Raħeb** marks the southeast tip of the beautiful, if exposed, bay of Fomm ir-Riħ. There are very few inhabitants in the triangle of land north of Dingli and south of Rabat. This is languid rural Malta. Old ladies sit under the sparse shade of a tree while their precious goats chomp away on grass and wild red flowers. The men work the fields' thin brown topsoil with hoes as their lazy *tal-feneks* (rabbit or pharaoh hounds) snooze nearby. The crops and tiny vineyards are ambushed by the sinister shadows of prickly pears, thoughtless fly tipping and encroaching wild bamboo before the harder coralline limestone and sweet-smelling maquis nearer to Dingli take over.

The empty quiet spaces and opportunities for peaceful walks are the main reason for venturing to these parts, but it is also the only way down to the bay of Fomm ir-Riħ. Off the point of Ras ir-Raħeb, only accessible by boat, there is a tricky dive site for the experienced. The road to the point and the small car park for Fomm ir-Riħ runs through the village of Baħrija, once the site of a fortified village in 800 BC. Out from underneath the southern walls of Rabat, the road runs past a sign for the distinctly unimpressive Chadwick Lakes and on into the village, where you would think you were south of the Mexican border as the poor road surrenders to a wide dust bowl.

By car, the terrible road to the footpath goes through Baħrija and is about 4½ miles (7.5km) from Rabat. For those who suffer from major (or even minor) bouts of vertigo and don't fancy the footpath, the clifftop of Fomm ir-Riħ can only be approached by an even worse track that branches left off the Mosta–Mġarr road half a mile (1km) before Żebbieħ. There are no facilities in the area. Do not be deterred by the bay's name – Fomm ir-Riħ means 'mouth of the wind'.

## *Festas* West of St Paul's Bay

On 8 September there is a national holiday to celebrate the end of both **Great Sieges**.

Mellieħa's *festa* is the **Birth of the Blessed Virgin**, on the first Sunday in September.

Mġarr's *festa* is the **Assumption**, which is held on 15 August.

## Where to Stay West of St Paul's Bay

### Mellieħa
****Mercure Selmun Palace**,
t 21 521040, *www.mercure.com* (€€€).
At the main roundabout just before Mellieħa town. Owned by Air Malta, this discreet and well-run hotel is a favourite with those who like a more hushed poolside environment. Set in the palace grounds, the hotel's 150

rooms are big on modern comforts but short on soul (near to the pool there is a sign that forbids early-morning reservation of sun loungers, which may bring a smile to some faces).

****La Salita**, Main Street, **t** 21 520923, *www.mariteammalta.com* (€€€). In Mellieħa itself, it would be hard to miss the modern 'Ascent'. This hotel, where you are a 'patron' rather than a 'guest', is a garish toothpaste blue; its 65 well-equipped rooms are decorated in unflattering pastel hues. Décor aside, there is a tinkling piano at weekends and the rooftop pool has a good view.

***Panorama**, off Valley Road, **t** 21 521020 (€€). A small, quiet place on the edge of town, popular with the British, and balanced almost on the ridge itself with an uninterrupted view of the bay.

### Mellieħa Bay

****Mellieħa Bay Hotel**, **t** 21 573841, *www.melliehabayhotel.com* (€€€). On the north side is this uninspired piece of late-1960s architecture, where the rooms are somewhat tired and the lobby and coffee shop poky, but the location scores a lot of points. All 302 rooms have uninterrupted sea views. The garden runs almost to the water's edge and there is a very good range of facilities for water sports and children.

****Seabank Hotel**, Marfa Road, **t** 21 521460, *www.seabankhotel.com* (€€€). Located on the south side of the bay, and offering facilities for the disabled. The 180 generous and calmly decorated rooms are air-conditioned, and have decent balconies. There is a pool and it is one minute from the beach and, unfortunately, the road.

*** Mellieħa Holiday Centre**, Għadira Bay, **t** 21 573900, *wwwmhc.com.mt* (€€€). Just behind the Mellieħa Bay road you'll find this excellent Danish-owned complex offering 150 two-bedroom bungalows set in manicured gardens thick with butterflies. There are a big children's adventure playground, a good restaurant, a decent pool and a private tunnel

giving access to the beach, as well as a well-stocked supermarket to ease self-catering worries.

### The Marfa Peninsula

****Paradise Bay**, Ċirkewwa, **t** 21 521166, *www.paradise-bay.com* (€€€). Constructed in a curved sweep to give every room a view of the snug bay and its fish-shaped pool. Through a short tunnel it has a private beach for water sports. The hotel is self-contained with squash and tennis courts and recreational facilities for children, much needed in this cut-off end of the island.

****Ramla Bay Resort**, Marfa, **t** 21 522181 (€€€). A small hotel with more amenities than the rating would indicate, but rather worn out. Try to arrive at night or the ghastly approach road (no fault of the hotel) might make you turn and flee. The pleasant beach lido and pool are open to non-residents.

## Eating Out West of St Paul's Bay

### Mellieħa

Coming into Mellieħa, by the main roundabout is the **Belleview**, a long-established and massive bakery with excellent substitutes for overpriced and indifferent beach food; it is also a good pit stop if you are returning from Gozo in the small hours.

**The Arches**, 113 Borg Olivier Street, **t** 21 523460 (€€€). Smartly dressed staff lead you up a curving staircase to a large and sometimes noisy restaurant. It is a little starchy, but a worthwhile treat. Stay with the pasta or the fresh fish. *Dinner only; closed Sun.*

**Giuseppe's**, 8 St Helen Street, **t** 21 574882 (€€€). Mellieħa's best. His kitchen can be relied upon to create imaginative food from a menu that varies according to his mood and available produce. A small place with a wine-bar feel downstairs, and a more intimate atmosphere upstairs. *Dinner only (booking essential); closed Sun and Mon.*

**Il Mithna**, 454 Borg Olivier Street, **t** 21 520404 (€€). Built in a 17th-century windmill of dark weathered stone. The menu is simple and unfussy but the service is sound.

**Ix-Xatba Restaurant**, Marfa Road, **t** 21 521753 (€). Good fish and local dishes, this offers conspicuously good value for money. *Dinner only; closed Sun and Mon.*

**La Rampa**, **t** 21 520610 (€). For the more cosmopolitan palate, 50 yards away from the Rover's Return. Omelettes, salads, pizzas and Italian coffee are competently cooked and served, both inside and out.

**Rover's Return**, 4 St Anne Street, **t** 21 520921 (€). At the top of steep Borg Olivier Street, in a far more imposing building than its UK counterpart. No prizes for guessing the house style, but the kitchen produces reliable fare.

None of the many restaurants and snack bars on Mellieħa Bay beach is noteworthy, but you could try the **Great Dane** or **The Pizzeria**, **t** 21 573116 (€), both at the Seabank Hotel. They serve crusty pizzas and especially fine seafood ones. Both are open for lunch and dinner every day.

### The Marfa Peninsula

**The Beachcomber**, Armier Bay (€). A conventional beach establishment, but the fish and the salads are always fresh and the beer ice-cold.

**Ray's Lido**, Little Armier (€). You will need dark glasses at Ray's. Painted snow-white, not even the big square canvas umbrellas are able to dull the glare of the Mediterranean sun. You can eat either inside or outside. The excellent, home-made, grilled Maltese sausages are definitely not for the health-conscious.

### Golden Bay

**Apple's Eye**, Golden Bay, **t** 21 573359 (€). The 'Great British Breakfast' as interpreted in the car park is cooked until 1pm every day. Lunch is in a similar vein.

### Mġarr

**Charles Restaurant**, 10 Jubilee Esplanade, **t** 21 573235 (€). Located opposite the church, one of the places for *fenkata* (*see* p.56) in Malta, and well worth going out of your way for. Here it is bunny, bunny and more bunny; choose the pasta with rabbit sauce, the rabbit stew with garlic and white wine, or other local dishes. On Saturdays be prepared for noise, bustle and the all-permeating aromas of a Maltese kitchen. This one is not to be missed.

**The Sunny Bar**, Jubilee Esplanade, is a nice place to sit on the west-facing steps at sunset.

**Victor's Bakery** by the Ġnejna road will provide the basics for a picnic.

### Baħrija

**North Country Bar and Restaurant**, **t** 21 456688 (€). On the north side of the village. Should you want horse meat, they prefer reservations, 24 hours in advance (cash only). If you don't, however, there is a good choice of rabbit, steak or fish. A bottle of Baħrija wine, non-vintage, will cost you very little (the nearby vineyards are a great comfort after the first few glasses). *Open Tues–Sat for dinner, and Sun lunchtime.*

If you only want a cold drink, the **New Life Saloon** is opposite.

# The Southwest Coast

*The southwest is a friendly area with a slow tempo, somewhere to picnic, walk or simply daydream. The landscape is too wild and too lunar for concerted tourism, and that is its charm, being disconnected from the air-conditioned hullabaloo of the northern shores; one small 'aparthotel' is the sum total of the accommodation available. Yet the area has more than its share of interesting places to visit and things to do, including Dingli Cliffs, the Verdala Palace, two prehistoric sites, a forcefully extravagant Baroque church and a seductively charming medieval one. You can take a luzzu ride to the Blue Grotto or a stroll around the mysterious pattern of limestone ruts known as 'Clapham Junction'.*

# 10

## Don't miss

**1** Malta's high points
Dingli Cliffs **p.194**

**2** Baroque splendour
Church of St Nicholas, Siġġiewi **p.199**

**3** Cave swimming
Għar Lapsi **p.200**

**4** Prehistoric stunners
Ħaġar Qim and Mnajdra **p.200**

**5** Medieval evocations
Two churches at Ħal Millieri **p.206**

*See map overleaf*

# The Southwest Coast

Ras ir-Raheb

Fomm ir-Rih Bay

V i c t o r i a       L i n e s

Dwejra Lines

Bingemma Gap

Il-Blata

Baħrija

Ghemieri

Chadwick Lakes

Mtarfa

Mdina

National Stadium

Rdum tal-Vigarju

Tal Merħia

Is-Sikka

Is-Swatar

Hal Bajjada

Rabat

Ras id-Dawwara

Ta'Gfien

Rdum Depiro

Dingli

Verdala Palace

Buskett Gardens

Magdalena Chapel

Ghar il-Kbir

Clapham Junction

Inquisitor's Palace

Laferla Cross

Dingli Cliffs

M e d i t e r r a n e a n

Il-Kullana

Ix-Xaqqa

N

1 km

1 mile

Gozo

Malta

Mosta
Ta'Mlit
Il-Qashija
Il-Bwieraq
Gzira
Sliema Creek
Manoel Island
Marsamxett Harbour
Lija
Balzan
Birkirkara
Ta' Xbiex
Floriana
Ta'Qali
Tal-Mirakli
Msida
Pieta
Santa Venera
Gwardamanga
Hamrun
Grand Harbour
Attard
Il-Kortin
Hospital
Qormi
Marsa
Kaldin
Tal-Filas
Hal Muxi
Hospitals
Rahal Gdid
Żebbuġ
Hal Mula
Paola
Hal Dwin
Luqa
Santa Lucia
Siġġiewi
Girgenti Valley
St Mary
Ta' Bir Miftun
Gudja
Mqabba
Malta International Airport
Madonna Tal-Providenza
Kirkop
Cavalier Tower
Hal Millieri
Qrendi
Zurrieq
Safi
Xarolla Windmill
Ħaġar Qim
Mnajdra
Il-Maqluba
Għar Lapsi
Ras Hanzir
Ras il-Hamrija
Ras il-Bajjada
Blue Grotto
Il-Mizieb
To Rjfja
Il-Minkba
Hal Far Industrial Estate

p.212

# Don't miss

1 Dingli Cliffs **p.194**
2 Church of St Nicholas, Siġġiewi **p.199**
3 Għar Lapsi **p.200**
4 Ħaġar Qim and Mnajdra **p.200**
5 Ħal Millieri **p.206**

*Cedant Curae Loco:*
*'Here cares end'*

Grand Master
de Verdalle's motto,
Verdala Palace

Of all the sights along this coast, the cliffs at **Dingli** are the most impressive – at 850ft (260m) the highest point in Malta. From here the Mediterranean appears benign, even when the white foam angrily whips the indigo water below. The horizon brims full of mirages; it is easy to believe you can actually see North Africa.

Further south, on the barren coralline rocky outcrops, are the prehistoric temples of **Ħaġar Qim** and **Mnajdra**, where scholarly history tells of an ancient people who worshipped pagan gods and symbols of fertility. Inland, the landscape becomes more fertile and terraces are cut into the low hills, like a giant's staircase. From the hilltops the horizon is dominated by the domes of parish churches or Verdala Palace, the erstwhile opulent summer residence of Grand Master de Verdalle.

# Around Dingli to Mnajdra via Siġġiewi

Along the coast are some of the archaeological and scenic highlights of Malta, as well as villages that still feel remarkably off the beaten track. Circled numbers below refer to the map (opposite) of this mini tour.

## Dingli

The village of **Dingli** ①, at 785ft (240m), is the highest village on Malta; it is a dozy farming community you will drive through in order to reach Dingli Cliffs. There is something calming about the cliffs despite the angry sea below. Tommaso Dingli, a noted 16th- and 17th-century Maltese architect, and Sir Thomas Dingley, an Englishman said to have had a house nearby in the 16th century, are given equal credit for the village's name.

## Dingli Cliffs

⭐ Dingli Cliffs

Dingli Cliffs ② fall 850ft (260m) to the sea and the area is a paradise for daydreamers and walkers with its spring/autumn carpets of crocuses and narcissi. Yet here, most of all, it is the Mediterranean itself that impresses – wine-dark, like a great ocean, it just does not look like an inland sea.

---

### A Spy Story

During the Second World War, a consistent irritant to the Axis high command was its inability to infiltrate Malta with so much as one spy. At 2am on the night of 18 May 1942, Caio Borghi, also known as Carmelo Borg Pisani of Senglea, rowed ashore from an Italian torpedo boat to the cave at Ras id-Dawwara, 1½ miles (2.5km) north of Dingli Cliffs. Pisani was a Maltese Fascist sympathizer educated on a scholarship in Rome. To feed his ideology and repay his moral debt, he volunteered to recce the defences and supplies prior to the planned Axis invasion of Malta, Operation Herkules. The sheer cliffs above him were impossible to scale, however, and within 48 hours all his rations had been washed away by the sea. Following his frantic waves to the British patrol boats, he was arrested and subsequently confessed. The British hanged him as a spy, aged 28, on 28 November 1942.

## Getting to and around Dingli and Siġġiewi

The infrequent **no.81 bus** goes via Rabat and terminates here. By **car**, the road out of Rabat forks right to Dingli opposite the Dominican monastery, but if you continue straight the road leads to Buskett from where you can still reach Dingli and the cliffs. It can be a nice **walk** from the village and the cliffs are half a mile (1km) further on.

**Clapham Junction** is not well signposted. The **road** by the Buskett Forest Aparthotel (see p.204) forks into a 'Y'. The right fork will take you to Dingli and 300 yards down the left fork is Clapham Junction.

**Buskett** is 2½ miles (4km) out of Rabat on the **road** to Dingli, and is signposted. For the woods, turn left at Verdala Palace and twist your way down to the bottom where there is a small car park. The Dingli bus, no.81, drops you on the road, leaving you a brief downhill walk.

By car along the road from Rabat is the easiest way to get to **Siġġiewi**, even though it does not look it on the map. Bus no.89 runs to Siġġiewi; there's also no.94, which runs June–Sept from Siġġiewi to **Għar Lapsi** (4 times on Thurs, 7 times on Sun); otherwise it's about a 2½-mile (4km) hike.

The cliff road stops alarmingly at the precipitous edge. The track to the left eventually links back to Buskett. One mile (1.5km) along, with only Filfla as neighbour, is the chapel dedicated to the patron saint of prostitutes, **St Mary Magdalene** (1646). For 364 days a year it stands alone and silent, but at 7.30pm on 22 July each year a delightful Mass is said on its steps at the cliffs' edge as the sun dips into the sea behind. To the right the road is smoother, and with the sunset and the onset of dusk it becomes 'steamy window alley'. Cars park along the cliffs' edge and lovers gulp in romance.

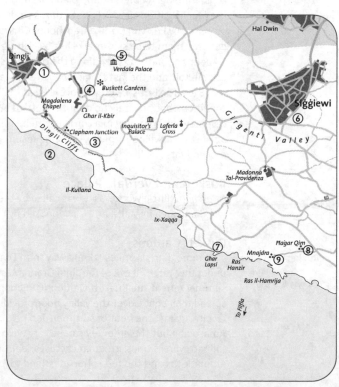

(Malta is a small and Catholic island where privacy can be hard to find.) Further along is the Bobbyland restaurant.

The village **church of the Assumption** with its tall silver-coloured cupola and twin bell towers is as visible as a lighthouse. The church, of no particular merit, is only approximately 100 years old.

## The Clapham Junction Mystery

**Clapham Junction** ③ is the nickname given to the largest convergence of Bronze Age (approximately 1500 BC) cart ruts yet discovered in Malta: parallel concave grooves 5ft (1.5m) apart and 16–24in (40–60cm) deep, cut or worn into the coralline stone.

Cart ruts occur in Malta and Gozo – and in parts of Sicily and Greece – especially where outcrops of hard stone are found. Mystery and speculation surround their origin and use. One of the saner theories attached to the site states that the ruts were a complex series of tracks for people to drag their goods around on stone-shod carts. Unfortunately this theory does not explain the absence of scarred wearing, or why some of them disappear off the cliffs' edge, or why, as is the case here, they converge like a railway siding. The BBC carried out tests for a documentary many years ago, but all they came up with was that a wheeled structure kept jamming. A different and plausible notion suggests they were used for irrigation channels, but far less credible is the theory proposed by Erik von Daniken, author of *Chariot of the Gods*, who declared them to be skid-marks left by visiting aliens.

About 200 yards further along the outcrop is the shrubbed crater **Għar il-Kbir**, and the last troglodyte cave in Malta, inhabited until the 1830s. The British, publicly incensed at the insanitary conditions, but privately no doubt unsettled by the thought of cavemen living happily in a corner of their Empire, moved them against their will to Siġġiewi – where presumably their descendants still live.

## Buskett and Verdala Palace

*Boschetto* (little wood), as it was called by the knights, is the only woodland area in Malta and is overlooked by the Verdala Palace.

### Buskett Gardens

**Buskett Gardens**
*open all year;*
*picnicking is permitted*

No more than 1¼ miles (2km) away from Dingli cliffs, and sitting under the watchful eye of Cardinal Grand Master de Verdalle's summer retreat, are Buskett Gardens ④. Panoplies of foliage spread their shade over the valley floor, providing a welcome respite against the heat of summer; don't expect anything Amazonian but the greenery can be very welcome. Orange trees, tall sad cypress trees, irregular cactuses, leguminous carobs, aromatic firs and the Judas tree (destined to foretell Easter with its pink blossom, and the tree from which Judas is said to have hanged himself) are some of the randomly planted flora. A sign warns that picking fruit will lead to prosecution – pity there's no similar legend about littering. In spring and autumn, Buskett bristles with hunters hoping to bag birds migrating over Malta, resting in the trees.

## Verdala Palace

**Verdala Palace**
*the summer residence of the president and sometimes used as accommodation for visiting dignitaries; usually closed to visitors, but check with the tourist board*

Grand Master de la Valette was a humble man of granite Christian morals who was content with a tiny hunting lodge in the *Boschetto* from which he would hunt with his crossbow. Cardinal Grand Master de Verdalle, who reigned only 14 years later, was less the warrior and more the sybarite. The Verdala Palace ⑤ was his specially commissioned *palazzo*, disguised as a castle; somewhere he could escape the oppressive summer heat of Valletta and feed his voracious appetite for the trappings of state. The site he chose was on top of the hard rock overlooking the *Boschetto*, from which he could see nearly all his archipelago. The design of the three-storey palace is credited to Gerolamo Cassar and construction began the year he died, 1586. Initially, all the palace's stone was quarried from the site and the excavations formed the existing dry moat. In each of the four corners – the plan is basically symmetrical – is a bastioned tower rising above the top floor. At the garden entrance Grand Master de Vilhena, another later epicurean, added the elaborate balustrade and his gigantic escutcheon.

Inside the main door is a further signpost to its egocentric creator. A marble bust shows off his Byzantine collection of facial features: a tall slender forehead over hard eyes and flared nostrils set in a tight face that ends in a goatee on a virile chin. This is the face of a man who did not find his penchant for piracy incompatible with holding the office of cardinal to the pope (the only grand master to receive this honour). On his deathbed de Verdalle bequeathed to the Order all his vast wealth – even his quint – which he had accumulated with the Order's laws, thereby silencing from the grave his many detractors.

The ceiling above the ground floor is by Paladini, whose frescoes show the high points of de Verdalle's illustrious life. Note the broad shallow steps of the oval staircase (knee-joints in a 77lb/35kg suit of armour were not very flexible). In the adjoining hall two chessboards carved into the stone floor are by French officers imprisoned here by the British during the Royal Navy blockade of 1800 (there is another in the top garret). The bastioned towers are divided into passages, grim little cells and torture chambers for anyone who fell foul of the grand master. From the roof you can

### Filfla – a Far-flung Isle

Filfla is an uninhabited and somewhat foreboding rocky islet, 5 miles (8km) offshore and clearly visible from the southwestern cliffs. It has always been treated as the archipelago's unwanted orphan, until in 1970 it was declared a nature reserve.

Filfla is the unhappy victim of the nasty (and absurd) legend of Il-Maqluba (*see* Qrendi, p.208): the evil inhabitants of Il-Maqluba so displeased God that he tore the ground from beneath them and sent them crashing through to hell. So base were they that not even hell could hold them, and in desperation the devil threw the depraved sinners (and the earth, trees, etc.) out of hell and back into the night sky. The tangled mass of rock, vegetation and godless souls landed in the sea and thus created Filfla. From such an egregious birth as that, its fate was set.

The next, and more tangible, calamity to befall Filfla came at the hands of the Royal Navy and the Royal Air Force, who used it for target practice. For more than 25 years they bombed it in the full knowledge that it was home to the only known colony in the world of a large dark green and red spotted lizard (*Lacerta muralis* var. *filfolensis*). Miraculously, the lizard and a rare species of Mediterranean stormy petrel that breeds on the islet have managed to survive, albeit in greatly reduced surroundings.

The waters run very deep around Filfla, which was used as a refuge by local fishermen until the Second World War. The parish priest of Żurrieq would journey out once a week to say Mass in the small medieval cave chapel. Some of the delicate icons have been saved and can be seen in St Catherine's in Żurrieq. Today it is forbidden to land, moor a boat or dive near its peaceful, rocky shore, as not all the British ordnance detonated upon impact.

see most of Malta through 360° as well as the southern Ta'Ċenċ cliffs of Gozo.

In the gardens and abutting the palace is the **chapel of St Anthony the Hermit**, built at the end of the 16th century. The work by Preti, *The Madonna and Child*, is in need of restoration and is therefore overshadowed by a garish sculpture of the Madonna holding the dead body of Christ. Note the granite **milestone** at the entrance to the palace drive: it is one of the many on which the distances were chiselled off by the Allies during the Second World War in the daft hope that invading Axis forces would get hopelessly lost.

## Siġġiewi

If you are only going to see one old village in Malta, make it **Siġġiewi** ⑥. One of the 10 original parishes created in 1436, Siġġiewi lies midway between Rabat and Żurrieq in the fertile Girgenti Valley, which begins near the cliffs of Dingli. It is from the fruits of this valley that the sleepy village has grown. Today about 6,000 people live hereabouts. There is a southern Italian air about the oversized square with its wooden benches upon which the villagers rotate like the hands of a clock, keeping one step ahead of the sun. At high noon in summer not even a cat will cross the square, and the Friend to All Bar is eerily quiet. St Nicholas stands aloof on a roundabout in the centre of the L-shaped sloping square, in front of his extravagant Baroque church.

## Around the Town

 **Church of St Nicholas**

The **parish church of St Nicholas**, one of Malta's most august Baroque churches, dominates the centre of Siġġiewi. Lorenzo Gafa finished it, his first Baroque church, in 1693. Perhaps because it was also his first major commission, he adopted certain elaborate Italian and Sicilian idioms, but its classical Baroque features retain a feeling of light and space.

The west-facing façade and the huge dome were not Gafa's design but were added in 1864 by a resident of Siġġiewi, Dr Nicola Zammit. To ensure his dome was visible from the bottom of the sloping square, he extended the height of the drum so it would not be lost between the two bell towers. Quentin Hughes, the noted historian of architecture, wrote: 'The treatment of the façade is truly dynamic. Like a ship in full sail, thrusting its bow forward, it is set trailing its two campaniles in the wash.' Most of the lavish decorations – including the eight segments of the dome – were added long after Gafa had completed his brief. The altarpiece is Preti's last and unfinished work, a painting of St Nicholas.

Behind the bus terminus is the **chapel of St John the Baptist**, built in 1730, by Fra Salvatore Cutaja, who is buried underneath the centre marble. The chapel is small and unremarkable except for a truly gruesome picture of St John's beheading. The Madonna looks on unperturbed from the left-hand wall. The chapel is seldom open but the viewing window enables you to see most of the gore. Opposite and next to the petrol station is the crumbling, box-like **chapel of Our Lady**, which only opens during the *festa*.

A mile or so (couple of kilometres) south of town, on the road to Għar Lapsi, is a very beautiful chapel, **Madonna Tal-Providenza**, set in the middle of a field, the portico of which was designed by Michele Cachia. This tiny octagonal chapel was built in 1750 and looks no more than a dome and a bell cote. Fable has it that the church grew weak after being struck by lightning and the dainty portico was added to lend support in 1815. The whole is a study in the main elements of pantheon design; note the small statues against the roof line. Mass is said here just once a year, on the first Sunday in September. At all other times the portico and the bell cote are used exclusively by the birds. A viewing window will provide you with a glimpse of the nave; the cannonball on the right of the altar is, according to hearsay, from the Great Siege of 1565. (Nissen huts and other deleterious buildings have been built with mind-numbing insensitivity next door.)

About 2½ miles (4.5km) west from Siġġiewi, on the secondary road that just about links Dingli to the head of the Girgenti Valley, are the Inquisitor's Summer Palace and the Laferla Cross or Tas-Salib. The **Inquisitor's Summer Palace** was built in 1625 by Inquisitor

## Getting to Ħaġar Qim and Mnajdra

Take the **road** to Żurrieq and then towards the Wied iż-Żurrieq (Blue Grotto). The road is signposted 'Ħaġar Qim' on your right, half a mile (1km) before the Blue Grotto. Alternatively, you can take a short detour through Qrendi, again following the Blue Grotto sign; this route goes right past Il Maqluba; *see* above. **Buses** nos.38 and 138 stop at Ħaġar Qim. **Taxis** park near the terminus.

For the **disabled**, Ħaġar Qim is accessible, and Mnajdra less so, but just about feasible with the help of a companion – the smooth and straight 480-yard path that leads to it falls away steeply in a 1:13 gradient.

---

Visconti, who perched this narrow building on a ledge overlooking a wild valley of bamboo and pomegranate trees. The little chapel was added in 1760. It suffered years of disuse (in the Second World War it housed records from the Grand Master's Palace) but is now the official summer residence of the prime minister and cannot be visited. **Laferla Cross** or **Tas-Salib**, at an elevation of 715ft (218m), is clearly visible from most of the roads leading to Siġġiewi. As neither the cross nor the chapel is impressive, it is only worth climbing up for the views – the Verdala Palace stands to the northwest like a bold sentinel, to the east is Marsaskala, and to the south is the islet of Filfla.

From this vantage point the church domes spread out below and, like signatures, tell instantly which town is which. The hill has been a romantic rendezvous for years; the earliest of the neatly carved names on the steps of the cross dates back to 1907.

### Għar Lapsi

⭐ Għar Lapsi

Għar Lapsi ⑦, 'the cave of Ascension', was a fishermen's secret hidy-hole until a direct road replaced the path, and is often referred to as Siġġiewi's beach; it is a good spot for diving. Traditionally the local people swim here on Assumption, 15 August.

For half of the year Għar Lapsi looks like a deserted frontier town, a windswept area with one low-built restaurant, a car park, some wind-eaten and derelict buildings, a children's play area and a few hardy divers. In the summer it is awash with three generations of Maltese families picnicking and enjoying themselves.

At the bottom of the steep steps and slipway at the water's edge are fishermen's *luzzus*. The caves and easy access from the little jetties and rocks into the water make it a favourite with swimmers and cave divers; this part of the coast is octopus territory. For those who don't want to swim there are paths in the direction of Wied iż-Żurrieq (Blue Grotto) or benches to sit on and gaze out to Filfla and the sea.

## Ħaġar Qim and Mnajdra

⭐ Ħaġar Qim and Mnajdra

The structures of Ħaġar Qim and Mnajdra date from the Ġgantija and Tarxien phases (3600–2500 BC). They are believed to be temples where prehistoric man worshipped goddesses of fertility, although there has been some controversy over the true purpose of Mnajdra; see pp.203–4. At the Museum of Archaeology in Valletta many of the original finds are displayed, as well as helpful three-dimensional models. At the time of writing a project was under way to conserve both structures, which may result in covers being erected over both of them to protect them from the elements.

## Ħaġar Qim ⑧

**Ħaġar Qim**
www.heritagemalta.
org; open 9–5, last
admission 4.30; closed
Good Fri, 24, 25, 31 Dec,
and 1 Jan; adm

Ħaġar Qim (meaning 'sacred stones' or literally 'stones of worship') is a megalithic structure situated in a commanding position on a barren rock plateau overlooking the sea and the craggy islet of Filfla. The site remained buried under mounds of earth until its discovery in 1839, when clumsy attempts were made at excavation; the site was not properly revealed until 1910. The orthostats (upright stone slabs) here are the only ones in Malta to be made of the soft globigerina limestone, and they have been weathered by a combination of sun, wind and sea air.

There appears to be no specific reason, solar or otherwise, for siting the main five-apse temple with a southeastern aspect. The restored trilithon façade (two upright stones supporting one stone lintel) with its striking entrance belies the confused layout within.

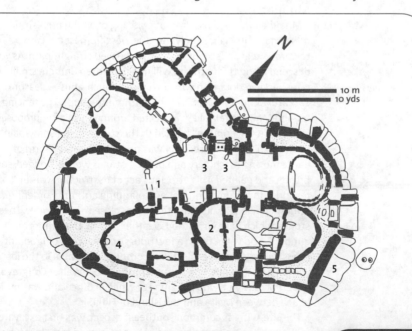

10 m
10 yds

Ħaġar Qim

The Southwest Coast | Around Dingli to Mnajdra via Siġġiewi: Ħaġar Qim and Mnajdra

Unlike any other temple site, the prehistoric builders of Ħaġar Qim did not adhere to a trefoil arrangement (symmetrical layout of three chambers); the chambers and apses connect with one another but not in a uniform plan. Each was built almost as an individual place of worship and it is supposed the whole later evolved into one temple, when it is believed to have been entirely roofed.

Points of note (numbers refer to the site plan, p.201) are: the seven headless **'Fat' deities**, each 10in (25cm) tall, believed to represent symbols of fertility [1], the so-called headless and nude *Venus of Malta*, and the exquisite pitted **altar** with its growing plant motifs [2] (found here and now on display in the Archaeological Museum). Also note two pedestalled altars [3], a betyl or tall cylindrical stone [4], and the largest megalith, more than 23ft (7m) long and approximately 20 tons [5]. The little boulders strewn about the site were used like castors on which the orthostats were inched into place.

True knowledge of prehistoric man's beliefs, habits and culture is hard to ascertain; much is scholarly guesswork. The evidence unearthed here and at Tarxien strongly suggests a highly sophisticated culture; just look at the intricacy of the designs and the engineering of the robust structures themselves.

## Mnajdra ⑨

**Mnajdra**
*www.heritagemalta. org; open 9–5, last admission 4.30; closed Good Fri, 24, 25, 31 Dec, and 1 Jan; adm*

**Mnajdra** has the most dramatic setting of all the prehistoric monuments in Malta: 480 yards due west from Ħaġar Qim towards sheer cliffs along a steep and paved straight path. As you descend along this path you will notice a dozen or more small ramshackle redoubts in which, during a much-abused season, *kaċċatur* or hunters trap and shoot migrating birds. The fencing around Mnajdra temple was erected around 1999 after proposed changes in the hunting laws led to the stones being spray-painted. In 2000, this minimal security was breached by some form of earth-moving machinery and over 80 stones were dislodged, some broken and painted. This atrocious act of destruction was in response to the environment and planning authority ordering the removal of illegally built hunting hides close to the temple. These stones, which have withstood weather and earth tremors for almost 6,000 years, fell in a few hours at the hands of ignorant men. The restoration project was completed in 2002. To the left of the path by the cliffs' edge is a **memorial to Sir Walter Congreve**, a governor of Malta, who died in 1927 while in office and was buried at sea between Malta and the island of Filfla.

The **site**, with its common southeast aspect, was first excavated in 1840 and reveals smaller and better-preserved temple structures than Ħaġar Qim. The outer walls are made from the harder coralline limestone which has survived the worst weather.

The Mnajdra complex which spans the Ġgantija and Tarxien phases (3000 BC to 2500 BC) comprises three temples set around a semicircular forecourt (numbers refer to the site plan below): the oldest and hardly recognizable **Trefoil Temple** [1], Middle Temple, the last to be built [2] and the now controversial Lower Temple [3]. The concave walls surrounding all three suggest this was a roofed complex. The **Middle Temple** gives a further indication that the deities worshipped were ones of fertility and rebirth. The plan, with its two elliptical apses, suggest a primeval female form with the worshippers entering through the womb-like entrance in a rite of fertility. Decoration, such as scarring and pitting on the trilithon inner entrance of the Lower Temple, is more elaborate than at Ħaġar Qim. Apart from minor artefacts there have been no other finds here.

The **Lower Temple** was until as recently as the 1980s assumed to be an adjunct to the Middle Temple. It is now suggested that it is a highly sophisticated solar observatory, capable of predicting the

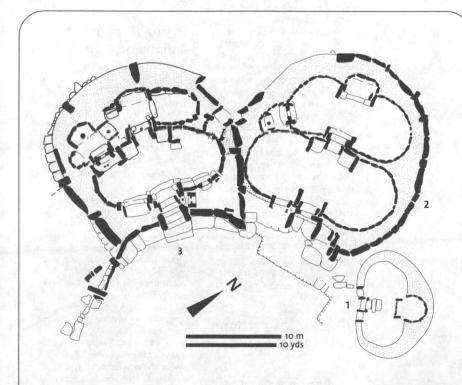

10 m
10 yds

**Mnajdra**

four annual solstices using the sunrise and sunset. Prehistoric man would undoubtedly have needed the information that such a 'calendar' might offer for agricultural and religious rites.

Mathematics supports the calendar theory. The main trilithon entrance runs, with the exit, almost exactly along the same east–west axis as the sun's rays at the time of an equinox. On summer and winter solstices the rays of the sun clip exactly at the very edges of the stones. Most impressively, the odds against this happening have been calculated at 26,000 x 26,000 x 26,000 to 1. In addition, while attempting to prove the theory that man developed an accurate and practical calendar, those involved in the recent study have applied their own date to Mnajdra: 3700 BC.

# Festas around Dingli and Siġġiewi

In **Dingli**, the *festa* of **Holy Mary** is held on 20 August.

In **Clapham Junction, L-Imnarja**, the feast of St Peter and St Paul, celebrates the summer harvest. Its name is a corruption of the Latin *luminaria*, which referred to the bonfires of Mdina and Rabat that illuminated the feast (*see also* p.250). The *festa* begins on the evening of 28 June and runs through the night. At the Mnarja races the next day, donkeys, mules and horses are all ridden bareback, with much hilarity, down Racecourse Street. The tradition dates back to the days of the knights and today the winners receive an elaborate cloth, the *paliu*, from Malta's president, which the winners' church will use as an altar cloth. The Maltese eat and drink more rabbit and local wine than seems feasible at this feast.

On the last Sunday in June, **Siġġiewi** celebrates the *festa* of St Nicholas of Myra (and later Bari), sometimes known as Santa Claus. He is also the patron saint of sailors and pawnbrokers.

# Where to Stay around Dingli and Siġġiewi

## Dingli

**\*\*Buskett Forest Aparthotel,**
t 21 454266/454328 (€), is the only hotel to be found in this area.

Situated about half a mile (1km) beyond Verdala Palace on the Buskett road, it is a small, family-run and modern complex of hotel rooms and self-catering apartments. Facilities include a rooftop pool, restaurant and glittery bar. It is a pity about the crane park next door.

# Eating Out around Dingli and Siġġiewi

## Dingli

On a sunny day a picnic by the cliffs is the best idea. Fresh bread, tomatoes, tangy goat's cheese and fruit can be gathered from the **Mollu Store and Corner Confectionery**, 70 yards before the bus terminus. About 30 yards before the terminus, there is a **takeaway** serving chicken and chips or burgers.

**Bobbyland**, Panoramic Road, t 21 452895 (€€). There is, as with most things Maltese, a tale behind the seemingly absurd name, and it is best revealed by Reno the owner. The huge restaurant is very popular with locals, especially at weekends, when you'll encounter every stratum of Maltese society from burly stevedores to politicians. The food is like the atmosphere – bustling, generous and frank, but service can lag at busy times. Rabbit and lamb are specialities and you can eat inside or out. The owner and waiters are all avid hunters. Anyone who does not see the particularly Maltese thrill of standing in a small field blasting anything that moves should ask for an explanation here. *Open for lunch and dinner all week except Mon; booking essential at weekends.*

**Buskett Forest Restaurant,** Buskett Road, t 21 454328 (€). Halfway down the road which threads past Verdala Palace to Buskett Gardens, this is for those with fond memories of Butlin's-style holiday camps. They serve lunch and dinner every day, with live music in the summer. *Closed Fri–Sun eves in winter.*

### Siġġiewi

**Friend to All Bar,** in Pjazza San Nikola serves all manner of drinks. There is also a small **baker's** facing the church on the right.

### Għar Lapsi

**Blue Creek Bar and Restaurant,** t 21 462800 (€€€). Nicely positioned for some lovely sea views, this restaurant offers a decent choice of Mediterranean food, including lighter food at lunchtime. The food is a bit fussy but the portions are generous. *Open Wed–Mon.*

# Żurrieq and Around

Some people say the real heart and soul of Malta lies in this backwater. In the countryside that surrounds these villages and along the Wardija Ridge in the north, the air feels drier and the wild herbs and flowers are so pungent they almost claw your nose. The dry-stone walls are built higher to protect the crops from the wind and a few hardy trees remain undefeated and bow just a little bit. A canopy of tall palms lends a North African air to the open spaces and village squares; invariably this was where the sirocco and the Barbary corsairs struck first.

The villagers in this corner of Malta are a devout people; religion is the foundation stone upon which their lives are built. Historically, their lot in life has been to serve the more influential citizens of Mdina and Valletta, to man the watchtowers, to farm and grind corn or to quarry stone in Mqabba. Each village developed its own character or industry and there exists a fierce but friendly rivalry over the *festa*: who can out-firework whom, and which band club can make the more euphonious din.

## Żurrieq

The name Żurrieq is apparently derived from the Arabic *Israq*, which means azure or blue, associated with the clear blue waters of Wied iż-Żurrieq (Blue Grotto), some 2 miles (3km) away. It also accounts for the delightful idea that if you come from Żurrieq you will have blue eyes (in the late 11th century Aryan Normans founded a settlement here). Żurrieq is one of the original 10 parishes of Malta, and the largest landlocked village of the area. It has little of the charm found in its neighbours, but is close to the lovely medieval church at Ħal Millieri, and is en route to the Blue Grotto or to the temples of Ħaġar Qim and Mnajdra.

# Getting to and around Żurrieq and Area

For **Żurrieq**, take a good map. The quickest but least scenic route is to follow the signs to Luqa and the airport. NB: there is a signpost before you reach Żurrieq for Ħal Millieri, ignore it; if in a **car** this final path is impassable. There is a more scenic and longer route via Rabat. **Buses** nos.32 and 34 serve Żurrieq but do not go to the Blue Grotto. There is a **taxi** rank by the bus terminus, and a **market** on Thursdays in Mattia Preti Square.

For the **Blue Grotto**, by **car**, follow the signs for Luqa if you are coming from Valletta. Take the Mosta road and then the Żebbuġ or Rabat roads if you are staying on the north coasts. **Buses** nos.38 and 138 go to the Blue Grotto and Ħaġar Qim. Otherwise take 32 or 34 which terminate in Żurrieq, and take a taxi from the rank opposite the terminus. The walk from Żurrieq is a dull 2 miles (3km), downhill and then uphill. **Tour companies** offer narrated visits to the grotto, maybe coupled with a trip to the prehistoric sites of Ħaġar Qim and Mnajdra.

The road routes to **Qrendi** are either via Luqa or Siġġiewi. **Mqabba** is situated almost on the threshold of runway 06 of MIA, so follow the airport signs or go via Siġġiewi. Nos.32, 34, 35 and 39 buses stop at **Kirkop**. Alternatively, head for the airport and the village is just after the tunnel which takes you under the runway. Buses nos.34 and 39 stop in **Safi** en route to Żurrieq. Once in Kirkop, follow the signs for Żurrieq.

---

## Ħal Millieri

⭐ **Ħal Millieri**

This site is the highlight of the area and well worth traipsing to, even if you are all 'churched out'. To get there, turn right on the main road that runs from Żurrieq to Wied iż-Żurrieq just past the petrol station opposite the roundabout. It lies 1150 yards down this narrow track on the right; there is a signpost after 900 yards. Ħal Millieri was originally a medieval settlement until it became depopulated and ultimately deserted. Sandwiched between stone walls and surrounded by fields, all that remains are two 15th-century low-built churches – no bigger than chapels – and a cross.

Like a huge doll's house at the end of a garden brimming with flowers is the **church of the Annunciation**, probably built after 1430. A farmer used it as a stable for his donkey, paying the church Lm1 per annum in rent until 1968, when a fund was established to restore it. A simple door and three steps down into the dim interior almost give the impression of entering a cave; the walls are illuminated with angular frescoes of saints, partly restored but still showing the effects of humidity and salinity. The whole pretty structure epitomizes the simplicity of medieval Christian worship.

Outside the bigger, later **church of St John the Evangelist** is an old Roman olive-crusher that was once used as a baptismal font. The cross in front marked the centre of the settlement. The gates to the garden and both churches themselves are locked, but the parish priest of Żurrieq will open up by prior appointment.

## Around the Town

Back in Żurrieq, the **church of St Catherine** (1632), designed by Don Matteolo Saliba, the local parish priest, took over 25 years to build. Somewhat dull and overworked, it was built in a period before Maltese Baroque had evolved, a good example of what can happen when successive generations tinker with buildings in the vain hope of improving them. To be fair, Saliba's initial design was caught in that period when the influences on ecclesiastic architecture were evolving into what became Maltese Baroque. Furthermore, St Catherine's is not helped by being hemmed in by the police station and the large red banners of the Malta Labour Party, but the lights of the *festa* lend it a certain gravity.

The square format of the interior has been lifted by the work of Mattia Preti, who fled to the village to escape the plague of 1675 and ended up executing some magnificent paintings: behind the altar is St Catherine being freed by angels and in the nave St Andrew is depicted labouring magnificently under the weight of his cross. A triptych panel in the vestry dates back to 1604; it came from a cave chapel on the islet of Filfla, where the parish priest used to say Mass for the fishermen up to the outbreak of the Second World War.

**Parish priest's garden**
*open by permission*

In the **parish priest's garden** is part of a Punic tower, the only example on the island. The cornice has the telltale Egyptian lip. What is remarkable about it is the condition of the soft limestone structure, bearing in mind it must have been built between 5 BC and 600 BC. The massive bricks were laid without mortar, each having – like the pyramids – a concave and convex face to ensure a perfect fit.

At the end of Mattia Preti Square you can visit the **Armeria**, built as an armoury at the end of the 1600s and used by Grand Masters Pinto, Ximenes and de Rohan. It is a plain and classical structure that echoes a nobleman's town *palazzo*. The eight worn semicircular steps and the balcony hint that it may once have been something special and the twin dolphin door-knockers are traditional Maltese door furniture. The building was sold in 1784 to the Crispo family, a branch of which still own it today.

## Wied iż-Żurrieq (The Blue Grotto)

From a vantage point on the cliffs above **Wied iż-Żurrieq**, Grand Marshal Copier, together with a cavalry squadron, shadowed the Turkish Armada of over 181 galleys on the eve of the Great Siege of 1565.

Legend has it that the Blue Grotto was home to the sirens – sea nymphs – who serenaded sailors to their destruction with soft verse. Brightly painted boats and *luzzus* leave every 15 minutes, providing the sea is calm, for the seven principal natural caves and grottoes along this stretch of coast. The Blue Grotto is one of seven caves on the 25-minute trip. Try to go early in the morning when the queues are shorter and the sun is bright and reflects off the white sand of the sea bed. Each boat carries a maximum of eight people. If the weather looks dodgy, your hotel will ascertain the sea conditions in advance.

For those who turn queasy at the mere sight of a boat, there are benches, a shell collection and a filigree-jewellery shop. This is easy to spot: displayed outside is a life-sized cardboard troglodyte called Jean-Marc wearing a Maltese cross.

## Qrendi

**Qrendi** has a distinctive quasi-Moorish and Maltese feel to its twisty streets; you might only stop here on your way to the prehistoric sites of Ħaġar Qim and Mnajdra.

On the road in from Valletta is a little chapel dedicated to **St Matthew**. Right next door, in the shade, is a green-and-white sign pointing down some steps to **Il-Maqluba**, meaning 'overturned or upside down'. It is an overgrown geological fault – a large cave must have collapsed during an earth tremor – some 150ft (45m) deep (300ft/90m from the top) and 210ft (65m) across, with a green floor of tangled bamboo, fruit trees and shrubs. It is worth seeing simply for the dotty legend that accompanies it; *see* Filfla p.198.

It is suggested that Lorenzo Gafa was partly responsible for the **church of St Mary**, for he inherited an incomplete structure when he began work in 1685. What gives the church presence are the steps up to the *zuntier* (forecourt) and the huge carved wooden doors.

Altogether more fun is the octagonal **Cavalier Tower**, 200 yards off the west side of the square and surrounded by 16th-century dwellings. This is the only such tower in Malta, three storeys high with octagonal floor plans and roof terrace. From here the gallant inhabitants of Qrendi would pour boiling pitch, hoops of fire and any other handy projectiles onto the heads of those intent on slaughtering or enslaving them.

## Mqabba

The name 'Mqabba' is derived from the Arabic and may have referred to a domed building in the village which no longer exists. It is the largest of the four villages, with a population of 2,390, about 40 more than Qrendi.

Mqabba is the centre of the quarry area, there to fuel Malta's voracious appetite for building. As you approach the village, vast creamy pits appear on either side of the road, from which lozenge-shaped blocks are extracted, swarming with workers and antediluvian machinery.

Once in the village the narrow streets almost lean inwards and echo the North African feel of Qrendi. The **George V Band Club**, built in 1910, is a rather pompous building, unlike its neighbour the parish **church of the Assumption**. Tucked away behind it is the 16th-century **church of St Basil**.

## Kirkop

If it were not for the proximity of the runways, the triangular little square with its half-dozen evergreen trees and old benches would be a very pleasant place to while away an hour or two. The **church of St Leonard** was rebuilt in the 18th century and is a narrow gutted little building with two bell towers which squeeze all but the cupola on the dome out of view. The remains of St Benedict were donated to the church by Pope Pius in 1790 and are held inside.

## Safi

**Safi**, the smallest of the four villages, is almost a suburb of its bigger neighbour Żurrieq. Its name means 'clear' or 'pure'. Here more than anywhere in this area the North African stamp is evident: the palm trees are tall and their fronds generous, and a few of the buildings have forecourts with aromatic plants and herbs. Apart from the new band club, all the buildings have hints – in their window or door designs – of Moorish influence.

In the main square, *centru pastorali*, the green of the palms takes the hard glare off the stone and polarizes the sunlight. Between it and Żurrieq is the only interesting sight in the area, the **Xarolla windmill**. The now tumbledown windmill was introduced to the island during the reign of Grand Master de Homedes (1536–53); the Order maintained a monopoly on this revolutionary way of grinding corn. Other windmills were erected in the area by Grand Master de Vilhena 200 years later. Until approximately 20 years ago this particular windmill was fully operational, but during a terrible *gregale* the sails and mill were damaged beyond repair. Further into town on top of another cylindrical hulk of a windmill – now inhabited – are the horns of a cow: an old Maltese superstition holds that this guards against the evil eye.

### *Festas* in and near Żurrieq

**Żurrieq**: The *festa* of St Catherine of Alexandria falls on the first Sunday of September.

**Qrendi and Mqabba**: The tension mounts with the summer heat, for Qrendi and Mqabba share the same *festa*, the Assumption, on 15 August. Expect their respective band clubs to compete for volume, not tune.

**Kirkop**: St Leonard of Noblat was a French abbot who lived in the 5th century; a *festa* dedicated to him is held on the third Sunday in September.

**Safi**: Celebrates the Conversion of St Paul on the last Sunday in August.

### Eating Out in and near Żurrieq

#### Żurrieq

**Prima**, Main Street, to the right of the church. Hole-in-the-wall bakery that sells large squares of doughy pizza for 16c, *timpana* for 25c or *pastizzi* for 6c. *Open 5.30am to 7.30pm, except Sun when it closes at 9.30am.*

There is also an unmarked baker's facing the terminus on the right, which sells sandwiches.

### Blue Grotto

Half a dozen restaurants and bars, all inexpensive, none inspiring, offer the basic kind of fare on the lines of pasta, hamburgers or grilled fish. The best are the **Kingfisher** and the **Dolphin** (featuring a fearsome shark's mouth and photos of the largest Great White caught in the Mediterranean in April 1987; it was over 23ft/7m long and weighed 5,940lb/2,700kg).

**Congreve Channel**, Wied iż-Żurrieq, t 21 827928, provides cheese-filled jacket potatoes and salads.

### Qrendi

There is a choice of two bars: the **Hunter's** bar opposite St Mary's church and the **Nationalist Party Club**.

### Mqabba

The **New Life Bar** is on Melbourne View, behind the church.

**Anton's Bakery** has fresh bread as well as sweet rolls.

### Ħaġar Qim

**Ħaġar Qim Bar and Restaurant**, t 79 497329 (€). About 50 yards from the car park. *Open with the temples every day except Mon.*

# The South

*The south of Malta is often forgotten; the landscape has an isolated mood and the greedy god of tourism has shown little interest – he is too busy on the northern coasts. Yet the region has some of the oldest archaeological sites to be found anywhere in Europe. And if you hire a boat you will find bays that are uncrowded, and some good rock bathing between Marsaskala and Delimara Point.*

*The people of 'the forgotten south' have a surly, rebellious side that is especially evident during 'the hunt', both in and out of a much-abused season, which can make walking hereabouts somewhat daunting.*

# 11

## Don't miss

⭐ **A fishing tradition**
Marsaxlokk **p.213**

⭐ **Ice-Age bones**
Għar Dalam **p.215**

⭐ **Five millennia of history**
The Hypogeum **p.226**

⭐ **Mighty megaliths**
The Tarxien Temples **p.226**

⭐ **Ecclesiastical gem**
Church of St Gregory, Żejtun **p.231**

*See map overleaf*

Grand Harbour

Hamrun

Marsa

Il-Kortin

Senglea

Vittoriosa

Kalkara

Cospicua

Xghajra

Ras il-Gebel

Il-Hofra

Newport (Marsa) Cr

Kordin

Zabbar Gate

Fort St Leonardo

Żabbar

Ghajn Dwieli

Raħal Gdid

Hypogeum

Tal Borg

Fgura

Ta' Grazzia

Zonqor

Fort St Thomas

Ħal Saflieni

Paola

Tarxien Temples

Marsaskala

Zonqor Point

Wied ta' Mazza

Wied il-Għajn

Marsaskala Bay

Il-Kappara

Luqa

Santa Lucia

Tarxien

Tal-Barrani

Il-Minzel

Wied iż-Żiju

Il-Ħamrija

Il-Gżira Point

Mamo Tower

Mignuna Point

St Mary

Żejtun

St Gregory's

St Thomas Bay

Ta' Bir Miftuħ

Gudja

Għaxaq

Bir id-Deheb

Il-Munxar

Malta International Airport

Tas Silġ

Tas Silġ Battery

Island Bay

Xrobb il-Għaġin

Marsaxlokk

Ras il-Fenek

Il-Ħofra ż-Żgħira

Safi

Ghar Dalam

Borġ in-Nadur

Il-Blez

St Lucian's Tower

Peter's Pool

Tumbrell Point

Delimara

Il-Mizieb

Birżebbuġa

Pinto Battery

Kbira Point

Marsaxlokk Bay

Fort Delimara

Long Bay

Slug's Pool

Delimara Point

Hal Far

Tal-Papa

Kalafrana

Delimara Lighthouse

Hal Far Industrial Estate

Benghisa Point

Ghar Hasan Cave

Fort Benghisa

N

1 km
1 mile

Gozo

Malta

## Don't miss

1 Marsaxlokk **p.213**

2 Għar Dalam **p.215**

3 The Hypogeum **p.226**

4 The Tarxien Temples **p.226**

5 The church of St Gregory, Żejtun **p.231**

# Marsaxlokk Bay

⭐ Marsaxlokk

*Marsa* means 'harbour' and *xlokk* is the Maltese name given to the sirocco, the hot southern wind that blows in from North Africa. Until the 20th century **Marsaxlokk Bay** was known as Marsasirocco Bay. Nowadays, sadly, this historic bay is in a somewhat unkempt state.

The single largest bay in Malta and geographically orphaned in the south, Marsaxlokk has proved ideal for two massive government development projects: a new electricity-generating plant and a freeport. Damage to the environment, the bay's natural beauty and marine life has been immense. More positively, the freeport generates valuable foreign exchange, and the power cuts and surges which once bedevilled the island are now mostly events of the past.

The coves on the Delimara peninsula have escaped development, and the fishing village of **Marsaxlokk** is a genuine 'photo opportunity'. Here at any one time more than a hundred *luzzus* of all sizes swing at anchor in the shallows of the bay, their primary colours splashing an air of tranquillity as they have always done.

## History

Throughout Malta's history the almost circular shelter of Marsaxlokk Bay has provided hospitable waters (safe in summer and winter except during the very worst *gregales* and siroccos), and an ideal landing point for invaders. At noon on Saturday 19 May 1565, the day the **Great Siege** began, the Turkish Admiral Piali anchored his 181-strong fleet and disembarked Mustapha Pasha's army of 35,000 from here. The *gregale* is a fierce winter wind, its lungs exhausted by the end of March, but Piali believed it could blow any time. So, fearing for his Sultan's precious fleet, he overruled Mustapha Pasha's well-formulated plan to wage a land war from Marsaxlokk and to blockade the Grand Harbours from the south. Instead he insisted on the safer anchorage of Marsamxett Harbour, which meant Fort St Elmo had to be taken first. His decision was the first of many catastrophic errors that led to the Turkish defeat.

The Turks tried their luck again in 1614 with a much smaller force of 60 galleys but were repulsed by the mighty defences of Fort St Lucian; they then headed round Delimara Point for Marsaskala, managing to reach Żejtun before being driven back by a squadron of the knights' cavalry.

On 10 June 1798 **Napoleon** disembarked the bulk of the French army in the bay under General Dessaix. Of the seven landing sites he had chosen, Fort St Lucian was one of the very few of the Order's defences to offer any resistance. During **Nelson**'s ensuing

## Getting to and around Marsaxlokk Bay

A **car** is imperative to reach **Birżebbuġa**. Due to the condition of the roads, borrow or hire one: don't use your own.

The area is officially served by the nos.11, 12 and 13 **buses** from Paola but these can be erratic, and the journey from Valletta can take as long as an hour. In many instances, you will find that Birżebbuġa is abbreviated to *B'buġa* or *B'buġia*.

Three **buses** serve **Marsaxlokk**: the no.27 from Valletta, the 427 from Buġibba and the 627 from Paceville.

One **road** goes out to **Delimara Point** from Marsaxlokk; towards the end it peters out into a rough track. By the signposted turning is one of the few remaining British milestones defaced by the Allied commanders during the Second World War (*see* p.198). There is no **bus** service.

---

blockade of the French, Marsaxlokk Bay was used as one of three victualling and repair stations for his warships.

Between the two **World Wars** the relatively calm waters of the bay at Kalafrana provided the perfect landing site for the magnificent flying seaplane hotels of Imperial Airways as they plied their pioneering routes to the ends of the then predominantly pink globe. At the outbreak of the **Second World War**, Kalafrana (now home to the very unglamorous but profitable freeport) became the Fleet Air Arm's base. It was on this jetty, crated for dispatch, that the four Gloucester biplanes that defended Malta in the summer of 1940 were found.

Swordfish seaplanes and the mighty four-engine Sunderlands roared in and out of the bay in all weathers during the Second World War. In the middle of a horrific sirocco, on the night of 13 October 1940, one such Sunderland flight carried Anthony Eden, then the British Secretary of State for War, who came within inches of being embedded into the limestone of Delimara Point; only the pilot's skill saved all on board. Meanwhile, the Axis was planning the invasion of Malta at Marsaxlokk Bay, **Operation Herkules**, but by the end of 1942 the plan was abandoned so that Hitler could pursue his fatal obsession with Russia.

The Allied forces in the bay and at Kalafrana suffered terribly at the hands of the Axis bombers right up to 8 September 1943, when the armistice with Italy was signed. By the end of that month 76 ships of the surrendered Italian Navy were anchored around the island, predominantly in the bays of Marsaxlokk and St Paul's. With great sang-froid, Admiral Cunningham cabled the Admiralty in London: 'Be pleased to inform their Lordships that the Italian battle fleet now lies at anchor under the guns of the fortress of Malta.'

# Birżebbuġa

This region once had hardy olive trees in abundance (*bir* means 'meadow' and *żebbuġ* is both Malti and Arabic for 'olives'). Once a simple fishing village and a quiet summer resort, over 6,000 people now live on the headland and coastal sprawl that seeps from Kalafrana to Fort St Lucian on **Kbira Point**. Maltese women still love to sit in the shade on upturned beer crates and play *tombla* or cards, or gossip in small groups under the shade of the Southend Apartments. Their uninterested men, meanwhile, swim with their children in the sometimes polluted waters off the sandy beach of **Pretty Bay** – a sad misnomer.

There is much more to see than to do here; the waters are sometimes polluted, but the surrounding area is rich in prehistory.

The cliff **cave of Għar Hasan**, well-signposted about 2 miles/3km from Birżebbuġa. is admittedly a secondary sight. It is imbued with Saracenic legends and has fine views of the sea. An old man sitting in the shade of the desolate car park will rent you a dim torch for 30c. Access is via steps (a rusty railing is all that separates you from the sea 435ft/130m below, so be very careful – it is muddy and slippery when wet) until you reach the cave itself, where Hasan, the last of the 11th-century Saracens, is supposed to have lived. The view of the deep-blue sea from the natural 'window' in the cliff face on the right as you go in is as spectacular as the legends about Hasan are unreliable.

Many stories are told of the heathen and his harem of young Maltese women, and how he sold his harem into slavery by lowering them on a rope into ships below. The best tells of how he fell in love with a member of his harem – they lived a blissful existence until, hearing Count Roger's Christian soldiers coming, they leapt hand-in-hand to their deaths into the sea below. (The Catholic version of this story says the lady in question was kidnapped and held unwilling hostage.)

# Għar Dalam

**⓲ Għar Dalam**
*signposted 600 yards from the St George's Bay end of Birżebbuġa on the Żejtun road. open 9–5; closed Good Fri, 24, 25, 31 Dec, and 1 Jan; adm; attendants will help the disabled as far as the small museum or the terrace overlooking Wied Dalam and the gardens*

Of more interest and significance is Għar Dalam, 'the Cave of Darkness', an extraordinary prehistoric cul-de-sac containing the bone remains of animals stranded on Malta at the end of the Ice Age.

The cave was first scientifically investigated in 1865 but was not opened until 1933 – during the Second World War it was used as an air-raid shelter. Sadly, the most important and irreplaceable relics (such as four tusks of a dwarf elephant and the skull of a Neolithic child) were stolen from the museum in a commissioned theft on the night of 7 April 1980, presumably at the behest of a mysterious private collector.

The bone deposits of long-extinct fauna, such as dwarf elephants, bears and hippopotami that date back approximately 180,000 years, make Għar Dalam unique. Together with the even earlier deposits of bone-free material they offer a window of understanding into the Pleistocene era.

The history and story of Għar Dalam spans the entire Quaternary period (1–2 million years ago), from the early Pleistocene epoch to the late Pleistocene era (the Ice Age). The Ice Age was punctuated by climatic fluctuations of rain, thaw and freeze. During a part of the Ice Age there were thousands of years of rain – the pluvial age – when Malta's valleys were formed. A torrent of water coursed through what is now the Wied Dalam, and its river slowly ate into the limestone rock fissures of the river bed, causing a subterranean tunnel imperceptibly to erode over the centuries, creating the cave that exists today.

During the interglacial periods of thaw the climates normalized, and European fauna, like modern man, migrated south to warmer climes. Malta was at the time joined to Sicily and the continental European landmass – but not Africa – via a swampy land bridge and was as far south as the fauna could go. Gradually, as the ice melted and the rivers drained into the inland (Mediterranean) sea its level rose, trapping hippopotami, elephants, brown bears, giant swans, deer, wolves, voles and mice on the newly created islands; at this stage Marsaxlokk Bay was a freshwater lake. Imprisoned and unable to swim north or south, the animals underwent remarkable adaptive changes, becoming smaller and smaller, requiring less food and so increasing their chances of survival.

When the stunted animals eventually became extinct, starting with the hippopotami 180,000 years ago, their bones were sucked down through the holes and fissures in the river bed and solidified into bone *breccia* in the clay. Layer upon layer was built up over the years as each species died. The mystery (and there always is one) occurs after the deer became extinct 18,000 years ago. In 1981 the curator, Dr Zammit-Maempel, recorded a thick layer of volcanic ash on a similar Pleistocene deposit in central Malta which would indicate an unexplained cataclysmic occurrence such as untold years of constant volcanic eruption and earthquakes; whatever caused it will never be known for sure.

The illuminated cave is 475ft (145m) long (260ft/80m of it is open and not in any way claustrophobic) with one entrance where you can see across the valley to what was the other end of the cave. The single most fascinating part is the freestanding layered sandwich section that, like a 180,000-year-long egg timer, clearly shows part of evolutionary history.

Għar Dalam is undoubtedly the best-maintained site in Malta. The flowers leading down to the cave are flagged and watered, the paths swept, and the cactuses and carob (which normally wear summer clothes of opaque dust) glisten.

### Around Għar Dalam

Between Pretty Bay and St George's Bay, the old **Pinto Battery** of 1752 has long been an oil depot, and opposite is the bizarre monument erected in December 1989 to the Bush–Gorbachev summit. Its sympathies must be with the old Soviet Union: it is agricultural in appearance, neglected, rusting and falling apart. The inscription has already faded.

Further on, just before the Żejtun road, is the interesting **St George's Chapel**, the impact of which is somewhat diminished by the public convenience next door. Built by the knights in 1683 on the site of a medieval chapel, it is the only fortified church on the coastline. Access was via a drawbridge and portcullis at the back of the small church. The knights often wintered their galleys in the bay and Mass was said here before a voyage. The path behind the church leads to the historically significant **Borġ in-Nadur**; the hilly area all around here and Wied Dalam was a late Bronze Age settlement. A 4-D imagination is needed today, however, for all that exists is an overgrown wasteland of boulders, shotgun cartridges and bird traps.

# Marsaxlokk

**Marsaxlokk** is the fishing capital of the island. Strong traditions and a tightly knit community have allowed it to remain a village of cosy charm. Around the harbour a ribbon of houses is protected by oleander bushes in different shades of rose and white. Nothing, except of course the church, rises more than three storeys. The colours of the *luzzu* flicker off the still waters, their Eyes of Osiris staring balefully back at onlookers. Men sit on the quay with their legs apart, making sense of the tangles of spaghetti-like nylon that are miraculously transformed into nets every night. Sometimes their tired faces in the early morning light tell the true size of a catch long before even the wily urban wholesaler has noticed. This is an easy place in which to lose a couple of days.

Two *cippi*, low marble sepulchral pillars, were discovered in 1697 near the village of Marsaxlokk. Their carved inscriptions in Phoenician and Greek of vows to Melkert, Lord of Tyre, were the key pieces in the linguistic jigsaw that unlocked the Phoenician dialect – just as the Rosetta stone deciphered the secrets of Egyptian hieroglyphics. One *cippus* was given to doomed Louis XVI by Grand Master de Rohan and is still in the Louvre – the other is in the Museum of Archaeology.

At the **fish market**, the best of what can be fished in Maltese waters (and probably some sea bass poached from the government fish farm) can be purchased most Sundays till late in the afternoon. Try to arrive early, if only to see the increasingly rare Mediterranean swordfish.

The **swimming** is cleaner off the rocks between Fort St Lucian and Marsaxlokk village than at Birżebbuġa. Finding a fisherman to take you **fishing** is not too hard if you ask around the quay or the bars. Haggle playfully. A **tourist market** on the waterfront sells mostly machine-made lace tablecloths and, even in 95°F (35°C), thick locally knitted Aran sweaters and a comprehensive line in T-shirts.

**Fort St Lucian** was built by Grand Master Alof de Wignacourt in 1610 and designed by Vittorio Cassar to dominate and protect the bay. That's a hard brief for 2¾ square miles (7 sq km) of water and 5½ miles (9km) of coast, but one they fulfilled with equanimity. The massive fort, sitting broad-shouldered on the high ground of Kbira Point and encircled by a deep trench, successfully saw off a Turkish invasion of 60 galleys in 1614. With uncanny foresight Grand Master de Rohan (whose escutcheon is above the main gates) strengthened the fort and the seaward battery in 1795. Three years later the garrison of 160 men kept the French at bay for 36 hours, and were eventually defeated only by lack of rations. Today, somewhat ironically, the fort accommodates the government-owned **fish farm** and is not open to the public.

On the secondary road between Delimara and Żejtun is **Tas-Silġ**, a pair of sites steeped in history and not much else. Limestone walls encircle the barely discernible ruins of four different periods: a temple from the Tarxien period (3000 BC–2500 BC), a Bronze Age settlement, a Graeco-Punic temple to the goddess Astarte (Juno to the Romans) and an early Christian (AD 4–6) place of worship. The Italian Archaeological Mission unearthed the remains of the Graeco-Punic temple during its 1960s excavations. Pottery, ivory and stoneware were uncovered to suggest it might have been the Temple of Juno which was looted lock, stock and chalice by Verres, the kleptomaniac Roman governor of Sicily and Malta between 73 and 70 BC. During Verres' subsequent impeachment in Rome, Cicero stated in his charges, 'I do not know where you obtained those 400 jars of honey or such quantities of Maltese cloth or 50 cushions for sofas or so many candelabra, but what could you want with so many garments as if you were going to dress all your friends' wives?' As the evidence mounted against him, Verres, evidently not wishing to end his days as a lion's snack, fled to the Levant, presumably to plunder the mosques. You can climb over the walls, but otherwise the keys are available from the Museum of Archaeology in Valletta.

# Delimara Point

**Delimara Point** offers excellent uncrowded rock swimming, sunbathing, walks and an education in the barbarous activities of the *kaċċatur* or hunters, which can be quite intimidating, as men stroll about with arsenals of firepower. This desolate limestone peninsula of wild green maquis, inhabited solely by geckoes, juts south-wards, forming one of the first and last landfalls for exhausted migratory birds. Unfortunately, primeval traps and redoubts have mushroomed unchallenged, marring the beauty of the landscape, frightening innocent walkers, and corrupting the heady natural aromas even more than the new power-generating plant. In the four summer months, when the hunting season closes, those who observe the law (and that, sadly, is by no means everyone) sit on the rocks that edge into the sea, watch the incandescent apricot sun sink into Africa, and listen to the gentle wop-wop-wop as the fishermen chug slowly out to sea in their small *luzzus*.

## Beaches on Delimara Point

The inlets for bathing on the eastern coast are **Peter's Pool**, **Long Bay** and **Slug's Pool**. Access is tricky for the elderly and very young; take care if there is a swell. North of Peter's Pool are twin bays separated by Ras il-Fenek (Rabbit Point), the larger being **Island Bay**. You need to charter a boat to reach them but it is well worth it: they are free of day-trippers and the clear waters offer some of the best swimming and snorkelling on this coast. Turn a blind eye to the radio masts. The dive off the tip of Delimara Point is for the experienced only.

**Peter's Pool** has been signposted by an enterprising local who sits in the rubble-strewn field of a car park, and collects a few coins for the privilege. Rudimentary steps lead down to a flat rock which looks like a through-section of an industrial-sized layer cake; the wind has kindly formed it so that it provides a little shade. A few crude steps have been cut into the water, providing easier access than the other pools. Young summer love has been here for generations, and countless hearts and promises are tattooed into the golden limestone.

**Long Bay** had a restaurant which closed many moons ago but left a good, free car park. Steps go down to the pencil-shaped inlet, smaller and shadier than Peter's Pool. If the sea has been rough, seaborne rubbish can collect here. **Slug's Pool** is invariably deserted on account of its name and position. The swimming is excellent, but the rocks are jagged and shade is scarce.

## *Festas* in Marsaxlokk Bay

The grim-sounding **St Peter in Chains** is Birżebbuġġa's patron saint, and the *festa* dedicated to him always takes place on the first Sunday in August.

**Our Lady of Pompeii** is celebrated noisily in **Marsaxlokk** village square by the waterfront on the first Sunday in August; the fireworks light up the *luzzus*. Maltese women traditionally stipulated in their marriage contracts that they were to be taken to two *festas*, **L-Imnarja** and the **Pilgrimage to the church of St Gregory** in Żejtun (*see* pp.230 and 232) on the first Wednesday after Easter.

## Where to Stay and Eat in Marsaxlokk Bay

### Birżebbuġa

There is little choice of accommodation.

**\*\*\*Sea Breeze Hotel, t** 21 651499, *www.tcin.com/seabreezehotel* (€€). Overlooking Pretty Bay, the Sea Breeze is the best option. It is clean, the restaurant is air-conditioned, the rooms comfortably furnished, and the staff attentive. If you don't mind the extra noise, the rooms at the front of the hotel are blessed with large triangular balconies.

**Al Fresco Restaurant**, Intercontinental Hotel, St George's Bay, **t** 21 653422 (€€). Has a large terrace with generous umbrellas and a welcoming interior. It specializes in fish, with fresh catches when available, and it has a decent children's menu.

### Marsaxlokk

**\*\*Golden Sun Aparthotel**, Kajjik Street, **t** 21 651762, *www.goldensun hotelmalta.com* (€). Accommodation in Marsaxlokk is limited to this hotel in a dusty side street. It jollies up inside, with a bar that harks back to an English pub. The stone-floored rooms are cool in summer, and there are swimming pools as well as a restaurant. Inexpensive apartments are also available.

Fresh fish – which can sometimes be surprisingly expensive – is always on the menu around here.

**Hunter's Tower**, Wilga Street, **t** 21 651792 (€€€). A long-established place at the end of the quay next to a decaying old villa; its slightly uninspired menu consists mainly of fish. It does have some very nice views and a new playground where you can keep an eye on the kids. It is also a favourite haunt for a romantic tryst.

**Ir-Rizzu**, 89 Xatt is-Sajjieda, **t** 21 651569 (€€€). An excellent restaurant on the seafront, offering a variety of steamed fish, steaming being the traditional local method of cooking. It is particularly recommended. *Closed public hols.*

**Is-Sajjied**, Xatt is-Sajjieda, **t** 21 652549 (€€). Large restaurant which commands good views of the sea and the local fishing fleet going about its everyday business. Specializes in fish dishes. *Closed Mon.*

**Pisces**, 49/50 Xatt is-Sajjieda, **t** 21 654956 (€€). Popular with the locals, in spite of being located next to the police station. The cooking is excellent with generous portions, all of which are unfortunately accompanied by packet French fries. They plain-grill fish to perfection, but tend to lose their touch with sauces. Ask for a table by the window on the first floor. *Closed Wed.*

**La Capanna**, 80 Xatt is-Sajjieda, **t** 21 657755 (€). Delicious, original food is served up here, and it represents excellent value for money.

# Marsaskala and St Thomas Bay

Defenceless **Marsaskala** was the scene of the last Turkish invasion of Maltese soil in the late spring of 1614, a revenge attack on the knights for plundering grain. The 5,000-strong force,

# Getting to and around Marsaskala and St Thomas Bay

Unless you are coming on the **main road** from Żabbar, bring a compass, distress flares and tranquillizers. The signposts have either disappeared or been used as target practice by the *kaċċatur*, turning the **secondary roads** into a maze fit to confound Daedalus. From Valletta, 8 miles (13km) away, the best route is Marsa–Paola–Fgura–Żabbar, after which the signposts (two of them) begin. Three buses, nos.19 and 20 from Valletta and no.22 from Cospicua, serve the area.

repelled at Fort St Lucian, came ashore here but was driven back to its galleys once it reached Żejtun.

The long thin creek of Marsaskala was the favoured fishing port of the Sicilian community from the north of Żejtun. It became known as Marsa Ta'sicali, 'The Sicilians' Harbour', and was frequented by the well-to-do from Żabbar. Now 2,200 people live on the slopes that rise up from the sea, but numbers sometimes quadruple at the very peak of summer. It is the most developed village of the area, but has managed to maintain its identity as a fishing community. The buildings that snake from Zonqor Point to Fort St Thomas are mostly low and small; the topography prevents high-rises craning for a sea view. Families tend to vacation here and enjoy the evening *passeggiata* along the head of the bay while the action-seeking young prefer to be sardined along the northern coasts.

In winter, after the salty sea air has welded shut the shutters on the summer apartments and the tourists have returned to even chillier climes, Marsaskala is another place where time, like a *luzzu*'s anchor in a storm, can easily come adrift.

The headland of **Il Gżira** separates the bays of St Thomas and Marsaskala, and was the most suitable place on which to construct a fort. In 1614, just after the last Turkish invasion, the prolific team of Grand Master Alof de Wignacourt and Vittorio Cassar hurriedly began Fort St Thomas at the enormous cost of 13,450 *scudi*. Cassar designed the tall bulky fort with its four corner towers and seaward battery to be garrisoned by 100 men in times of emergency, and to field eight cannon and a mortar. The seaward battery was eaten by the elements and finally demolished in the 1970s to make way for the Jerma Palace Hotel. **Fort St Thomas**, its imposing walls not yet completely covered in matted green clumps of wild shrubs, now houses a restaurant.

On the Żejtun to St Thomas Bay road is the 17th-century **Mamo Tower**, a miniature fort built in the shape of the cross of St Andrew, with one floor and a vaulted ceiling. St Thomas Bay, with its wide undefended coastline, was a favourite of the North African slavers, for the shallow waters made it easier to drag the Maltese peasants off to their new lives. Understandably, the Mamo family found it hard to attract labour for their nearby estates, and so they constructed the tower as an early example of an employee benefit.

Later the family used it as a summer residence; the small chapel 50 yards away was its place of worship. It has recently been restored by the Malta National Trust.

**Zonqor Point**, the northern tip of Marsaskala Bay, houses the **National Swimming Pool**, where important water-polo matches are played. The local team play on the north shore of the bay itself where the team and spectators are catered for by the 'ET, at your Service' café. **St Thomas Bay** takes its name from a long-since demolished church and is not very attractive, but has reasonable swimming and snorkelling. Very popular, it can congest with four generations of Maltese at the weekends. In May and June you'll find the old men sitting on crates next to the shingle beach lovingly painting their *luzzus*. From Delimara Point or Marsaxlokk it is a reasonably easy 2–2½-mile (3–4km) walk and the cliffs along the south coast are not unnervingly high. Diving off the Munxar reef is only for the skilled. Many ships have been caught unawares by the reef along this coast.

**National Swimming Pool** *for information on water-polo matches, contact the National Swimming Association,* **t** *21 829369*

## Festa in Marsaskala

The Marsaskala *festa* of **St Anna** is celebrated on the last Sunday of July.

## Where to Stay in Marsaskala and St Thomas Bay

### Marsaskala

**\*\*\*\*Corinthia Jerma Palace Hotel**, **t** 21 633222, *www.corinthiahotel.com* (€€€€). The part-Libyan-owned Jerma Palace is situated on the very tip of Il Gżira Point. Designed to take in the sea on all sides, it has many amenities including indoor and outdoor pools, gym and recreation rooms. A good hotel of 350 rooms and suites, nearly all with sea glimpses, it is let down slightly by a journeyman kitchen and sombre public rooms. Good kids' club in the summer.

**\*\*\*Cerviola Hotel**, Qaliet Street, **t** 21 823287, *www.cerviolahotel.com* (€€). Recently refurbished and upgraded, with rooftop pool and 50 air-con rooms. The entrance hall is reminiscent of a 1960s airport lounge and is not aided by the proximity of the kitchen. There is a sun deck and a karaoke bar. Fine if you want a cheap base.

**\*\*\*Etvan Hotel**, Bahhara Street, **t** 21 636203 (€€). Near the Cerviola is this modern guest house; the rooms at the front all have uninterrupted views of the bay.

**\*\*Porto Scala Hotel**, Bahhara Street, **t** 21 633961, *portoscala@waldonet.net. mt* (€). Small hotel with no pool, but close to the sea.

**Apartments** are plentiful: enquire at **Dahlia**, 31 Marina Promenade, **t** 21 684491, or the **Shik Complex** 100 yards away at the Piazza Mifsud Bonnici, **t** 21 829949.

### St Thomas Bay

**\*\*Ramla Lodge**, **t** 21 637596, *ramla_lodge_hotel@msn.com* (€). Caters predominantly to Germans. The 31 rooms and public rooms are clean and ordered, and everything on sale is German. There is a pool, and the beach is less than 100 yards away.

## Eating Out in Marsaskala and St Thomas Bay

### Marsaskala

**La Buona Pasta**, Marina Street, **t** 21 684050 (€€€). This small place serves home-made pasta at reasonable prices.

La Favorita, Il-Gardiel Street, t 21 634113 (€€€). A definite favourite with locals, this restaurant serves first-class food, especially the fish. Highly recommended.

Grabiel, 1 Mifsud Bonnici Street, t 21 634194 (€€€). By the roundabout at the head of the bay and named after a wrecked oil tanker. Popular and capable, if a bit starchy. Closed Sun.

Il Re del Pesce, t 21 634178 (€€€). On the way to St Thomas Bay. Good fish restaurant.

La Spigola, Zonqor Street, t 21 634288 (€€€). Towards Zonqor Point is this fish restaurant, with a tiny terrace overlooking the picturesque bay and a romantic air despite bizarre décor. The food is 'mid-Med' with the emphasis on fish. Worth a visit. Open for dinner daily exc Tues; also open Sun lunchtime.

Tal Familja, Gardiel Street, t 21 632161 (€€€). A large restaurant with good food and equally good service. Closed Mon.

Al Kafe, t 21 637956 (€). On the promenade. Good for pizzas, salads and ice creams, and a place where people congregate all day and well into the night.

There are also a few smaller seafront promenade cafés, such as Tiny Mint and Lemon 'n' Lime, which can provide a pleasant pit stop on a walk along the coast. Marsaskala has a penchant for small eateries; further along Marina Promenade and next door to the youthful La Playa, is a Chinese takeaway the size of a broom cupboard, for those who want to sit by the water in the still evenings and see if the fish eat fried rice. In recent years, quite a number of Chinese and Oriental restaurants have set up business in this area.

Jakarta, Il-Gardiel Street, t 21 633993 (€€). Serves Asian food.

### St Thomas Bay

Fisherman's Rest, t 21 632049 (€€€). Unpretentious family-run restaurant specializing in local and fish dishes.

San Tomaso, t 21 639394 (€€). Out of the beach lido mould, but luckily none the worse for that.

# Inland: Żabbar, Żejtun and Around

The two casals (villages) of Żabbar and Żejtun are similar in many ways. They both grew out of agricultural communities — Żabbar means someone who prunes trees – and both enjoyed the dubious honour of Grand Master von Hompesch's patronage. (Żabbar was elevated to city status in 1798 with the immodest new name of Città Hompesch – it never caught on.) Today both are political hotbeds, left of centre. Tough and hard men come from these parts.

## Żabbar

As Malta's economy became increasingly dependent on the harbours, the villages diverged. Żabbar, on the doorstep of the Three Cities, became urbanized and lost its old country feel. With 13,500 people, it has grown into the area's largest community. Rural features remain, but there are fumes and especially noise now in the centre of town by the church of Our Lady of Graces.

### History

On 18 May, the dawn of the **Great Siege** of 1565, the Turkish invasion forces trampled the older Żejtun and set up their camp at

# Getting to and around the Żabbar and Żejtun Area

It is easy to get lost in this area, where one town seems to melt into the next, but **Żabbar** is flanked by the Hompesch Arch and the Żabbar Gate; anywhere between is bound to be Żabbar. By **car** take the Paola road from Valletta and then follow the signs for Żabbar or Fgura. The **bus** terminus of Żabbar is halfway down the main street, Santwarju Street – five buses stop here, the nos.18, 19, 21 and 22 from Paola and the no.22 from Cospicua.

A total of 18 different **buses** go to **Paola**; 10 carry on to Tarxien. For both the **Hypogeum** and **Tarxien Temples**, alight at the main terminus in Piazza Paola. The temples are 450 yards to the east of it, and the Hypogeum 300 yards to the south in Burials Street; neither is well flagged. By **car**, head for Paola and park in the square, which sometimes hosts a market.

There are five **buses**, nos.32, 34, 35, 36 and 39, which serve the **Luqa** area from Marsa. By **car**, follow the signs for the airport, then turn right towards the old terminal instead of left towards the new.

There is only one **bus** serving the **Gudja** and **Għaxaq** area, the no.8 from Paola. Follow the road to Luqa and the airport, and from there Gudja is signposted. Għaxaq is tripped over easily after leaving Gudja on the Żejtun road. Gudja has a particularly good public garden near the bus stop, with swings, etc.

By **car**, follow the signposts via Marsa and Paola for **Żejtun**, which is about 4½ miles (7.5km) from Valletta. By **bus**, the area can be reached on the nos.26, 27 or 29 from Paola and the no.28 from Cospicua.

the village of Żabbar; life outside the fortified protection of the Three Cities was uncertain. It was not until 1670, when Grand Master Nicolas Cotoner began the construction, funded from his own purse, of the 3 miles (5km) of defences known as the Cottonera Lines that the villagers felt more secure: at the first sign of an invasion, the principal entrance into the fortifications, the Żabbar Gate, was only a 1-mile (1.5km) dash.

In 1800 Żabbar and Żejtun (*see* p.230) became one of the three **British** land-force bases and the headquarters of the Maltese insurgents who blockaded the French within the walls of Valletta and the Three Cities. The guns of the French garrison did immense damage to the village and destroyed the dome of the parish church. Further damage was done in the **Second World War**, when the area's proximity to the Grand Harbour meant that it fell prey to stray Axis bombs. The last civilian to be killed by enemy bombing, shortly after midnight on 26 July 1943 and 24 hours after Mussolini's fall, was Vincent Attard of Żabbar.

## Around the Town

The fussy, confused-looking parish church of **Our Lady of Graces** sits alone on an island site. Designed by 50-year-old Tommaso Dingli in 1641, it has since been added to by others less skilled, and detracted from by human and seismic violence. Dingli's design sensed the wind of architectural change blowing south from Italy and did not call for the bold bell towers; these were added between 1738 and 1742. The façade, built in 1730, is by Giovanni Bonavia. The dome, erroneously credited by some to Lorenzo Gafa, was badly damaged over the years and finally replaced in 1928. The stunning barrel vault in the nave, the bays of which are decorated in a linear pattern, is one of the best surviving features of Dingli's

## The Last Grand Master to Reign in Malta

Guarded by the later and unnecessary addition of two rusty cannons on an isolated roundabout is a triumphal arch erected in honour of Grand Master von Hompesch, who was the last grand master to reign in Malta. The arch, like the man, is neither grand nor flamboyant, and was a gift from the people of Żabbar, one which crowned his sad life.

The Bavarian Ferdinand von Hompesch was elected in 1797 and was the only German grand master in the Order's history. He had a tremendous regard for the Maltese and was the only grand master to speak their language. History's chroniclers have not been kind, however, partly because of his almost eager surrender to Napoleon 11 months into his reign in June 1798. By the time he assumed the magistracy, the Order had become a faction-ridden and none-too-exclusive club of petty despots, fifth columnists and drunken aristocrats.

As a weak but kindly leader, he lacked the resolve and ability to reform the Order militarily or spiritually, being no more than a supplicant to those – especially the knights of French *langues* – he was meant to lead. The reason for the Order's existence, the 11th-century Holy Crusades, seemed to have been forgotten.

original design. The church has undergone some restoration work in recent years, prompting congregations of elderly men to gather outside twiddling their rosaries and speculating over the next modification to their beloved mongrel church, while the town elders still lament the 'new dome' erected in their now-distant childhood.

**Our Lady of Graces parish church museum**
*open Sun am only*

The church has a small **museum** established in the 1950s, consisting of votive paintings from sailors miraculously or fatefully rescued from the seas by Our Lady of Graces.

# Tarxien, Paola and the Temples

There are two reasons to visit these towns: the **Tarxien Temples** and the **Hypogeum**. Other less touristy sights include the **prison**, **Addolorata Cemetery**, the **Mosque** and **Qaddafi Gardens** where the great man planted a cypress in 1973.

There have been agricultural settlements at Tarxien since the time of the early temple builders (3000 BC). The streets follow the infuriatingly delightful plan of the old *casals* or villages and wind aimlessly around the 17th-century parish church of **Our Lady of the Annunciation**. Today Tarxien is the home of the former prime minister, Dom Mintoff, and 7,000 others.

**Paola** is the 17th-century 'new town' sewn into the north edge of Tarxien. Called Casal Nouva when it was founded by Grand Master de Paule in 1626, it was designed for the higher ground above the harbour to catch the sea breezes of summer. It did not catch on immediately, partly because new towns never do, and partly because it was outside the harbour area fortifications and near the burial ground for plague victims. Today it has over 12,000 inhabitants.

Vittorio Cassar's church of 1626, **Santa Ubaldesca**, 350 yards west of the prison, had been outgrown by the turn of the 19th century. To accommodate the parishioners (and as a sign of the parish's growing importance), an imposing new church to **Christ the King** was begun in 1924. Designed by Giuseppe Damato (better known for 'The Rotunda' in the Xewkija, Gozo, *see* p.291), it has a neoclassical style and was built using modern techniques and materials.

## The Hypogeum at Ħal Saflieni

⭐ **Hypogeum**

*tours daily 9–4; book well in advance as tickets are often sold out weeks ahead, through t 21 825579, www. heritagemalta.com, hypogeum@gov.mt or in person from the Hypogeum Visitor Centre at Paola, the Archaeological Museum of Archaeology at Victoria on Gozo, the National Museum of Archaeology at Valletta, or the Ġgantija temples on Gozo; guided tours to the Hypogeum are restricted to 80 people per day; no children under 6; adm*

The Hypogeum is Malta's finest archaeological monument as well as being a World Heritage site. It was closed in 1991, but reopened in 2001 after extensive work to try to stabilize the site and minimize damage caused by visitors. The tour begins with an introductory exhibition and a multilingual film.

Hypogeum is a word derived from Greek, meaning an underground burial vault. The vault comprises a complex of interlinking subterranean curvilinear chambers on three levels hewn by hand out of the limestone rock to a depth of 35ft (10.6m), and dating back to approximately 3200 BC.

**Ħal Saflieni** is a part of Paola, and the Hypogeum was, like so many other archaeological sites, a chance discovery. In 1902 a builder crashed through the roof of the upper chamber of the burial site while excavating for a new housing development. Unfortunately, he kept his discovery quiet until he had finished his entire project, resulting in more avoidable damage. Detailed excavations were begun in 1905 under the direction of Dr (later Sir) Themistocles Zammit. By 1909, the bones of 6–7,000 people had been found in the side chambers along with pottery and personal artefacts. As the excavation progressed, it became apparent that the complex was more than a burial site. Informed speculation suggests that the main chambers were used for initiation and training in rites associated with those enacted at the nearby Tarxien Temples.

Because it is underground it has survived (Maltese builders notwithstanding) the elements and the ravages of war for more than 5,000 years; its overall condition is remarkable. It also miraculously escaped the Axis bombing of the Grand Harbour area when it was used as an air-raid shelter.

## The Tarxien Temples

⭐ **Tarxien Temples**

*open 9–5; closed Good Fri, 24, 25, 31 Dec, and 1 Jan; adm*

The temples are the most important megalithic structures on Malta, and are powerfully impressive, despite the fact that they are hemmed in by 20th-century buildings. Historians agree that what remains in **Tarxien** today was part of a much greater settlement, but modern developments seem to have precluded the possibility

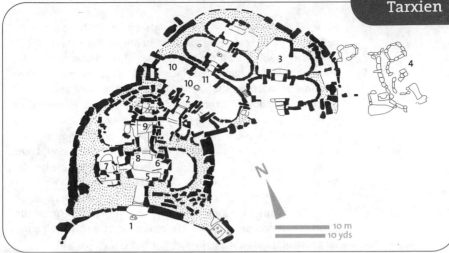

of further exciting discoveries. A visit to the Museum of Archaeology in Valletta is advisable, to help translate what can appear at first sight to be an impressive but random collection of large rocks. The museum has a helpful three-dimensional model of the site and an artist's impression of what the structures originally looked like. It should be noted that many (easily discernible) preventative repairs have been made, and that the altars, statues and friezes are copies. The originals and other finds are housed in the museum.

Not long before the First World War, and after the discovery of the Hypogeum, a farmer complained at the constant blunting by large stones of his plough. The antennae of Dr Themistocles Zammit twitched and in 1914 he began his five-year excavation of the site.

Three main temple structures and the remains of a small fourth (numbers refer to the site plan) were unearthed: The **South** [1], the **Central** [2], the **East** [3] and the **Early** [4]. All except the last structure to be built, the Central Temple, are sited in a southeast quadrant. With the exception of the Early Temple, which dates back to the older Ġgantija phase, the three principal temples date back to the eponymous Tarxien phase (3000–2500 BC). These were the last of the temple structures to be constructed by prehistoric man in Malta.

In the four-apsed **South Temple** is the huge and sadly headless statue of an elephantine female, possibly the **'fat' goddess of fertility** [5] (she must have stood more than 8ft/2.5m tall). Dr Trump, the former curator of the Museum of Archaeology, has eloquently described her: 'She wears a very full pleated skirt. It would be ungentlemanly to quote her hip measurements, and her calves are in proportion. She is supported, however, on small, elegant, but seriously overworked feet.' To her right is an **altar** niche [6] above delicately carved spiral stonework. The space behind the niche revealed a collection of animal bones and a flint knife presumably used for sacrifices. There is no indication of human sacrifice having taken place. To the left or in the west apse are more **animal friezes** [7], although less recognizable, and in the centre a **pitted bowl** [8]. Through what was the temple's inner door is the decorated **central niche** [9].

The **Central Temple**, more than 75ft (23m) high, is unique in Malta for having three pairs of apses rather than two and was built after the South and East Temples. The predominant feature is reddening of the stone, possibly caused by an inferno that marked the end of the temple-building period 4,500 years ago. The further you go inwards, due to the lie of the land, the more the structure's condition improves. The central court is striking, if only for the manner in which man was able to fit huge slabs of limestone together.

There are two bowls in the **left apse** [10], the larger of which was hewn from one piece of rock. Entry to the third pair of apses, and what may have been the priests' inner sanctum, is barred by the finest and most powerful carving here, the oculus **motif stone** [11]. Very little is left of the **East Temple**, even less of the oldest **Early Temple**. The large stones outside were part of the enclosing wall.

While it seems pretty unlikely that the Tarxien Temples saw anything other than religious rites, try to bring an inquisitive mind. They might, after all, have been the site of a cattle market.

## Luqa

*1987: Money No Problems – 1992: Problems No Money*
inscription outside the Labour Party Club, Luqa

**Luqa**, although named after the white poplar tree, is synonymous with arriving and departing. The fate of this friendly village of 5,650 people has been inextricably linked to that of the nearby airport. Brought into commission in June 1940, Luqa was the islands' main and only concreted airfield during the Second World War. Wellington bombers flew from here, and when inclement weather or Axis bombs shut down Ħal Far or Ta'Qali it became Malta's only airfield. Without air-strike capability, the islands would have been doomed. Not surprisingly, Axis bombs almost levelled the village (an agricultural community since 1634), but the airfield's longest inoperational period was a remarkable 48 hours. The new airport, which is located around 2 miles (3km) away from the old one and has been named **Malta International**, will always be known as Luqa.

Much of the village has been sympathetically restored since the war, along the same old winding street. Buildings take a long time to complete in Malta but the unfinished one opposite the parish church must take first prize – it was begun in 1946. There is some ambiguity as to who actually oversaw the design of the parish church of St Andrew but it is credited to Tommaso Dingli between 1634 and 1665, although it is built in the style of Cassar's St John's.

The faithful post-war restoration took over 25 years. It is no masterpiece, but the benches underneath the trees outside are ideal for people-watching. To the west is the small **Chapel of the Assumption**, with a fine little bell cote. Peer in through the viewing window at the tessellated marble floor covering those buried beneath. By some fluke it survived the war unscathed.

## Gudja, Għaxaq and Around

**Gudja** stands alone and **Għaxaq** almost forms part of Żejtun. Both villages, of 2,350 and 3,860 inhabitants respectively, date back to the 14th century when they were probably agricultural satellites of Żejtun. The medieval church of St Mary Ta'Bir Miftuħ and the narrow twisty streets of Gudja attest to how long these villages have existed. Gudja was the birthplace of the remarkable Gerolamo Cassar, architect of many of Valletta's buildings.

Ever since the airport began to expand in the 1970s, the village of Gudja has found itself uncomfortably close to the runways. The new terminal roads encroach even further, and Ta'Bir Miftuħ looks sadly out of place next to its new neighbours. People tend to live behind closed doors here; the sense of community is underwhelming, owing in part at least to the cramped village square where even the church seems to gasp for air.

The church of **St Mary Ta'Bir Miftuħ** (St Mary of the Open Well), on the Luqa–Gudja road before the town itself, was mentioned in, and possibly predates, the 1436 report of the 10 original parishes. Double the size and a few years younger than the church at Ħal Millieri (see pp.206–7), it is constructed in the same box-like idiom and has been added to over the centuries. The most notable features are the Cyclopean window above the Norman-influenced door, and the simple late 16th-century bell cote. The very high parapet conceals not only the pitched roof but five long waterspouts. Inside, some tantalizing pieces of original stone-painted frescoes of the *Last Judgement* have just about survived.

In between Gudja and Għaxaq is the **Villa Bettina** or Dorell Palace, known to the villagers as Il Palazz. Built in 1770, it has survived as one of the finest private houses in Malta and is not open to the public. Bettina Muscati married the French Marquis Dorell and became lady-in-waiting to Carolina, Marie Antoinette's sister and wife of the King of Naples and the Two Sicilies. After jealously upsetting the queen, she returned to Malta and assumed the role of grand hostess. Among others, she is said to have entertained Napoleon here (it is one of the more sympathetic and likely refuges the Corsican might have sought).

During the blockade of the French in Valletta, however, she showed the élan of a capricious host, when the villa's keys were put at the disposal of General Thomas Graham, the British commander-in-chief. She reached the summit of her social mountain in May 1800, when Nelson, accompanied by Sir William and Lady Hamilton, dined at the villa. Little is known about her luckless French husband, who presumably footed the bill for his enemies' entertainment.

# Żejtun

*Żejt* means oil and the village was famous for its olive oil, yet not one tree remains. Situated midway between the Grand Harbour and Marsaxlokk, it prospered as a market garden through Punic and Roman times to become the main parish hereabouts. Today it is a welcoming village of 12,000; the stares from the men outside the band clubs or on the church steps are not hostile, just curious. One of Malta's finest old parish churches, the church of St Gregory, falls within its boundaries while its present parish church is a monumental and powerful 17th-century edifice by Lorenzo Gafa.

Contrasting with the slow tempo of the village is the temperament of its people. The tight-knit population has fostered under a myriad differing yokes a fierce sense of independence and pride. The villagers are outsiders and, while the inhabitants of Żabbar might disagree, the men here are probably harder.

## History

By the time the long-expected **Turkish invasion** got under way in May 1565, the village of **Żejtun** was prepared: completely emptied of people and livestock, on de la Valette's orders. Grand Marshal Copier's cavalry, which had the unfortunate job of patrolling the Żejtun area and the cliffs up to Għajn Tuffieħa, encountered the first detachment of Turks as they headed for Żejtun. The first blood of the Great Siege was spilled in an engagement that would later prove crucial. Two young knights, one French and one Portuguese, were captured, and the lies they uttered to Mustapha Pasha's skilled torturers before they were killed helped to seal the fate and failure of the Turkish invasion.

The Turks landed again in 1614 at Marsaskala and the 5,000-strong army were forced to retreat by a cavalry detachment after ransacking the south of Żejtun. This was the last Christian-Muslim skirmish on Maltese soil.

## Visiting the Village

The village has many noteworthy buildings. See them at their best when the bells for evening Mass sound and the sun throws long shadows and a rich light onto the honey-coloured stone. A handful of the less devout sit resolutely on chairs spilled out from clubs and bars; the day's work is done.

The centre of the village is dominated by the fortress-like **parish church of St Catherine** (1692–1722), which is a fine example of Maltese Baroque shaped by Roman and not Sicilian influences. It is possibly Lorenzo Gafa's finest parish church. The whole site has been used to great effect and purpose. The wide façade with its seven bays retains a horizontal feel from the clever use of single Doric and Ionic pilasters; the two perfectly scaled bell towers are encircled with Corinthian pilasters. Side screens and arcades-which-lead-you-nowhere-but-everywhere maintain the coherence of the design.

Gafa became a master craftsman of domes as a result of his Roman training. The great octagonal dome here was structurally a less successful forerunner to his masterpiece at the Cathedral in Mdina, its vault having to be replaced in 1907. Yet the style of the interior shows more restraint and is more satisfying than his earlier St Nicholas at Siġġiewi.

Opposite, in St Catherine's Street, are less meritorious buildings, but all are worth a quick look. On the right as you go down is the sensibly inconspicuous right-wing **Nationalist Party Club** which used to be the old law courts. Next door to it is another smaller church, the only one in Malta dedicated to the **Holy Ghost**, built at the same time as St Catherine's and credited to Gafa. At the bottom of the hill is **Casa Perellos**, once the country home of Grand Master Perellos. Today it is a sad victim of family inheritance squabbles and is falling apart. On the right-hand pilaster is his Aragonese symbol, the Perellos or pear. During the procession of the feast of St Gregory the nobility would watch the pageant from the balcony supported by four wonderful gargoyles, as it passed en route to the eponymous church.

The former parish church of St Catherine, now known as **St Gregory's**, is the best of Malta's older churches. It was built in 1436, the year Żejtun became one of the island's 10 parishes, in an amalgam of styles: military, puritanical and Italian. The only parts that remain from the original structure are the nave and the façade, with its perfectly proportioned bell cote.

The west-facing Renaissance main door with its fluted pilasters – it was thought that all churches should face west to Mdina, then the capital – was added in the mid-16th century just after the Order arrived in Malta. The knights' austere Rhodian style coupled

**⭐ Church of St Gregory**
*open at the weekends when Mass is said; for a more detailed tour, including the secret passages, contact the parish office,*
*t 21 693704*

with seven years in the Mediterranean wilderness turned their architectural clock back, so their additions were already dated. For example, notice the Gothic-style diagonal vault and the transepts, both added in 1606. At the eastern end the wall slopes away like a battlement to the road. The reddish dome, thought to be the earliest in Malta, dates from 1495; its saucer shape belies its depth.

The feeling of serenity inside the building is amplified by the flagstones, the almost throne-like confessional, and the shaft of incandescent light that rotates with a sundial's precision from the eye of the dome. If you stand at the main door, you will notice that it is left of centre. The reason for this, it is said, is to confound the devil, who always walks in a straight line and is therefore prevented from interfering with a liturgical service.

It would be very un-Maltese if a church such as this did not have a secret or two. In the vestry, a small spiral staircase leads up to two narrow passages first discovered in 1909 by two children who were too frightened to tell anyone. In 1969 the parish verger, Mr Debono, rediscovered the bones of 50 or so people, possibly those missing in Dragut Rais's raid of 1547. It is assumed they died from the smoke caused by the Muslim soldiers desecrating the church.

St Gregory's has had a chequered life: it has been a fishermen's store, a British hospital during the French occupation, a dormitory in the Second World War, and finally a store for the Royal Engineers, who blithely whitewashed over all the precious old wall-paintings.

## *Festas* around Żabbar

**Żabbar**: Our Lady of Graces is on the first Sunday after 8 September.

**Paola:** celebrates Our Lady of Lourdes, on the first Sunday after 15 August and Christ the King on the fourth Sunday in July.

**Tarxien:** marks the Annunciation on the fifth Sunday after Easter.

**Luqa:** the *festa* of St Andrew takes place on the first Sunday in July.

**Gudja and Għaxaq:** both have *festas* celebrating the Assumption, 15 August; Gudja also has its *festa* of St Joseph on the first Sunday in June.

**Żejtun:** celebrates St Gregory on the first Wednesday after Easter, with a procession leaving from St Clements. It was once customary that a bride would have written into her marriage contract that her husband would take her to this feast, the true origins of which are uncertain. There is also a conventional *festa* for **St Catherine** on a floating date in June.

## Where to Stay and Eat around Żabbar

There is nowhere to stay or eat in **Żabbar** or **Tarxien** so head for Valletta, Marsaxlokk or Marsaskala.

There is nowhere to stay in **Luqa**, but there is an array of typically Maltese bars such as the colourful **Phoenicia Café**, adorned with racing pictures. To the left of the church as you face it is one of the friendliest **fruit vendors** in Malta, tucked into a small hole in the wall.

There are many bars and clubs near the imposing St Catherine's church in Żejtun. All serve pizza slices and *pastizzi*. Or have a picnic in the walled-in shade of the Luqa Briffa Gardens, 100 yards from St Gregory's. The dedication plaque (erected by George III and Governor Ball) above the entrance is wrong; the village built it in the early 18th century as a fruit orchard.

# Mdina, Rabat and the Inland Towns

Few sights in Malta are as impressive as Mdina, one of the few remaining fortified medieval cities in the Mediterranean. High on a plateau in the middle of the island, away from the busy coasts, it still is Malta's patrician old capital; set back in time, another age caught within its mellow walls.

Outside the walls are Rabat, with acres of catacombs, and a Roman villa. Further afield, in Mosta, is the most contemporary of Malta's ecclesiastic extravaganzas, the parish church of St Mary, known as the Mosta Dome. The seamless suburbs of Birkirkara, and the Three Villages, have a great wealth of Renaissance and Baroque architecture, including five churches worth going out of your way to see, and the public gardens in the San Anton Palace.

# 12

## Don't miss

- **1** Wandering in the old capital
  Central Mdina p.234

- **2** An essay in Baroque
  St Paul's Cathedral, Mdina p.240

- **3** Eerie depths
  St Agatha's catacombs, Rabat p.249

- **4** The perfect souvenir
  Ta'Qali Crafts Village p.250

- **5** Veterans of the skies
  Aviation Museum p.253

*See map overleaf*

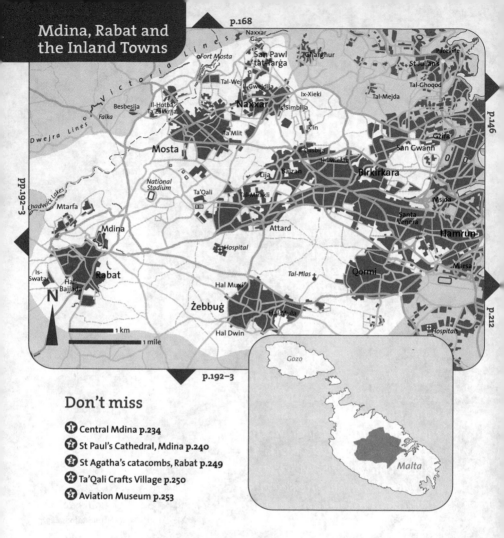

p.168

p.146

pp.192–3

p.212

p.192–3

## Don't miss

1. ⭐ Central Mdina **p.234**
2. ⭐ St Paul's Cathedral, Mdina **p.240**
3. ⭐ St Agatha's catacombs, Rabat **p.249**
4. ⭐ Ta'Qali Crafts Village **p.250**
5. ⭐ Aviation Museum **p.253**

# Mdina and Rabat

⭐ **Central Mdina**

Put **Mdina** at the top of your 'sights to see' pile, above historic but sometimes wearisome Valletta. For more than 2,000 years Mdina has played a key role in the island's history. The 'tourist powers that be' have finally woken up to the exploitability of Mdina; hence you'll find many 'Experiences', some better than others. The best 'Mdina experience' by far is a leisurely 4pm-ish stroll through the city itself.

Mdina, in Arabic 'a walled-in city', was the old capital of Malta. Two hundred years after the Arab occupation ended in 1224 it was renamed Città Notabile, and in 1571, when Valletta became the capital, Città Vecchia, 'the old city'. Today, within its panoramic bastions and cool narrow alleys there is evidence of a civic self-

*Città Notabile
della mia Corona
(Notable City of
my Crown)*
King Alfonso V of
Aragon, 1428

## Getting to and around Mdina and Rabat

The **road** to Mdina and Rabat is signposted from Mosta, Msida and Valletta. Despite poor signposting, the Ħamrun/St Venera bypass is the quickest route from both St Julian's and Valletta. Visitors' cars are banned in Mdina and the ticket-issuing police tend to lie in wait where tourists gather – so it is best to use the car park by Howard Gardens.

By **bus**, from Valletta nos.80 and 81 run to the towns.

**Taxis** can be found lurking in the shade around the car park and streets outside the Main Gate, Saqqajja Square and occasionally Parish Square.

Unlike its Gozitan twin, the Citadel, Mdina is reasonably level and **wheelchair access** to many places is comparatively good.

---

*One of the smallest and most compact of historic cities, and entirely and wholly complete within the circle of its walls. No sooner has one set foot in Mdina, one has only to walk through this gateway, then time rolls back and one is in another age.*

Sachverell Sitwell, *Malta*, 1958

respect not found anywhere else in Malta: it is clean, only residents' cars are allowed inside, and even the street signs are elegantly scripted on china plaques. There is charm and enchantment in its twisting streets where shadows, as in an old master, are thrown onto the honey-coloured stone walls. (Do not be deceived by such apparent confusion; the shadowy alleys were built to keep the town cool and confuse invaders.)

This is the only true Maltese city; the knights' influence is restricted to a few, albeit fine, buildings including the magnificent **Palazzo Vilhena** and the stunning Baroque **Cathedral of St Paul's**. Mdina's zenith was during the darker medieval times of the Normans and Spanish and, though all Arabic traces have long been eradicated, some of the existing architecture pre-dates the Order by hundreds of years – from the medieval **Palazzo Falzon**, where the grand master received the keys to the city in 1530, to the original Roman city walls.

Today Mdina has the smallest urban population in Malta, of just 500 people. By contrast, over 13,000 live in the sprawling suburbs of neighbouring **Rabat**, a grimy town with little to commend it. Its sites, however, are worth taking in: the **Roman villa**, St Paul's **Chapel and Grotto**, and the **catacombs of St Agatha and St Paul**. Rabat was once no more than a suburb and necropolis to Mdina, created under an ancient Roman law which stated the dead had to be disposed of outside the city limits. However, before the Arabs reduced Mdina by four-fifths to its present, easily defendable size, the old city wall used to encompass Rabat's northern quarter, where the numerous catacombs still honeycomb the subterranean rock.

### History

Mdina's history is, for what was the capital city of one of the central Mediterranean hubs until the late 16th century, remarkably uneventful. The usual cast of aggressors – Romans, Arabs, Turks and French – have all at one time besieged and/or occupied this fortified city, 620ft (190m) high. The **Romans** were the first, excluding **Neolithic man** and the **Phoenicians**, to colonize the plateau seriously. Their settlement, named for simplicity the same as the island, 'Melita', was the seat of their *municipium*. The city walls spread into Rabat and afforded them in the northern and eastern quadrants good natural defences.

The **Arabs** adopted Melita as their capital in AD 870, renamed it Medina ('the walled city'), reduced it to its present size, dug a moat and strengthened the southern walls. The defences proved strong enough for 220 years, until Christianity spread south; in 1090 it was taken by Count Roger the Norman. He found a crumbling city, built a new rectangular-plan cathedral and introduced a north European feudal system.

Between 1194 and 1530, under Swabian, Angevin, Aragonese and Castilian influence – known under the collective misnomer, the '**Spanish Period**' – Mdina not only prospered but became an aristocratic Maltese city. In the 14th century it accommodated the almost mute Università, or governing body, established by the Spanish viceroy in Sicily. Alphonso V of Aragon visited in 1428, rejuvenated flagging morale, vowed the city would forever remain Spanish, and renamed it **Città Notabile** (a public relations coup similar to George VI's awarding the island the George Cross in 1942.) In 1530 **Charles V** broke his ancestor's promise and ceded the islands to the wandering **Order of the Knights of St John**. Grand Master de L'Isle Adam received the silver keys to Città Notabile in Palazzo Falzon from the Hakem of the Università soon after his arrival in the autumn of 1530. His promise to maintain all their privileges and rights was promptly broken.

The Order was a seafaring body, the harbour was its base and, in all but name, its capital. Città Notabile, therefore, became increasingly less important. During the ensuing **Great Siege of 1565**, Città Notabile was a refuge from which the cavalry squadrons and local militia, under the command of the Portuguese knight **Don Mesquita**, harried the Turks' camps on the Marsa and Corradino. After the Turks finally withdrew, defeated in September 1565, a limp second attack on Città Notabile was made from the beach at St Paul's Bay. Like their first invasion it was a badly executed and mistimed disaster.

Mdina was eclipsed with the building of Valletta, and became known as **Città Vecchia**, 'the old city'. For most of the 17th century it was in decline. People left and, with the exception of Grand Master de Redin's polygonal southern and eastern bastions, the defences were weakened. So the earthquake of 1693 came as a blessing here, an opportunity for a new start and a fitting end to the century. The first of the major reconstructions was the cathedral in 1702, and by Grand Master de Vilhena's reign (1722–36) the Order, wealthy now and used to silk not cold armour, was lavishing money on the city. As the century progressed, the gracefully ageing stone palaces of Città Vecchia silently witnessed the slow, inevitable crumbling of the Order that had built them.

By midday on 10 June 1798 the keys to the city were formally in the hands of **Napoleon**'s governor designate, General Vaubois, and the Order's reign was over. Napoleon's war effort urgently needed funds, and within three months the French set about auctioning treasures looted from the city's Carmelite church. Incensed, the devout Maltese rioted, killed the French commander and set in train the rebellion that led to the French being besieged inside Valletta and eventually, with the aid of the British, overthrown.

The **British** abolished the powerless Università in 1819 and Mdina, no longer referred to as Città Vecchia, retired like an old and weary campaigner behind its quiet walls for more than 130 years. The **Second World War** brought very little damage to the city, despite the proximity of the fighter airfield of Ta'Qali at the foot of the plateau, but a few stray bombs damaged Rabat.

## Mdina City Sights

Mdina is pedestrianized, and you can walk to all the notable places to visit and historical landmarks in half a day (numbers given below refer to the city map on p.237). If you would rather read or soak up the sun, however, head for the open-air Fontanella Tea Garden on the northern bastions.

### From the Main Gate to the Cathedral Museum

**[1] Main Gate** (1724). Designed by de Mondion, the triumphal gate was built by Grand Master de Vilhena to replace the older gateway to the right. It is a fine, if top-heavy, example of restrained Baroque by one of the Order's most prolific builders. The escutcheon bears his arms – the growling lions in front are a part of them – and the inscription records the restoration of parts of the city walls.

Following the election of a new grand master, he and his procession left Valletta for Mdina, where he was met at this gate by the head of the Università, or the Hakem, Captain of the Rod. Having received the silver keys to the city, the new grand master promised to 'observe the privileges, and franchises and usages of this city' – a promise all too often and readily broken.

On the inside façade are three statues of **St Publius**, **St Paul** and **St Agatha**, the island's and the city's patron saints, all of whom carry palm fronds to symbolize their martyrdom. The remaining escutcheon is that of the island's oldest nobles, the Inguanez (*see* p.245), while the blank one was defaced by the French in 1798.

**Mdina Dungeons**
*open daily 9.30–5,*
*winter 9.30–4; adm*

**[2] Mdina Dungeons.** Spookily set in the old cells below the Courts of Justice (*see* [6] below), the walk through more than 20 different waxwork set pieces offers a study in man's ingenuity in

**N**

100 metres
100 yards

BASTION SQUARE

MAGAZINE STREET

CARMEL STREET

ST PETER STREET

ST SOPHIA STREET

ST ROQUE STREET

De Redin Bastion

ST PAUL'S SQUARE

GATTO MURINA ST

VILLEGAIGNON

MESQUITA SQUARE

MESQUITA STREET

INGUANEZ STREET

SAN PAWL STREET

STREET

Roman Villa and Museum

to Rabat

different methods of extracting information, until the British abolished torture in 1813. Children invariably love it.

**[3] Torre dello Standardo**. The Signal Tower of the Standard was once a guardhouse and is now the police station. De Vilhena tinkered with the original 16th-century building which formed part of the island's chain of signalling stations.

**[4] Palazzo Vilhena/Museum of Natural History** (1730). This is one of the most rewarding examples of Grand Master de Vilhena's benign and somewhat egocentric compulsion to erect impressive buildings. Inside on the main staircase is a white marble bust of de Vilhena which shows his well-composed and dainty features: a small feminine mouth and flowing bouffant locks, marred only by bloodhound eyes.

The building was designed as de Vilhena's summer residence, on the site of the Università, either by Maltese architect Giovanni

**Palazzo Vilhena/ Museum of Natural History**

*open daily 9–5; closed Good Fri, 24, 25, 31 Dec, 1 Jan; adm*

Barbara or, more likely, the resident French architect de Mondion. The fulsome three-sided *palazzo*, built on an irregular French plan around a central courtyard, imitates an auditorium and – with its arched balconies and boxes – the Manoel Theatre in Valletta, also built by de Vilhena (*see* p.120). The entrance screen is embellished by his fanciful and ubiquitous escutcheon and leads to a main door, gathered in by magnificent French banded columns with de Vilhena immortalized in a bust of bronze relief set above.

In 1908 the *palazzo* became the Connaught Tuberculosis Hospital, named after King Edward VII's brother, then naval commander-in-chief, and did not shut until 1956. In 1973 it was converted into the Natural History Museum. The admission fee can only be justified by the *palazzo* itself and not the unspeakably dull collection of tired exhibits housed within, the most interesting of which is a chip of the moon given to Malta by President Nixon in 1979. A stroll around the courtyard is free.

[5] **Herald's Loggia**. From the security of the first floor, the herald or town crier would shout out the orders for the day to those gathered in the small square formed by the Xara Palace Hotel and the Corte Capitanale. The orders, known as *bandi*, were issued by the Università and are preserved in the Cathedral Museum.

[6] **Corte Capitanale/The Courts of Justice**. The Courts of Justice formed part of the Palazzo Vilhena and except for the dungeons (*see* [2] above) are closed to the public. The figures on the left and right of the balcony symbolize *Justice* and *Mercy*. A secret underground passage used to lead from the courts to the Archbishop's Palace.

[7] **Xara Palace**. A local nobleman's house, which once belonged to the Strickland family, it served as an RAF officers' mess during the Second World War. Until quite recently it was a delightfully Fawlty-esque hotel. It has now been reborn as a 5-star de luxe Relais Châteaux hotel.

[8] **Archbishop's Palace** (1722). The present building was constructed in the wake of the 1693 earthquake. Mdina was the seat of the bishops of Malta until 1816 when St John's in Valletta became the Co-Cathedral. The bishops, appointees of the kingdom of Spain and the grand inquisitor – himself a papal appointee – were often vocal and powerful irritants to the Order's power. The French General Vaubois dined here in 1798 as the guest of his conquered enemy.

**Cathedral Museum**

*open Mon–Fri 9.30–4.30, Sat 9.30–3.30; closed Sun and public holidays; adm*

[9] **Cathedral Museum** (1733). Commissioned as a seminary by Bishop de Bussan, the design is often and incorrectly attributed to Giovanni Barbara who died five years earlier. The unknown architect (possibly Andrea Belli) produced a crisp and impressive structure with effusive Sicilian decorations that complement the earlier cathedral. The concave window and balcony supported by

12 Mdina, Rabat and the Inland Towns | Mdina City Sights

two Atlantean figures on the first floor neatly separate the façade. Cicero stayed in a house on this site while preparing his case against the thieving Roman governor, Verres (*see* p.218).

The museum sprawls over two floors around an airy central courtyard and, unlike the Natural History Museum, houses articles of importance, beauty and value including the cathedral's and Inquisition's archives. Many of the artefacts, including the Dürer collection, were bequeathed by Count Saverio Marchese in the early 19th century. Notable exhibits include a comprehensive collection of coins and medals from ancient Malta through to the present day, vestments of ancient lace, Dürer woodcuts from the early 1500s (no.64 of St Jerome, with his ever-present skull, is worth the entrance fee alone), relics of the pre-1693 cathedral including the dramatic early 15th-century Spanish-school polyptych altarpiece depicting the life of St Paul, and paintings by de Favray and Preti. The ground floor displays a collection of Roman and Punic artefacts.

## [10] St Paul's Cathedral (1697)

**② St Paul's Cathedral**
*open Mon–Fri 9.30–4.30, Sat 9.30–3.30*

Of all the churches on the islands, St Paul's Cathedral is the finest and most mature example of Maltese Baroque; not fussy and ornamental but the work of an articulate pen imbued with all the influences – Roman, Sicilian and Italian – from which the idiom evolved. From all perspectives, this monumental church with its bold swathes takes charge: at the screen façade, from a distance, in silhouette and from inside.

Tradition states the cathedral is built on the site of the villa belonging to the Roman governor, Publius, where the shipwrecked St Paul healed Publius's father and converted the grateful governor himself to Christianity. (Publius later became the first bishop of Malta and was martyred in Greece.) The simple 12th-century Norman structure of Count Roger was enlarged in 1419, and the present cathedral was built following the earthquake of 1693 which destroyed much of Malta. A new cathedral had been talked about before the earthquake; Lorenzo Gafa had added a new choir in 1679 and after the earthquake he was commissioned to create the new building. The site on the northeast corner of Mdina must have flattered Gafa's inspiration (this domed cathedral would be seen from afar) and the structure went up rapidly: five years after the foundation stone was laid in 1697 it was consecrated.

St Paul's Cathedral sits on a low podium at the end of the eponymous rectangular square. The near-square façade with its three cleanly divided bays gives it a light but solid air. The Corinthian order of pilasters below the composite ones span the entire façade without interruption, leaving above the two side doors brave expanses of honey-coloured masonry. The bell towers –

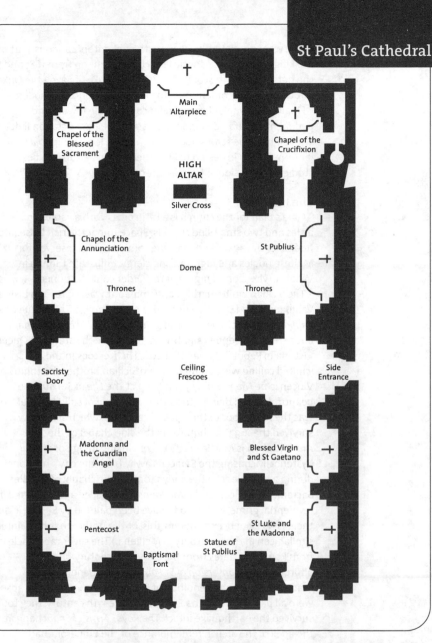

Main
Altarpiece

Chapel of the
Blessed
Sacrament

Chapel of the
Crucifixion

**HIGH
ALTAR**

Silver Cross

Chapel of the
Annunciation

St Publius

Dome

Thrones

Thrones

Sacristy
Door

Ceiling
Frescoes

Side
Entrance

Madonna and
the Guardian
Angel

Blessed Virgin
and St Gaetano

Pentecost

St Luke and
the Madonna

Statue of
St Publius

Baptismal
Font

each with six bells – are squat, adding to the façade's heaviness, but with Gafa's deft touch they appear lighter, for the twin clocks nudge into the lower lip of the cornice. Note, in relief at the top of the bell towers, St Paul's viper twists out of the flames. Above the main door on the left is the escutcheon of Grand Master Perellos (during whose reign the cathedral was built) and on the right that of Bishop Palmieri, who consecrated it in 1702 two years before the dome was completed. In front are the obligatory cannons, part of the knights' ordnance: to the left a Dutch cannon from 1681 and to the right, bearing the coat of arms of the Duke of Savoy, the Duke's gift cannon to commemorate the knights' defence of Rhodes.

Finally, sneaking out from under cover of the towers and pediment, is Gafa's dynamic swan song, the light octagonal dome, with eight stone scrolls above a high drum leading up to a neat lantern. Similar in design to St Catherine's in Żejtun, it is best studied from inside or from a distance.

## The Interior

Gafa's plan for the church is a Latin cross with a vaulted nave, two aisles and two small side chapels. Space under the rich tessellated floor of extravagant and macabre tombstones is reserved for Maltese nobles and high-ranking clergy, unlike at St John's in Valletta, where only knights of the Order could be buried.

The Sicilian white marble **baptismal font** was a gift from Bishop Valguarnero in 1495 and survived the earthquake. The **statue** of *St Publius* and the two **lecterns** of *St John* and *St Luke* by the main altar are by Giuseppe Valenti, who also made the statue of Queen Victoria in Republic Square, Valletta. The **frescoes** in the cross-vaulted ceiling were painted by two Sicilian brothers, Antonio and Vincenzo de Manno, in 1794 and depict the *Life of St Paul*. The beautiful carved **door** to the sacristy is made of solid Irish oak and was the main door to the original cathedral which somehow survived the 1693 earthquake. In the side **chapel of the Annunciation** is Mattia Preti's unconvincing image of *St Paul* hysterically chasing the Saracens away from the city's bastions during a brief siege in the early 1400s. In the **chapel of the Blessed Sacrament**, the icon of the *Madonna*, bejewelled and shrouded in reverential grime, is alleged to have been painted by St Luke. (Sadly there is no evidence to support this, or the notion that he painted a similar icon in the Sanctuary in Mellieħa.) The silver tabernacle is from Rome and dates from the early 18th century. The main **altarpiece**, the *Conversion of St Paul*, the side panels and the marvellously graphic rendition of St Paul's shipwreck in the apse were all painted by Mattia Preti in the late 17th century; they too survived the earthquake intact. The *Royal Arms of Spain* hang at the apex of the arch in remembrance of the Emperor Charles V who gave the islands to the Order in 1530. The two Italian oval portraits by the front pillars are marble mosaic compositions of photographic clarity depicting *St Peter and St Paul* and date from 1873. Rarely on display is the **silver cross** brought by the knights from Rhodes. A weak supposition states that Godfrey de Bouillon carried it into Jerusalem in the First Crusade in 1099. The two thrones are reserved for the bishop of Malta and the grand master.

The original paintings in Gafa's splendid dome were ruined by inclement weather and the present images represent the Divine Mission of the Church and were painted in the 1950s. Like the other side chapel, the **chapel of the Crucifixion** has delicately inlaid marble floors resembling a carpet and sombre black and gilt 18th-century gates. The crucifix was fashioned by a Franciscan monk in the 17th century. The altarpiece of the *Martyrdom of St Publius and his Baptism by St Paul* has sometimes been attributed to Preti but is only his school.

## Banca Giuratale to Howard Gardens

[11] **Banca Giuratale** (1730). The Order referred pompously to prosaic civil records offices as a Municipal Palace or Banca Giuratale, and this is still a records office. It is also an exquisite example of de Mondion's Baroque handiwork. Two storeys of crisp detail, florid carving and elaborate windows are set beneath two equally elaborate corners of what look like limestone flowerpots of dotty ornaments. It housed for a time the Università, which was politely ejected from its old site, on which Palazzo Vilhena was being built.

Nearly opposite at No.11 Ville Gaignon St, known as the **House of Notary Bezzina**, in 1798 the luckless French officer Captain Masson was pitched off the balcony to his death by the bloodthirsty Maltese mob, after his countrymen's attempt to auction off the plundered treasures of the Carmelite church.

[12] **Fontanella Tea Garden**. A refuge for light refreshment at the very edge of the north bastion (*see* p.251).

[13] **Bastion Square**. Bastion Square was the old parade ground and 40 yards away in Magazine Street the munitions were stored. The old firing bastion, the Bastione de Vaccari, has a superb panorama of Malta – from Valletta, the Mosta Dome (in the middle), to St Paul's Bay. Part of Camilla's Gift Shop is on the site of what was the Jewish Synagogue before the Jewish community was expelled from the island by King Ferdinand of Aragon in 1492. **Villegaignon Street**, the 350-yard main street which runs from the Main Gate to Bastion Square, is named after Nicholas de Villegaignon who defended the city against Dragut Rais's corsair raid of 1551. Its other names have been Tal Muyeli or the Street of the Gentry and Strada Reale.

**Palazzo Falzon/**
**The Norman**
**House**
*museum open 9–1*
*and 2–5, viewing by*
*appointment only,*
*t 21 454512*

[14] **Palazzo Falzon/The Norman House** (1495). In 1530 the first of Malta's grand masters, the Frenchman de L'Isle Adam, received the keys to the city here after the knights were given the islands by Charles V. (There is a painting of him receiving the keys in the Grand Master's Palace In Valletta.) The building is in fact medieval not Norman and, in keeping with medieval design, the living quarters were on the first floor – the ground floor was for kitchens,

stables, etc. – hence the more intricate arched windows with their colonettes above the twin cornice of triangular corbels. There is a small private **museum** on the ground floor.

**[15] Medieval Times Adventure.** Housed in the Palazzo Costanzo, this features a journey through a medieval 'Time Tunnel' featuring various garish fibreglass tableaux designed to demonstrate Maltese life in the 14th and 15th centuries. In truth, it is gloomy and not worth a detour. There is a rather uninspired **restaurant** next door in the **Palazzo Notabile**.

**Medieval Times Adventure**
*open daily 10–4.30; multilingual commentary; adm; restaurant in Palazzo Notabile open Mon–Fri 10–4.30, Sat 10–4.30 and 7–11pm, Sun 10–4*

**[16] Carmelite Church** (1660). Designed by Francesco Sammut and 12 years in the construction, the church and its associated monastery is also known as Our Lady of Mount Carmel; the Carmelites were a Sicilian Order who came to Malta in 1370. The interior with its seven altars and Palladian pilasters under an oval and well-lit nave-cum-dome is unexpectedly rich, despite the French army's looting of the church in 1798 to fund Napoleon's war effort.

**[17] Chapel of St Roque** (1798). St Roque is the patron saint of diseases, often invoked during the plague-infested 14th–19th centuries when the sick would congregate and pray for succour. Grand Master de Vilhena demolished the earlier chapel of St Roque which was uncomfortably close to his intended summer residence, the Palazzo Vilhena, and built this one much further away.

**[18] Palazzo Santa Sophia** (1233?). The date plaque may be unreliable. The first floor was added in 1938 to what is still probably Mdina's oldest building.

**[19] Casa Testaferrata.** The Testaferrata family still live behind the red main door. The Marquisate was created by Grand Master Pinto in 1745. (The majority of Maltese titles were created during the reign of the knights.)

**[20] Palazzo Gatto Murina.** Tucked away in Gatto Murina Street, the early 15th-century *palazzo* has a fine example of restored arched windows above strident arcaded coursework. The eponymous *murina* or lamprey motif is set above the spindly colonettes. The building is off Mesquita Street, named after the Portuguese knight Don Mesquita who commanded the cavalry garrison and governed the city during the Great Siege of 1565. It is said that after the fall of St Elmo he hanged one Turkish prisoner every morning from the walls of the city until the siege ended. The six rooms on the top floor have been turned into an exhibition, **Tales of the Silent City**, similar in nature to the Medieval Times display in the Palazzo Costanzo (*see* [15] above). Again, various stages of Maltese history have been illustrated through the use of waxwork tableaux and multilingual commentary. The show starts with a representation of Neolithic times, passing through the arrival of St Paul in AD 60 and the Arab invasions of the Middle

**Tales of the Silent City**
*open daily 10–5; adm*

Ages to the Knights of St John. Napoleon's arrival, British rule and the resistance of the Maltese people during the Second World War are also represented. The exhibition has been designed by the same people responsible for the London Dungeon.

[21] **Casa Inguanez**. Occupying an entire block, the house has been the Inguanez home since the 14th century. Cicco Gatto was created Baron in 1350 for quelling an uprising of the Gozitans against their Aragonese masters, and his direct descendants, the Inguanez, are the oldest of Malta's 29 noble families. In 1432 King Alfonso V of Aragon stayed here, as did Alfonso XIII of Spain in 1927.

**The Mdina Experience**
*open daily 9.30–4.30, with shows every 30 mins; adm*

[22] **The Mdina Experience** is in Mesquita Square, a leafy gap under the evergreen ficus trees. This attraction is a well-converted old building with a cool ground-floor café and the inevitable souvenir shop. Linguistically, and as if to out-do the 'Malta Experience', this audiovisual show is in 12 different languages; the history of Mdina is recounted. There's also a Knights of Malta walk-through experience on offer.

[23] **Chapel of St Nicholas** (1550). This is one of the oldest and most tranquil *quartiers*, and many of the 16th- and 17th-century buildings have survived. The little chapel was remodelled in 1692.

[24] **Magazine Street and the Greeks' Gate**. The gate, like so much of Mdina, owes its restoration to de Vilhena. It was named after a small Greek community that lived in the southwest of the city in the 16th and 17th centuries. The steep slope leads out to the defensive ditch surrounding this part of the city, and there is a separate entrance known as 'the hole in the wall' in Magazine Street. Easily visible from a short distance away in the valley below is the old Valletta–Mdina railway station, now a restaurant. During the Second World War the tunnel was part fuel dump, part shelter.

[25] **Nunnery of St Benedict and chapel of St Peter (St Benedict)**. The building dates from the 15th century, as does the Benedictine community. The Order is a very strict and devout one: no man is allowed into the convent without the bishop's permission, with the exception of a doctor and, traditionally, the whitewasher who in times of plague would disinfect the walls; nor are any of the 20 or so nuns allowed out. Until 1974, even after a nun had died she had to be buried within the grounds of the convent. The chapel was restored in 1625 and the altarpiece is another work by Preti.

[26] **Chapel of St Agatha** (early 15th century). St Agatha is said to have fled to Malta from Sicily in AD 249, following persecution by the Emperor Decius, after refusing to marry Quintianus, the governor of Catania. Upon returning to Catania in AD 251 she was imprisoned and on the orders of the spurned Quintianus met with a grisly end. Her left breast was cut off – statues like the one on the city side of the Main Gate often depict her holding either her

breast or the shears used to remove it – and then she was burnt to death over hot stones. The chapel was remodelled in 1694 by Lorenzo Gafa. Mass is said here on 5 February, the day on which St Agatha died.

[27] **Howard Gardens**. Named after Malta's first prime minister (1921–3), the gardens were made public in 1924 and ramble down towards the Roman villa. The old cross is said to have been a gift from Count Roger the Norman, to celebrate the reinstatement of Christianity after he took the islands from the Arabs.

## Rabat

The easiest way to see Rabat is on foot; leave Mdina by the Main Gate. The five principal places that are worth visiting (numbers refer to the map opposite) are a short walk down St Paul's Street from the Roman *domus*, or house. You can invariably park near Parish Square or outside the Roman *domus*.

[1] **Roman *Domus***. The *domus* probably belonged to a wealthy Roman merchant or a senior official; its position and size confirm this. The siting has an Italian flair, looking west over the valley towards what is now Mtarfa.

The *domus* and its grounds were first excavated in 1881. The clean neoclassical temple museum building now camouflaged by a forecourt of citrus trees was built in 1921–4 during the second round of excavations. Not all the museum's exhibits were unearthed within the *domus*'s grounds. However, they are all of a domestic nature and appropriate to this type of Roman dwelling.

The corner stairs lead down to what remains of the *domus* itself. The main attraction is the (now roofed) square mosaic-covered peristyle, or central court, enclosed by 16 columns, only one of which is original. The *impluvium* gathered water and channelled it into the *compluvium* – an internal water feature designed to impress visitors. The two rooms off the peristyle were, on the left, the *triclinium* or dining room (which housed the mosaic in the museum) and a reception room (or *atrium*). Some heavy-handed restoration in the Arab period has left the remaining mosaics in poor order. In the annexe are relics from later Arab graves found within the grounds.

Other items in the courtyard include the famous but disappointingly small motif of an astonished open-mouthed woman from a mosaic's border, a blurred scene of either a satyr being teased by *maenads* (orgiastic nymphs) or Delilah and Samson, and marble statues and busts including *Antonia* – the daughter of the Emperor Claudius – who looks handsome only in profile.

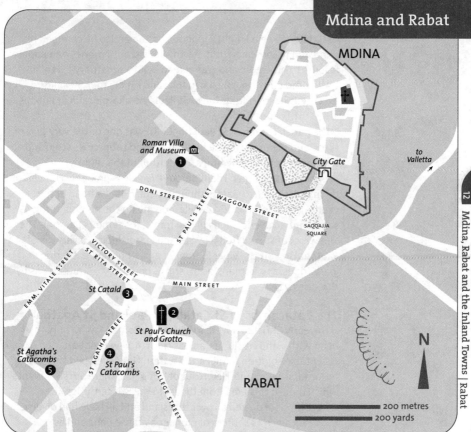

MDINA

Roman Villa
and Museum ①

to
Valletta

City Gate

DONI STREET

ST PAUL'S STREET

WAGGONS STREET

SAQQAJJA
SQUARE

VICTORY STREET

ST RITA STREET

EMM. VITALE STREET

St Catald ③

MAIN STREET

ST PAUL'S Church
and Grotto ②

ST AGATHA STREET

St Agatha's
Catacombs
⑤

St Paul's
Catacombs ④

COLLEGE STREET

RABAT

N

200 metres
200 yards

**Grotto and parish
church of St Paul**
*open 9.15–1.30 and
2–5; a guide is usually
on hand to deliver a
deadpan explanation;
if so, leave a tip*

[2] Grotto and parish church of St Paul Tradition has stated that
during his enforced three-month stay in Malta, and while a
prisoner of the island's Roman governor, Publius, St Paul eschewed
the comfortable surroundings offered to him and chose this
subterranean **grotto** instead. It seems unlikely that one of Emperor
Nero's more valuable prisoners would have been allowed to pass
the winter in an exceedingly damp and cold cave; he probably just
preached from here. Other widely held and even less plausible
beliefs are that St Paul's presence imbued the stone walls with an
antidote to poison, and that however much stone is chiselled away
the grotto will remain exactly the same size. The statue of *St Paul*
was donated by Grand Master Pinto in 1748 and the silver galley
hanging from the ceiling was the gift of the Knights of St John in
1960 to mark the 1900-year anniversary of St Paul's shipwreck. The
eight coats of arms are of each of the *langues*. Pope John Paul II
prayed in the grotto while on his visit in May 1990.

Annexed to both the church and the grotto is the **sanctuary of
St Publius**. A Spaniard, Juan Beneguas, came to Malta in about

1600 to become a knight. Upon seeing the grotto he changed his mind and became a hermit. By 1617 he had both money and papal favours to his credit, and was able to build a sanctuary. Lorenzo Gafa completely reworked it in 1692 and his brother Melchiorre executed the marble statue of St Paul. The altarpiece of St Publius is by Mattia Preti.

The **parish church of St Paul** (1656–81) was one of the very first of the island's churches to be built on a grand Latin-cross scale and has been altered many times. The author of the slightly overworked three-pediment Baroque façade is probably Francesco Buonamici. Lorenzo Gafa is thought to have had a hand in the vaulting and dome in 1692 while working on the neighbouring sanctuary. In an enormous gilded frame, the famous painting *The Shipwreck of St Paul* (1683) by Stefano Erardi depicts a very dry St Paul shaking off the viper in front of an astonished gathering of 'barbarians' and Romans, as his ship is pounded to smithereens by the stormy seas.

## The Catacombs of St Catald, St Paul and St Agatha

The early Christians were forbidden by Roman law to bury their dead within the city limits, and as cremation was not an acceptable solution families and fraternities developed the intramural catacomb. Hewn out of living rock there are six variants which date in this area from the 1st to the 8th centuries AD. Catacombs are dotted all over the island and all have had diverse uses ever since as sources of plunder, as cattle pens and as air-raid shelters.

**St Catald**
*open during daylight hours*

[3] **St Catald**. Just outside the perimeter ditch of the Roman city and diagonally opposite the parish church is the tiny 18th-century

---

### Catacomb Terminology

*Loculus*: a small rectangular recess cut into a wall, for infants and children.

**Canopied table tomb**: the most common normally consisting of two graves exposed by two or four arches above 3ft (1m) from the ground. The graves were sealed by separate stone slabs to leave a flat surface under the arches.

**Saddle-backed canopied tomb**: similar in height and positioning to the table tombs, and with the same arched appearance, in this instance the body would be interred underneath the pitched roof via an opening in the lower wall.

*Arcosolium* **tombs**: also known as window graves, they resemble an arched window cut into the rock at a lower level.

**Floor graves**: these graves are cut into the ground with head rests or divots and sealed with a stone slab.

**Agape table**: unique to Malta, and made up of a circular table and a semicircular bench. A highly civilized ceremony, not unlike a wake, would take place at the burial. The family, friends and a priest would gather to pray, mourn and feast. The agape would also be used for religious rites, and it is usually found near the entrance to a catacomb.

church of St Catald, built on the site of one said to date back to AD 400. Beneath it is a small group of catacombs dating from the late 2nd and early 3rd centuries in what was originally a Punic burial shaft. One of the best examples of an agape table is to be found on the left at the bottom of the stairs, and the majority are fine canopied tombs.

**St Paul**
*adm, includes audio-guide, available in various languages*

**[4] St Paul.** About 70 yards from the square into St Agatha Street is the main entrance to a large labyrinth of catacombs dating from the 3rd century. In all it accommodated more than a thousand corpses throughout its 23,680 sq ft (2,200 sq m). Not all are accessible, but all types can be seen. A useful little map is included in the back of the historical pamphlet on sale at the ticket office.

At the bottom of the steep steps, 23ft (7m) into the catacombs, are two striking rooms divided by a central pillar. The main crypt, just to the right, has a high ceiling, and at either end a raised plinth and agape tables. Down a couple of steps, the crypt to the left has been called a chapel and has a recess at the far end which may have been an altar. Stand with your back to the entrance steps (note the sad *loculi* tombs) and use the main crypt as a reference point; the area to the right is more extensive and two long corridors, each about 80ft (25m) long, lead to groups of canopied and saddle-backed tombs. To the left it is even spookier and, apart from another group of canopied tombs, there is a long twisty passage leading to a lower level.

**❸ Catacombs and Museum of St Agatha**
*open Mon–Fri 9–12 and 1–4.30, Sat 9–12.30; closed Sun and public holidays; adm*

**[5] Catacombs and Museum of St Agatha.** Flagged 100 yards past St Paul's are the more exciting catacombs and frescoes of St Agatha. Entrance to the catacombs is down a few steps via the crypt, again hewn out of rock, where St Agatha (*see* p.245) is said to have spent her time in exile praying and teaching. On the walls are 31 detailed frescoes in varying states of restoration from the 12th to 15th centuries, many of which are of St Agatha in pious poses. The tour of the catacombs lasts 20 minutes and takes in only 10 per cent of the honeycomb necropolis which is said to cover nearly 43,000 sq ft (4,000 sq m). The ceilings are disorientatingly low, but the tombs, including the *arcosolium*, are well lit. Claustrophobics should stay in the crypt.

The museum contains a little of everything – related and unrelated. Among the exhibits are coins, vestments, ancient pottery, an eccentric mineral collection and a 3ft (1m) statue of St Agatha, carved from a solid piece of alabaster in 1666, and originally the crypt's altarpiece. Look out too for some fine examples of bones of pigmy hippos which lived in Malta in the Pleistocene period.

⭐ Ta'Qali Crafts
Village >>

## Tourist Information in Mdina and Rabat

Try to arrive as early or late as possible, before 9.30am or after 3.30pm, unless you enjoy being swamped by tour groups. Outside the Main Gate are public conveniences and a large map.

### Festas

**Mdina** celebrates the conversion of St Paul on the last Sunday in January, and **Rabat** the *festa* of St Paul on the first Sunday in July.

The traditional festivities during the national holiday of **L-Imnarja** (the Feast of St Peter and St Paul) on 29 June include horse and donkey races. They begin in the Siġġiewi Road (Racecourse Street) and end at the dotty winning post, the extravagantly Baroque Casino Notabile or Loggia.

## Shopping in Mdina and Rabat

### Mdina

Mdina has a handful of shops all obviously geared to the tourist. There are also numerous small art galleries.
**Camilla's**, Bastion Square. Books, paintings and the occasional interesting antique curio.
**Galleria Cremona**, Mesquita Square. Local artists' ceramics and paintings.
**Greenhand**. Has fashions, wallets, belts, handmade leather bags and caps, and a good selection of Maltese lace, as well as a range of glassware.
**The Maltese Falcon**, Villegaignon Street. Silver filigree and films.
**Tales of the Silent City**, Villegaignon Street. Extensive souvenir shop with books, silver filigree, knitware, pottery, Maltese food and wine.

### Rabat

**Empire Arts and Crafts Centre**, between St Paul's Church and the catacombs. A huge craft emporium selling lacework, paintings, glass and ceramics, with craftspeople on hand to provide demonstrations. This is a good place for souvenirs; for not much you could pick up a plaster-cast Eye of Osiris.

**Mike's Jewellery** and the **Rabat Lace Shop** are pleasant places to spend a browsing hour.

Ta'Qali Crafts Village in the Nissen huts of the disused Second World War airfield (*see* p.77). Anyone determined to get rid of their money will not have missed the signposts on the main Rabat road for this attraction. A favourite attraction here is **Mdina Glass, t** 21 415786, where glass-blowing, etching and crystal-cutting are all demonstrated on site by skilled craftsmen.

## Where to Stay in Mdina and Rabat

### Mdina

**\*\*\*\*\*Xara Palace-Relais Châteaux**, Misrah il-Kunsill, **t** 21 450560, *www.xaraplace.com.mt* (€€€€). Luxurious bijou hotel with 17 rooms perched high on the bastions of Mdina. Fabulously restored and decorated, this is without doubt the most beautiful hotel in Malta. It does not have a pool, and there is no real 'life' within walking distance, so this one may not be perfect for everyone. Yet, for a magical step into another time and world, this is the one. There are two restaurants (*see* right).

### Rabat

**Point de Vue**, Saqqajja Square, **t** 21 454117, *www.pointdevuemalta.com* (€). Guesthouse, 50 yards from the gate to Mdina, providing a base from which to explore this part of the island. Destroyed during the Second World War when it served as an RAF mess, it is now an adequate family-run guesthouse with 17 rooms (nos.1, 2 and 11 have large balconies). There is no standing on ceremony in the hotel, or either of its two restaurants.

## Eating Out in Mdina and Rabat

### Mdina

**De Mondian**, Xara Palace, **t** 21 450560 (€€€€). This is the smart restaurant of the Xara Palace, which serves excellent food at a price. In summer, meals are served on a terrace with views of the whole island – some evenings the fireworks of three or four towns can be watched at once. *Dinner only; closed Sun.*

**Ciappetti,** 5 St Agatha's Esplanade, **t** 21 459987 (€€€). A great spot to sit and gaze. The upstairs open-air terrace tea garden has excellent panoramic views of the bastions and beyond. Maltese favourites such as spaghetti with rabbit and beef olives. Gluten-free items available. *Closed Sun eve and Mon.*

**The Medina,** 7 Holy Cross Street, **t** 21 454004 (€€€). Down a narrow street opposite the cathedral. The courtyard garden, with its large tree, hanging oleander and rough-hewn walls, is the most memorable feature of this established converted-townhouse restaurant. The food is reliable, but the small menu also has old-fashioned French pretensions. The puddings are either home-made or come from the Fontanella. *Sometimes open for lunch; call to check.*

**Trattoria AD1530,** Xara Palace, **t** 21 450560 (€€). Good pasta, pizza, salad and other 'light' meals.

**Fontanella Tea Garden,** 1 Bastion Street, **t** 21 454264 (€). Situated above a small citrus courtyard on the edge of the north bastion with panoramic views. Even when it is deserted the service is diabolical, and the tea almost undrinkable, but it is redeemed by the best home-made apple and chocolate cake in Malta (they also serve pizzas). Wash the cake down with bottled refreshment and, if you are hungry, and patient, they will contrive to deliver a good toasted sandwich some time on the same day.

### Rabat

**Grotto Tavern,** Misrah il-Parrocca, **t** 21 455138 (€€€). Cosy restaurant in the main square of Rabat. The chef and owner is French, and the menu features oddities such as fondue.

**Stazzjon Restaurant,** Mtarfa Road, **t** 21 451717 (€€€). Under the same management as Peristyle, a 'theme' restaurant built in an old train station from the time of the old steam route which ran between here and Valletta until 1931. Customers are served in a waiting room and order from a ticket office. The food itself is standard fare – pasta, grills and fish. *Open Fri and Sat eves, Sun 10.30–8, plus Sun eve in summer.*

**Peristyle Restaurant and Bar,** opposite the Roman villa and museum, **t** 21 451717 (€€). Peristyle has attempted a classical sort of décor to match its surroundings, and offers reasonable pizzas and local wines at reasonable prices.

**Il Veduta,** Saqqajja Square, **t** 21 454666 (€€). The main attraction is the view; the restaurant has a huge open terrace facing Mdina's bastions – perfect for idle summer evenings' contemplation. Mainly a pizzeria, but there are other dishes too.

**The Garden of Eden,** 150 yards from the main Mdina gate (€). Kiosk, serving cod and chips and toasted sandwiches.

**Point de Vue,** 5 Saqqajja Square, **t** 21 454117 (€). Outside the city walls and part of the guesthouse. It has a restaurant and a pizzeria, apart from serving snacks all day both inside and outside.

A proliferation of **snack vendors, fruit vans** and **cafés** are grouped in and around Parish Square, which during the summer becomes a convention centre for bad-tempered coach drivers. Flee.

## Nightlife in Mdina and Rabat

**Ta'Gianpula** nightclub, nearly 2 miles (3km) off the Rabat–Siġġiewi road, **t** 21 450238. Follow the headlights snaking their way like fireflies to the club. Open only in the summer months, this smart open-air discotheque is in the grounds of an old farmhouse. The music, while not exactly Barry Manilow, is less techno than in Paceville's two haunts and the usual crowd will never see their teens again. *Summer, Sat only; adm.*

**Tattingers, t** 21 451104. On the main road coming up the hill to Rabat, Tattingers is a proper neon, mirror-ball disco. Pay it a visit and you will be able to see the locals undressed to impress.

# Mosta and Naxxar

## Mosta

Situated near the very middle of the island, **Mosta**'s name derives from the Arabic for 'centre'; around 13,000 people live in this thriving and not particularly attractive hurly-burly town atop the safety of the Victoria Lines. Ever since the Second World War, the spread of new building around its older centre has continued at a rapid pace. From many places in Malta, the dome of St Mary's stands out like a beacon. Relegated to fourth-largest in Europe by the upstart Xewkija parish church in Gozo, **Mosta Dome** can still, however, claim third place on volumetric measurement; either way, it is well worth seeing.

### Parish Church of St Mary (Mosta Dome or the Rotunda)

*Parish church of St Mary (Mosta Dome or the Rotunda)*

*open 9–12 and 3–5; wheelchair access; wardens are on hand to answer questions; no shorts; visits to the top of the dome by permission only*

As a symbol of a simple farming community's devotion, the huge 19th-century church of St Mary's is remarkable. Unlike St John's at Xewkija (Gozo's great rotunda), St Mary's was begun in 1833, long before immigration had enriched its then-tiny population; it must have appeared a daunting and possibly ludicrous concept. From day one, the church was dogged by misfortune and controversy. First the collection of building funds was diverted to help with a cholera epidemic in the 1830s. Next the architect, George Grognet de Vasse, was embroiled in an infantile scandal with the Académie Française over the provenance of a piece of Mdina stone he alleged came from the lost city of Atlantis, of which he averred Malta was the northwest tip! Finally, even the bishop snubbed the project by refusing to lay the foundation stone in 1833; he sent a minion priest instead. The bishop, like others, thought de Vasse's departure from cruciform to a circular 'mosque'-style plan had pagan associations.

The church took 27 years to build and the entire dome was constructed without the use of scaffolding, around and partly supported by the old parish church which was then dismantled. De Vasse's design takes a lead from the massive twin rows of six pillars in the Pantheon façade. The whole has been likened to the Pantheon itself, but the likeness stops with the façade. The two intricately decorated belfries do not sit comfortably with the curves of the massive dome behind (inside it is 23ft/7m wider than that of St Paul's in London). The local limestone has a warm apricot hue even in winter and has weathered to a deeper colour than other buildings on the islands. The real mastery and fun, however, is to be seen inside.

## Getting to and around Mosta

Mosta is as near to a cross-route hub as the **bus** system has. The easiest route by **car** from Valletta, 5½ miles (9km) away, is via Birkirkara and Balzan. From the north the road going through Bur Marrad is best. **Taxis** can be found near the bus terminus next to St Mary's.

Underneath the towering and mercifully simple dome with its 16 windows spiralling up to the lantern are six **side chapels**. The **floor** is an intricate geometry of two different marble inlays – no tombstones here – that weave an interplay of patterns with the ceiling. The **murals** were painted by Giuseppe Cali early in the 20th century. Before the main altar and to the left is the sacristy. Displayed among the usual souvenirs is a replica of a large **Luftwaffe bomb** that pierced the dome at 16.40 on 9 April 1942 as more than 300 people milled around awaiting early-evening mass. It was one of three to hit the dome – two bounced off – and like the others was designed to explode after a delay. The bomb rolled across the floor, startling the congregation; miraculously, it never exploded.

### Fort Mosta

*Fort Mosta*
*open Mon–Fri*
*9.30–12.30; visitors*
*must join one of the*
*three tours at 9.30,*
*10.30 or 11.30*

Built over 7th-century catacombs, this is one of a string of forts built by the British at the end of the 19th century with the aim of protecting Valletta and its harbour. In the event, the fort never actually saw action, but is nonetheless an interesting example of Victorian Military Architecture.

Despite the earnest signposts, give the **National Park** a wide berth. Hurriedly built in 1990, it has since fallen into a sorry state of neglect. The central pond is full of everything except water.

### Aviation Museum

*☉ Aviation*
*Museum*
*open daily 9–5, except*
*Good Fri, Easter Sun, 15*
*August, Christmas Day*
*and New Year's Day;*
*adm; children under 6*
*free*

Situated in between the Crafts Village and the National Stadium and housed in a Second World War Royal Air Force Station, this will prove a hit with anyone who was a big fan of Airfix in their youth. Its blue-riband exhibit is a rebuilt Spitfire, although the collection also includes a Douglas DC3, a Beachcraft and a Hawker Hurricane, as well as salvaged items from Second World War aircraft. The RAF squadrons are listed and there is a comprehensive array of photos.

## Naxxar and San Pawl tat-Tarġa

**Naxxar**, one of the original 10 parishes of 1436, was once a sleepy farming village close to Mosta. Now overbuilding has linked the two communities in places and, with a population of just 7,000, it

# Getting to Naxxar

**San Pawl tat-Tarġa** is less than half a mile (1km) northwest from the terminus in **Naxxar** (take the Birkirkara Road). From Sliema, take the road through San Gwann. The Naxxar Gap corkscrews down the Victoria Lines towards the northern coasts.

Naxxar can be reached on nos.54, 55 and 56 **buses** from Msida.

*Palazzo Parisio*

*gardens open Mon–Fri except public holidays; guided tours of the palace and gardens, on the hour 9–1; coffee shop open 9–2; adm*

is half the size of its neighbour. The urban spawl now spreads to Għargħur too.

**Palazzo Parisio**, opposite the church, is Naxxar's principal attraction. An ornate palace with extensive gardens. is also a coffee shop. The annual International Trade Fair is held in Palazzo Parisio's grounds in July. Further north, towards the lip of the Victoria Lines, San Pawl tat-Tarġa has one of the earliest of the knights' defences. Both towns are linked to St Paul. Naxxar translates as 'to hang clothes to dry', and it is claimed that it was here that St Paul was first received and dried his robes over the fire after the shipwreck – a doubtful supposition as St Paul's Bay is a difficult 5-mile (8km) hike even in summer, let alone in soggy robes on a winter's dawn after a terrifying shipwreck. Naxxar also relates phonetically to *Insara* meaning Christians, and San Pawl tat-Tarġa, meaning 'St Paul of the Step', refers to the step from which he is supposed to have first preached.

## San Pawl tat-Tarġa

Gathered around the little church, the suburb of San Pawl tat-Tarġa has a genteel air of lace curtains and prying neighbours; in fact everything but a privet hedge. The neighbouring residence of the British high commissioner, with its fluttering Union Jack, is probably to blame.

On the *zuntier* or forecourt of the elegantly humble **church of St Paul** (1696) is a statue of *St Paul* partly sheltered by a cooling umbrella of pine trees. Tradition says he preached from here so forcefully that his voice was heard in Gozo.

Behind the church, and located within the natural defence of the Victoria Lines, is the private **Gauci Tower** (1548). This is one of the first of the island's defences, built with Grand Master de Homedes's permission after a stealthy corsair raid when members of Cikko Gauci's family were carted off into slavery. The drop boxes on the roof, from which Mr Gauci hoped to pour hot oil and drop projectiles, echo the design of the older octagonal tower in Qrendi.

On the other side of the road is the (private) **Torri tal-Kapitan**, the Captain's Tower (1558), built by the knights to keep a vigil on the northern plain and coasts.

## Tourist Information in Mosta and Naxxar

Almost a provincial capital, **Mosta** has many services grouped together to the left of the church facing Constitution Street: the **police station**, a **polyclinic** (medical centre), **post office** and **public conveniences**. The ticket-issuing police are white-hot around here; park in a side street if there is no space in the meagre car park.

### Festas

**Mosta** is one of eight parishes to celebrate its *festa*, the **Assumption**, on 15 August. St Mary's looks even more spectacular when dressed and illuminated.

**Naxxar**'s *festa* is the **Birth of the Virgin Mary**. It is held on 8 September, which is also Victory Day, a national holiday.

## Eating Out in Mosta

**Cosa Nostra**, t 21 431007 (€€€). An Italian-style restaurant in a converted village house, this serves good pasta and fish.

**Lord Nelson**, 278 Main Street, 300 yards from the centre, t 21 432590 (€€€). Mosta is not somewhere to seek out culinary gems but the Lord Nelson is worth a trip. This has been a bar in some form for a hundred years. The present proprietor, Jim Camilleri, presides over a small but adventurous establisment. Its distinguishing feature is the central Garigor-style spiral staircase going up three floors.

The menu includes fishcakes with pesto, excellent home-made puds and peppered pineapples with vanilla ice cream. *Dinner only, Tues–Sat.*

**Ta'Marija**, Constitution Street, t 21 434444 (€€€). This too-well-advertised place is not worth a special trip, although it does have a narrow first-floor balcony which makes a prime spot for taking pictures of the dome. It is aimed directly at the tourist as a Maltese-speciality restaurant serving local dishes – which it does, although only the very brave choose *Fritturi tal-mohh* (brain fritters) – but their 'Folk Evenings' in the old-farmhouse setting are all pretty tacky and part of the kitchen is in the dining area, adding unwelcome 'authentic' aromas. Not many Maltese eat here. *Closed Mon.*

**La Deliziosa** (€). Look left, obliquely across from the church, find the large red Coca-Cola vending machine, and squeezed into a cupboard is this *pastizzeria*. If *timpana* and *pastizzi* on the hoof are too unhealthy, usually there is a fruit van opposite.

**La Fragola**, Constitution Street (€). A tiny shoe-box café, which serves freshly squeezed orange juice, pies and eight different flavours of local nougat. Snacks are the order of the day in Mosta.

There are a couple of other sound places to water at such as the **Olympic** or, towards the end of Main Street, 200 yards from the Main Square, the **City Café Bar** – note the Queen Victoria letterbox in the wall – which has a pleasant shaded front *zuntier* or forecourt.

# Birkirkara, the Three Villages and Żebbuġ

## Birkirkara

**Birkirkara** is the single-largest town in Malta; more than 21,000 people live within its confusing maze of streets. The town is bisected by the main road that links the Valletta suburbs with both Rabat and Mosta and has become somewhere to drive through rather than to. Stay awhile and ferret around some of its antique

## Getting to and around Birkirkara

**Birkirkara** is often abbreviated to 'B'kara' and all **roads** lead to it; from Valletta go via Ħamrun (avoid rush hours) or take the longer route via Msida and the Regional Road. From the south, go via Luqa then Valletta. It is signposted from Mosta and Rabat.

and *brocante* (bric-a-brac) shops or visit some of the area's numerous churches.

### Around the Town

The **parish church of St Helen's**, north of the main road heading west to Rabat, is big, flashy and lively. Begun in 1727 and completed in 1745 towards the end of the rainbow of the Maltese Baroque period, the pen of the designer has been obscured by time (it could have been that of the young Domenico Cachia or Salvu Borg, and was probably a joint effort). It does not matter, for whoever undertook it had a great command of the language. Sneaking into the sunlit square from narrow and dark St Helen Street is poor preparation: design details make this Sicilian-influenced façade one of the islands' finest, with tightly coupled pilasters and angels gesticulating wildly around the intricate bell towers; there is a rhythm to the three ground-floor door and window pediments that even the strangely out-of-sync centre window can't disturb. Inside it is conventional Latin-plan, a little heavy but lightened by rich frescoes, and in direct contrast to the bubbly façade.

Designed by Vittorio Cassar at the beginning of the 1600s when Renaissance was merging with Baroque, with Tommaso Dingli's façade completing the older Cassar's work in 1617, the old **parish church of the Assumption** (south of the main road) had fallen into terrible disrepair and almost collapsed. It is now undergoing a total and deserved restoration. It will be some years before the works are finished but it is still worth a look. Still evident is the painstakingly delicate detail on the twin superimposed Corinthian columns and the crisp motifs above, all set beneath the shallow, now broken, triangular pediment. In the shoe-box idiom is the old railway station next door to the Assumption. The restored Birchircara (as it was spelt) **station** area has a third-class carriage and a good children's park. The railway line and trains – in Malti, Xmundifer (prounounced *shmun-di-ferr* and a phonetic play on the French *chemin de fer*) – began in 1883. British-manufactured steam trains puffed their way between Valletta and Mdina, stopping at Ħamrun, Birkirkara and Attard. Although they carried over 1,500,000 passengers a year in the 1920s, the enterprise was a financial disaster and ceased in 1931.

# The Three Villages

Beyond Birkirkara's indefinable limits are the Siamese triplet villages of **Attard**, **Balzan** and **Lija**, known collectively as the Three Villages. During the last three to four hundred years these small settlements gathered around village churches and among fertile groves have grown into solid and wealthy towns, where even the stray cats are plump. Though comparatively young, they are not brassy like Madliena; the pace is slower, and amateur watercolourists sit peacefully in the shade on tiny stools, picking out architectural details. San Anton Palace is one of the many fine houses in this area: it is now the official residence of the president of Malta.

## Attard

In 1620, Grand Master Antoine de Paule began to enlarge his country house near **Attard**. When he became grand master three years later, he so disliked the long journey to the traditional summer palace at Verdala that he adopted **San Anton Palace** as his summer retreat. The palace has been tinkered with by successive grand masters. During the siege of the French in 1799, Sir Alexander Ball and the National Congress were based at San Anton and the formal surrender of the French was signed here. It later became the governor's summer residence, replacing the palace in Valletta as the permanent residence in 1928. Since 1974 it has been the official quarters of the president of Malta.

*San Anton Palace gardens*
*open every day until sunset; the main garden entrance has de Paule's and Sir Arthur Burton's escutcheons above, and a smaller entrance is in St Anthony Street; meagre car parking by the main gate*

The public section of the **gardens** were opened in 1882 by Governor Burton. The oldest part of the well-maintained and mature grounds is the **Eagle Pond** dating from 1623, at the opposite end of the palace. In addition, there is a small aviary and most of the trees, plants and flowers are flagged. Among the numerous species are Washington palms, jacarandas, Norfolk Island pines, citrus, avocado, bamboos and the wonderfully twisted old roots of the fat-leafed *Ficus benghalensis*. A limited part of the

---

## A Lavish Grand Master's Court

The reign of Grand Master Antoine de Paule (1623–36) was for many the very beginning of the end for the Order. As a Frenchman he gave full vent to his self-indulgent and sybaritic ways; no expense was ever spared. For his celebratory dinner feast at the San Anton Palace he entertained an immodest 600 guests so bounteously that it sent Inquisitor Chigi – later Pope Alexander VII – into a pre-papal tirade. The lieutenant governor of Malta (1930–38), Sir Harry Luke, describes his outrageous (even by the standards of an eastern potentate) court thus: 'Besides the seneschal, the chaplains and the physicians, the gamekeeper and the falconers, the drummers and the trumpeters, the valets and the pages, grooms and a host of other domestics in descending order of importance, there were the wigmaker and the winder of clocks, there were even a rat-catcher and a baker of black bread for the hunting dogs.' Conveniently, de Paule ignored his vows of poverty and chastity and despite his excesses soldiered on unabashed until he died a ripe 85 in June 1636.

# Getting to and around the Three Villages

The road out of Birkirkara forks left for **Attard** and right for **Balzan** just after St Theresa's, the nadir of contemporary church architecture, a grubby dollop of concrete resembling an upended mushroom. For Lija take the right fork, signposted Naxxar, before St Theresa's. If you get lost, ask – local knowledge goes a pretty long way in these narrow one-way streets. The three villages are served by a variety of **buses**: for Balzan, you can catch pretty much anything going west from Msida, no.40 for Attard via Lija and nos.80 or 81 for Attard via Balzan.

palace terrace is open to the public; de Vilhena's chapel of 1722 to Our Lady of Pilar is on the right at the start of the tunnel to the St Anthony Street entrance. Occasionally, on summer evenings, a Shakespeare play will be performed here; the Bard's words obviously fascinate the local wild felines, who often meander on stage mid-performance.

**St Mary's parish church** is the best, and probably the last, of the handful of Renaissance-style churches built on Malta. Architectural design had passed over the cusp into the more effervescent Baroque when work commenced in the early 17th century; the date inscribed on the wall is 1613, which possibly indicates the church was begun 10 or more years earlier. Its design is attributed to an ageing Vittorio Cassar or a youthful Tommaso Dingli, who was born here – it was probably Cassar. The façade is nearly identical to that of the Assumption in Birkirkara (also credited to Dingli), and is a pleasing relief from the Baroque style, with an elegant temple front and a neat triangular pediment above a circular window; the main door columns are finely detailed stone carvings and the six niches are occupied by saints. The campanile was added to the cruciform plan in 1718. There is a small **pastoral museum** to the right of the church.

*Pastoral museum in St Mary's Church*
*open Sun*

## Balzan

The most interesting part of **Balzan** is in **Three Churches Street** (It-Tliet Knejjes) at the eastern corner of the square: 120 yards from the square, in the oldest part of the village and grouped together around an old meeting or cemetery cross there are, not surprisingly, three old churches. Little **St Roque**, sophisticated in its simplicity, was built in 1593 during a terrible plague. (Roque is the patron saint of plague-fighters.) For what must have been a rapid building programme there is some fine, if naive, detail. Note the Cyclopean circular window above the door which uses a set of six ordinary intertwined semicircles to form a striking pattern. Above its setting, a crude moulded square, is a charming tiny triangle pediment enclosing a delicate flower. The other two churches are the earlier **Annunciation** and **St Leonard's**, which is now a house (during the Second World War it was a refuge).

*St Roque*
*open every Sun, but Mass is said only once a year*

## Lija

The **parish church of St Saviour** was designed by Giovanni Barbara in 1694 when he was just 24. It is an austere building in an equally cold square, but most of its detail is original and the lights of the *festa* lift its sombreness. To the right of the church, past a statue of *St Peter*, is the earlier 16th-century parish church to St Saviour, now shaded by ancient, gnarled olive trees.

Further afield is Tal-Mirakli, **Our Lady of Miracles**, said to be built at the precise centre of the island. To find it, follow the one-way system out of the square, turn right at the Three Villages Bar into Annibale Preca Street, and it is at the end, about 1,250 yards from the square. Built by Grand Master Cotoner in 1664 on the site of an earlier church, it is a neat building with an unusually generous dome. The thoughtful main altarpiece, unkindly served by poor illumination, is of the *Virgin and Child* by Mattia Preti. To the right is the much-venerated 16th-century wooden triptych of the *Madonna*. According to legend, tears flowed from her eyes during the earthquake of 1743. Opposite the church is an old farmer's shed with a different kind of superstition attached: the horns of a bull to ward off the evil eye.

## Żebbuġ

This is 'old-banger country' where ancient vehicles and busted machinery are brought to be sold, or to die. If you want a second- or tenth-hand car, **Żebbuġ** is the place. It was not always so. Żebbuġ means olives, and the village grew from a handful of tiny *casals* knitted together around the common industries of olives and cotton. Żebbuġ cotton was woven into a high-quality heavy sailcloth and exported all over Europe. Neither crop is farmed any more, but as one of the original 10 parishes recorded in 1436 it was and is a wealthy country village. Unfortunately, it has turned its gaze inwards: the village is well kept but the de Rohan arch signalling the entrance to the village is in a sad state. Żebbuġ was once the home to Antonio Sciortino, one of the few Internationally recognized Maltese artists.

Grand Master de Rohan adopted Żebbuġ and elevated it to a city, renamed it **Città Rohan**, and built what is today a sorry-looking **triumphal arch** at the entrance to the village. In its older streets off St Anthony Street and Hospital Square (Misrah L-Isptar) and behind the church are many generous old houses which serve to date it. Some of the cuboid buildings here go back to the 16th century. The villagers and the nuns of Żebbuġ are devout; niches and churches proliferate. In the main square the **parish church of**

## Getting to Żebbuġ

Żebbuġ is south of the Rabat–Qormi road, but the easiest, signposted route is via Attard. The no.88 **bus** from Ħamrun stops at Żebbuġ.

St Philip (the patron saint of the area), begun in 1599, was initially the work of the Cassars, *père et fils*, but Dingli finished it 60 years later. It is far more ornate and even fussier than Gerolamo Cassar's most famous church, the striking St John's Co-Cathedral, built over 25 years before. The two towers seem squeezed together in the screen façade, isolating the twin domes either side. For a lavish interior, study the north and south transepts and the coffered semicircular vault. The locals are obviously impressed with the structure – the majority of Żebbuġ's male population is called Philip.

About 350 yards behind St Philip's, on the corner of St Roque and Kbira, is the **chapel of St Roque**. It is hardly a striking edifice and is easy to miss. Inside is a restored mini-museum of Żebbuġ containing various artefacts, from Roman pottery pieces to Pisari's sketches. To be shown round, ask for Philip (naturally) in the shop opposite or wait until the St Philip's festival in June, when it stays open all weekend.

On the northern outskirts of Żebbuġ is the little church of **Tal-Ħlas**, dedicated to mothers in labour. In the early days of the Order it was on the main route between Mdina and the Three Cities, and was used by travelling knights. (Today it is not so easy to find:

### An Enlightened Grand Master

*I can't be King; I won't be Duke: I am Rohan.*
Motto of the noble de Rohan family

When de Rohan was elected to the magistracy in 1775, a spell was broken over the French *langues*, which had not provided a grand master since Adrien de Wignacourt in 1697. But the regal celebrations in the French *auberges* could not conceal the Order's troubles for a split second longer than the fireworks illuminated the bastions of Valletta – de Rohan had inherited a near-bankrupt Order in moral disarray. Nevertheless, his 22-year reign was to be an enlightened and reforming one. A cheery, optimistic and – by grand-master standards – young man of 57, he was not only popular with his peers but with the Maltese, 10 of whom – one-third of the entire Maltese nobility – he ennobled. He made himself accessible, revised taxes and abolished the more brutal acts of torture enshrined in the penal code; the Code Rohan still forms a part of Maltese common law. The Order's library in Valletta was completed the year before he died, and he was the first to admit women to court.

Nevertheless, his generosity of spirit and loyalty to his doomed monarch, Louis XVI, was to speed the Order's inevitable demise. Despite the parlous state of the knights' finances, de Rohan sold silver plate to pay for the French royal family's disastrous flight to Varennes in 1791. Their capture brought on a near-terminal apoplectic fit, and he limped through Louis XVI's execution in 1793 to the summer of 1797, when he died, convinced he would be the last grand master to reign in Malta.

One year later Napoleon, with his elephantine memory, informed de Rohan's successor von Hompesch that the knights could not plead with impunity that theirs was a neutral and religious order: had they not, only seven years before, been strident Royalist sympathizers?

50 yards before the roundabout to Siġġiewi on the Rabat–Qormi road, turn left down a hilly track at Raymond Auto Dealer, 700 yards later by a field is Tal-Ħlas.) Partly shaded by a weaving old tree-climbing evergreen, the tiny church is charmingly simple. The original building dating from 1500 was destroyed by the 1693 earthquake, but, in between rebuilding St Paul's Cathedral in Mdina, Lorenzo Gafa found time to rebuild it. It is said the organ came from the wreckage of St Paul's in Mdina. The unusual twin-porticoed loggias on either side were added in 1699 to provide shelter for pilgrims, and the escutcheon is that of Pope Clement XI. A good example of priestly self-preservation, common in many of the small churches, are the heavily barred windows in the façade; during corsair raids they enabled the priest to remain locked safely inside, and say Mass to the congregation outside.

## Tourist Information in Birkirkara, the Three Villages and Żebbuġ

There is a **children's play park** behind St Helen's church in Birkirkara, but a much better one in the gardens of the old railway station next to the church of the Assumption.

### Festas

**Birkirkara** has three *festas*: **St Joseph the Worker** on the first Sunday in July, **Our Lady of Mount Carmel** on the third Sunday in July, and **St Helen's** on the third Sunday in August.

**Attard** has one of the eight *festas* to the **Assumption** on 15 August and **Balzan** the **Annunciation** on the second Sunday in July.

**Lija** is famous for having one of the more lively and pyrotechnically accomplished *festas* – the firework displays are terrific. It is on 6 August and celebrates **St Saviour**.

In **Żebbuġ** the *festa* of **St Philip** is held on the second Sunday in June, and the *festa* of **St Joseph** is on the last Sunday in July.

### Shopping

In **Birkirkara**, **Paul Borg Antiques** and **Versailles Antiques** are in Naxxar Road. **Wignacourt Antiques** is in Valley Road and **TouchWood** is in Mannarino Street (with a larger shop in **St Venera**).

Nearly all Malta's **antiques** and *brocante* (bric-a-brac) dealers are situated in the **Three Villages** area. Don't be afraid to haggle, but be warned – the Maltese dealer has a very stubborn streak. For different souvenirs of a less expensive kind, try the pottery studio, the **Ceramica Saracina**, in **Attard**.

**Ceramica Saracina**, 87–8 St Anthony Street, Attard, near to the secondary entrance to Palace Gardens. All kinds of handmade and home-fired oddments from vases to old-fashioned piggy banks via plates and tiles. Prices are reasonable too.

**Benny's Antiques**, 234 Main Street, Balzan. A small emporium of *brocante* and antiques.

There is also a branch of Nicholson's supermarket in Balzan; you can't miss it.

## Where to Stay in Birkirkara, the Three Villages and Żebbuġ

**\*\*\*\*\*Corinthia Palace Hotel**, De Paule Avenue, Attard (opposite San Anton Palace), t 21 440301 (€€€€). Following a major rebuilding programme in the early 1990s, this has 150 rooms, a business centre, three restaurants, a tennis court and an interesting megalithic-shaped pool complex. The décor is a bit tired, but the gardens are nicely tranquil. Its principal restaurant is oriental and is ideal for those wishing to flee the *costa* scene, while the health club Athenaeum offers a wide variety of spa treatments.

## Eating Out in Birkirkara, the Three Villages and Żebbuġ

Most of the restaurants in this area are housed within the Corinthia Palace Hotel.

**Villa Corinthia Restaurant, t** 21 440301 (€€€€). The hotel's main restaurant, serving international cuisine in very formal surroundings. *Open for dinner and Sun lunch.*

**Rickshaw, t** 21 440301 (€€€). Serves a mixture of different Asian foods in elegant surroundings. Very popular. *Dinner only.*

**Melita, t** 21 470663 (€). This is the only restaurant that is not part of the Corinthia Palace. There is a small bar, and the restaurant serves a straightforward range of fare – salads, pizzas, burgers and the like indoors or out. A little uninspiring.

**Pizza, Pasta, Basta, t** 21 440301 (€). Alfresco restaurant serving inexpensive pizza and pasta. *Open May–Oct, dinner only.*

If you just want a drink, the **Three Villages Bar** at the north end of St Anthony Street is a small and friendly place with moody wood-panelling and just about every conceivable liquor on its dusty shelves.

# Gozo and Comino

*Gozo is further in spirit from Malta than the 5-mile (8km) channel Il-Fliegu which separates the two islands would suggest. Some visitors to the comparative fast lane of Malta cannot comprehend the idea of spending more than one day in sleepy Gozo, while Gozo's visitors, an eclectic mixture of discerning wealthy Europeans and divers on a budget, would never contemplate setting foot in Malta.*

# 13

## Don't miss

⭐ **A formidable fortification**
The Citadel, Victoria
**p.270**

⭐ **The charm of the village square**
Xagħra **p.276**

⭐ **Pagan place of mystery**
Ġgantija **p.277**

⭐ **Twentieth-century wonder**
The Rotunda **p.291**

⭐ **Island paradise**
Comino **p.300**

*See map overleaf*

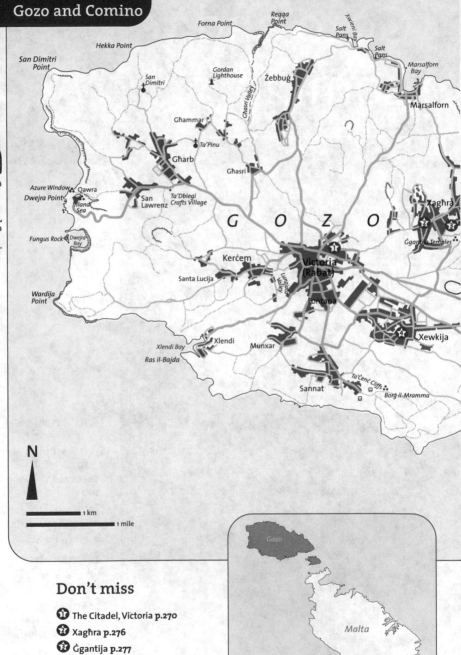

# Gozo and Comino

San Dimitri Point

Hekka Point

Forna Point

Reqqa Point

Salt Pans

Xwieni Bay

Salt Pans

Marsalforn Bay

San Dimitri

Gordan Lighthouse

Żebbuġ

Marsalforn

Għammar

Għasri Valley

Ta'Pinu

Għarb

Għasri

Azure Window

Qawra

Dwejra Point

Inland Sea

San Lawrenz

Ta'Dbiegi Crafts Village

G O Z O

Fungus Rock

Dwejra Bay

Xagħra

Ġgantija Temples

Kerċem

Victoria (Rabat)

Santa Lucija

Lunzjata Valley

Wardija Point

Fontana

Xewkija

C

Xlendi Bay

Xlendi

Munxar

Ras il-Bajda

Ta'Ċenċ Cliffs

Sannat

Borġ il-Mramma

N

1 km

1 mile

Gozo

Malta

## Don't miss

1 The Citadel, Victoria **p.270**

2 Xagħra **p.276**

3 Ġgantija **p.277**

4 The Rotunda, Xewkija **p.291**

5 Comino **p.300**

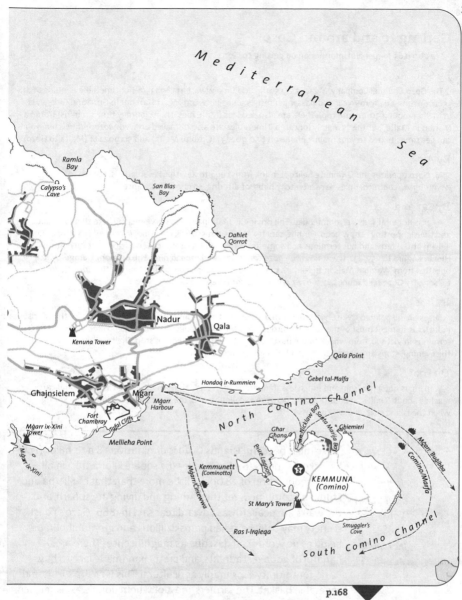

p.168

**Gozo**'s proud emblem of three green hills (said to be Żebbuġ, Xagħra and Nadur) over a blue sea is the first silhouette of landfall; peaceful villages cling like limpets on to the sides of the fertile and flat-topped hills. The greens of the landscape and valleys are a welcome surprise after the summer has baked Malta into a dusty brick. This is not a place for a wild bacchic party; it is about first gear, a slow pace. To a Gozitan, *pace* (prounounced *par-chey*) is a common surname, not something that governs anyone's life.

## Getting to and around Gozo

*See also* p.65 for general information on getting to Gozo.

### By Sea

**The Gozo Channel Company**, Mġarr, **t** 21 556114, and Ċirkewwa, **t** 21 580435/6 (for timetable enquiries **t** 21 556016), runs a daily ro-ro car and passenger ferry service between Mġarr Harbour in Gozo and Ċirkewwa in Malta (about a 30-minute trip). There are also services (Mon, Tues, Thurs; journey time 90 mins) from Sa Maison in Malta, but this is mainly for cargo. Timetables are also displayed on *www.gozochannel.com*; you can get times texted to your mobile phone on **t** 50 902233 (Gozo to Malta) and 50 902244 (Malta to Gozo).

### By Air

**Air Gozo** operates the 12-minute helicopter link from Luqa to Xewkija. Reservations: **t** 21 561301, *www.airgozo.com*. Schedules have a twitchy habit of altering, so check in advance.

### By Car and Taxi

A **car** is not vital, but is recommended. The driving is marginally less nerve-racking here than on Malta and the signposting is now good. For **hire cars** try **Mayjo**, **t** 21 556678, *www.mayjo.com.mt* in Victoria. **Taxis** line up at the ferry and bus terminus and sometimes in It-Tokk, Victoria, otherwise contact **Adventure Car Hire** in Xagħra **t** 21 557632, *www.adventuregozo.com* (taxis and moped hire), the **Belmont Garage** (which operates from 'Wombat Maison' in Nadur), **t** 21 556962. For **jeep and walking tours** with added Gozo folklore, try **Gozo Jeep Tours**, **t** 21 566267, *www.gozo.com/jeeptours*.

### By Bus

Buses are all painted civil-service grey with a spruce red stripe, and their prime concession to the tourist industry is to meet most of the summer ferries from Mġarr Harbour. You will be deposited at the central terminus in Victoria, from where all the buses originate, depart and often stop. The service ceases early in the evening; stops anywhere other than the main villages are rare.

### On Foot

Walking is not a hardship and much less dangerous than on Malta – in rural Gozo a donkey and cart reaches about 6 miles an hour (10kph). There are excellent walks, the most fragrant time being spring when the island is at its most colourful.

> *'Gozo is different,' concluded the priest Don Salvatore.*
>
> Nicholas Monsarrat,
> *The Kappillan of Malta*

Like most peaceful islands Gozo is diminutive – 8 by 4 miles (13.5 by 6.5km) at best, 26 square miles (67 square kilometres) in all – and its population of 28,000 is little more than that of Sliema and St Julian's combined. Yet the bathing and diving are superb, and the walks are peaceful; as Edward Lear said in 1866, 'Gozo's coast scenery may truly be called pomskizillious and gromphibberous, being as no words can describe its magnificence.' There are a handful of good restaurants, and pretty handmade lace to buy.

The community is primarily agricultural. This is Malta's fruit and vegetable basket. The farmers, most of whom double as fishermen, have used traditional implements to work the blue clay soil of the hillside fields for generations. Their weathered and leathery faces are coarser than those of the Maltese, but they are a lot more house-proud; the whole island is neater and cleaner than Malta.

Gozo's landscape has made it vulnerable to invasion, and over the centuries the islanders have developed a healthy suspicion of foreigners – and that includes the Maltese. This insularity has coalesced the community into a proud and traditional one, and slowed down the rate of change. (Being a few steps back in time is the island's charm.) Fortunately, over the past 35 years or so the Gozitans' natural wariness has eased into friendliness. They have now accepted that not all tourists are direct descendants of 16th-century Turkish slave-traders, but just people who have come to wander around their island. Centuries of self-sufficiency have bred a culture built around folklore, and the villagers have countless tales to tell – from the legend of Calypso ensnaring Odysseus in her cave above the red sand of Ramla Bay to the metamorphosis of an altarpiece of San Dimitri in Għarb. This capacity for faith is manifested in the islanders' energetic devotion to their church. For weeks before the lively local *festas* they wind themselves up with a torque wrench of anticipation, then celebrate with more gusto and warmth than anywhere else.

## History

A self-sustaining agricultural community has inhabited Gozo for about 5,500 years (as evidenced by the ancient temples of Ġgantija). Because it lacks a natural harbour it held no attraction for the seafaring nations that roamed the Mediterranean, all of whom gave it a cursory name. The Phoenicians called it *Gwl*, meaning 'round ship' (the Greeks and the Romans chose something similar). The Byzantines called it *Gaudos* and, finally, the Arabs in the 9th century settled on *Ghudash* (*Għawdex* in Malti), a name which is still used today. It was the Aragonese and the knights who christened it Gozo. The island's fate has, not surprisingly, always been linked with Malta's. Largely undefended, for a while its sole and unwitting purpose was to be the provider of a steady flow of slaves to passing Barbary Coast pirates or Turks; the bays of Marsalforn, Xlendi and Ramla being safe enough to anchor in while a few villagers were rounded up to be sold in the markets of Tripoli or Constantinople or, if lucky, ransomed. (Until 1637 every inhabitant had to be within the walls of the citadel at Victoria by sundown.)

The scourge of the central Mediterranean, **Dragut Rais**, was attracted to Gozo like a magpie to silver, his raids providing recreation in between serious missions like devastating Naples or Sicilian shipping. There was, however, a reason for his spite. During

### Gozo's Stockpile

During the Second World War the failure of convoys to provide adequate foodstuffs during the hot summer of 1942 brought an already desperate situation to a head. The newly appointed governor, Lord Gort, calculated a target date at the end of August when starvation alone would force him to replace the Union Jack with the white flag of surrender. But the Gozitans had, like squirrels for winter, stockpiled much of their produce. Furthermore, many are said to have sailed in small boats at night across the 60-mile (100km) channel to enemy-occupied Sicily to barter for provisions. Only after a direct appeal to the bishop of Gozo, Michael Gonzi, did the Gozitans open their cache – enabling Lord Gort to move his pencilled date back a few weeks in anticipation of the next convoy.

an attack in 1544 – only 14 years after the Order had arrived in Malta – his brother was captured and killed. The governor of Gozo refused to return the body and burned the corpse. Dragut, a man who thought revenge was a dish best eaten cold, waited before he hit back. In July 1551, he and Sinan Pasha besieged the citadel. The islanders finally surrendered on 27 July, but not before some survivors had taken desperate action – Bernardo Duopuo, a soldier, put his wife and two daughters to death rather than allow them to be captured. Almost the entire island's population of 6,000 was then hauled away into slavery. The only survivors were the infirm, who could not be sold, and those who had escaped over the citadel's walls. The island was only resettled three years later, by **Grand Master de la Sengle**, who bribed many Maltese to cross the channel by waiving their last four years' debts.

The island endured six more raids during the latter half of the 16th century. It was only in the early 17th century, when the Order realized how potentially destructive a Gozo-based Turkish army could be, that they grudgingly took action. St Mary's Tower (1618) on Comino was the first link in what was to become a chain of defences that stretched from Gozo across Malta. It took a century before the island was sufficiently well fortified to ward off incursions – the last pirating raid the Gozitans had to endure was as late as 1708.

When the **French** invaded in June 1798 they met with little resistance from the enfeebled garrison of knights. Yet, soon after, the Gozitans rebelled against French rule, recaptured the countryside, and besieged the 50-strong French garrison in the citadel until its surrender in 1800. Ironically, it was during this brief two-year period of French rule that the Gozitans enjoyed their only spell of political independence from Malta. The **British** had little use for the island, which they regarded as a nuisance, another Scotland, with little to contribute and there only to be protected. However, during the siege years of the Second World War their approach changed when Gozo provided food and accommodation for many of Malta's evacuees.

## The Constitution

Politically, Gozo is part of Malta. The Romans organized both islands as separate *municipia* and until the arrival of the Order in 1530 Gozo's self-governing local council, the Università, was headed by the Hakem or Captain of the Rod. After another of Dragut's raids in 1551 the Order perceived Gozo as a security risk and brought the island under its jurisdiction. Since 1987 the island has had its own ministry, sending five representatives to the 65-seat House of Representatives. It has been a separate diocese since 1864.

## The Future

Progress in the concrete sense of the word is being made in Gozo: building activity has increased hugely, with large apartment blocks covering green fields and old village houses being replaced by garish new builds. Despite this Gozo has not yet sufffered the urban sprawl of Malta, and terraced green fields still for now separate one place from the next. But large resorts and marina projects are in the pipeline.

Gozo's ecology, environment and infrastructure are as fragile as Meissen china. The island is still greener and cleaner than Malta, but the manic greedy building has started. Even the Hotel Ta'Ċenċ, once one of Gozo's loveliest hotels, is now the site of a massive project of apartments and hotel accommodation. It has taken great effort from local heritage committees and environmental organizations to downscale the size of the project. So while old Gozo can still be seen in quiet village squares and enticing beaches, so too are the sad predictions of irreversible change much in evidence. All Gozo's legends warn of the blindness of greed that leads to the inevitable comeuppance. Ironically, the moral is going unheeded now.

In this chapter the island has been divided into five areas: the capital Victoria, and the north, west, south and east. Victoria is at the centre and with one or two exceptions all points lead from it, to it and through it. It is often referred to by its pre-1897 name of Rabat and the main street is known officially as Republic Street, more popularly as Racecourse Street.

# Victoria (Rabat)

To celebrate Queen Victoria's Diamond Jubilee of 1897 the capital of Gozo, **Rabat**, changed its name in her honour (although to hear the Gozitans talk you would never know; it is still Rabat to the majority). This Lilliputian capital of 6,200 people is lively in the mornings, gently nods off in the afternoons, twitches with energy again from about 6pm to the sound of birdsong from the trees of It-Tokk and St Francis Square, before retiring early. The old quarter behind It-Tokk began to take shape more than 350 years ago and is made up of narrow alleys that mould themselves into a cohesive little maze of dark angular shadows and bright sunlight, distorting the delightful local balconies out of proportion. All is made more mysterious by the mix of aromas that waft through the nameless streets.

The citadel, with its patriarchal history, four museums, cathedral and panoramas of the whole island is well worth visiting, as is the **Collegiate Basilica of St George** behind It-Tokk.

## Getting to and around Victoria (Rabat)

All **buses** go from the terminus in Main Gate Street, but times coincide with school and work hours, not the whims of tourists. There is a large map depicting the different routes, and a ferry company board warns of delays. Bus no.25 goes to and from Mġarr – during the summer, the last one leaves around 9pm. Between 7.30am and 5pm, part of Republic Street and Sir Adrian Dingli Street is one-way, adding to Victoria's already confusing one-way system.

Park your **car** behind the terminus in the free car park; the three-minute walk to the centre of town is less aggravating than trying to find a space. Free parking on the streets of Victoria is limited to 90 mins in any one place. Parking clock dials can be obtained from local council offices and on board the Gozo ferry, though Gozo hire cars should have them anyway.

# The Citadel

 **Citadel**

Victoria's citadel, like Mdina's, sits on a high ledge. From the semicircular battlements running from east to west there is an unrivalled panorama of Gozo, each of the pocket-sized villages being identifiable by their anything but pocket-sized churches. The immense dome of the Xewkija rotunda to the east looks even more splendidly over-the-top from here. Apart from its dramatic vantage point, the citadel's attraction lies in the colour of its old limestone buildings, whose pallor has warmed with age. There is a diversity of styles within the fortifications: the Baroque cathedral, diminutive Palazzo Bondi, the derelict Norman area, the bastions and the gutted little alleys.

The original citadel dates back to the Romans, who probably used the 500ft (150m) high bluff, in the centre of the island, as an acropolis for their settlement below. Hardly any traces of this or the 9th-century Arab occupation have survived, however. The 12th-century Norman citadel or Gran Castello was destroyed by Dragut Rais during the disastrous short siege of 1551 (until 1637, the island's population had to pass the night in the citadel in order to avoid being captured by pirates). The town, within its fortified walls, was rebuilt in fits and starts on the existing plan by a series of grand masters. The present entrance to the citadel was cut through into Cathedral Square in 1957; the original and much smaller one 25 yards further on, known as the Mdina Door, is marked by a Roman inscription dating back to the 2nd century AD.

### The Cathedral of the Assumption

The cathedral, originally the *matrice* until Gozo became a separate diocese in 1864, is built on the site of three or more older places of worship, including Roman and Phoenician temples. Construction commenced in 1697, four years after the 1693 earthquake had damaged its predecessor and destroyed large tracts of southeast Sicily. (The cathedral at Mdina was another victim of the earthquake, and Lorenzo Gafa was commissioned to design replacements for both.) By the end of the 17th century

Maltese Baroque had become more sophisticated, the simple swaggering effect having more impact than mere ornamentation. Here, the rectangular façade with its gown of stairs coming down from the Corinthian pillars lends height, and the escutcheon is that of Grand Master Perrellos in whose reign it was built. From the outside the façade gives the impression of a gloomy nave, but inside it is surprisingly small and light due to a course of windows above the high vault and distended pilasters on the ornate tessellated floor of tombstones. The single most interesting feature is a pure example of Gozitan ingenuity: due to lack of funds a dome was not added to the structure, so the Sicilian Antonio Manuele was commissioned in 1739 to paint a meticulous trompe l'œil in its stead. The clever perspective is at first too difficult to grasp – watch out for others walking around in dizzying circles craning their necks. From a distance, the domeless cathedral oddly fits in with the decapitated Gozitan hills. It is ironic that poor Gafa did not have the funds at his disposal to add his signature, a dome, in this, the last work of his life.

The irregular **Cathedral Square**, guarded by two toy-sized 17th-century cannons, once housed dwellings on the now vacant south and west walls. The two remaining buildings on the north side house the **Law Courts**. The building on the right was the **Governor's Palace**, built by Grand Master Alof de Wignacourt in the early years of the 17th century with the hallmark 'fat' Melitan

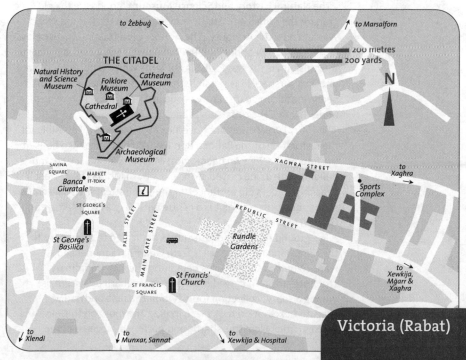

Victoria (Rabat)

windows; that on the left was the old **Public Registry** from where decrees were read out.

## The Five Museums of the Citadel

**Citadel Museums**

*all museums and temples open 9–5, last adm 4.30, closed Good Fri, 24, 25, 31 Dec, 1 Jan; adm (free for Old Prisons), combined ticket available; free for under 16s, over 65s and holders of student cards; the prehistoric temples of Ġgantija and the Windmill (Il Mitħna), both in Xagħra, have combined entrance fee*

The **Cathedral Museum** is 70 yards up Fosse Street. The vault in the basement displays ecclesiastical silverware. On the ground floor there is the bishop's British-made landau of 1860 and clerical oddments. On the first floor, take a look at the expressions of Gozo's influential bishops and dignitaries in the picture gallery. Bishop Cassar with his viciously stern expression led the local insurrection against the French; nearby Dr Nicola Mahnuk, a prosperous 17th-century merchant, is portrayed as comically smug. Note also the early 16th-century cathedral altarpiece, a gentle polyptych of tempera on wood to *St Maria*.

Housed in a row of three well-restored 15th-century buildings (the windows display the Siculo-Norman influence) is the excellent little **Folklore Museum**, and opposite the entrance is where Bernardo Duopuo fell in 1551 (*see* p.268) at the end of Dragut's siege. The exhibits reflect the simple yet hard Gozitan life through the ages: a blacksmith's and carpenter's workshop, looms, and primitive grain-milling and grape-pressing equipment. The social and sporting side of Gozo is also well documented with 18th-century guns, fishing paraphernalia, mortars for the *festas* and costumes.

The **Natural History and Science Museum** is opposite the old granary, the British garrison's headquarters in the Second World War and now the Armoury. (The Armoury is a frustration – displays of the knights' weaponry are behind permanently barred gates.) In the museum is the tragic display of birds which innocently strayed into local airspace; it is possible the once-proud Mediterranean peregrine falcon on display was one of the very last pair to nest under the Ta'Ċenċ cliffs.

Sir Harry Luke, lieutenant governor 1930–38, was responsible for the restoration of the Palazzo Bondi which has since 1959 housed the impressive little **Archaeological Museum**, a small but grand building with a fine carved stone balcony in Mdina Door Street near the citadel's old entrance. (In the same street are small crafts shops and at the end of it is a centre with displays of Maltese and Gozitan products.)

The **ground floor** of the museum is dedicated to **prehistory**. In the right-hand room are relics from Ġgantija; a model and watercolours of the temples help bring these extraordinary structures to life. A carved relief of a snake (hard to discern) is among a sparse collection found when the first, and badly executed, excavation took place in 1827. The room on the left houses earlier Neolithic shards and pottery discovered in the

Xagħra area to the north. Punic, Roman and Arab relics are on the first floor: the Xlendi room (on the left) is named after the deceptively treacherous and narrow bay to the south where two merchant ships sank, one in the 2nd century BC, the other in the 5th century AD; the anchors, countless wine jars and amphorae on display were uncovered in 1961. On the landing tucked away in a niche is a beautiful Majmuna tombstone (1174), inscribed with the pitiful yet sad Kufic (early Arabic) lament of a distraught father at the death of his 12-year-old daughter. The largest room is reserved for Gozo's Punic and Roman finds including: pottery and tiles from the old Roman villa in Ramla; the grisly remains of a split Punic burial amphora found underneath stones in Santa Marija Bay, Comino; and a coin collection found in 1937 near St George's, an old part of Victoria that is believed to have fallen within the boundary of the Roman *municipium*. On the coins, Nero (AD 54–68) is depicted in lampooning profile, with a boxer's neck, weak jaw and pusillanimous nose. The unflattering image of the despotic and insane emperor (apart from playing a fiddle while Rome burned, he put St Paul to death) raises the question as to the unknown artist's fate.

The **Old Prisons** are situated next door to the Gozo Courts and date from the 16th century. De la Vallette himself was once imprisoned here.

# Outside the Citadel

**Citadel Theatre**
*Shows every half hour from 10.30–3.30, except Sun and national holidays 10.30–1; adm*

Just outside the Citadel on Castle Hill is the **Citadel Theatre**, currently showing 'Gozo 360°', the smaller island's version of the Malta and Mdina Experiences. This 30-minute show uses 1,000 colour slides with commentary in eight languages (English, French, German, Italian, Spanish, Dutch, Danish and Maltese), designed to illustrated the island's culture.

The **Banca Giuratale** (1733), a pretty bow-fronted Baroque building in It-Tokk, was Grand Master de Vilhena's present to the people of Gozo after his visit in 1723. The 'civil building' (the knights referred to them grandly as Municipal Palaces or Banca Giuratale) became the seat of the Università, the almost powerless local governing body, whose authority amounted to the ability to lend money to the poor, collect taxes and conscript able-bodied farmers into the diminutive 90-strong garrison. The privileges of the jurats (officers of the Università) were equally hollow – the right to a special pew and incense at high Mass. It is still a government building, and houses the occasional local art exhibition.

Behind It-Tokk is the **basilica of St George**, the original parish church, built in 1678 as no more than a simple nave. The façade was altered in 1818 and the aisles, dome and transepts were all added between 1935 and 1945. Despite architectural meddling, the church has remained a pleasing structure. Its interior, however, is the product of a contemporary and somewhat overenthusiastic Baroque school, and is only muted when the sunlight filters through the stained-glass windows. The bronze and black canopied altar with its barley-twist columns is a small copy of Bernini's in St Peter's, Rome, and the ornate vaulted ceiling and dome show colourful episodes from Saint George's dramatic life. Hidden among the remodelled exuberance of its interior, the church possesses some important paintings. Mattia Preti's *St George* (1678) in a heroic pose differs greatly from the artist's version which hangs in St John's Co-Cathedral, Valletta. In this composition the saint is diminutive to the point of harmlessness, with cherubic cheeks and a slight pot belly. His foot rests cautiously on the freshly severed and extinguished dragon's head while his sword flashes mysteriously clean. Francesco Zahra, one of the finest of 18th-century Maltese painters, shows yet another interpretation of St George with two equally powerful works, one of which includes his beheading. The 150-year-old statue of the saint by another local artist was carved in one piece from a tree trunk. Finally, the bells of St George's, unlike those of other Gozitan churches, chime at 11am – tradition states this was to remind the women to begin kindling the fire for lunch.

**Rundle Gardens** at the bottom of Republic Street next to the Duke of Edinburgh Hotel were planted in the last two years of Sir Leslie Rundle's governorship (1909–15), and have remained Gozo's main public gardens. Formally laid out, they contain, apart from the indigenous *Ficus nitida* tree, an avenue of olives, tall canary palms and an aviary of noisy chirping birds. An annual **agricultural fair** takes place here on 14–15 August, the feast of Santa Marija or the Assumption.

## Tourist Information and Services in Victoria (Rabat)

(i) **Victoria ›**
*Tigrija Palazz, Republic Street, Victoria, t 21 561419 (open Mon–Sat 9–12.30 and 1–5; Sun and public holidays 9–12.30)*

The **MTA** is centrally located near the Citadel. When the new ferry terminal is complete another office may open there.

Grouped together on both sides of Republic Street, and impossible to miss, are **Maltacom**, the main **post office**, the **police station** and the **banks**.

There are **public conveniences** under Banca Giuratale in It-Tokk, next to the bus terminus and at the entrance to the citadel.

**Gozo General Hospital, t** 21 561600, is signposted on the Xewkija road just outside Victoria. There is a **clinic** for minor complaints 100m out of St Francis Square in Enrico Mizzi Street. The **Gozo Sports Complex** in Victoria, **t** 21 560677, has excellent amenities: tennis, squash, basketball, volleyball, gym (*open Mon–Fri 8am–9pm, Sat 9–6, Sun 8–5*).

**Religious Services: Church of England services** are held on Wednesday at 11am at the Seminary in Victoria. **Roman Catholic Mass** can be heard on Sundays, Wednesdays and holy days in English at 9.30am at the Sacred Heart Seminary in Victoria, at 10am at the Franciscan Sisters in Nadur and at 10am at Our Lady of Mount Carmel in Xlendi.

### Festas

Victoria has two very excited feasts that are steeped in rivalry: the cathedral's *festa* of the **Assumption** (Santa Marija) on 15 August, when half of Malta invades Gozo; and the *festa* to **St George** on the third Sunday in July. The battlements of the citadel make the ideal launching pad for an increasingly colourful palette of fireworks. In Republic Street (also known as Racecourse Street) there are horse races the day after.

## Shopping in Victoria (Rabat)

Shops on Gozo tend to shut for the weekend at Saturday lunchtime. Even if they post notices of opening and closing times, remember these are Gozitan times and therefore elastic.

Victoria hosts a **daily market** in It-Tokk, meaning literally 'the meeting place' (*early morning until 1pm-ish*). It is basically a clothes market, displaying bolts of gaudy cloth destined to be fashioned into expressive Sunday dresses. Shops in the square sell **fresh fruit** and **vegetables**. Beside the Banca Giuratale at the west of It-Tokk a couple of **fish hawkers** always set up a stall. Better still, go to **Bugeja Fish Market** (*open Mon–Sat 8–12 and 4–7*) before the Gozo Heritage on the main road to Victoria.

**Foreign wines and spirits** and local **cheroots** can be bought from one of three shops in St George's Square. One of the most drinkable **local wines** is Razzett, which can be sampled and purchased at 4 Fosse Street in the citadel.

Next to the MTA office is the reputable **Palm Pharmacy**, and not far away is **Abelas Health and Beauty Centre**, impressive and well stocked. Another store, **PlayPen**, stocks all the stationery, cards and toys you don't need as well as offering **copying**

facilities; it is in Main Gate Street across from the bus terminus.

The swishly modern **Palazz Centre**, next to the police station in Republic Street, is discreetly executed; among the services and stores is a **fitness centre**. In a typical example of eccentric Gozitan charm **British Sunday newspapers** are available on Sunday morning from the lower ground floor of the Palazz Centre – during the week **English-language books and newspapers** can be obtained from **Book Rose** opposite. At the eastern end of Republic Street is the **Tower Bakery**; it is not the only one, but the easiest to find. Further away (700 yards east from It-Tokk) is **Arkadia**, Gozo's latest, largest and hopefully last mall. Selling everything from cars to hair accessories, food to furniture, Arkadia is the top shopping centre in Gozo.

**Handmade lace**, for which Gozo is famous, is hard to find. (Beware, sometimes there are 'handmade' labels on what is machine-made.) Try **Bastion Lace** in Bieb il-Imdina Street for creamy hand-made lace; they are next door to the Archaeological Museum in the citadel. (For some of the best handmade lace, *see* p.289.) The **Cittadella Centre**, 14–16 Sir Adrian Dingli Street (a continuation of Republic Street) is a refurbished mall with a **jeweller's**, a **souvenir shop** and a **perfumery** as well as a bar and a restaurant. **Prestige Gifts**, a few doors along at No.2, also has a good selection of souvenirs. Seventy yards away in Savina Square is a **brocante stall** (*open every day except Mon*) where all the old merchandise – some good and some tat – is hung from the outside walls. Two hundred yards along the Xlendi road, at 35 Enrico Mizzi Street, out of St Francis Square is **Gozo Antiques, t** 21 562422. The dealer keeps idiosyncratic hours and principally sells furniture as well as a few more portable knick-knacks and curios. In the citadel, at 4 Fosse Street among the souvenirs is **local wine**, **anisette** and **honey**. For something truly unique, the **Sacred Heart Bazaar** in Sir Arturo Mercieca Street has **religious icons and paraphernalia**.

The island's best **supermarket** is to be found in Arkadia Commercial

Centre. If you are staying in one of the villages there's no need to shop for food in Victoria, as you can buy from **local farmers** – their produce will be the freshest and best.

## Where to Stay and Eat in Victoria (Rabat)

The building boom over the past few years in Gozo has led to a dramatic increase in the quantity of holiday accommodation, although there are still no **hotels** or **guesthouses** in Victoria. MTA has lists of licensed apartments.

Useful **agencies** for the island include **Gozo Farmhouses, t** 21 561280, *www.gozofarmhouses.com* (for self-catering), 25 superb houses dotted through the island; **Dhalia**, 49b Republic Street, Victoria, **t** 21 551984, *www.dhalia.com*, which offers flats and houses; **Frank Salt**, Fortunato Mizzi Street, Victoria, **t** 21 560169/70, *www.franksalt.com.mt*; and **Legend**, Republic Street, Victoria, **t** 21 558855, *www.legend.com.mt*.

Victoria is not a gourmet's mecca either. The following is a selection of the best **restaurants** on offer.

**Brookies Restaurant**, 1 Wied Sara Street, **t** 21 559524 (€€€). Offers a decent choice of Mediterranean food; outside terrace in summer and wine bar serving platters and pasta. *Closed Tues.*

**Il Panzier**, 39 Charity Street (€€€). Simple delicious Sicilian cooking: try home-made pasta or the pork *vulcano*.

**It Tmun Victoria**, Europe Street, **t** 21 566667 (€€€). Excellent food and service and extensive wine list; the 'tasting menu' has six courses with wines to match.

**Riccardo**, 4 Fosse Street, **t** 21 555953 (€). Around noon you can't do better than go and see Riccardo, up from the cathedral in the citadel. At the back of his conventional souvenir shop are a couple of tables. Here you can eat aromatic local tomatoes, fresh bread, olives and Gozitan *gbejniet* (peppered goat's cheese) washed down with a glass of his heady local red wine.

**Silver Jubilee Cafè**, next to the Cittadella Centre (€). Open in the early hours for *pastizzi* and sweet tea. All the other bars around It-Tokk serve *pastizzi* but sell out by about 11.30.

**Tamarisk**, Fortunato Mizzi Street, **t** 21 551382 (€). Cheap and cheerful pizzeria.

**Tal-Ħwawar**, down the Kerċem Road, 300 yards beyond the citadel. For sweet teeth, this is an excellent confectioners, selling tasty, not to say sticky, toffees.

# North of Victoria

## Xagħra

 **Xagħra**

Xagħra, meaning 'a large open place', boasts the most enchanting **village square** on the island, and the twisty hairpin road up to the plateau is lined with pink and white oleander trees. Xagħra was probably the de facto capital of the island in ancient times and was certainly the site of man's first efforts to cultivate Gozo. It now has 3,300 inhabitants and is the second-largest village after Nadur.

The **Ġgantija Temples** are nearby, as is the major non-event of the island – the boulder-strewn hole that is alleged to be Calypso's Cave.

# Ġgantija

**Ġgantija**

*open Mon–Sat 9.5, last entry 4.30; adm; bus nos. 64/65 from Victoria*

The two prehistoric structures known as Ġgantija are the most impressive and well preserved of all the 'temples' in the Maltese islands. Along with Ta'Ħaġrat and Skorba in Malta, they are believed to be the oldest freestanding monuments in the world. Although they lack the fine artistic treasures of the later Tarxien Temples, they make up for it with brute size – poised at the edge of a plateau, they are a daunting sight. In keeping with everything else on Gozo, the complex itself is well kept and colourful; the wild bougainvillea and the flower beds contrast gently with the massive deep-honey-coloured stones. (Numbers in the text relate to the site plan below.)

The temples date back to the Ġgantija phase (3600–3200 BC) of the Copper Age and were first formally and badly excavated in 1827. The site comprises two similar structures (one with five apses, the other with four) and the whole is enclosed by a shared outer wall of megalithic proportions. The outer walls were made from hard coralline limestone; softer, more versatile globigerina limestone was used for the inside walls. A roof, which has not survived, would have covered the structures.

Walk across the threshold of each and there is a sensation of being 'inside', contained by the concave walls. The larger, and as you face it left-hand, temple is the older of the two and, like Mnajdra and Ħaġar Qim, is orientated southeast (the significance of this is unknown). The southerly five-apse temple has, in contrast to any

13 Gozo and Comino | North of Victoria: Xagħra

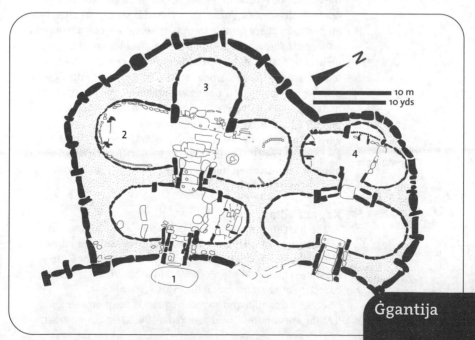

Ġgantija

## Sansuna

Copper Age man was an extraordinarily talented builder, but it must have taken decades, possibly generations to move, position and erect the boulders for Ġgantija's perimeter wall and the temples. Legend tells of a giantess from Qala named Sansuna who built the temples 5,500 years ago and owed her gargantuan stature to an awesome diet of broad beans and water. Her job was to carry on her head the stones from the quarry site at the Ta'Ċenċ cliffs. The settlers were apparently an ungrateful lot, and Sansuna ended her days sapped of strength by a dearth of beans, and living alone and unwanted in a cave.

similar structure on the islands, smaller outer than inner apses. It also has the largest **threshold slab** [1] of the temples. The left-hand of the two inner apses (which together span 77ft/23.5m) is stirring, with its walls, 20ft (6m) high, curving inward; it was here [2] that the **snake relief-carving** now on display in the Gozo Archaeological Museum was found. The central apse is raised higher and has similar pitted decoration to that at Tarxien. To the rear [3], **two stone heads** believed to belong to the headless female 'Fat' deities were discovered in the niche. These are on display in Valletta's Archaeological Museum.

On the right in the smaller temple (64ft/19.5m long) there is little of note other than the small raised **altar** [4] in the central niche at the end. But the single most striking element of Ġgantija is the perimeter wall. The stone wall reaches 20ft (6m) high in places, and the largest of the slabs measures 20ft (6m) by 21ft (6.5m).

As with all the megalithic structures in the islands, the nature of the god or gods worshipped here can only be guessed at. The dramatic shape of Ġgantija (and others on Malta) has often been likened to an obese female form, with the threshold marking the entrance to the 'womb'. This has led to assumptions that prehistoric man worshipped deities of fertility and symbols of rebirth, an idea that is carried forward by the obese little figurines discovered in many of the sites. Nevertheless, the theory has no material basis whatsoever, and assumes that the figurines preceded the structures and therefore influenced their form, whereas in fact they are known to postdate the structures. That said, the supposition could be correct, even though the evidence is missing. Keep an open mind – who is to say they never contained a series of market stalls?

## Xagħra Village

At 10 Triq Gnien Xibla (behind the church and opposite the Marsalforn turning) is the **Pomskizillious Toy Museum**, named after Edward Lear's fictional adjective used to describe Gozo's coastline; children like it. Victor Wickman has an impressive private collection of **naval memorabilia** in his Xagħra home.

Between Ġgantija and Xagħra's square is the prominent **Il Mitħna** or windmill, now restored as the latest government

**Pomskizillious Toy Museum**
*t 21 562489; open April Thurs, Fri and Sat only 10–1; May–mid-Oct Mon–Sat 10–12 and 3–6; winter Sat and public holidays only 10–1*

**Naval memorabilia collection**
*visits by appointment only, call t 21 690254*

museum. All the various implements a miller or farmer would use are displayed, but visit on the same day as Ġgantija and use the same entrance ticket – it is not worth the separate entrance fee.

For an entertaining diversion, you could stop and have a look at **Nino's and Xerri's grottoes** (to the north and south of the square respectively); these are two underground caves of stalactites and stalagmites, which are often found in limestone strata. The entrance to Nino's, the smaller of the two grottoes, is through the owner's front room and the cave is not deep. The descent to the much more substantial Xerri's Grotto, through a house called 'God Bless Australia', is more precarious: 10 yards down a tiny spiral staircase off another sitting room. (The modest entrance fee is justified on the grounds that 24 light bulbs are needed to illuminate the rock formations, and not by the more enticing fact that it takes 1,000 years for a single centimetre to form.)

The church in Xagħra, like everything and everybody in Gozo, has a nickname – Il Bambina – after the church's 19th-century French statue. The large church, **Our Lady of Victory** (1815), has an interior with wide columns and 10 small chapels and follows the idiom of the day, the marble work being rich and ornate. Apart from Christian scenes of victory over heathen enemies, there is an apse painting of the *Nativity of the Virgin* by Giuseppe Cali.

## Calypso's Cave

*The cave was sheltered by a copse of alders and fragrant cypresses, which was the roosting place of wide-winged birds, horned owls and falcons and cormorants with long tongues, birds of the coast... It was indeed a spot where even an immortal visitor must pause to gaze in wonder and delight.*

The Odyssey, Verses 63–74, Book 5, Homer

Either Homer (*see* quotation, left) was a daydreamer *extraordinaire* or time has been unkind in its treatment of what is purported to have been **Calypso's Cave** (it is signposted from Xagħra, and all over the north and east of the island). Despite her many charms, it is highly unlikely that Calypso enticed Odysseus to remain here for as much as seven minutes, let alone as many years. Although it is set promisingly on a craggy bluff, with a panorama of the Mediterranean sea, the fertile Ramla Valley and the red sandy beach of Ramla below, the cave itself is little more than a grubby, cramped hollow that was created by a rockslide in the Xagħra cliffs. A loud youth is invariably on hand at the site to light a candle, drip hot wax on his and other people's feet, and receive a tip for his considerable trouble.

## Marsalforn

**Marsalforn** is an old fishing community which has evolved into Gozo's main summer destination – apart from seven hotels there are numerous rental apartments. A mixed bag of tourists head here: diving enthusiasts, people over from Malta for a few days and Europeans wishing to escape.

In the height of the season it never quite jumps (nowhere does in Gozo), but it becomes touristy and the seafront, overrun with cafés

## Getting to Marsalforn and Żebbuġ

For **Marsalforn**, at Victoria turn right and head straight down the Marsalforn Valley to the sea (about 2½ miles/4km). There is ample **car parking** behind the bus terminus. The **no.21 bus** comes here from Victoria.

To reach **Żebbuġ** by **car** you can ascend via Xwieni and along the saltpans or by turning north off the first main road west out of Victoria. The **no.91 bus** stops at Żebbuġ on its circuit of the northwest coast of the island.

and shops, is the forum for the evening and Sunday *passeggiata*. Out of season, the hotels remain open and the esplanade has the eerie calm of an English seaside town in winter. Sometimes the strong north wind causes the waves to crash over the sea wall, leaving snakes of seaweed on the slippery road, and the sea spray welds the shops' shutters with rust.

Marsalforn is a base, somewhere to return to in the evening, not somewhere to linger. The small beach underneath the seafront is not very attractive, cramped and more often than not untidy; there is much better swimming elsewhere. The **Calypso Diving Centre**, next door to the Calypso Hotel, is licensed for beginners and experienced divers. There is free **diving** along the coast and off the saltpans at **Qbajjar** and **Xwieni**. The nearest organized dive site is 2 miles (3km) away off **Reqqa Point**, the most northerly point on the islands. It is not a dive for the inexperienced, but the clear waters and caves are good for fish-spotters.

In the tiny harbour, Il Menqa, again in front of the Calypso Hotel, there is normally a fisherman who is willing to take visitors out on fishing trips. **Xlendi Pleasure Cruises** operate from here on a circuit via San Blas Bay and the Blue Lagoon in Comino. It alternates its departure point for trips around Gozo and Comino between here and Xlendi. Once a week it goes to Popeye Village in Anchor Bay, Malta (*see* p.183) – a total waste of time.

**Xlendi**
**Pleasure Cruises**
*t 21 559967,*
*www.xlendicruises.com*

## Żebbuġ

**Żebbuġ**, meaning 'olives', is one of the highest of the villages straddling the spine of a ridge. It is Gozo's windy city, where it is said the people live longest. Żebbuġ has wide-running views but

### The Clockmaker's Saltpans

Legend tells of a clockmaker from Żebbuġ whose greed propelled him to think of new and devious methods of fulfilling his lust for money. Blinded by avarice, he cut new saltpans on the clifftop far above the sea. Then, in order to harness the thundering winter waves and so fill his pans with sea water, he dug a steep shaft down to the water's edge. When the winter came the sea water shot up through his man-made funnel and filled his saltpans. But the mercenary clockmaker had cut them into soft, porous globigerina limestone, not the hard coralline limestone, and the sea water disappeared long before the valuable crystals could form. Worse – the salt-water spray continued to erupt through the funnel and destroyed his neighbour's crops until the clockmaker was sued into bankruptcy.

there is not much to see in the village itself, apart from the rich marble interior of the early 18th-century **parish church of the Assumption**. The local inhabitants were fortunate enough to have had a rich seam of marble, now exhausted, which covers the walls of their church and was used in parts of St John's Co-Cathedral.

This part of the exposed northern coastline is pockmarked with **saltpans** (squares carved in the hard coralline rock) which yield coarse sea salt. Salt is still harvested today and has long been a source of both income and legend. The lip of soft limestone rock stretching from unattractive Xwieni to the Għasri valley provides somewhere to sunbathe and clamber into the sea.

## Festas North of Victoria

**Victory Day**, 8 September, is a national holiday so the **Xagħra** *festa*, the **Nativity of Our Lady**, is held on the Sunday closest to the 8th. Xagħra has a friendly rivalry with Nadur, and both their festive pyrotechnics can be elaborately daft.

**St Paul** is **Marsalforn**'s patron saint and he is said to have preached here; as yet Marsalforn is not a parish and does not have a *festa*.

**Żebbuġ** is one of Gozo's six original parishes and its *festa* of the Assumption is celebrated on the first Sunday after 15 August.

## Where to Stay and Eat North of Victoria

### Xagħra

****Cornucopia**, 10 Gnien Imrik Street, t 21 556486 (€€€). Originally a farmhouse, the Cornucopia, on the edge of the valley looking down to Marsalforn, has 44 comfortable, air-conditioned rooms. The rooms are well equipped and quiet. Two adjoining farmhouses offer larger or more private accommodation as well as use of the hotel's facilities.

**Oleander**, 10 Victory Square, t 21 557230 (€€). In summer, Mario can become a victim of his own success at the gay-friendly Oleander. The service here is sometimes erratic but the menu changes regularly, with old favourites such as pasta with rabbit sauce, marinaded and roasted rabbit, pouched [*sic*] local fish, and chicken stuffed with all manner of things

sitting alongside more adventurous fare such as squid stuffed with breadcrumbs and olives, barb fish and tuna cooked in red wine. In summer, dine outside under the oleander trees and bougainvillea. *Open for lunch and dinner.*

**Gesther's**, 8 September Avenue (off Victory Square), t 21 556621 (€). Tiny Gesther's serves traditional Gozitan cooking by two sisters Gemma and Esther. Forget about the rudimentary tables and décor and try their *bragioli*. Good home-made pickles, spiced peels, etc. for sale.

### Marsalforn

*****Calypso Hotel**, Marsalforn Bay, t 21 562000, *www.hotelcalypsogozo. com* (€€€). Dominates the east side of the bay. Recently refurbished, with fresh, simple rooms, two restaurants and two bars.

***Marsalforn Guest House**, Rabat Road, t 21 556147, *on2wheels@gozo.com* (€). For more basic accommodation, this is the most central option, just behind the seafront on an island site. Most of the rooms have balconies and there is a small restaurant on the ground floor; it is clean and unpretentious. Nearby is a block of six two-bedroom apartments that come under the same management.

The choice of where to eat is split between places supplying pasta or pizza to 'fuel' another day's diving, and more ambitious eateries. 'Downtown' Marsalforn is full of the former.

**Il Kartell**, t 21 556918 (€€€). A good place for local fish. There is a first-floor bar. *Closed second half of Jan.*

**Ta'frenc**, about a mile (1.5km) out of Marsalforn on the Victoria road, t 21 553888 (€€€). One of Gozo's upscale restaurants and a favourite with locals and visitors. It offers a range of great Mediterranean food, with a well-chosen selection of wines.

The farmhouse setting is charming. *Closed Tues; Jan–Mar open Fri–Sat lunchtime only.*

**The Ritz Café**, Valley Street, t 21 558392 (€). A popular stopping place with tourists and local cognoscenti for late-night/early-morning breakfasts.

# West of Victoria

## San Lawrenz

You are likely to pass through the little village of **San Lawrenz** en route to the wholesome scenery and cliff walks around Dwejra and the Inland Sea, areas which offer some of the best diving in the central Mediterranean. San Lawrenz, where Nicholas Monserrat, the late author of Second World War classic *The Cruel Sea*, once lived, is the westernmost settlement of Gozo, and the only village to take its name from its patron saint (whose emblem is a palm frond on a gridiron; poor St Lawrence was roasted to death in AD 258).

### The Inland Sea

The **Inland Sea** is a geological fault, similar to but much more spectacular than Il-Maqluba (*see* p.208). It was created when the roof of what must have been an immense cave collapsed some 80–100 yards, leaving a landlocked basin of sea water opening into the Mediterranean via a massive gothicky arch. This is a quiet and not too touristified spot with little to do other than let the day evaporate: soak up the sun, swim in the clear water and watch the fishermen toying with their *luzzus*. You could haggle for the short trip out through the arch and the Azure Window, or simply sit in the shade of the one café and read; on windy days the swallow-hole formation turns into an effective windbreak.

Most days, tourists on whistle-stop day trips from Malta are disgorged from their coaches in the late morning, shatter the peace and spend 10 minutes photographing everything in sight before a guide hauls them off.

## Fungus Rock and Dwejra Bay

**Fungus Rock** is the affectionate nickname for Il-Ġebla tal-Ġeneral, 'the General's Rock'. This monolith, which is 200ft (60m) high, guards the entrance to an almost circular black lagoon with a spooky seaweed-covered bed. Apparently a general of the knights' galleys discovered a rare tuber plant (*Fucus coccineus melitensis*), which grew on the rock's flat top. The knights believed the

## Getting to and around West of Victoria

If you go **walking** around **San Lawrenz**, the landscape demands stout shoes and care should be taken near the cliff edge.

By **car**, the west road to **Għarb**, 2½ miles (4km) from Victoria, goes past the remains of the 19th-century Victoria aqueduct and is clearly flagged. The **no.91 coastal bus** service stops at Għarb from Victoria.

For **Għasri**, by **car** from Victoria all routes are clearly signposted; just turn right by the large tree and derelict watchtower on the Victoria road. Again, if you are travelling by public transport, you want the **no.91 bus**. If you are staying in one of the many farmhouses, try to unravel a ball of string in your imagination as you go, or you will never find your way home – asking is invariably of no use, because the villagers don't know the house by its smart brochure name.

---

repulsive-smelling plant had medicinal properties when brewed into an even more foul-smelling concoction; it was used as a styptic dressing for wounds and a cure for dysentery. Grand Master Pinto decreed the rock out of bounds in 1746 – trespassers were punished with a three-year spell in the galleys – posted a permanent guard and built a precarious cable-car basket to the mainland 50 yards away. Later it was discovered that all Pinto's efforts were for naught; *Fucus coccineus melitensis* has no medicinal properties whatsoever. The climb to the top is only for aspiring mountaineers.

If dark waters don't put you off, Dwejra Bay is a placid place to swim. There are two small grottoes, and plenty of fish for divers to spot off Fungus Rock. In calm weather the bay (17–23ft/5–7m deep) is an idyllic spot to anchor for the night. You will be awoken in the early morning by goats on the clifftop, as their shepherd leads them away from the weather-devoured **Dwejra Tower** to another meagre patch.

### Diving and Snorkelling

It is often said that the diving between Dwejra Point (by the Inland Sea) and Wardija Point (the southwestern tip of Gozo) is the finest in the Mediterranean, with the **Blue Hole** dive off Fungus Rock one of the best. All dives here are for experienced and team divers only; Fungus Rock is 150ft (45m) plus.

Among other dives are: a 115ft (35m) tunnel dive from the Inland Sea out into the open sea where the floor falls away dramatically, a dive under the Azure Window, a blue hole dive, and a long drift-type dive off Crocodile Rock, named after the shape of its back jutting out above the surface. There are caves, groupers and all manner of marine fauna in the clear waters.

The clear but dark sea and deserted, ragged coastline make this ideal territory for keen snorkellers. Care should be taken on anything other than calm days: getting into the water with a swell is easy, getting out can be treacherous. The points of ingress over the battered coralline are laceratingly sharp under foot.

# Għarb

**Għarb**, meaning 'west', is the oldest and main western village, with its own unintelligible dialect. Tourists are as ubiquitous as legends in the west, and Għarb is where they both meet. So much building and refurbishment is going on that it is beginning to resemble the suburbs of the late 1980s. Fortunately, the village itself has remained tranquil and unspoiled; essentially this is still hard farming country. On their way to the unforgiving fields, you still see elderly farmers creaking their laden and ancient single-geared bicycles through the square.

Għarb has the tastiest and most aromatic tomatoes in Gozo, an exquisite parish church, fine old carved stone balconies and two good restaurants.

The foundation stone of the **parish church of the Immaculate Conception** was laid in 1699, 20 years after Għarb had become a parish and had outgrown its older church of St Mary's, known as Taz-Żejt (600 yards from the village square towards Birbuba). One of the many narcissistic elements Baroque needs in order to thrive is space for admiration, and here three old boundary tracks have neatly formed a wide sweeping square, leaving the church isolated on an island site at one end. In a fit of immodesty the villagers instructed their architect Giuseppe Azzopardo to model the design on the Sant'Agnese in Piazza Navona, Rome. Azzopardo's more parochial work does have the obvious Roman Baroque swathes of the day, but otherwise can hardly be said to resemble Sant'Agnese. The concave façade is split by a razor of a balustrade and the two dominant bell towers are set back from it. The upper façade neatly hides the drumless dome, collecting the whole into a uniform and manageable size; notice how the church works with the village houses and not against them by following the contours of the square. The three statues of *Faith* (middle), *Hope* and *Charity* (on either side) complete the fine building. Inside, the plan is circular and the main altarpiece, the *Visitation of Our Lady to her Cousin*

## A Tale of Greed

Still in use today and shaded at the bottom of its own pastoral little valley is the 16th-century **church of St Mary** known as Taz-Żejt, 'of the oil'. The legend and its simple moral tells of an old spinster, conveniently named Marija, whose only solace in her abject poverty was two daily visits to the church. Her sorrow deepened each winter because she was unable to earn enough money to replenish oil in the lamp in front of the church's Madonna to whom she prayed. One night, the Madonna appeared to her and mysteriously told her to take a jar to the 4am Mass. When Marija arrived at the church she glimpsed, coming from underneath it, a spring of oil glistening in the dawn light – the answer to her prayers. Once the miracle became known, however, people came from all over Malta and Gozo to bottle and profit from the oil which was intended to illuminate the Madonna's statue. The priest's protestations and warnings went unheeded, and one day Marija's river of oil dried up as quickly and miraculously as it had flowed.

*St Elizabeth*, was a gift from Grand Master de Vilhena in the early 18th century. An inscription on the right-hand clock face reads 'heed precious time'.

## The Folklore Museum

**Folklore Museum**
*open 9–5; adm*

In Church Square, this latest addition to the cultural life of Għarb is Gozo's best museum by far. Built in what used to be Carmela Grima's house (*see* p.286), its 28 rooms feature a wealth of original Maltese and Gozitan exhibits and effectively evoke Maltese folk life in centuries past. Most of its rooms are dedicated to one particular craft: there is a blacksmith's room, a wine room with wine presses, a fisherman's room with lobster pots, a cheese room, a weaving room, a candlemaker's room, a shoemaker's room and a bread-making room with various implements of bread-making paraphernalia including carts, fuel, farmers' tools and, of course, bread.

There are also some other interesting exhibits such as a jam-making mill, an old children's hearse which would have been pulled by four white horses and, taking pride of place, an 18th-century printing press.

## The Loneliest Chapel on Gozo

Right in the middle of a field is the loneliest chapel on Gozo, **San Dimitri** (it is 1 mile/1.5km to the west of Għarb and signposted). The beauty of the little square building, like the Magdalena chapel on Dingli Cliffs, lies in its windswept isolation. The front door is always open. Behind the security bars is the altarpiece of San Dimitri on his white steed, keeper of probably the best and certainly the dottiest of Gozitan legends (*see* 'San Dimitri's Miracles', below).

### San Dimitri's Miracles

Back in the time of savage corsair raids there was a pious woman called Zgugina, who had a son and prayed every day to San Dimitri. One day a pirate ship hove into view, and finding nothing worth plundering in the village the corsairs seized as many able young lads as they could find, including Zgugina's son. Zgugina immediately crept back to the chapel, where she prayed to San Dimitri. As she did so, the altarpiece came to life and San Dimitri rode out of the chapel towards the sea, galloped across the water and returned with her son. Zgugina vowed to keep an oil lamp alight in front of the altarpiece for the rest of her life.

Nearly 200 years later the original chapel fell victim to an earthquake and sank to the bottom of the sea. Years passed, until one day a ship anchored in the vicinity of the cliffs. The ship's anchor became snagged and divers were sent down to free it. All of them disappeared beneath the waves, however, and were assumed to have been drowned. Then, miraculously, they surfaced unharmed and told of a beautiful chapel lying intact on the seabed and how they had walked into it, breathed in fresh air and seen an altarpiece to San Dimitri illuminated by an oil lamp.

Fishermen say that on especially calm days you can still see the glow from the seabed, and farmers believe that two indentations in the hard rock near the present chapel were those made by the hooves of San Dimitri's horse as he galloped back from the slavers' boat with Zgugina's son.

# Għasri, Għammar and Ta'Pinu

**Għasri** is Gozo's smallest village, with a total population of 350 people, and **Għammar** is no more than a hamlet in between Għasri and Għarb. One of the best-kept secrets of the island is to be found at the bottom of the Għasri valley, a minuscule gem of a beach. The national shrine of Ta'Pinu underneath evergreen Għammar hill, and the views from the top of the Gordan Lighthouse, are other reasons for prowling around this agricultural area.

As in Għarb, many of the farmhouses on either side of the Għasri valley have become holiday homes. The farmers continue to be bewildered as to why northern Europeans should wish to come to this picturesque but comparatively barren spot and pay exorbitant prices for rubbly old animal sheds. Being Gozitan, they don't question it, they just bank it.

## Ta'Pinu

*Ta'Pinu closes 12.30–1pm every day and during the numerous packed Masses; visitors must wear long trousers or knee-length skirts; guides and multilingual information machines are available; take bus no.61 or 91.*

The huge basilica of **Ta'Pinu** with its solitary campanile, 154ft (47m) high, is the national shrine and a church of pilgrimage, not a parish church. Built in a neo-Romanesque style, at an architecturally uninspiring time between the two World Wars, the taut exterior stands in austere isolation amid the surrounding cultivated fields. By direct contrast the interior is plain, reverential and moving. A place of worship has existed on the site since the early 16th century. In 1575 the original structure was condemned, but the demolition never took place; according to folklore, the first hammer strike broke the wrecker's arm. The original church remained, and lurched between repair and disrepair until the late 17th century when the family of Filippino Gauci – abbreviated to Pinu – repaired it for the last time. Today the old structure is incorporated into a small chapel behind the apse.

On 22 June 1883 a peasant woman from Għarb, Carmela Grima, heard a voice calling to her from the isolated chapel. It requested that she say three Hail Marys, 'In memory of the three days My Body rested in the sepulchre'. She told only one man, Francesco Portelli, who said that he too had heard a voice on six occasions. Three years later both attested to their experiences at the insistence of Bishop Pace. Since then, miracles and narrow escapes have been attributed to the grace and intercession of **Our Lady of Pinu**. There are numerous votive offerings in the church. In the groves of Għammar hill overlooking Ta'Pinu is a **Way of the Cross**, with 12 life-size marble statues.

From dozy one-horse Għasri village square, turn right down a shocking road for the mini-beach at the bottom of the **Għasri Valley**. The track peters out and you can park on the coralline outcrops at the top of a precipitous fjord. At the end of this 400-yard long, needle-thin fjord between the cliff faces is the tiny, often deserted, fine-pebble beach. Some rudimentary steps have been cut for the steep climb down to sea level. Bring an air bed if you are too lazy to swim to the mouth, and a picnic. Sometimes the whole day passes without interlopers. Swimming and access are suitable for children.

Over the other side of the valley and past Ta'Pinu is **Gordan Lighthouse**, 475ft (145m) above sea level; on clear nights the powerful beam can be seen from more than 25 miles (40km) away. The final third of the road is too steep to drive up, but the hike is worth it for the panoramic views.

## *Festas* West of Victoria

The *festa* of **San Lawrenz** is held on the second Sunday in August. The **Visitation of Our Lady to St Elizabeth** on the first Sunday in July is **Għarb's** *festa*. A celebratory Mass is said at **San Dimitri** on the Sunday after 9 October. **Għasri's** *festa* is Christ the Eucharist, held on the first Sunday in June.

## Shopping West of Victoria

En route to **Għarb** is the **Ta'Dbiegi Crafts Village** (*open summer 8.30–6.45, winter 8–4.45*); it has traditional Maltese crafts, including knitware, silver filigree, pottery and replicas of medieval armour.

**Gozo Glass** is before the craft village next to Jeffrey's Restaurant and the souvenirs are more original, but the local garishly coloured glass is not to everyone's taste.

## Where to Stay and Eat West of Victoria

### San Lawrenz

*****Kempinski** San Lawrenz Resort and Spa, Triq ir-Rokon, **t** 22 110000 (€€€€). Gozo's latest five-star offering may be a little gaudy and marbled for some tastes, but it has beautiful gardens, children's programmes and a spa.

**L'Ortolan, t** 21 558640 (€€€). The main restaurant of the San Lawrenz Resort (*see* above). In summer, there is a lovely terrace overlooking the pool area. The food is as you would expect from a hotel restaurant, albeit in a five-star establishment, hence it is priced accordingly. *Open for breakfast and dinner daily.*

**Tatita's,** San Lawrenz Square, **t** 21 566482 (€€€). Mediterranean fare, notably fish. *Closed Nov–Feb.*

### Għarb

**Jeffrey's,** 10 Għarb Street, **t** 21 561006 (€€€). At the turning into Għarb is a simple rustic restaurant, serving good food, including courgettes, rabbit, fresh fish and Mexican specialites, in a small converted farmhouse. The menu changes daily. Nothing has changed very much here since Joe, the owner, won the National Lottery in 1992 – a good omen. The service is friendly and there is an open courtyard at the rear. *Dinner only, Mon–Sat, closed Nov–Mar.*

**Salvina,** 21 Rock Street, **t** 21 552505 (€€€). Two hundred yards to the right of the parish church in Għarb (third street) in a little townhouse with a fine balcony. It is bigger and swankier than Jeffrey's, with a busy bar, but there is still a family mood. Flies make the terrace a no-go area for lunch in summer, but it is ideal for dinner when the insects have gone to bed. Stay with the local dishes, such as fish or *bragioli*.

# South of Victoria

## Kerċem and Santa Lucija

Approximately 1,500 people live in the villages of **Kerċem** and **Santa Lucija**, which are located 1¼ miles (2km) and 1½ miles (2.5km) southwest of Victoria respectively. On the outskirts of the tranquil village of Kerċem an Italian company drills to a depth of 3 miles (5km) for oil. The eyesore rig stretches 200ft (60m) high into the air and, without any trace of irony, is called Il-Madonna taż Żejt (Our Lady of the Oil).

### Two Walks

The **Lunzjata Valley** peels away on the left as you come into Kerċem. There is a pleasant 15-minute walk through this, the most fertile part of the island. The valley was a game preserve of the knights who built several, now decayed, watchtowers for hunting (grand masters erroneously believed sport exorcized the impure thoughts of young knights). The walk begins at an old arched entrance and guardhouse and opens into a verdant oasis of plants and fruit trees. Part of the small **chapel of the Annunciation** (half in a cave and still in use) dates back to 1347; most of the present structure dates from the early 17th century. As you walk the dusty track, the rustle of bamboo on the valley floor amplifies the sound of running water, the rarest of sounds on the Maltese islands. Fat and vivid dragonflies buzz around pools of water in the sadly forgotten remains of a public spring over which Grand Master Perellos built an arch in 1698. On the way back up the path past the chapel, tempting plump figs dangle from a tree overhanging the dry-stone wall.

For a much longer walk, with a destination in mind, drive west out of Kerċem past the daftly positioned parish church, to a small car park where the path begins. The cliff walk towards an old tower near **Wardija Point**, not quite the westernmost point of Gozo, is one of solitude above what is a higher continuation of the Ta'Ċenċ cliffs. The desolate peace of the countryside is sometimes shattered by the *kaċċatur*, or hunters, shooting blindly at migrant birds, in and out of the so-called season. Nevertheless, it is an enjoyable walk.

## Sannat and Munxar

**Sannat** is Gozo's most southerly village, close to the Ta'Ċenċ cliffs. **Munxar**, a small village, perches between Sannat and Xlendi on the eastern slope of the valley.

## Getting to and around South of Victoria

By **car** the road for **Sannat** leaves Victoria through St Francis Square and is well signposted. For the Hotel Ta'Ċenċ, head southeast round the village square, where the hotel's own signposts take over. For **Munxar**, the easiest route is to take the Xlendi road and turn left onto a terrible road 500 yards after Fontana. By **bus**, both towns are served by the **no.50** from Victoria.

**Xlendi** is just over 2 miles (3km) south of Victoria. The road is straight, downhill all the way, and there is a large car park at the bottom. En route, in **Fontana**, there is an old arched public wash house built by the knights; opposite this there is a comprehensive souvenir store. By **bus**, Xlendi can be reached on the **no.87** from Victoria.

The village of **Xewkija** sprawls along and off the main Victoria–Mġarr road, and is well signposted. **Buses nos.42 and 43** from Victoria stop here.

Sannat's various attractions include the 475ft (145m) high **layercake cliffs**, with their quite breathtaking scenery and views, a fairly energetic and long track walk down to the sea at **Mġarr ix-Xini**, the famous **Hotel Ta'Ċenċ**, and somewhere for visitors to buy examples of hand-made traditional Gozitan lace.

Sannat was the traditional centre of the island's lace-making cottage industry, and on occasions, if you are lucky, you can still chance upon women sitting on their stumpy chairs in the shade of the 18th-century parish church of St Margaret, their fingers working the bobbins with both fury and precision (*see* box below).

**Ta'Ċenċ Cliffs** and **San Dimitri Point** were once the breeding grounds of the Mediterranean peregrine falcon, the **Maltese falcon** (*see* p.290). The species, despite a 1980 declaration of protection, is now – as far as the Maltese islands are concerned – extinct. The last-known pair 'disappeared' from these cliffs in the mid-1980s. Apart from shooting or trapping the birds, the *kaċċatur* would let

**13**

**Gozo and Comino | South of Victoria: Sannat and Munxar**

### Lace

*8 x 12 pairs long and 8 x 12 pairs short mits, besides a scarf.*
An order from Queen Victoria, 1838

Sannat lace is a creamy off-white colour and very hardwearing. Nearly all the patterns are traditional and are laid over the *trajbu* or lace pillow. Pins are placed in the pillow and the bobbins are thrown over them to produce the weave.

Black lace, the type worn by Queen Victoria, is not found any more: working with black thread strains the eyes. In the tiny square behind Sannat church and next to Main Street is the **Old Lace House** where many of the skilled women worked. It is now a private house but there is a plaque commemorating the visit of Princess Elizabeth and the Duke of Edinburgh on 2 April 1951.

When you buy, try to resist the temptation to haggle. A tablecloth for Lm400 represents over 12 months' work and a set of napkins can cost as little as Lm6. Both women listed below have various items for sale and distinctive styles. Mornings or early evenings are good times to visit.

**Rosina** sometimes weaves and sells lace in Xlendi and her house, which is not named or numbered, is opposite the main entrance to the school on the way into Sannat. Persevere; her work has a fine edge. She is an ebullient woman, the eldest of 17 children, and learned to weave at the age of four.

If **Marianne Cordina**, 140 Ta'Ċenċ Street, Sannat (50 yards past the church on the left) is not working in her garage workshop, knock on the front door. Marianne has a large selection of lace and locally made knitted goods.

themselves down the cliff face by rope, some 475ft (145m), in order to steal the young or the eggs.

This sad story now means there are tranquil walks along the cliffs. Two tracks out of Sannat lead down to the **beach at Mġarr ix-Xini**; take the first turning left out of the square for the more direct route or follow the track past the hotel. Along the way there are a few **cart ruts**, two **dolmens** and the meagre plan of the old temple-period site of **Borġ il-Mramma**. If you leave the track, the lip of the vertigo-inducing limestone cliffs should be treated with great respect.

## Xlendi

The old fishing village of **Xlendi** used to have a peace, a magic, and was Gozo's most beguiling spot. Now, it is just another stop for the tourist bus, and has been well and truly trampled. From the head of the bay the entire left side as far as the knights' tower is a seamless colonization of characterless apartments. The right-hand side is safe only until an engineering wizard figures out a way to build on its craggy face. Yet there is a good diving school, an over-supply of reasonable self-catering accommodation and an excellent nightclub.

If you are yachting here, you should take note that the bay offers up on first impression deceptively safe shelter from all but westerlies. Tremendous care should be exercised as a **shallow reef** – 5ft (1.5m) below the surface – straddles the mouth. Many ships have come to grief here; the relics of two, one from the 2nd century BC and another from the 5th century AD, are on display in the Gozo Archaeological Museum.

Under the meagre shelter of the tamarisk trees at the head of the bay is a small but always crowded **beach**; the rocks going out to the tower (1658) are also staked out with tourists who leap in and out of the water like penguins. In front of the statue to **St Andrew**, the patron saint of fishermen, is a flight of steps cut into the limestone which lead up over a large rock to a small and secluded natural cove. The steps were cut to allow private bathing for the local nuns, who seldom use it today.

**St Andrew's Diver's Cove** offers beginners' courses, and a full range of dives around the island, including night dives. They hire

**St Andrew's Diver's Cove**
*St Simon Street,*
*t 21 551301*

---

**The Maltese Falcon**

In 1980 the Maltese falcon was declared a protected species, yet here it has been hunted, trapped and shot into extinction. There is an irony to this tragedy. The Act of Donation dated 24 March 1530 (preserved and displayed in the Bibliotheca Valletta) by which the Spanish Emperor Charles V ceded Malta to the Order, states the none-too-onerous annual rent for the islands – a single live falcon was to be presented on All Saints' Day to the viceroy in Sicily.

**Xlendi Pleasure
Cruises**
*t 21 555667*

out equipment, and apartments. Four days a week the **Xlendi
Pleasure Cruises** boat leaves from Xlendi (from Marsalforn on
the remaining alternate days; *see* p.280) for trips round Gozo
and Comino.

# Xewkija

**Xewkija** is famous for its contemporary **parish church to St John
the Baptist**, known simply as 'the **Rotunda**'. Not only does it
dominate the village, it dominates the entire island. The village,
with its population of fewer than 3,000, has an eccentrically
suburban air for an agricultural community. Men on ancient lilac-
coloured Vespas roar noisily through the streets wearing
soup-bowl helmets and shotguns slung across their backs; young
boys goad a donkey and cart full of pungent manure through the
main square; a handful of people too old to work the fields sit
beside their bamboo-slatted front doors awaiting the cool of the
day, while tourists gawp at their church.

## The Rotunda Church

✪ **The Rotunda**

To understand the rationale behind building a cathedral-sized
parish church that just happens to be marginally higher than
Mosta's (though volumetrically smaller) is to begin to understand
the intensity of Maltese-Gozitan rivalry.

The Rotunda does look a little eccentric stuck in the middle of the
Gozitan countryside surrounded by diminutive cuboid village
houses, but it is mightily impressive. It has the second highest
dome, internally, in Europe (after St Peter's in Rome), is 20ft (6m)
taller than St Paul's in London and can accommodate nearly three
times the village's population. The villagers wanted such a church
and it was constructed and paid for entirely by local volunteer
labour and donations.

Construction began in 1951 around the structure of the existing
17th-century Baroque church. The design, neither quixotic nor
plagiaristic, is by Giuseppe Damato in homage to Santa Maria della
Salute in Venice. The fanatical dedication and skill of the
stonemasons is remarkable but the single-most impressive feature
is the dome, a 45,000-ton structure set on eight columns. Seen
from within, the 16 clear-glass windows of the dome and 16
smaller windows in the lantern illuminate the milky limestone,
invoking more space than actually exists. If you stand at a distance,
in the fields opposite Għajnsielem at sunset, the dome presents a
striking silhouette as the orange light powers through it. The
interior is restrained and simple in its execution. Above the six side
altars are six paintings depicting the *Life of St John the Baptist*,
which culminate in another rendition of his martyrdom (for

rebuking an adulterous King Herod, and at the behest of Salome). The image of the price he paid for speaking his mind is violent, without the temperance of Caravaggio's in St John's Co-Cathedral. Part of the rich interior of the old church has been dismantled like Lego, and rebuilt stone by stone in what is called the **Museum of Sculpture** to the left of the Carrara marble main altar.

## Mġarr ix-Xini

From Xewkija it is 2 miles (3km) to the pebbly **beach** at **Mġarr ix-Xini** (meaning 'the galley's landing place'). Fork left about half a mile (1km) out of Xewkija – the road is not for the drunk or faint-hearted. The swimming in the small fjord at the bottom of the steep single track is clean and suitable for children. Gozo's south coast has the same topography as Dingli cliffs: the waters are dark, deep and clear against the sheer cliff face, offering good diving and snorkelling. Fishing lazily off **Fessej Rock** is a peaceful if not always fruitful way of passing the time and around the tiny headland to the west is the private lido and bar of Hotel Ta'Ċenċ.

Mġarr ix-Xini tower was built in 1658, more than a hundred years too late, for this was a favourite landing place for the Barbary slavers and the spot from which most of the population was carried away in Dragut's catastrophic raid of 1551 (*see* p.49).

### *Festas* South of Victoria

The two *festas* at **Kerċem** are **St Gregory the Great**, held on the second Sunday in March and, on the second Sunday in July, **Our Lady of Perpetual Succour**.

In **Sannat** the *festa* of **St Margaret** is held on the fourth Sunday in July.

**Munxar's** *festa* to **St Paul** takes place on the last Sunday in May.

On the fourth Sunday in June, **Xewkija** celebrates its *festa* to **St John the Baptist**, patron saint of the knights of Malta.

### Shopping South of Victoria

On the outskirts of Kerċem, opposite the old knights' wash house, is a souvenir emporium stashed full of a range of products from the local knitting and lace-making cottage industry.

### Where to Stay and Eat South of Victoria

#### Sannat and Munxar

*****Hotel Ta'Ċenċ**, Sannat, **t** 21 556810 (€€€€). Now sadly lacks the Italian touches that made it so famous, and food and service are not what they were. Facilities include two large pools, tennis and volleyball courts, and a restaurant which sprawls under the sinewy branches of a magnificent 150-year-old carob tree. At dusk, the long walk back from its private lido as the sun flops into the sea over the cliff's edge is a singular attraction.

****Andar Hotel**, Munxar, **t** 21 560736 (€€€). Munxar has its own very pleasant 40-room hotel set in the countryside. It is a family-run establishment with a decent pool, generous public rooms, bar and restaurant and games room. The rooms are air-conditioned and each has satellite TV. Only the noise of the church bells will detract from its appeal if all you want is to escape and recharge. The hotel is not clearly flagged and is best approached from the Xlendi road.

**Noel's**, on the beach in Mġarr ix-Xini (€). Wonderful beachside shack restaurant, this is pleasantly basic, with half a dozen metal tables. Simple grilled fish, prawns and steak and chips. *Open summer only.*

### Xlendi

Nearly all the cafés and restaurants have 'apartments to rent' signs for flats in improbable-sounding blocks such as the 'Xlendi Hilton'; take your pick.

**\*\*\*\*St Patrick's Hotel**, 12 Xlendi Seafront, t 21 562951, *stpatricks@vjborg.com* (€€€). Opened in 1993 with 63 rooms, 20 facing the sea (the topmost ones have fabulous views), and a mini rooftop swimming pool; in reality an industrial-sized bath.

**\*\*\*Hotel San Andrea**, t 21 565555, *hotelsanandrea.com* (€€). Modern 28-room hotel. It offers comfortable, pleasantly decorated rooms set up with satellite TV and Internet connection facilities.

**\*\*Hotel Serena Beach Club**, Punici Street, t 21 553719, *www.serena.com.mt* (€€). Family-run by friendly owners, the Serena has a 26 serviced apartments overlooking the bay, a large restaurant and terrace on the roof, a private pool and a mini-market. The top two floors have the best outlook.

**San Antonio Guest House**, t 21 563555, *www.clubgozo.mt* (€€). Plain and pine-furnished, but clean and a few minutes from the beach. Lovely terrace with pool.

**Paradise Bar and Restaurant**, Mt Carmel Street, t 21 556878 (€€€). Specializes in grilled king prawns. *Closed Mon.*

**Il-Terrazzo**, St Simon Street, t 21 562992 (€€€). Popular restaurant, overlooking Xlendi Bay, serving local fish and a variety of pasta dishes. *Lunch and dinner Thurs–Tues.*

**It-Tmun**, 3 Mt Carmel Street, t 21 551571 (€€€). The family-run It-Tmun is the best restaurant in Xlendi. Set way back from the seafront, it prepares and serves local fish, meat and pasta dishes well. *Closed Tues and mid-Nov–mid-Dec.*

**Stone Crab Pizzeria**, St Andrew Street, t 21 556400 (€€), is at the water's edge yet far enough away from the bustle of the seafront. Try the Stone Crab pizza – it has got more ingredients than a Chinese feast. The owner has just opened a bar in the knights' tower at the mouth of the bay.

**Moby Dick**, Xlendi Seafront, t 21 556151 (€). Downstairs is an all-day snack bar and pizzeria and on the fifth-floor terrace by the harbour there is a more formal barbecue restaurant (*evenings only*). They have apartments.

## Nightlife
## South of Victoria

Just outside Xlendi, the nightclub **La Grotta**, on Xlendi Road, has a superb position above the bamboo floor of Xlendi Valley. Half in a grotto and half alfresco, it has everything a good summer resort nightclub needs: loud music, quiet nooks, and three bars. It is at its best on a Friday (Saturday is sardine night) and keeps its own hours – but a full head of steam is not reached until 2am. Parking can be a nightmare.

# East of Victoria

## Mġarr and Għajnsielem

**Mġarr** means simply 'a place to where goods are taken or a landing place' but today PT Barnum could be Mġarr Harbour's ringmaster. Under the big top of summer the shenanigans that

# Getting to and around East of Victoria

## Mġarr and Għajnsielem

The **Gozo Channel Co.**, *www.gozochannel.com*, enjoys a highly profitable monopoly **ferrying** people and cars betwen Malta and Gozo. In daylight hours in the summer, ferries shuttle between **Mġarr** and **Ċirkewwa** once an hour. During the winter, ferries depart every 90 minutes, and at times of huge demand, such as the *festa* of Santa Marija in August, the timetable is abandoned and a shuttle service operates. Arrive at least 30 minutes before the advertised departure time. Unlike most things in Gozo the services are punctual. If you are driving, there is a ticket booth as you drive into the queue for the ferry. Tickets are only purchased from Ċirkewwa (not Mġarr). A monstrous new ferry terminal is being built.

The **road** between **Mġarr** and **Victoria** is Gozo's main road, and the port is well signposted. At most times of the day **bus no.25** greets the arriving ferries and goes only to Victoria.

**Taxis** park on the quayside, but can be hard to find otherwise, so unless you are being met, phone in advance; the only alternative is to walk 500 yards up to the main road and catch a bus into Victoria.

The **heliport** is stuck in a field outside Għajnsielem a mile (2km) or so west of Mġarr, down a lane by the St Cecilia Tower and opposite the Gozo Heritage.

## Qala

By **car** the easiest way to get to Qala is to take the road north out of Mġarr or follow the signposts from Xewkija. To get there by **bus**, take either the **42 or 43** from Victoria.

## Nadur

The **road** out of Victoria to Xagħra winds its way up past the Kenuna Tower to the village of Nadur, a journey of 3¾ miles (6km). As an alternative, from Mġarr the village is only 1½ miles (2.5km) up the hill. Again, take either the **42 or 43 bus** for Victoria.

---

take place here in Gozo's principal harbour, bottle-necked front door, tradesmen's entrance, yacht marina and emergency exit can be truly comical. Unfortunately, it is the sort of place that needs a second chance to make a good impression, for any sane person, tourist or local, will turn and flee from the dysfunctional world that greets them.

Ferries barge, hoot and churn the waters in lopsided tussles with incompetent yachtsmen and obstinate fishermen 365 days a year. Tourists lost in the one-way maze of queues are ignored by mean-looking policemen, while Gozitan men in their stained singlets (which never quite stretch over their bellies to meet their overtight shorts) gesticulate wildly and release a bonanza of obscenities that is only curbed when a priest ambles by.

Amid the apparent chaos, fishermen tinker with their *luzzus* and mend their nets. In the cool of the day, under the watchful eyes of the mock-Gothic church, Fort Chambray and those on the balcony of the Gleneagles Bar (hub of the Mġarr cosmos), Gozitans tenderly bathe the fetlocks of their chestnut trotting horses in the shallows of the harbour (*see* opposite). On the slopes above the harbour, the village remains aloof, ignoring the circus below.

### History

**Mġarr** is the closest shelter to Malta and a service linking the two islands dates back to the late 13th century. During the reign of the knights a communication of sorts was maintained despite the plundering attentions of pirates holed up in Comino. Until the advent of steam in the mid-19th century the islands relied upon the infrequent visits of sailing craft subject to the vagaries of the wind and strong currents of the channel. In June 1885 the first formal service was begun in a brand new iron steamer, *Gleneagles*, 135ft (41m) long, and with it came the beginning of the end of Gozo's isolationist ways. The jetty and breakwater was extended in the 1930s and again in 1970 to its present protective size.

**Fort Chambray**, high above the harbour on the blue-clay Tafal Cliffs, was originally planned as far back as the mid-17th century as a mini-Valletta. In the 18th century when the project resurfaced, the knights finally accepted Gozo's need for somewhere more secure than the citadel. But the Order was by now in moral and financial decline and the fort proved to be its last major defence project. The original plan was scaled down by the prolific builder, Grand Master de Vilhena, but he was still forced to seek private funding. Retired Admiral Jacques de Chambray, a wealthy and disgruntled sea dog fed up with the cancerous disintegration of the Order he had joined aged 13 as a page, offered to fund the new fortress town himself and so became the governor of Gozo. Work began in 1749 and was completed in 1761, but few Gozitans were willing to buy plots of land as the threat of the Barbary corsairs no longer existed. Since then, apart from a brief and spirited defence against the French on 10 June 1798, Fort Chambray has had a chequered and miserable life: first when it served as an unpopular British garrison post, then in a new role as a mental institution and, imminently, as a tourist village. All but the outer structure is closed to the public.

**Mġarr Harbour** is an interesting microcosm of local life. In 1992 the government lassoed the fishermen's *luzzus* and yachts and coralled them into order. Locally, unmitigated disaster was predicted, as no Gozitan, least of all a fisherman, was going to be told where to moor. Moreover, they predicted, the harbour's unique charm would be gone for ever. Fortunately, the harbingers of doom have been proved wrong. Gozitans and yachtsmen have taken to the new pontoon facilities and the harbour has lost none of its quirky charm. The spoiler, though, is the hideous new ferry terminal here – grossly outsized for such a small place.

**Gozo Heritage**
*t 21 561280; take bus no. 25; open Mon–Sat 9.45–4.30 and national holidays 9–1; adm*

The **Gozo Heritage**, Għajnsielem, is an excellent thematic walk – in five languages – through Gozitan history. The tour starts with Neolithic man and wanders colourfully through more than 5,000 years of local history, aided by cleverly designed audiovisual techniques and static sets on themes including the legend of Calypso, the Romans, Dragut Rais, the Second World War and a contemporary harbour scene – all well worth seeing.

# Qala

Not a lot goes on in **Qala**, but there are two places to swim nearby. It is Gozo's most eastern settlement, with 1,300 inhabitants. The winds, especially the northeastern *gregale*, whip across the headland of Qala Point and the exposed village. The knights built many windmills, a couple of which remain in use. Nowhere is further from the citadel than Qala, and as befits what must have been a desolate part of the island many legends are woven into the village's history.

Tucked away just inside the front door of the chapel is a basement shrine to Kerrew (*see* 'Kerrew the Hermit', below). His bones lie in a pile on the small altar which, like the grotto in Mellieħa, is visited by families with unwell children. The chapel is about a mile/1.5km east of Qala, and usually open during the day.

There are two entirely different places to swim on the southern coast below Qala. The easier and therefore less rewarding is **Hondoq ir-Rummien**, signposted (none too clearly) from Qala. A small sandy beach suitable for children, it faces the bays of Santa Marija and San Nicklaw on Comino. The sea runs up through the channel and is always clean, but it can become crowded at weekends with families of picnicking Gozitans.

The clear and sheltered waters off **Qala Point**, with its lone and now crumbling redoubt, are tantalizingly visible from Comino's northern headland – but it is quite difficult to reach. There is a rudimentary footpath in an old quarry area, which peters out into a scramble ending west of the rock **Ġebel tal-Ħalfa**, but it is infinitely easier journey by boat. (On foot, this is a destination for the whole day, not just for a quick dip.) The swimming and snorkelling in the inlets are superb, the sea bed shelving away in sand and rocks. In any weather other than a strong *gregale* or sirocco, Qala Point is a very pleasant and peaceful place to drop anchor for the night.

# Nadur

From **Nadur**, which literally means 'lookout point', the knights were able to keep vigil over the channel between Malta and Gozo

## Kerrew the Hermit

One of the oldest Gozitan legends involves the trials of a hermit, named Kerrew, and the partly 13th-century little chapel of the Immaculate Conception. Kerrew was an unassuming and religious man from Mosta who, like most hermits, lived in a cave. When a jealous prank was devised to induce him to break his holy ways, he fled from the doomed village. Arriving at the northern channel separating Gozo and Malta, he threw his moth-eaten old cloak onto the water and miraculously floated on top of it across to Hondoq ir-Rummien, Qala's sandy cove. Here, in a new cave on the road from Qala to Hondoq ir-Rummien, he continued his holy ways until eventually he died a venerated, peaceful death.

at all times. The village, with its imposing houses, is the largest and wealthiest of Gozo's settlements after Victoria, with 3,500 inhabitants including many immigrants. (Come the *festa*, probably the island's best, half of the rooftop flags are American, Australian or Canadian.)

The Nadurese themselves may have emigrated to seek their fortune, but invariably they return with at least a part of it. Those who remain farm the fertile fields and slopes which fall away to the northern beaches of Ramla, San Blas and Daħlet Qorrot, where once Grand Master Alof de Wignacourt came to hunt and now much of the island's fresh fruit grows.

In the five days preceding Ash Wednesday, Nadur has the wildest and most bizarre carnival celebrations of the Maltese islands.

## Visiting Nadur

It would be surprising if Nadur did not have a powerful and edifying church to complement its affluence. Folklore says the position of the original church was determined by a holy man's donkey laden with stones which would not budge from the site, and that the foundation stone was taken from those on the donkey's back. The present church, dedicated to Saints Peter and Paul and nicknamed **iż-Żewġ**, 'the twins', was begun in 1760 and designed by Giuseppe Bonnici. The wide, robust and symmetrical building took 20 years to complete. The façade, and the dome with stained-glass windows, were added in the mid-19th century (alterations are easy to detect from the contrasting colour of the ageing stones).

The interior is splendidly ornate with extravagant marble inlaid floors, walls and pillars. Around the beginning of the 20th century, the Maltese painter Lazzaro Pisani painted no fewer than 150 canvases to be attached to the vaulted ceiling; the images and the stories told are the liveliest of many such ecclesiastical works on the islands. In the right-hand aisle is a twinned processional statue of the saints, made in 1881 in Marseille for the then-huge sum of Lm50.

Also on the right, in the transept is the macabre skeleton of St Coronatus, which was brought here intact along with a cup of his blood soon after he was martyred in AD 100. His skeleton is now, thankfully, clothed save for the peepholes.

## Where to Swim

Side by side and to the north of Nadur lie three good bays: **Ramla**, **San Blas** and **Daħlet Qorrot**. The most accessible and best for children is Ramla with its wide red-sand beach, but the most rewarding swimming is off the rocks of San Blas.

**Ramla**, meaning 'sandy beach', is Gozo's largest beach and it is here that the nymph Calypso and Odysseus are supposed to have played out their one-sided seven-year affair (*see* p.279). The beach can be approached from both Nadur and Xagħra, although the Nadur road is the easier one. Both routes are steep – if you hoof it down the bamboo valley road, around 4pm a taxi normally appears to save you making the long trek back up. The coarse sand, the colour of burnt almonds, the water-sports concessions, three cafés and a stall selling everything from English newspapers to inflatable sharks have made it too touristy for many and at weekends it gets crowded. There is a strong undertow in rough weather, and you can scratch any notion of a picnic when the wind is from the north unless you like sand sandwiches. The very few campers who visit the Maltese islands pitch their tents on the bay's western ridge or beside the cafés.

**San Blas Bay** is named after St Blaise. Along with the miniature fjord at Wied Għasri it affords the best bathing in Gozo, but access is poor. The road down the valley is narrow and steep, with fewer than half a dozen places to park at the end. From there it is a scramble down to the rocks and gravelly sand. Arrive early with a picnic, and like a seal secure yourself a rock for the day; because of San Blas's position and unsuitability for children, it is unlikely you will be disturbed. (Note: there is a sewage outflow in San Blas. It is supposed to pipe sewage out to sea but in practice is often damaged, leaving San Blas too polluted to swim in safely. Check with the local MTA office at time of travel; *see also* 'A Few Words of Caution', p.87.)

**Daħlet Qorrot**, to the east of San Blas, is a popular spot with the Gozitans. It is a small, uncommercialized sandy beach devoid of honeypot concessions, and easier to get to than San Blas; an ideal place for a quick dip. There is plenty of parking space, and a cold-drinks vendor.

### Not with a Bang but a Whimper

An unknown Roman citizen built a large villa on the western edge of Ramla Bay (some of the finds are in the Gozo Archaeological Museum). In the 18th century the knights wished to make the beach as impregnable as possible; the remains of some of the interlinked defences are still clearly visible: a redoubt (a few courses of brickwork remain above the site of the Roman villa); and an undersea wall linked on the east headland with a *fougasse*, a fiendishly clever device which resembles a deep and primitive mortar hewn out of living rock which was packed with explosives, shrapnel, rocks and anything else that would decimate the enemy.

The Order's military engineers dreamed up the theory that an invader would enter the bay and ram into the unseen wall, thereby leaving the soldiers enough time to detonate the *fougasse* and attack the dazed enemy with cannon- and musket-fire from the redoubt. However, when the French landed in the bay in 1798, the only time that the theory was put to the test, the soldiers fled and surrendered without firing a single shot and, to quote the historian Dr Trump, 'so ended ingloriously the knights' rule of Gozo'.

## Tourist Information
## East of Victoria

The **MTA office** should be opening once the new ferry terminal is completed in Mġarr.

There are pontoon facilities in Mġarr Harbour for up to 151 visiting boats (*see* 'Yachting Information', p.93).

### Festas

**Għajnsielem** has a *festa* on the last Sunday in August. Celebrations are in Għajnsielem square in front of the huge mock-Gothic church to **Our Lady of Loreto**.

**St Joseph's** *festa* in **Qala** is on the first Sunday in August.

**Nadur's** main *festa*, on the Sunday following 29 June, is not to be missed; it has sometimes been known to run on literally for days. A procession to commemorate **St Coronatus** is held on the second Sunday in November.

## Shopping
## East of Victoria

Some of the simplest and best of the local souvenirs around are **hand-carved stone objects** by Joe Xuereb at **Ta Peppi**, Baggara Street, Għajnsielem, t 21 553559.

## Where to Stay
## East of Victoria

### Mġarr

Terminus hotels can invoke grimy nightmares; happily, that's not so with Mġarr's.

**\*\*\*\*Grand Hotel**, 56 St Anthony Street, t 21 556183 (€€€). Quietly located is the immodestly named Grand, built on the site of an old guest house. It opened in Easter 1997 and has eight floors, 46 rooms including family suites (16 have a sea view). Each room has satellite TV and balcony, and the walls are decorated with Anna Grima's illustrations.

### Qala

**St Joseph**, Immaculate Conception Street, Qala, t 21 556573 (€). Not far from St Joseph Square is this five-room guesthouse. The owners, the Bartolo family, also run a small and very popular **restaurant** on the ground floor, which is open for lunch and dinner.

## Eating Out
## East of Victoria

### Mġarr

**Kċina tal-Barrakka**, known to all as **Sammy's**, underneath Gleneagles Bar (*see* below) at the waterfront, t 21 556543 (€€€). Sammy, the overworked brother of Tony from Gleneagles, runs the restaurant. The menu consists of whatever the fishermen hauled in that day and a few staple items such as pastas and steak. Tables are shoe-horned in place resulting in slow Gozitan service, but more often than not the food is excellent – try the king prawns. In summer dinner is alfresco under a bamboo canopy; in winter it is cosy inside and full of warm kitchen aromas. Highly recommended, book in advance.

**Manoel's**, t 21 560721 (€€€). Owned by Noel (late of a restaurant in Marsalforn called the Pink Panther). Right next door to Sammy's. You won't go wrong here either.

**Park Lin**, opposite Manoel's, further up the road, t 21 5561967 (€€€). Family-run restaurant which makes an effort – there is even a vegetarian dish of the day.

**The Seaview**, Mġarr Harbour, t 21 553985 (€€€). Next door to the police station, this restaurant is often referred to after its owner, **Lino**. He offers plain grilled fish and a few Italian meat dishes in more ordered surroundings, and has a surprisingly varied wine list. In summer you can sit outside on the balcony and wolf down local garlic bread. Pity about the adjacent concrete ramp to the new ferry terminal, which has spoilt the atmosphere. Booking is advisable.

**Gleneagles Bar**, also known as **Tony's**, 150 yards up the hill from the harbour. Almost as famous as Calypso herself is Tony, the proprietor. Everyone meets here. The drinks are generous, the décor is 'eclectic fishermen's style' with old lobster pots and taxidermed fish, and the balcony overlooking the harbour is a perfect *tal-barrakka* or lookout. Only fearless swimmers should ask Tony for the photos he keeps behind the bar of the 23ft (7m) Great White shark caught locally.

### Nadur

Apart from the none-too-appetizing food that is on offer at the **beach** concessions in Ramla Bay, Nadur has three **bars** in the village square and one of the best bakers in Gozo; fill your tuck box with local cheeses and tomatoes. This is also the best place to sample the *ftajjar* or Gozitan pizza. Call either Grace, **t** 21 553025, or Evan, **t** 21 556877, who will bake them after the bread is done every day (except Sundays), from 8am to 6pm.

## Comino (Kemmuna)

 Comino

Comino takes its name from the cumin herb, one of the few plants that grow wild in the inhospitable topsoil of this basically uninhabitable island. For centuries, Comino sat orphaned in the middle of the channel separating Malta and Gozo. Now it is a prized jewel, albeit sun-baked and barren; it is one of the few places left in the Mediterranean where there are no cars or roads and the land, including its airspace, is a wildlife sanctuary. The indigenous population remains in single figures, and with the exception of the residents of the one hotel all visitors and day-trippers depart before sunset, leaving only yachtsmen to linger for the night in the bays where 400 years ago Saracen pirates lay in wait.

Time your visit correctly – before 10.30am or after 4pm – and Comino offers the finest bathing, snorkelling and diving for hundreds of miles around. Time it incorrectly and parts of the island, especially the translucent waters of the Blue Lagoon, can be more unpleasant, noisy and populous than Bognor Regis or Coney Island on a hot August weekend.

Yet despite its daily invasions, Comino has retained that rarest of commodities – an unhurried temperament in a hurried world. It is a kindly and gentle island where even the sinister prickly pear seems to cast long-defeated shadows.

### History

A 3rd-century BC Phoenician amphora containing an adult skeleton and anointment oils has been uncovered in Santa Marija Bay. There is no logical explanation for the find (the Phoenicians were far too wise to colonize Comino) and it is now on display in the Gozo Archaeological Museum. Almost the only individual who is known to have survived a troglodytic life here was the 13th-century author and prophet **Abraham ben Samuel Abulafia**, otherwise known as 'the Spanish Messiah'. Selfless and harmlessly unhinged, his quest in life was to be at the vanguard of a new religion, uniting in one faith Christianity, Judaism and Islam. Abraham tried to convert Pope Nicholas III (who died of an

## Getting to Comino

*See also* p.65 for general information on getting to Comino.

There are three different ways of getting to Comino from **Malta**, and one from **Gozo**. The schedules are for an extended summer period (*April–Oct*); no service exists when the Comino Hotel is shut (*Nov–Mar*). Anyone wishing to visit in winter should enquire of the fishermen in Mġarr Harbour, Gozo.

From **Marfa**, a mile (1.5km) before Ċirkewwa, '**Gozo Charlie**' runs a service every day in summer on the hour every hour in the *Royal 1* for the 15-minute trip to the Blue Lagoon. The Comino Hotel operates its own service from **Ċirkewwa** seven times a day, starting at 7.30am, with the last departure at 6.30pm; and seven times a day from **Mġarr Harbour** from 6.30am–11pm (fares are the same, either from Ċirkewwa or Mġarr). The **Captain Morgan** fleet (*www.captainmorgan.com*) has day trips from the **Sliema Ferries**: departing at 9.15, arriving in the Blue Lagoon 1½ hours later and returning at 5.30pm in Sliema (*May–Oct daily, Mar three a week, April and Nov Mon–Fri; departure 10am all months other than May–Oct*).

However temptingly close the shores of Comino look from Gozo, do not attempt to swim across the 1-mile (1.5km) channel; the strong currents are likely to wash your corpse up in Sicily.

---

apoplectic stroke the day Abraham espoused the idea), and had to flee Rome as his execution pyre was lit. The poor man eked out a subsistence on Comino until the end of his days. Here he wrote up his cabbala philosophy and best-known work, the *Book of the Sign*.

Even after the arrival of the knights in 1530 the island was no more than a pirate's lair, with corsairs lying in wait under the lee of the southwestern cliffs for ships crossing the channel. In 1618 **Grand Master Alof de Wignacourt** finally built St Mary's Tower, which linked a line of defence and communication from Valletta to the citadel in Victoria. Doomed efforts were made during the Order's reign to populate the island and Comino remained just another game preserve, where a trespasser 'armed with gun, dog, ferret or net' could be sentenced to three years as a galley slave.

The **British** legacy to Comino (and Filfla) was not a proud one. In 1800, after Nelson saw off the French, some 2,000 prisoners-of-war were interned on the island before being sent home. At the beginning of the First World War, the British built an isolation hospital, now the village, in an effort to contain the many frightful diseases imported with the sick and dying servicemen of the Crimean campaign. During and after the Second World War, their imperialistic habits continued, as the Royal Navy fired torpedos at it for practice; the waters were so clear that the unexploded torpedos could be retrieved from the sea bed. Their final act in 1961 was to sell the island to a British development company who subsequently built both the Comino Hotel and Club Nautico. Their 150-year lease was surrendered back to the independent Malta government in the 1970s.

# What to See on Comino

A tower on Comino to guard the troublesome channel was first mooted in the early 15th century when King Alphonso V of Aragon levied a local wine tax to pay for it, but having collected the money he squandered it elsewhere. Nearly 200 years later, in 1618, Grand Master Alof de Wignacourt built **St Mary's Tower** to the design of Vittorio Cassar. As a partnership they had already beefed up the coastal defences with the Wignacourt Tower, and Forts St Lucian and St Thomas; St Mary's Tower was their final and most costly effort. Commanding the high ground on the southwestern cliffs, St Mary's is smaller but no less robust and fierce than its Maltese forerunners; Cassar had by now perfected his technique. The classical four-square fort has a commanding presence of both channels from its raised podium and it housed a permanent garrison of 30 men. Today it is a lookout post for the Armed Forces of Malta and a snoop around it to see its far-reaching rooftop views is at their friendly discretion. The crumbling escutcheon above the makeshift drawbridge is de Wignacourt's. The fort has struggled with the elements for nearly 400 years and is not in good condition, but when crossing the channel at night the powerful uplighting imposes its strength on the channel once more. St Mary's Tower featured as the feared prison of Château d'If in the 2002 movie of the *Count of Monte Cristo*.

The old **isolation hospital** is 300 yards away but is not really worth visiting. Scattered around in front of what is daftly known as Liberty Square is the detritus of bygone conflicts and ancient rusty machinery which no one has bothered to cart away.

Along the oleander-lined solitary dirt track to **Santa Marija Bay** (named Congreve Street after a British governor who died in office in 1927 and was buried at sea off Filfla), is the island's chapel, dedicated to Our Lady's Return from Egypt. Comino falls under the parish of Għajnsielem on Gozo but has had its own chapel dating back to the 13th century. Its setting is more Greek than Maltese; the small white-fronted building with its little picket gate, tamarisk trees, three hooped bells and snout-like water spouts was built not long after the fort. Mass is said at weekends, when the priest comes over from Qala.

## Activities

Comino is justly famous for the colour of its water, **bathing**, **diving** and **general aquatic recreations**. With no cars the island, especially in spring, is good for lazy walks; the rugged landscape is tranquil but botanically dull. Temperatures can soar in summer, so bring a bottle of water and a hat.

The stretch of water between the leaf-sized beach on Comino and Cominotto, the **Blue Lagoon**, has a South Pacific quality: limpid crystal turquoise water over a white-sand sea bed. In June 1993 the very core of the lagoon was roped off to the flotillas of small boats;

you will be safe from the lunatic fringe of speedboat show-offs here. The day-trippers' boats and other yachtsmen can still anchor outside the area. In the peak of summer it can get extremely overcrowded; the best time to pay a visit is before 10.30am and after 4pm. If you drop anchor for the night (the holding is good), swim at dawn and flee after breakfast.

Past the little hideaway caves of uninhabited **Cominotto**, and under the lee of the fort, the swimming is less frantic and the snorkelling more rewarding. The caves in the cliff face are worth a look, but unfortunately can become fouled with boats' exhaust fumes. When the wind comes from any direction but the southwest the deep bay is a perfect venue for water-skiing, especially in the late afternoon.

Round the headland from the Blue Lagoon and approximately 15 minutes' walk away, are the **San Nicklaw** and **Santa Marija** beaches. The immediate foreshore and beach in front of the **Comino Hotel** in San Nicklaw Bay is private and the management guard their unique (for Malta) territorial rights vociferously. Use of all the hotel's facilities for the day, such as the pool and the beach, are available to non-residents at a fairly hefty price. The beach by **Club Nautico** in Santa Marija Bay is not private. The swimming, providing a few underwater rocks and seaweed don't put you off, is excellent, and the tamarisk trees provide privacy and shade. It is a picnic beach and one of the best sand beaches in Malta, not least because there are no water or food concessions. Also, idiotic speedboat drivers rarely venture in. Even more secluded is **Smugglers' Cove**, a small cove on the south channel. Head for the fort and walk downhill in a southeasterly direction in order to get there.

There are three good **diving locations** in Comino's waters. The southwestern tip of the island is called **Ras l-Irqieqa**, and the deep dive is sheer down to 130ft (40m). The fast currents running through the channel keep the area well stocked with fish. Among the easiest and most exciting dives are the cave dives off **Ghiemieri**, around the Santa Marija headland – a good dive for photographers, since the caves are full of fish as well as the occasional moray eel. The easiest dive in Comino is the slow relaxing plod along the sea floor and the reef off the west in between **Għar Għana** and the Blue Lagoon. The Comino Hotel has its own diving school.

**Snorkellers** should swim in pairs and take extra precautions with a marker buoy; all the dive and snorkelling areas are in the speedboats' line of fire.

# Tourist Information on Comino

Comino's **police station** is unusually attractive – a cream-painted one-man outpost, set above a boathouse at the water's edge in Santa Marija Bay and proudly flying the Maltese flag.

The island's only **telephones** are at the Comino Hotel and Club Nautico and their use is at the owners' not always helpful discretion.

The only **public convenience** is 50 yards above the Blue Lagoon. There is no shade on the island, other than at Santa Marija Bay, so bring **protective clothing** and a bottle of **water**.

## Festa

The island's small *festa* is organized by the parish priest from Qala. Attended by both Maltese and Gozitans, it takes place on the fourth Sunday in July and is dedicated to the Sacred Heart of Jesus.

# Where to Stay on Comino

***Comino Hotel**, t 21 529821, *www.cominohotel.com* (€€€).

Encompasses what was two hotels: the Comino Hotel (San Nicklaw Bay) and the bungalow-style Club Nautico (Santa Marija Bay). Both were built during the bleak architectural period of the early 1960s with lashings of cheap cement and acres of aluminium windows. The Comino Hotel has more than 90 rooms, but unfortunately their décor is still locked in the regrettable 1960s time capsule; however, the Club Nautico has been modernized, air-conditioned and now comprises 45 suites in three grades set in a cleverly landscaped garden at the water's edge. It positively bristles with facilities, many of which are extremely expensive. There is a 'Club Med' atmosphere but you are a captive; it is fine for young children but teenagers can get bored. *Closed Nov–Mar; bungalows open in May*. Between the two hotels there are no fewer than 10 sand tennis courts, three swimming pools, a windsurfing and diving school, a large children's play area, water-skiing off the private sandy beach as well as a private boat service to Malta and Gozo. Residents of both the hotel and Club Nautico can use each other's facilities.

# Trips to Ionian Sicily

*Sicily is the largest island in the Mediterranean; beautiful, stirring, mysterious and crammed to the very peak of Mount Etna with history and myth. Malta once formed a part of the Sicilian landmass from which it is now separated by a comparatively shallow 58-mile (93km) channel, only 90 minutes by boat. The Sicilians and the Maltese share an Arab sense of fatalism and solemnity; the cultural, topographical and anthropological similarities are easy to discern.*

14

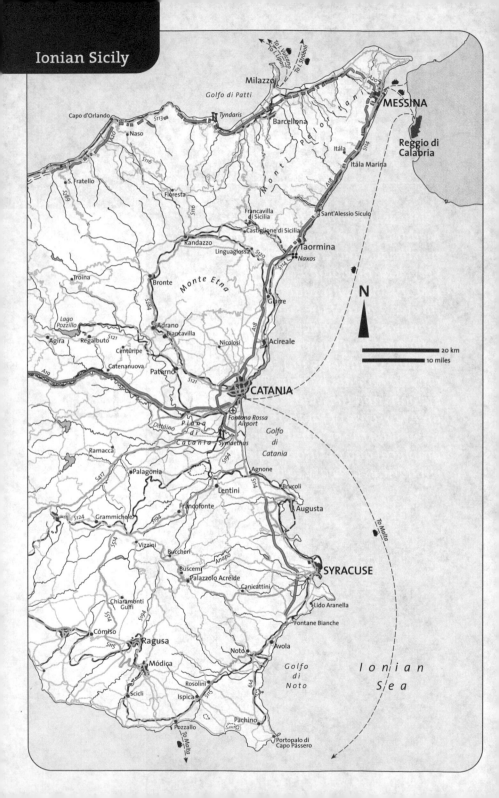

# Ionian Sicily

*'Like Sicily extremely – a good on-the-brink feeling – one hop and you're out of Europe: nice, that.'*

D.H. Lawrence, 1920

Despite the cultural links with and proximity to Malta, when you visit Sicily you will find an entirely different country. Sicily is not really like anywhere else. An island surrounded by three seas – Ionian, Tyrrhenian and Mediterranean – and set in between the two republics of Italy and Malta, it has a character quite different from that of mainland Italy.

Along the Ionian coast of Sicily are the superb Greek and Roman archaeological treasures of **Syracuse**, the menacing anger of the active volcano **Mount Etna**, the idyllic beauty and romance (especially in spring) of **Taormina**, and the exciting market in the forever bustling city of **Catania**. The signposting of the sites, hotels and towns is faultless, a welcome change from Malta, enabling you to explore freely and without frustration.

# Syracuse

*The most beautiful and noble of the Greek cities*

Livy (59 BC–AD 17)

The rubber stamp of tourism has yet to be printed on the wobbly faded terracotta streets of Syracuse. It is strange to think that this sleepy old southern Sicilian town divorced from violent headlines was the centre of the civilized world 2,000 years ago. The archaeological treasures found and lodged here rank among the finest in central Europe; the **Museo Archeologico Paolo Orsi** (1988) and the **Neapolis Archaeological Park** alone are worth a special trip. The original centre of ancient Syracuse, the tethered island of **Ortygia**, is a maze of narrow and twisted streets where the Baroque and medieval buildings are cleansed by the sea air and bleached by the diffused Mediterranean light. Here the less site-minded can eat well, sip an espresso or meditate. Plato walked the same streets 2,350 years ago; as did Archimedes, who was born here 130 years later.

## History

The city of Syracuse was founded by **Corinthians** in 733 BC. Like Malta, its destiny was foretold by its position and its protected harbour, Porto Grande, as well as by the sometimes calamitous underground twitches from Mount Etna 37 miles (60km) to the north. The nearby southern coastal town of Gela had a tyrannical leader called **Gelon**, who after a victory over the Carthaginians in 480 BC at Himera in the northwest of Sicily declared himself master of Syracuse. Gelon's influence extended over half of Sicily and the golden era of his adopted power base began. Syracuse's rise eclipsed Athens and lasted until it fell – in spite of **General Archimedes**'s ingenious weapons – to the Romans in the Second Punic War of 211 BC. In those 270 years Syracuse was governed both by wise rulers and by monstrous tyrants, during whose reigns the

## Getting to and around Ionian Sicily

The **Virtu Ferry Co.** runs a year-round service to **Pozzallo** (90mins) and **Catania** (3hrs); there may also be summer sailings to **Reggio**. In winter there are three or four crossings a week to Pozzallo and one a week to Catania; in summer there are two to three crossings a day four times a week

Two different one-day **excursions** via Pozzallo are organized by Virtu; one takes in Mount Etna and Taormina (*April–Oct, depart 7am, return 11pm*) the other Catania, Módica and Mount Etna (*all year; returns 9pm in winter*).

The high-speed ferries leave from Pinto Wharf in the Grand Harbour. Day-return tickets are quite a bit cheaper than ordinary returns, and for a small charge you can upgrade to club class – good value if you hate queuing: you not only get more comfortable seats but are allowed to disembark first – no small blessing when the ferry is full and there are only two immigration officers on duty at 11pm. There is a departure tax for each person or car, which is not included in the fares. However, the travel levy applies only to Maltese nationals and residents.

Pozzallo sailings are shorter and more frequent, and Pozzallo is a nice seaside town. The quay at Pozzallo can be hard to find: follow signs to 'Porto' then 'Gozo Channel'. The local police (*carabinieri*) are quite used to providing an escort for those who get seriously lost.

**Timetables** change over the year – the above services only apply from July to September. For a full timetable, or to make a reservation, contact **Virtu Ferries Ltd**, 3 Princess Elizabeth Terrace, Ta'Xbiex, **t** 21 228777 (Malta), 0932 954062 (Pozzallo) or 095 535711 (Catania); *www.virtuferries.com*.

If you hate the sea, **Air Malta** flies four times a week to Fontana Rossa, Catania's airport, and twice a week to Palermo in the high season. Call **t** 21 662211 for times, fares and reservations (*www.airmalta.com*).

---

ancient monuments that can be seen today were built. **Hieron I** (478–466 BC) and the paranoid and black-hearted **Dionysius I** (405–367 BC) stand out as shining examples of tyrants. Dionysius I had a wastrel son and heir, **Dionysius II**, who in spite of being tutored by Plato ended his days, according to Plutarch, 'loitering about the fish market, or sitting in a perfumer's shop drinking the diluted wine of the taverns, or squabbling with common women'. Only Syracuse's last two rulers, **Timoleon** and **Hieron II** (who died in 216 BC), displayed peaceful and democratic intentions.

Under the Roman governorship of **Verres**, 73–70 BC, a master of Roman-Maltese relations (*see* p.218), Syracuse reached its nadir; 90 years later **St Paul** stayed here for three days en route to Rome from Malta. Except for the Byzantines who briefly made Syracuse their capital in AD 663–8, it was largely ignored by the Arabs, Normans and other north European powers.

During the **Great Siege**, on 25 August 1565 the Spanish viceroy, Don Garcia, finally embarked his relief force of 8,000 men and 58 galleys from Syracuse to Malta. When the long-overdue force arrived in Malta on 7 September Grand Master de la Valette had all but claimed victory over the Turks.

The earthquake of 1693 wiped out the town **Noto Antica** and destroyed much of the city. In so doing it provided a clean sheet for the embryonic Sicilian Baroque. In 1865 the city once again became the provincial capital. The **Second World War** saw bomb damage inflicted by both sides. Many of the buildings were restored following the most recent **earthquake** of December 1990.

# Getting around Syracuse

There are several **bus** lines serving the archaeological sites in Neapolis. All can be caught outside the post office in Ortygia. The no.11 goes closest to the Euryalus Fort.

There are also **cruises** available in the summer months around the city's two main harbours, t 0931 62776; the cost includes a picnic lunch.

## Seeing Syracuse

The town of Syracuse is divided into five areas: the principal attractions are in Tyche, Neapolis and Ortygia. Achradina is the commercial centre and in the suburb of Epipolae 5 miles (8km) to the west are the remnants of Euryalus Fort, the last important Greek fortification in the Mediterranean. Further afield is the River Cyane with its banks of withering Egyptian papyrus.

**Neapolis**
*open Tues–Sun; adm; keep your ticket until the last site*

The archaeological park is in **Neapolis**. The park comprises four very different sites. By the main entrance is the **Greek Theatre**, bigger than the theatres at both Delphi and Athens, and still in use today; plays and concerts are performed here biannually in even-numbered years from May to August. It was hewn out of the rock in the 5th century BC and was enlarged by Hieron II to accommodate an audience of 15,000. At the top of the auditorium is the Street of Tombs and an artificial *nymphaeum* of cascading waterfalls to clarify the actors' orations.

Further along the same path is the **Latomia del Paradiso**, Paradise Quarry, a warped misnomer in English, where Dionysius I kept 7,000 Athenian prisoners hacking away at the rocks for seven years to build Syracuse's fortifications, after the calamitous **Great Expedition**. (The so-called Great Expedition was the bungled but heroic attempt by Athens to wrest control of Syracuse from Dionysius I, in 413 BC, with one of the most impressive fleets ever assembled.) Part of the quarry is a cave, 75ft (23m) high, called the **Ear of Dionysius** by the painter Caravaggio in the 16th century due to its shape. According to legend, the remarkable acoustics – still evident today – enabled Dionysius I to indulge his paranoid delusions by eavesdropping from the small hole at the top on the scheming whispers of his prisoners below. The neighbouring cavern, visible but closed for safety reasons, is the **Grotta dei Cordari** or 'ropemakers' cavern'. Until recently, its damp air afforded ropemakers who worked here the constant moist temperature they needed to twist the hemp.

Further along is the **altar of Hieron II** and the Roman amphitheatre; the entrance to both is almost hidden behind the tacky souvenir stalls, a café and an information office. Only the outline remains of the altar of Hieron II, 650ft (200m) long, which consequently resembles an elongated football pitch. Built in the latter half of the 3rd century BC, its sole purpose was the ritual and sacrificial slaughter of animals. (The historian Diodorus records that on one occasion 450 oxen were put to the knife between flaming pyres – to celebrate democracy.) A row of nine sarcophagi leads to the even more gory early 3rd-century AD **Roman amphitheatre**. The huge 460 by 390ft (140 by 120m) elliptical theatre assuaged the Romans' appetite for circus-style games of death. The arena itself is out of bounds, but stand among what would have been the cheap seats at the top and appreciate the sheer scale of it. By the expensive front ringside seats and under the centre of the cavea is the vomitorium or corridor through which the animals would enter the fray. At the end of a contest, spectators would crowd around the animal carcasses to drink the warm blood and eat the raw livers (an early holistic remedy?).

On the east of town in **Tyche** and visible from everywhere in Syracuse is the **Santuario della Madonnina delle Lacrime**, looking like an immense concrete rocket. This bizarre structure houses a statue of the Madonna which apparently wept for five days in 1953. Opposite and subtly concealed in its own gardens is the famous **Museo Archeologico Paolo Orsi**. Spectacular relics from the many archaeological sites in Sicily are displayed in three sections: from the prehistoric to the Roman/Greek eras up to early Christian times. Among the almost too numerous exhibits are the dreamy, almost marshmallow-soft, white marble statue *Venus Anadyomene* coming out of the sea with a playful dolphin at her ankles, another headless statue, suckling twin babies, an ornate Roman marble sarcophagus from the 4th century BC, and a collection of vases from Camarina and Gela.

**Museo Archeologico Paolo Orsi**
*open Tues–Sat 9–2, Sun 9–1; adm; allow at least 2 hours*

A few hundred yards west along Viale Teocrito, and grouped together, are the **basilica and catacombs of St John** (San Giovanni) and the **crypt of St Marcianus** (San Marziano). The basilica has been a ruin since the 1693 quake and is pleasantly overrun with flowers, but you still need to go through it to reach the underground crypt where St Paul preached. Under Roman rule, Tyche was outside the Ortygia city limits and Roman law provided that all burials had to take place outside the city limits. Consequently, the catacombs are a vast Christian necropolis of more than 43,000 sq ft (4,000 sq m), and though the tombs have long since been removed the niches are still much in evidence.

**Basilica and catacombs of St John**
*catacombs open by accompanied tours only, on the hour 9–12.30 and 2.30–5, closed Tues; adm*

## Ortygia Island

**Ortygia** is tenuously joined to the mainland by two very short bridges, but it always appears eager to drift out to sea. The main bridge opens on to the Piazza Pancali and the sparse remains of the **temple of Apollo** (from the 6th century BC), the oldest Doric temple in Sicily. The morning market stretches off the piazza and down the Via Trento to the sea.

## A Love Story

In ancient Greece, the nymph Arethusa swam in the clear flowing waters of the river Alpheus. She was so beautiful that Alpheus, the river god, fell hopelessly in love. Artemis, the guardian of all virgins, rudely interrupted Alpheus's advances just as Arethusa was about to succumb to his charms. Artemis commanded the earth to open and the nymph vanished into the ground. Swiftly, she crossed underneath the Ionian Sea and metamorphosed as a freshwater spring, the Fonte Arethusa, in Ortygia. A distraught (and possibly frustrated) Alpheus disappeared under the Ionian Sea and joined her, and here their waters have mingled ever since. Today comical ducks play among the papyrus in the lovers' water and the fountain in Ortygia's Piazza Archimede romances Arethusa's transformation into the spring.

Even if you have feasted on (or drowned under) Baroque churches in Malta, don't miss the different Sicilian-Baroque buildings in the **Piazza del Duomo**. The Greeks built a temple to the goddess Athena on the present site of the **Duomo** – the Doric columns still form part of it – and the whole edifice nearly tumbled down in the 1693 earthquake which destroyed the cathedral in Mdina, Malta. The entire contents, including the huge doors of gold and ivory, were thieved by the governor, Verres, in 73–70 BC. The ornate Baroque façade is magnificent and contrasts with the austere and voluminous interior. But there is much to see inside, including early Renaissance statues by Antonello Gagini (the most notable being the *Madonna of the Snows*, 1512). Also, peer into the interesting three chapels in the right-hand aisle. The **Palazzo Beneventano del Bosco** (1779), in an open courtyard, has an imposing staircase; it became the local headquarters of the Knights of Malta as the Order was disintegrating.

**Museo Regionale d'Arte Medioevale e Moderna**
*open 9–1*

South of the Piazza del Duomo, 200 yards away, is the **Museo Regionale d'Arte Medioevale e Moderna,** housed within the Palazzo Bellomo, which had to undergo a sustained period of refurbishment as a result of the 1990 earthquake. Constructed around a small courtyard, this hybrid building houses a superb collection of medieval art. Within its 13th- to 15th-century walls are the world-famous 15th-century *Annunciation* by Antonello da Messina and one of Caravaggio's last paintings, *The Burial of St Lucia*, Syracuse's patron saint. He painted it in 1608–9 just after his escape from Malta and two years before his death (*see* p.109). This darkly evocative depiction of the saint's burial shows Caravaggio's talents at their zenith.

A few hundred yards away from the Palazzo Bellomo at the water's edge is the **Fonte Aretusa** (*see* A Love Story, above). Below the Fonte Aretusa, the **Foro Italico** (where the car ferry for Malta embarks) is lined with a handful of cafés, trinket and nut vendors; it is the stage for the evening *passeggiata*. If you want to swim, there's a tiny sandy beach in town near the Fonte Aretusa, and **Fontane Bianche** 9 miles (15km) to the south has a long sandy beach. Avoid swimming in the polluted waters north of Syracuse.

## Tourist Information in Syracuse

ⓘ **Syracuse >**
*Via San Sebastiano
43/45,* **t** *0931 481232,
www.apt.siracusa.it*

The main **AAST tourist office** is near the archaeology museum, and there is a small office in the railway station.

There are **APT Information Offices** in the archaeological park and opposite the catacombs of St John. All have free maps, and hotel and transport information, as well as details of festivals, the regular local puppet shows and cultural programmes.

## Where to Stay and Eat in Syracuse

**Syracuse** ✉ **961000**
****Grand Hotel Villa Politi**, Via Politi Laudien 2, **t** 0931 412121, *www.grandhotelsr.it* (€€€€). Grand old villa in the centre of town. Nice and leafy with a pool and tennis courts; Winston Churchill stayed here once.

****Hotel Gutowski**, Lungomare Vittorini 26, **t** 0931 465861, *www.guthotel.it* (€€€). Small 25-room hotel spread between two old buildings on the seafront in Ortygia. Stylish and fresh; great organic breakfasts. Ask for a sea view.

***Pantheon**, Via Foro Siracuso 22, **t** 0931 21010 (€). A nice old-fashioned *pensione*.

**Darsena**, Riva Garibaldi 6, **t** 0931 61522 (€€€€). Catering mainly to tourists, but reliably good food.

**L'Ancora**, Via Guglielmo Perno 7, **t** 0931 462369 (€€€). Excellent fish restaurant near to food market in Ortygia.

**Jonico 'a Rutta 'e Ciauli**, Riviera Dionisio il Grande 194, **t** 0931 65540 (€€). Conjures up Sicilian specialities and good pasta dishes on a modest terrace overlooking the sea within Tyche.

In Ortygia, **Al Gambero Rosso, Archimede** and **Osteria La Gazza Ladra** (both €€€) are also good.

# Catania and Mount Etna

## Catania

*Etna looked
like a toy,
but a rather
dangerous one.*

Lawrence Durrell,
*Sicilian Carousel,* 1977

Mount Etna is a consistently violent and psychopathic neighbour. Yet, paradoxically, the Catanese put up with it and in their own way mock it. Most aspects of life in this city of more than 400,000 inhabitants openly flout the powerful superiority of the volcano. Life is loud and never pauses, lest it be caught unawares – hence the horns, the market catcalls, the traffic, the capricious humour, the Mafia and its Machiavellian manoeuvring. Why conform, the people here seem to say, when you are sitting on a lit fuse?

### History

Catanese history is one long horror story beginning with Syracusan tyrants and followed by death and destruction from a succession of pirates, Normans, Angevins, plagues and volcanic eruptions. The most spectacular eruption began on 11 March 1669 in the Nicolisi area, when the earth opened up into a fissure 9 miles (15km) wide. Molten lava flowed through and past the city and out into the sea continuously for eight weeks. Charles II, with the magnanimity of a caring monarch, exempted what was left of the barbecued city from taxes for 10 years. In 1693, their tax holiday having barely ended, a Mount Etna-inspired earthquake wiped out

# Getting to and around Catania

Catania is the hub of all transport links in Sicily, with **buses** for most major points (including Taormina and Syracuse) leaving from the Stazione Centrale on Piazza Papa Giovanni XXIII. The city is on the Messina–Syracuse **rail** line, so you can travel there by train from Syracuse and Taormina.
**City buses** get you around the city centre, and there's a rather limited **metro** system.

two-thirds of the remaining inhabitants. In the 20th century alone there were six major eruptions; one in 1950 lasted 380 days and produced in excess of 800 million cubic metres of lava. The last eruption was in 2002; another, in 1992, prompted the Italian and US navies to attempt to hold back the relentless flow of lava by dropping concrete blocks in its path from helicopters.

## Visiting Catania

**Catania** has been rebuilt many times. Today, the city may look as if it is constantly being repaired, but it is not: it is just in a permanent state of propped-upness. Much of what you see was built after 1693, when a widely spaced grid plan was laid over the network of narrow streets; a lot of what remains from before 1693 is lava-encrusted. For sightseeing, the **Piazza del Duomo** with the city's totemic emblem, a foppishly grinning elephant carved from lava, is a handy reference point – everything worth seeing is within walking distance.

Unlike the more exuberant gold of Maltese stone, the greyish tones of the city's volcanic stone tends to suffuse the richly ornamental Baroque style of Giovanni Vaccarini's post-1693 buildings. Parts of the Duomo have survived since it was first built in the 11th century, but the exaggerated façade is mainly Vaccarini's handiwork. Inside, the fine Baroque chapel of the city's patron Saint Agatha is to the right of the choir. (She is also one of Malta's patron saints.) In the sacristy is a good snapshot painting of the 1669 disaster completed only eight years after the event. Catania's favourite son, **Vincenzo Bellini**, is buried next to the second pillar on the right which has a musical inscription from his opera *La Sonnambula*. Perhaps an even greater accolade is the naming of a pasta dish '*Spaghetti alla Norma*' (a Sicilian speciality), after his opera, *Norma*.

The **Porta Uzeda** leads down a few steps from the Duomo to the most enthralling **open-air market** in the Mediterranean. Stall-holders with hoarse voices, who sound as if they have gargled *grappa* and gravel all night, sell every kind of thing that is edible. The crowded market with its aromas and incredible displays of meat and fish – locally caught 360lb (165kg) tuna with flesh redder than steak, writhing displays of seafood, lambs sheared in half from head to tail – is not for vegetarians or the faint-hearted. See it, smell it and live it, but hang on tightly to your wallet.

14 Trips to Ionian Sicily | Catania

Further south, the entire area of land around the forbidding smut-grey 13th-century **Castello Ursino**, once Frederick II's cliff-edge fortress, was reclaimed by lava flows after the eruption of 1669. Inside the fortress is the **Museo Civico**.

**Museo Civico**
*open Tues–Sat 9–1 and 3–7, Sun 9–1; adm*

The two **Roman sites** are the theatre (400 yards west of the Duomo in Via Vittorio Emanuele II) and amphitheatre (650 yards north along Via Etnea) both built from blocks of the ubiquitous lava. The latter, which is railed off, seated roughly 16,000 and lies unexcavated under many buildings, but you can see its impressive shape from the steps of the church. The **theatre and the odeon** next door are also 2nd century AD and are accessible.

**Theatre and odeon**
*open Mon–Sat 9–1.30 and 3–7, Sun 9–1; adm*

**Museo Belliniano**
*open Mon–Sat 9–1.30, Sun 9–12.30*

Vincenzo Bellini died in 1835 at the early age of 34; his birthplace is now the little **Museo Belliniano** (300 yards along Via Vittorio Emanuele II). Crammed with memorabilia, including original scores, models of theatrical sets, his piano, and macabre death mask and coffin, it is worth looking in on.

The acoustic properties of the ornate neoclassical **Teatro Bellini** (1890), across Via Etnea in the Piazza Bellini, are said to be the third finest in the world.

# Mount Etna

*Etna spat out a mouthful of hot coals and then dribbled a small string of blazing diamonds down her chin.*

Lawrence Durrell,
*Sicilian Carousel*, 1977

Look at any map and you will see how **Mount Etna**, like an industrial-size burbling pimple, dominates the face of Sicily. The volcano was originally formed by a massive undersea eruption that forced its way up from the sea bed. It now has three craters and is the largest volcano in Europe, and one of the most active in the world: more than 135 fatal eruptions have been recorded.

From the summit, the views are extraordinary (on rare occasions you can see Malta); the odours are sulphurous and the winds fierce, although the landscape of once-vicious igneous lava is now benignly lunar. At the summit the strangest sensation of all comes through your feet: this is a tap into the earth's core, or even possibly one of the brimstone gateways to hell. Mount Etna's satanic power is hypnotic. Ignore your heart's quickened pace and the consequences that an immodest burp from below might have; the ascent should not be missed.

Mount Etna has always held a powerful fascination. The Greeks believed its quakes were the attempts of the giant Enceladus to free himself from his prison underneath Sicily. Vulcan, the lame son of Jupiter and armourer of the gods, is believed to have had one of his forges in the mouth of the crater, with branch offices in the Aeolian Islands off Sicily's north coast. Legend also tells how the mighty Cyclops Polyphemus, having been blinded by Odysseus (who paused here while on his way home from seven years on

# Getting to and around Mount Etna

## By Car or Taxi

From the centre of Catania, the first few hundred metres of Via Etnea are one-way, against you. Ask permission from a policeman in the Piazza del Duomo with all the effusiveness your stammering Italian can muster and he might let you proceed; it saves an age. Follow the signposts for **Nicolosi** (700 yards) and the **Museo Vulcanologico Etneo**. **Nicolosi Nord**, the 'base camp' (1910 yards) and **Silvestri Craters** are both well signposted.

An easier (but longer) way is to take the road to **Zafferana** past **Acireale**, heading north on the motorway to Taormina, from where the base camp is flagged. From the Silvestri Craters you can take a **cable car** (in winter you can ski down), then a **jeep** and finally a **guide** to as close to the central crater at the summit as safety permits (up to a height of 10,500ft/3,200m above sea level).

You can also join **tours** from Taormina. Bring stout shoes and a sweater; it can be very windy at the summit and the temperature falls 2°F every 1,066ft (325m) above sea level.

## The Circumetnea

Another highly worthwhile Etna-related excursion is to take the railway known as the **Circumetnea**, a private line that runs around the base of the mountain through an assortment of striking towns and villages, gaining some wonderful views on the way of the volcano and its surroundings. You can start this either from **Giarre-Riposto** on the main line between Taormina and Catania, or from **Catania Borgo** station, best reached by metro from Catania Centrale. If you want to explore some of the places on the route, you need to time the trip carefully, and get started fairly early in the morning. Some trains run through to **Riposto**, but most require a change at **Randazzo**, a rewarding little medieval town with plenty for a short stopover.

---

Calypso's Isle, Gozo), heaved three of Mount Etna's immense rocks at Odysseus's fleeing ships. Not surprisingly, he missed and thereby created the three rocks of Aci Trezza.

The demented 5th-century BC philosopher Empedocles came from Agrigento on the south coast. He was so convinced he was a god that he threw himself into the crater, in the belief that he would float on the gases and prove his divinity. The only traces of him that remained were his golden sandals, melting on Mount Etna's lip.

With true Sicilian perversity, the volcano has always symbolized Catania's inherent contradictions: it threatens the city below yet provides for it. The citrus fruits and vineyards of olives and grapes that grow in the famously fertile volcanic ash of the vast lower slopes are the finest to be found anywhere in the central Mediterranean. Patrick Brydone's words of 1773 still hold true: 'If Aetna resembles hell within, it may with equal justice be said to resemble paradise without.'

## Tourist Information in Catania

ⓘ **Catania >**
*Largo Paisiello 5, off Via Etnea just south of Giardino Bellini,* **t** *095 531802*

In addition to the main APT office in Largo Paisiello, there is a smaller one at the **train station**, **t** 095 531802, and at the base camp on **Mount Etna**.

**Fontana Rossa** airport, **t** 095 7306266, also has an office providing free maps, cultural information and transport timetables.

The **Sicilian Alpine Club**, Via Vecchia Ognina 169, provides information and guides for Mount Etna.

## Where to Stay in Catania

### Catania ✉ 95129

****Jolly Trinacria**, Piazza Trento 13, t 095 316933 (€€€). North of the town.

***Central Palace**, Via Etnea 218, t 095 325344 (€€). Centrally located, but noisier than the Jolly Trinacria.

## Eating Out in Catania

**La Siciliana**, Via Marco Polo 52, t 095 376400 (€€€€). A fine local restaurant with a cool garden.

**Sicilia in Bocca**, 16/18 Piazza Pietro Lupo, t 095 7461361 (€€€). Provides Sicilian cooking at its best.

**All'Alioto** (formerly Selene), 24 Via Mollica, t 095 494444 (€€). A few kilometres north of Catania, in the direction of Aci Castello, this seaside restaurant serves a huge variety of antipasti, fish and shellfish. Highly recommended.

**Stella Antica Friggitoria Catanese**, Via Ventimiglia 66, t 095 325429 (€€). Savour a little piece of history and have a meal at this restaurant, which has been operating continually since 1830; they must be doing something right.

**Trattoria Tripoli** (€€). Those with a strong constitution should try eating at this lively place right in the heart of the heaving market; *lunch only*.

# Taormina

*Taormina should be let out by the Italian government, as an open-air asylum for Anglo-Saxons who live their lives according to the adage 'time is money'. It would cure their restless efficiency. Nobody ever looks at a clock in Taormina.*

Walter Starkie, *The Waveless Plain*, 1938

Without its views, **Taormina** might just have slipped by unnoticed like so many other hilltop Sicilian villages. Even the hundred or more hotels that share the craggy lair, 700ft (213m) high, in the Peloritani Mountains with the locals have not diminished the almost too-lyrical beauty of the place. Taormina is touristy and only Mafia scares can empty the place (as they did in 1992) – though this is, happily, a thing of the past. In August it can be an Anglo-Saxon jungle, but in the mellow golden light of late September, or the crisper days of April–May, when the bougainvillea tumbles like a purple waterfall, it becomes a moocher's nirvana.

## History

Nearby **Naxos** was the first Greek colony in Sicily and foolishly allied itself to Athens during the Great Expedition, which forced the ill-tempered and conquering Syracusan Dionysius I to reduce it to rubble in 403 BC. Led by Andromachus in 358 BC, the few survivors settled in Tauromenium on Monte Tauro, and ever since then Taormina's fortunes have been tied to those of Syracuse. By 215 BC it was a *civitas foederata*, a **Roman** federated city, and when Syracuse fell it became capital of Byzantine Sicily until the **Saracen Arabs** sacked it in AD 902.

The town was slowly rebuilt and by the 11th century it flourished again under the Norman, Count Roger; many of the buildings bear the Norman hallmark. During the **Sicilian Vespers** (1282), the town sided luckily with the victorious Aragonese. In 1410 the Sicilian parliament sat in the Palazzo Corvaja to elect a successor to the

## Getting around Taormina

Taormina is 32 miles (52km) equidistant from Catania in the south and Messina in the north. Forget the car. Most of the town is pedestrianized and you are better off driving up and parking wherever you can on the outskirts. Alternatively, there is a **cable-car** service which runs every 15 minutes from near the shore at Mazzaro to Via Luigi Pirandello in the centre of town. The **bus terminal** is also in Via Luigi Pirandello, with frequent buses from the wonderfully architectural **rail station** at the bottom of the hill. **Taxis** are in the Piazza Vittorio Emanuele and the Piazza del Duomo.

extinct line of Aragon. The town remained Spanish – except for a brief French interlude when Spain was short of funds – until the 1860 arrival of the **Bourbons**.

It remained undiscovered as a tourist destination until the 19th century. A German, **Baron von Gloeden**, put it on the map when he returned to the chilly climes of northern Europe with an armful of sepia photographs depicting hot-blooded young Sicilian men and boys demurely naked save for laurels of ivy (you can buy reproduction postcards in town.) While not quite becoming an early Club 18–30, it was firmly positioned on the itinerary of the Grand Tour where it has remained ever since. Field Marshal Kesselring had the unfortunate good taste to turn the San Domenico Convent into his headquarters during the **Second World War**, resulting in Allied bomb damage both for itself and the town in July 1943.

### What to See

Taormina is the archetypal picture-postcard subject and the town itself is the main attraction. Whether you look down from the old Saracen fort beneath Castelmola or up from the beach at Giardini-Naxos, its pedestrianized streets, alleys and piazzas have a self-conscious charm; Taormina is just meant to be admired.

No wonder that the ancient Greeks ruled the civilized world; their eye for a site was faultless. From the top of the cavea of the **Greek Theatre**, you can frame the smouldering spire of Mount Etna, the Ionian Sea, terracotta roofs, the mountains and valley through a camera viewfinder. The position of the theatre is Greek, but the fabric is Roman. It was built in the middle of the 3rd century BC by Hieron II and like all Greek theatres it functioned as their omnipotent media forum. Partly by hewing out the rock, the Romans enlarged it to its present size to cater for their more gladiatorial tastes in the 2nd century AD. Their changes were drastic, the new arched openings and columns obscuring much of the natural view, with the obvious intention of keeping the audience focused on the slaughter at hand. The semicircular theatre, the second largest in Sicily after the one in Syracuse, is 360ft (110m) in diameter. It held approximately 6,000 and is still used today during the summer arts festival. For romantics, the best

**Greek Theatre**
*open 9–one hour before sunset; adm*

time to go is just before sunset; otherwise go at 9am for the morning light. There is a small museum by the entrance containing a few tablets from ancient Taormina.

The main *corso*, **Umberto I**, begins at the Porta Messina and ends at the Porta Catania. Everything of note is on it or off it. Inside the Porta Messina, by the old forum, off the Piazza Vittorio Emanuele, is the **Palazzo Corvaja** (1372), a handsome but somewhat frigid Norman building with lancet windows and inlays of black lava and white stone. The public rooms off the courtyard staircase house local art exhibitions. This is where the Sicilian parliament met in 1410 and now, more prosaically, the tourist office occupies part of the ground floor. Next door are the submerged, dull remains of a 2nd-century AD Roman **odeon** which crops out through the floor of the **church of Santa Caterina**. Further up the hill (Via Cappuccini and Via Fontana Vecchia) is the old villa where DH Lawrence lived from 1920 to 1923, now a private house marked by a plaque and a pair of cypress trees.

The evening fun is played out in the large open terrace of the **Piazza IX Aprile**. On a clear windy day, look up above the skull-and-crossbones escutcheon over the main door of the 17th-century **church of San Giuseppe** at the clouds racing through the sky, and the backdrop of Castelmola appears to move while all around is stationary. It seems to confirm the sense of time suspended. If the night-time views don't bowl you over, you can have a cartoon drawn or sit in the Caffè Wunderbar under the watchful eye of the **Torre dell'Orologo**, the 12th-century clocktower built above the **Porta di Mezzo**, and people-watch during the evening *passeggiata*.

Through the Porta di Mezzo lies the **medieval part of town**. Down to the left is the old **monastery**, now the San Domenico Palace Hotel (*see* p.319). The many nook-like piazzas are sheltered, colourful in spring and cool in summer. The **Piazza del Duomo** is typically discreet and shares its insignificant piazza with cafés and a spluttering early 17th-century fountain, the steps of which are still a rendezvous. The **Duomo** (dating from the 13th century, but completely remodelled during the Renaissance) is restrained and unexciting save for its lofty wooden-beamed ceiling and a 15th-century alabaster statue of the *Madonna* by Montinini. Before you reach the Porta Catania with its Aragonese coat of arms, on the left, you will see the **Palace of the Dukes of St Stephen** (1330). The 2nd-floor mullioned lancet windows with intarsia decorations, and the lava and limestone frieze above are the best remnants of the Norman period.

**Palace of the Dukes of St Stephen**
*open 9–12.30 and 3–6*

The **Public Gardens**, laid out at the turn of the century by an eccentric Englishwoman, are worth a look. Among the follies is an extraordinarily bizarre monument: a reconditioned *mezzo d'assalto della marina* or two-man submarine with a 660lb (300kg)

## Tourist Information in Taormina

**(i) Taormina >**
*Palazzo Corvaja at the junction of Corso Umberto and the Piazza Vittorio Emanuele t 0942 23243, www. gate2taormina.com*

The **AAST tourist office** is half-heartedly multilingual but very helpful: they can tell you anything from where to rent a Vespa to how to track down a hotel room in August. The free large-scale map is excellent.

## Where to Stay and Eat in Taormina

### Taormina ✉ 98039

There are over a hundred hotels and *pensioni* in and around Taormina. Eating out is hardly a problem, either.

**\*\*\*\*\*San Domenico Palace**, Piazza San Domenico 5, t 0942 613111, *www.sandomenico.thi.it* (€€€€). In a 15th-century monastery, very, very special and stupendously expensive.

**\*\*\*\*Excelsior Palace**, Via Toselli 8, t 0942 23975, *www.excelsiorpalace taormina.it* (€€€). Less special but has a spectacular location and a pool.

**\*Pensione Svizzera**, Via Pirandello 26, t 0942 23790, *www.pensionesvizzera. com* (€€). An excellent-value hotel with sound plumbing and views.

**La Giara**, t 0942 23360 (€€€€). A pricey restaurant, but a good old-timer.

**Granduca**, Corso Umberto 172, t 0942 24983 (€€€). Specializes in Sicilian dishes; considered to be one of the best restaurants in Taormina. Even if you disagree, enjoy its spectacular view over the Greek theatre.

**Ristorante Luraleo**, t 0942 24279 (€€€). Has a secluded terrace and serves fresh fish.

warhead of the type used by the Italian navy during the siege of Malta in the Second World War. Somehow, it does not blend in with the trees and noisy cicadas. For the hearty there is a long-stepped climb, taking just over half an hour, from the Via Circonvallazione up to **Santuario Madonna della Rocca**. A further 200 steps lead up to the remains of the seemingly impenetrable **Saracen fort** or *castello*. Higher still is **Castelmola**, a dizzyingly sited hilltop village. In 1912 a donkey ride (return) to Castelmola was the equivalent of 6p or 9 cents – today you can take a bus or a taxi from Taormina. Lick an ice cream from the Café San Giorgio as you digest the stupendous panorama.

## Beaches

The cable car – when it works – goes down to the somewhat limited beaches of **Mazzarò** and **Isola Bella**, separated by the headland of **Capo Sant'Andrea**. Three miles (5km) further afield is the long sandy beach of **Naxos**, which attracts a younger crowd.

# Language

*Languages are the pedigree of nations.*
Samuel Johnson (1709–84)

If Samuel Johnson is to be believed, the Maltese nation is a true hybrid, a Heinz 57-variety country. The language of the Maltese islands, Malti, is a unique Semitic tongue woven from the linguistic threads of those who came either in peace or in war; the Phoenicians, the Arabs, the Italians, the Spanish, the French and latterly the English have all both corrupted and influenced spoken Malti.

To the visitor, it is particularly hard on the ear – like Turkish but without the chewy, gravelly noises. It becomes even more incomprehensible when spoken at speed, as it often is – then it is like the koranic incantations of a fanatical mullah. You will notice, above all else, that the Maltese speak like they drive – loudly, and with windmilling arms and hands, imbuing everyday life with a true sense of Latin drama.

Getting around the islands is not a problem. The Maltese are talented linguists, for until the 20th century Malti was purely a spoken language; the script with its modified Roman characters only evolved early in the 20th century. Italian was the official language of Malta until 1934, when it was replaced by English. Nearly all Maltese speak English, and many speak Italian. Menus are all in English, but road signs are for the most part in Malti. Problems usually only occur with bold attempts at pronunciation, which follow rules few people will be familiar with.

## Ground Rules

Dispel any notion of trying to learn the language – it is nigh on impossible. Almost every word conjugates byzantinely and has a gender; by comparison English is spectacularly simple. As an indication of the gurning skills required to master its complexities, try saying something as prosaic as 'What's the time, please?' – *Xħin hu jekk jogħġbok?* – or the even more tongue-twisting, 'Which way to?' – *Minn liema triq ngħaddi għal?*

For most visitors, the acquisition of a basic vocabulary and a few correctly pronounced place names is a solid accomplishment, and one that the native Maltese people will certainly appreciate.

## The Alphabet

The alphabet consists of 29 characters: 24 consonants and 5 vowels:

a, b, ċ, d, e, f, ġ, g, h, ħ, i, j, k, l, m, n, għ, o, p, q, r, s, t, u, v, w, x, ż, z

Of the 24 consonants, 14 sound similar to English; the other 10 are trickier and are therefore keys to correct pronunciation.

ċ as in 'ch' e.g. chapel

ġ is softer than an undotted g

j is soft like a 'y', e.g. *għajn* (well) 'ein'

ħ is spoken openly as in 'house' as opposed to 'hour' which is how the unlined 'h' is used

għ is a single letter and is usually silent. It has tonal variations when followed by an 'i' or 'u' and if it is found at the end of a word. The safest bet is a silent 'ahr', e.g. *għar* (cave) is pronounced 'ahrr'

q is usually a clipped 'k' except for when followed by a vowel when it's silent, e.g. *qala* is 'arla'

s is hissed, sssnake-like

x is a key letter. Just as in Chinese, it is pronounced 'sch', e.g. *Xlendi* is 'Schlendi'

unaccented z is soft, while ż is a Germanic 'tz': try *Żejtun*.

ll or l (or any of its other numerous manifestations) precedes many words and means simply 'the'.

# Basic Vocabulary

Notice the French and Italian phonetic influences, especially on phrases like 'thank you' and 'good night'.

| English | Malti | Pronunciation |
|---|---|---|
| yes | *iva* | eva |
| no | *le* | leh |
| please | *jekk* | eekk-y-ojbok |
| | *jogħġbok* | |
| thank you | *grazzi* | grat-see |
| goodbye/ | | |
| ciao | *saħħa* | sah-har |
| excuse me | *skuzzi* | skoossi |
| how much? | *kemm* | kehm |
| good | | |
| morning | *bonġu* | bon-jew |
| goodnight | *bonswa* | bon-swa |
| today | *illum* | ill-loom |
| tomorrow | *għada* | ahrda |
| yesterday | *il-bieraħ* | ill-bee-rahh |
| street | *triq* | trik |
| square | *misraħ* | miss-rahh |
| where is? | *fejn hu* | fey-noo |
| bread | *hobż* | hobsz |
| wine | *imbid* | im-beet |
| water | *ilma* | as written |
| ice | *silġ* | silch |
| church | *knisja* | k-neesya |
| cliff | *irdum* | ir-duum |
| beach | *plajja/* | plai-ya/ |
| | *spjaġġdoa* | spe-ajja |
| valley | *wied* | we-ed |
| harbour | *marsa* | marssa |

## Numbers

| | | |
|---|---|---|
| zero | *xejn* | shayn |
| one | *wiehed* | weehehd |
| two | *tnejn* | tn-ayn |
| three | *tlieta* | tlee-tah |
| four | *erbgħa* | airba |
| five | *ħamsa* | hum-sah |
| six | *sitta* | as written |
| seven | *sebgħa* | sehbah |
| eight | *tmienja* | tmee-eyn-ya |
| nine | *disgħa* | dissah |
| ten | *għaxra* | ash-rah |
| twenty | *għoxrin* | osch-rin |
| fifty | *ħamsin* | hamm-seen |
| hundred | *mija* | meeja |
| thousand | *elf* | as written |

# Place Names

Most of the villages and towns are pronounced as they are written, with the following exceptions:

| Location | Pronunciation |
|---|---|
| Balzan | Bal-tsan |
| Birżebbuġa | Beer-zee-booja |
| Buġibba | Buj-ibba |
| Ċirkewwa | Chir-kewwa |
| Dwejra | Dweyrah |
| Ġgantija | Jagan-teeya |
| Għajnsielem | Ein-seey-lemm |
| Għajn Tuffieħa | Ein-tofeeah |
| Għarb | Arb |
| Għargħur | Gargour |
| Ġnejna | Je-nayna |
| Gudja | Goodya |
| Gzira | Ge-zeera |
| Ħaġar Qim | Hajar-eem |
| Kerċem | Ker-chem |
| Lija | Leeya |
| Luqa | Loo-ar |
| Marsamxett | Mar-sam-schett |
| Marsaxlokk | Marsa-schlok |
| Mdina | Imdeena |
| Mġarr | Imjarr |
| Mġarr-ix-Xini | Imjarr-ish-sheeney |
| Mnajdra | Im-nigh-dra |
| Mqabba | Im-abba |
| Mslda | Im-seed ah |
| Nadur | Na-dour |
| Naxxar | Naschar |
| Pieta | Pe-etah |
| Qala | Ala |
| Qawra | Owwra |
| Qrendi | Rendi |
| Siġġiewi | Si-jee-wee |
| Ta'Ċenċ | Ta-chench |
| Ta'Pinu | Ta-pee-noo |
| Tarxien | Tar-sheen |
| Ta'Xbiex | Tash-beesh |
| Xagħra | Shahh-ra |
| Xewkija | Scher-keya |
| Xlendi | Schlendi |
| Żebbuġ | Tze-booje |
| Żejtun | Tzay-toon |
| Żurrieq | Tzur-rea |

15 Language

# Glossary

**auberge** the hall of residence of one of the *langues* of novice Knights of the Order of St John within the Convent (*see* pp.28–9)

**bastion** a fortified stone wall, often backed with earth, that thrusts out from the main fortifications at angles

**cavalier** defence work inside the enceinte and higher than the first line of defence, e.g. a bastion. Sometimes used as a gun platform and to store arms (*see* St James's and St John's Cavaliers, Valletta, pp.101 and 123)

**counterguard** acutely angled polygonal stonework built to protect a bastion (set lower than and in front of it)

**curtain** a sheer stone wall, bordered by a parapet, which usually joins two bastions.

**demibastion** a half bastion built to protect a curtain wall

**enceinte** a wall enclosing a fortified area, and/or the area enclosed (e.g. the fortifications that surround Valletta)

*ferreria* an arsenal

*festa* a weekend-long annual feast in honour of a village's patron and favourite saint – the high point of the year (*see* pp.45–6)

*gregale* a violent northeasterly winter wind

**hornwork** a defence work independent of the main fortifications

*kaċċa* the hunt (*see* p.46)

*kaċċatur* hunters (*see* p.46)

*każin* political clubs

*langue* a subdivision of the Knights of the Order of St John (*see* pp.28–9)

*luzzu* a Maltese fishing boat

**maquis** a type of shrubby, mostly evergreen, vegetation found mainly in Mediterranean coastal areas

**Melitan** (or **fat**) **mouldings** a triple roll of mouldings around windows and doors which get progressively fatter (the inner being thinner than the outer). They were typical to Malta in the 16th century

*nicci* boxes, dedicated to saints, placed in street walls; money is deposited and prayers said, in return for heavenly favours. There may also be a small altar

**parapet** a low, and sometimes indented, wall at the top of a rampart, which was built to protect the besieged

**pasha** a senior Ottoman rank (not a surname, as in Mustapha Pasha) of admiral or general or governor; the rank itself is divided into three grades

*passeggiata* a custom, originating in Italy, in which families promenade together just before dusk

*pilier* head of one of the *langues* of the Knights of the Order of St John

**quint** the one-fifth of a knight's wealth that he was not bound by statute to leave to the Order

**ravelin** a V-shaped defence built outside the main fortifications in front of a curtain wall, and with open access for the defenders at the rear

**sirocco** a hot southerly wind blowing in from North Africa

*tal-hut* a mobile fish vendor; most towns and villages are visited once or twice a week

*torba* a crushed compound of limestone and water used in floors

*zuntier* a forecourt; often where the men will meet up outside the parish church at the end of the day

# Chronology

**BC**
**Before 4,000** Arrival of man.
**Circa 3,600** Introduction of copper.
**Circa 2,500** First arrival of bronze-using people.
**Circa 1,500** Second arrival of bronze-using people.
**Circa 900–800** The Iron Age.
**Circa 800–480** Phoenician period.
**Circa 480–218** Carthaginian period.
**264–241** First Punic War.
**218–201** Second Punic War.
**218** Malta incorporated in Republic of Rome.
**149–146** Third Punic War.

**AD**
**60** Shipwreck of St Paul.
**117–138** Islands made municipalities during reign of Hadrian.
**395** Final division of Roman Empire.
**395–870** Byzantine period.
**870** Invasion by Aghlabite Arabs.
**1048** Byzantine bid to recapture the islands.
**1090** Norman invasion.
**1122** Uprising of the Arabs.
**1144** Byzantines again attempt to recapture the islands.
**1154** Bishops of Malta under the jurisdiction of the See of Palermo.
**1194–1266** Swabians (Germans).
**1266–83** Angevins (French).
**1283–1412** Aragonese (Spanish).
**1350** Establishment of Maltese nobility by King Ludwig of Sicily.
**1350–7** First Incorporation of Islands in Royal Domain.
**1397–1420** Second Incorporation of Islands in Royal Domain.
**1397** Establishment of *Università* (Commune).
**1425** Revolt against Don Gonsalvo Monroy.

**1428–1530** Third (and final) Incorporation of Islands in Royal Domain.
**1429** Saracens from Tunis try to capture Malta.
**1530** Order of St John takes formal possession of the islands.
**1535** First known date of celebration of Carnival in Malta.
**1561** Holy Inquisition officially established in Malta.
**1565** Great Siege.
**1566** Founding of Valletta.
**1578** Inauguration of St John's Co-Cathedral.
**1593** Inauguration of Jesuits' College.
**1768** Jesuits expelled from Malta.
**1775** Priests' Revolt.
**1784** Promulgation of the *Diritto Municipale* by Grand Master de Rohan.
**End of 18th century** General decline of the Order of St John.
**1798** The French, under Napoleon, occupy Malta. Abolition of the Inquisition.
**1799** Britain takes Malta under its protection in the name of the King of the Two Sicilies.
**1800** The French capitulate. Major General H Pigot is instructed to place Malta under the protection of the British Crown.
**1802** Peace of Amiens by which Malta was to have been returned to the Order of St John. Declaration of Rights.
**1813** The Bathurst Constitution. First issue of *Gazzetta del Governo di Malta* (changed in 1816 to *Malta Government Gazette*).
**1814** Treaty of Paris by which Malta granted to Britain.
**1819** Dissolution of *Università*.
**1828** Proclamation regulating state-church relations.
**1831** See of Malta becomes independent of See of Palermo.
**1834** Opening of Malta Government Savings Bank.

**1835** First Council of Government.

**1839** Abolition of press censorship and introduction of law of libel.

**1840** Council of Government with elected members.

**1864** Diocese of Gozo separated from See of Malta.

**1869** Opening of Suez Canal.

**1880** Malta Railway Company founded.

**1881** Executive Council – an entirely official body.

**1887** The Strickland-Mizzi Constitution.

**1903** Council of Government – largely a return to the 1840 Constitution.

**1914–18** First World War.

**1919** *Sette Giugno* riots.

**1921** The Amery-Milner Constitution granting self-government. Opening of first Malta parliament.

**1930** Constitution suspended.

**1931** End of Malta Railway Company.

**1932** Constitution restored.

**1933** Constitution withdrawn. Crown Colony government as in 1813.

**1936** Constitution providing for nominated members to Executive Council.

**1939** Macdonald Constitution: Council of Government to be elected. Lord Strickland's Constitutional Party returned.

**1939–45** Second World War.

**1940** First air raids on Malta (11 June).

**1942** Award of the George Cross for Gallantry to the People of Malta by King George VI (15 April).

**1943** Italians surrender (8 September).

**1946** National Assembly resulting in 1947 Constitution.

**1947** Restoration of self-government: Dr Paul Boffa's Malta Labour Party returned.

**1958** Dom Mintoff resigns as prime minister. Dr G Borg Olivier declines invitation to form alternative government and the governor takes over direct administration of the islands.

**1959** Interim constitution providing for Executive Council.

**1961** Blood Constitution published by Order-in-Council, providing a measure of self-government for the 'State' of Malta.

**1964** Malta becomes a sovereign and independent state within the British Commonwealth.

**1968** Establishment of Central Bank of Malta.

**1971** Sir Anthony Mamo becomes first Maltese governor general.

**1972** Military base agreement with Britain and other NATO countries.

**1974** Malta becomes a republic.

**1979** Termination of military base agreement. British Services leave Malta after 180 years.

**1989** US President George Bush, and Soviet leader Mikhail Gorbachev meet at Marsaxlokk for Summit (1–3 December).

**1990** Pope John Paul II visits Malta (25–27 May).

**1990** Prof. Guido de Marco elected president of 45th Annual UN General Assembly.

**1992** Her Majesty Queen Elizabeth II visits Malta for George Cross 50th anniversary celebrations (28–30 May).

**2003** Malta votes to join EU.

**2004** Malta joins EU.

# Architects and Artists

**Belli, Andrea** (1705–72). Little-known Baroque architect from Valletta who probably remodelled the Auberge de Castile et Leon and designed the Cathedral Museum in Mdina.

**Bonici, Giuseppe** (1707–79). Maltese architect responsible for Castellania, Valletta Customs House and Nadur church, Gozo.

**Buonamici, Francesco** (1596–1677). The Order's resident engineer from 1635 to 1659 who was probably responsible for the introduction of an early-Baroque style of architecture in major buildings. The Hostel de Verdelin, the Jesuit church in Valletta and the church of St Paul at Rabat are among his works.

**Cachia, Domenico** (c. 1700–90). Maltese architect of St Helen's at Birkirkara, and Selmun Palace on the outskirts of Mellieħa. The other, but less likely candidate, for the remodelling of the Auberge de Castile et Leon.

**Call, Giuseppe** (1846–1930). A portrait and ecclesiastical painter born to Neapolitan parents in Malta. Many of his works are to be found in parish churches.

**Caravaggio, Michelangelo Merisi da** (1571–1610). Regarded as the greatest Italian painter of the 17th century; a master of realism, his paintings are chromatically stunning.

**Cassar, Gerolamo** (1520–86). Famed Maltese architect and engineer who designed most of Valletta's buildings; his prodigious œuvre includes the Grand Master's Palace, St John's Co-Cathedral, and all the *auberges*.

**Cassar, Vittorio** (d. 1605/7). Son of Gerolamo, and like his father an architect and engineer. Formed a formidable partnership with Grand Master Alof de Wignacourt: together they built Forts St Lucian and St Thomas on Malta, and St Mary on Comino.

**Dingli, Tommaso** (1591–1666). Maltese architect who built many fine churches with certain Renaissance flourishes, notably St Mary's in Attard, and the Assumption in Birkirkara.

**Favray, Antoine de** (1706–98). French painter who adopted Malta; best known for his evocation of late 18th-century grand masters, especially Grand Master Pinto in the sacristy of St John's Co-Cathedral.

**Ferramolino, Antonio** (??–1550). Italian military engineer who worked for the emperor of Spain, Charles V. He advised Grand Master de Homedes on the vital fortifications of St Angelo and was the first to suggest building fortifications on Mount Sceberras (where Valletta now stands).

**Firenzuola, Vincenzo Maculano da** (b. 1578). An Italian engineer and Dominican friar who served the pope and built the Margherita Lines around the Three Cities in the mid-17th century.

**Floriani, Pietro Paolo** (1585–1638). Italian military engineer responsible for the immense Floriana Lines.

**Gafa, Lorenzo** (1630–1710). Doyen of Maltese Baroque architects. Trained in Rome and famed for his light touch; the dome is his signature. The cathedrals of Mdina and Victoria, and the parish churches of Siġġiewi, Vittoriosa and Żejtun are among the most notable of his works.

**Gafa, Melchiorre** (1635–67). Noted sculptor, brother of Lorenzo.

**Gruenenberg, Don Carlos de**. The emperor of Spain's engineer, who first came to Malta in the late 17th century at the request of Grand Master Perellos to advise on the Valletta Harbour fortifications. He built (and paid for) the batteries still standing at St Angelo, and was made a Knight of Grace.

**Laparelli da Cortona, Francesco** (1521–70). Italian architect and engineer who conceived and oversaw the masterplan for the new city of Valletta. He died in Crete just before the Battle of Lepanto.

**de Mondion, Charles François.** Outstanding French military engineer and architect, the Order's resident designer from 1715 to 1733. Apart from his work on the magnificent Fort Manoel (with de Tigné), he rebuilt much of Mdina after the 1693 earthquake for Grand Master de Vilhena; his buildings included the Main Gate and Banca Giuratale.

**Perez d'Aleccio, Matteo** (1547–1616). Rome-based Spanish painter who arrived in Malta in the wake of the Great Siege celebrations (1565). His most noted works are the cycles of frescoes in the Grand Master's Palace including 12 events of the Great Siege. He died in Peru.

**Preti, Mattia** (1613–99). Southern Italian Baroque artist who embellished many of the islands' churches. Best known for his work on the vault of St John's in Valletta and the influence left by his ecclesiastical paintings. The Order made him a Knight of Grace.

**de Tigné, René Jacob.** French military engineer who came to Malta in 1715 to help in the works on what became Fort Manoel. Not to be confused with Chevalier Tigne who designed, built and paid for the fort which bears his name.

**Zahra, Francesco** (1710–73). Gifted Maltese painter, some of whose works can be seen in St Catherine's in Żejtun.

# Further Reading

Books marked * are either out of print or probably only available at a library. Those marked ** are in print but may only be available in Malta. Sapienzas bookshop in Valletta has a good selection; books can be ordered from their website (*www.sapienzas.com*).

## Malta: History, Culture, etc.

*Balbi, Francisco, *The Siege of Malta* (Folio Society). Remarkable day-by-day diary account written by a humble foot soldier who survived the 5-month Turkish siege in the summer of 1565.

**Borg, Joseph, *The Public Gardens of Malta and Gozo* (Media Centre). A detailed horticultural guide with photographs.

**Bradford, Ernle, *The Great Siege* (Penguin). A highly readable history of the Turks' attempt to wrest Malta from the knights in 1565; many references are taken from Balbi's account (*see* above).

**Bradford, Ernle, *Siege: Malta 1940–1943* (Penguin). Written with insight, and clearly demonstrates how little siege warfare has evolved over the centuries.

Caruana Galizia, Anne and Helen, *Recipes from Malta* (Progress Press). Not just rabbit and *lampuki* dishes.

**Cini, Charles, *Gozo: The Roots of an Island* (Said). A lively coffee-table book with both written and photographic essays on Malta's sister island.

**Elliott, Peter, *The Cross and the Ensign* (Grafton). A riveting history of Britain's naval affair with Malta from 1798 to 1979; reads like a good novel.

**Galea, Michael, *Sir Alexander John Ball* (PEG). Biography of the first British administrator of Malta.

Lockhart, Douglas, *Landscapes of Malta, Gozo and Comino* (Sunflower Books). Walks around the Maltese islands for all abilities, including advice on where to stay to get the most out of your walking holiday.

Lucas, Laddie, *Malta: The Thorn in Rommel's Side* (Stanley Paul). An engaging 1992 biography of a 26-year-old Allied Spitfire pilot stationed in Malta.

**Mahoney, Leonard, *A History of Maltese Architecture* (Author). Masterful, detailed.

Mahoney, Leonard, *5000 years of Architecture in Malta* (Valletta Publishing).

Mifsud, A and Mifsud, S, *Echoes of Plato's Island* (Prehistoric Society). Presents evidence that civilization of Malta occurred much earlier than previously believed.

Mizzi, John, *Malta at War* (Bieb Bieb).

Niven, David, *The Moon's a Balloon* (Hamish Hamilton). The late star was posted to Malta, and his memoirs dwell amusingly on his less than hard army sojourn on the islands.

de Piro, Nicholas, *International Dictionary of Artists Who Painted Malta* (AVC Publications).

de Piro, Nicholas, *The Temple of the Knights of Malta* (Miranda Publications). One of a series of lavishly illustrated, huge coffee-table books about Malta. This one is all about St John's Co-Cathedral, Valletta. Others include *Sovereign Palaces of Malta* and *Malta 360°*, both of which feature stunning photographs by Daniel Cilia, among others.

**Schermerhorn, Elizabeth, *Malta of the Knights* (AMS Press New York). Wonderfully written in 1929, with tremendous understanding of, and sympathy towards, the Order's reign in Malta; it brings the knights into sharp focus.

Sultana, Donald, *The Journey of Sir Walter Scott to Malta* (Alan Sutton). Heavy going but detailed account of the dying writer's last year and last work.

**Sultana, J and Falzon, V**, editors, *Wildlife of the Maltese Islands* (Gutenberg Press). A comprehensive guide to the surprisingly extensive Maltese flora and fauna.

**Sultana, R and Baldacchino, G**, editors, *Maltese Society* (Mireva). A collection of contemporary essays on all aspects of Maltese society.

**★★Trump, Dr David**, *Malta: Its Prehistory and Temples* (Midsea Books). Guide to the mysteries of Maltese prehistory.

**★★Vella, Philip**, *Malta: Blitzed But Not Beaten* (Progress Press). Thorough and gripping account of Malta's role in the Second World War; excellent archive photos throughout.

**Waugh, Evelyn**, *Labels* (Methuen). No backpack for the 29-year-old Waugh as he takes a pleasure cruise and pauses at the great Mediterranean ports in the late 1920s.

## Malta in Literature

**Ball, David**, *The Sword and the Scimitar* (Arrow). The story of a Maltese brother and sister at the time of the Great Siege.

**Burgess, Anthony**, *Earthly Powers* (Penguin). The protagonist lives in Lija; this is a phenomenal book.

**Ebejer, Francis**, *The Maltese Baron* (Midsea Books).

**Monserrat, Nicholas**, *The Kappillan of Malta* (Pan). The author, one of the great contemporary storytellers, lived in Gozo. His love story set in the Second World War is a great read.

**Rinaldi, Nicholas**, *The Jukebox Queen of Malta* (Corgi Books). Another love story set in Malta during the Second World War … a Maltese *Captain Corelli's Mandolin*.

## Sicily

The largest island in the Mediterranean has caused more printer's ink to be spilled than anywhere else in the region. The books listed exclude titles in the *Godfather* genre which, although good reads, offer little more than background vignettes.

**★Blunt, Anthony**, *Sicilian Baroque* (Zwemmer). The late spy's cleverly anecdotal and witty walk through the intricacies of Baroque.

**Cronin, Vincent**, *The Golden Honeycomb* (Collins Harvill). What starts off as a search for Daedalus's proffered gift to Aphrodite ends up as an eloquent travelogue.

**★Durrell, Lawrence**, *Sicilian Carousel* (Faber). This excellent 1970s book is out of print.

**Fallowell, Duncan**, *To Noto* (Bloomsbury). Amusing and racy tale of the author's journey from London to Sicily in an old Ford.

**Gilmour, David**, *The Last Leopard* (Collins Harvill). Not only a biography of Giuseppe di Lampedusa (*see* below) but a sympathetic record of a bygone era.

**Holloway, R Ross**, *Archaeology of Ancient Sicily* (Routledge).

**di Lampedusa, Giuseppe Tommasi**, *The Leopard* (Collins Harvill). A desert island book; if you pack only one book for your trip, make it this one.

**Lewis, Norman**, *In Sicily* (Picador). The product of a lifelong fascination with Sicily. It is humorous, gentle and very readable.

**★Maxwell, Gavin**, *God Protect Me from My Friends* (Longmans). One of the very few Europeans to have a true grasp of Sicily. This book is about the famous 1950s bandit Salvatore Giuliano. His other book about the poverty-stricken west of the island, *The Ten Pains of Death* (Alan Sutton), might, however, be easier to find.

**Pirandello, Luigi**, *Short Stories* (Dedalus). One of the island's most famous poets, playwrights and novelists, Pirandello was born at Agrigento in 1867.

**Robb, Peter**, *Midnight in Sicily* (Harvill Press). Political corruption and violent crime.

**Sciascia, Leonardo**, *The Day of the Owl* (Paladin/Carcanet). Another Sicilian writer, who lived under the skin of the island's tortured psyche; his works are mostly short stories and political thrillers. Try also *The Wine-Dark Sea*.

**Simeti, Mary Taylor**, *Sicilian Food* (Grub Street). Countless ways to stuff vegetables and make the most of *melanzane* from an American who married a Sicilian.

# Index

Main page references are in **bold**. Page references to maps are in *italics*.

Abraham ben Samuel Abulafia 300–1
Ahrax Point 183
air travel **63–4**, 65, 266, 308
Alphonso V of Aragon 25, 26, 236, 301–2
Anchor Bay 183–4
antiques 84
Aragonese rule 25
archery 90
Armed Forces of Malta 79
Armeria 207
Attard **257–8**, 261
Aviation Museum 253
babies 78
babysitters 78
Baħar iċ Ċagħaq 165, 166
Baħrija 190
Baħrija phase 22
Ball, Sir Alexander 33, 34, 116
Balluta Bay 160, 164
Balzan 258
banks **63**, 85–6
bars 80–1
beaches 87–8
    Baħar iċ Ċagħaq 166
    beach clubs/lidos **88**, 156, 160–1, 176
    Comino 302–3
    currents and undertow 87
    Delimara Point 219
    gay 81
    Gozo **88**, 290, 297–8
    jellyfish 82
    Mellieħa Bay 88, **180**
    Mistra Bay 175
    North Coast 182, 184, 186–7
    Northeast Coast 160–1
    Sliema 155–6
    Taormina 319
beer 56
Bellini, Vincenzo 313
bicycles 69
    mountain biking 90
birds
    Maltese falcons 289–89, **290**
    trapping and hunting 46–7

Birgu *see* Vittoriosa (Birgu)
Birkirkara **255–6**, 261
    Station 78
Birżebbuġa 214–15, 220
The Blue Grotto 205, 206, **207–8**, 210
boats
    boat charters 66
    pleasure cruises **66**, 176
    Sliema Creek cruises 154
    Underwater Safaris 78, **178**
    *see also* ferries
Borġ in Nadur 217
Borġ in Nadur phase 22, 23
Bormla *see* Cospicua (Bormla)
bowling alleys 78, 80
British rule **34–5**, 41–2, 133, 169, 237
    and Comino 301
Brydone, Patrick 147, 315
Buġibba **176**, 177
    eating out 179
    where to stay 178
Bur Marrad 176
buses **68–9**, 98, 148, 166, 170, 174, 181, 185, 195, 206, 214, 221, 224, 258
    bus routes *70–1*
    coach travel to Malta 65
    Gozo 71, 266, 270, 280
    Ionian Sicily 309
Buskett Gardens 196–7
Byron, Lord 100, 150
Byzantines 24
camping 74
Captain Morgan Underwater Safari 78, **178**
car travel
    accidents 68
    chauffeur driven cars 68
    driving in Malta 66–7
    from the UK 65
    getting to and around Valletta 98
    Gozo **266**, 280
    hiring a car 67–8
    local drivers 40

car travel (*cont'd*)
    names and signs 67
    North Coast 170, 174, 181
    parking **67**, 154, 160
    rules of the road 68
    Sliema 154
Caravaggio, Michelangelo Merisi da 109
casinos **80**, 164
Castelmola 319
Catania 307, 308, **312–16**
    Castello Ursino 314
    Circumetnea 315
    eating out 316
    history 312–13
    Mount Etna 307, 312–13, **314–15**
    Museo Belliniano 314
    Museo Civico 314
    open air market 313
    Piazza del Duomo 313
    Porta Uzeda 313
    Roman sites 314
    Teatro Bellini 314
    tourist information 315
    where to stay 316
Catholic Church 42, 43, 87
caves
    Għar Dalam 215–17
    Għar Hasan 215
    Gozo 279
children 77–8
churches
    disabled access 61–2
    opening hours 86
    religious services and denominations 87
cinemas 78, 80
Ċirkewwa **183**, 294
Clapham Junction 195, **196**, 204
climate 58
clothes shopping **83**, 156
coach travel 65
Comino (Kemmuna) *265*, 300–4
    activities 302–3
    Blue Lagoon 88, 89, 300, **302–3**

Comino (cont'd)
Club Nautico 303, **304**
Cominotto 303
diving 302–3
getting to 301
Għar Għana 303
Ghiemieri 303
history 300–1
hotel 301, 303, **304**
Malta–Comino ferries 65, 183
Ras I Irqieqa 303
St Mary's Tower 268, **302**
San Nicklaw beach 303
Santa Marija Bay 88, 89, 302
Santa Marija beach 303
Smugglers' Cove 303
snorkelling 303
tourist information 304
Constantinople 24, 26
consulates 61
Copper Age 23, 278
Corinthians 307
Cospicua (Bormla) 97, 130,
131, **134**
couriers, international 87
craft shops 83–4
credit cards 63
crime 78–9
Crusades 26
currency 38, 62–3
regulations 61
customs 61
cycling 69
mountain biking 90
del Monte, Grand Master 100
Delimara Point 214, **219**
Dingli 194, 195–6, 204–5
Dingli Cliffs 72, 88, **194–5**
disabled travellers 61–2
discos 78
diving 78, **88–9** 176, 183
Comino 302–3
Gozo 280, 283, 290–1
Dragut Point 154–5
Dragut Rais 26, 27–8, **48–9**, 118,
155, 159, 267–8
driving see car travel
drugs 79
Durrell, Lawrence 312, 314
EHIC (European Health
Insurance Card) 62
El Alamein 36
electricity 80
embassies 61
emergencies 81
emergency telephone
numbers 76, **79**
entertainment 80
Etna, Mount 307, 312–13, **314–15**

European Health Insurance
Card (EHIC) 62
Eye of Osiris 52
farmhouses 74
ferries
Comino 301
getting around **65–6**, 148, 183
getting there 64, 65
Gozo 61, 65, 148, 183, 266, 294,
301
Ionian Sicily 308
*festas* **45–6**, 58
Birkikara 261
dates 59–60
Gozo 275, 281, 287, 292, 299
Gwardamanġa 148
Gzira 152
Marsaxloxx Bay 220
Mosta 255
Msida 149
Naxxar 255
North Coast 177, 188
Northeast Coast 161
Sliema 156
South Malta 232
Southwest Coast 204, 209
Three Cities 144
Valletta 127
festivals 58, 59
Filfla 198
First World War **34**, 160
fishing **89**, 218
Floriana 124–7, **125**
Argotti Botanical Gardens
124, **126–7**
Church of St Publius 126
Granaries 126
Independence Monument
126
Lines 124
Maglio Gardens 125-6
Mall 125-6
Porte des Bombes 127
St Philip's Gardens 124, **127**
Sarria Church 126
Valletta Waterfront 127
Wingacourt Water Tower 126
Fomm ir Riħ 187–8
Fomm Ir Riħ Bay 88
Font Għadir 156
food and drink **53–6**
eating out 54, **79**
markets and shopping 82–3,
156–7
restaurant price ranges 79
restaurants for children 78
specialities 55–6
see also under individual
places (eating out)

football 89
Fort Madliena 165
Fort Manoel 151
Fort Mosta 253
Fort St Angelo 131, 132, 133, 135,
**140–2**
Fort St Lucian 218
Fort St Thomas 221
Fra Ben Tower 170
French rule 25, 33
Gafa, Lorenzo 139
Garcia de Toledo, Don 28
Garzes, Grand Master 30
Gauci Tower 254
gay scene 80–1
Gelon 307
Ġgantija Temples 276, **277–8**,
277
Għadira 88
Għajn Razul 175
Għajn Tuffieħa 72, **184–5**
Għallis Tower 170
Għar Dalam 215–17
Għar Għana 88
Għar Hasan 215
Għar id Dud 156
Għar il Kbir 196
Għar Lapsi 88, 195, **200**, 205
Għarb (Gozo) **285–6**, 287
Għargħur 165–6
Għaxaq 224, 229
glassblowing 77
Gloeden, Baron von 317
Ġnejna Bay 81, 88, **186–7**, 186
Ġnejna Valley 185
go karting 77
Golden Bay **184–5**, 190
golf 90
Gort, Field Marshal Viscount 36
Gozo 263, **264–5**, 265–300
beaches **88**, 290, 297–8
Blue Hole 283
Borġ il Mramma 290
buses 69, 71, 270
Calypso's Cave 276, **279**
Daħlet Qorrot 297, **298**
diving and snorkelling 88, 89
Dwejra Bay 283
eating out 276, 281–2, 287,
292–3, 299
ferries 61, 65, 148, 183, 266,
294, 301
Fessej Rock 292
*festas* 275, 281, 287, 292, 299
Fort Chambray 295
Fungus Rock 282–3
Ġebel tal Ħalfa 296
getting around 266, 283, 289,
294

Gozo (cont'd)
 getting to 266
 Għajnsielem 294
 Għammar 286
 Għarb **284–5**, 287
 Għasri 286
 Għasri Valley 88, 286–7
 Gordan Lighthouse 287
 helicopter link 63, 65, 294
 history 267–8
 Hondoq ir Rummien 296
 Inland Sea 282
 Ir Ramla 88
 Kerċem 288
 lace 83, 275, **289**
 Lunzjata Valley 288
 Marfa Ridge 72
 Marsalforn **279–80**, 281–2
 Mġarr 89, **293–5**, 299–300, 301
 Mġarr ix Xini 88, **289**, 290, 292
 Munxar **289**, 292
 Nadur 294, **296–8**, 300
 nightlife 293
 Nino's grotto 279
 Pomskizillious Toy Museum
  77, **278**
 Qala 294, **296**, 299
 Qala Point 88, **296**
 Qbajjar 280
 Ramla 298
 Ramla Bay 74
 Reqqa Point 280
 Rotunda Church 291–2
 St Andrew's Diver's Cove
  290–1
 salt pans 280, 281
 San Blas 88
 San Blas Bay 81, 297, **298**
 San Dimitri chapel 285
 San Lawrenz 282, 287
 Sannat 83, **288–90**, 292
 Santa Lucija 288
 shopping 275–6, 287, 292, 299
 Ta'Ċenċ Cliffs 289–90
 Ta'Pinu shrine 286–7
 tourist information 299
 Victoria (Rabat) 86, **269–76**,
  271
 villas and farmhouses 74
 Wardija Point 288
 where to stay 276, 281, 287,
  292–3, 299
 Xagħra 276
 Xagħra Village **278–9**, 281
 Xerri's grotto 279
 Xewkija 289, 291–2
 Xlendi 289, 290–1, 293
 Xlendi Pleasure Cruises 280,
  291

Gozo (cont'd)
 Xwieni 280
 Żebbuġ 280–1
Great Fault 165, 166, 169
Grey Skorba 187
Gudja 224, 229
Gwardamanġa 148, 149
Gzira **149–50**, 152
Ħaġr Qim 200–3, *201*, 210
Ħal Millieri 206
Ħal Saflieni 226
health 81
helicopter sight seeing 78
Heritage Malta museums 86
history **19–38**, *20–1*
 British rule **34–5**, 41–2, 133,
  169
 Carthaginians 24
 Catania 312–13
 Comino 300–1
 Dark Ages 24
 First World War **34**, 160
 Fort St Angelo 140–2
 Fort St Elmo 118–19
 French rule 25, 32
 Great Siege (1565) **27–9**, 96,
  97, 132–3, 140, 141–2, 154,
  159, 180, 213, 223–4, 236, 308
 independence **37**, 42
 Manoel Island 150–1
 Marsaxlokk Bay 213–14
 Mdina 235–7
 medieval period 24–5
 Mellieħa Bay 180–1
 Mġarr (Gozo) 294–5
 modern Malta 37–8
 Order of the Knights of St
  John 26–7, **28–33**
 Phoenicians 23–4
 prehistory 22–3
 Romans 24
 St Paul's Bay 171–4
 Second World War **35–7**, 131,
  133, 174, 184
 Syracuse 307–8
 Three Cities 97, 130, **132–5**
 Żabbar 223–4
 Żejtun 230–1
holiday complexes 74
holidays, national 85
Homer 279
horse-drawn carriages
 (*karrozin*) 69
horse racing 90
horse riding 78, **89**, 184
hospitals 81
hostels 74
hotels 73–4
hunting 46–7

Hypogeum 224, 225, **226**
Il Għira 221
Il Karraba 187
il Maqluba, legend of 198
insurance 62
international couriers 87
Internet cafés 82
Ionian Sicily **305–19**, *306*
 ferry services from 64
 getting to and around **308**, 315
Island Bay 88, 219
Italian army, and the Second
 World War 35–6
John the Baptist, St 109
*kaċċa* **46–7**, 91
*karrozin* 69, 98
Kbira Point 215
Kennedy Memorial Grove 170
Kirkop 209
Knights of the Order of St John
 26–7, **28–33**
 Act of Donation **27**, 140
 bailiwicks 29
 Chapter General 29
 and Comino 301
 *commanderies* 29
 Convent 28
 conventual chaplains 28, 29
 decline of the Order 31–3
 and Gozo 268, 295
 Grand Masters 30
 Grand Master's Palace 62, 97,
  99, **112–15**, *114*
 and the Great Fault 169
 and the Great Siege of Malta
  112, 159
 history (before 1530) 26–7
 Knights of Grace 29
 Knights of Justice 28–9
 Maltese Cross 44
 and Mdina 236–7
 priories 29
 *Processi Nobilari* 111–12
 servants at arms 28, 29
 and Valletta 96
 and village *festas* 45
La Cassière, Grand Master Jean
 L'Evêque de 30, 105, 142, 143
La Sengle, Grand Master de
 268
La Valette, Grand Master Jean
 Parisot de 27, **47–8**, 96,
 98–9, 136, 139, 141–2, 170, 197
lace 83
Laferla Cross 200
language, Malti 67, **320–1**
Laparelli, Francesco 99
Lascaris, Grand Master Jean 31,
 **125–6**, 182

Lawrence, D.H. 307
Lazzaretto Creek 148
Lazzaretto quarantine hospital 148
L'Evêque de la Cassière, Grand Master Jean 142
libraries 82
lidos 88
Lija 259, 261
Lippla Tower 186–7
L'Isla see Senglea (L'Isla)
L'Isle Adam, Grand Master de 27, 48, 110, 132, 141
Little Armier 182
Long Bay 219
Lowell, James Russell 34
Luke, St 171, 173
Luqa 228–9
Madliena 165, 166
Maitland, Sir Thomas 34
Malta Labour Party (MLP) 37–8, 41, 42, 43, 44
Malta Marathon 91
Malta Tourism Authority (MTA) 60, 62, 72, 89
Maltacom 86
Maltese Crosses 44, 157
Maltese falcons 289–89, 290
Malti language 67, 320–1
Mamo Tower 221–2
Manfred, Swabian king 25
Manikata 72
Manoel Island 150–1, 152
Marfa 182
Marfa Peninsula 182–4
  beaches 182
  eating out 190
  St Agatha's Tower/Red Tower 182
  where to stay 189
markets 82, 83, 86
marrying in Malta 84
Marsa Racing Club 90
Marsa Sports Club (MSC) 89
Marsalforn (Gozo) 279–80, 281–2
Marsamxett Ferry 65–6, 98, 154
Marsamxett Harbour 101, 147, 148, 151
Marsaskala 220–3
  Razzett tal Hbiberija 77
  Sun City 80
Marsaxlokk 213, 217–18, 220
Marsaxlokk Bay 213–14, 216
  where to stay and eat 220
Mdina 233, 234, 235–46, 238, 247
  Archbishop's Palace 239
  Banca Giuratale 243
  Bastion Square 243

Mdina (cont'd)
  Carmelite Church 244
  Casa Inguanez 245
  Casa Testaferrata 244
  Cathedral Museum 239–40
  Chapel of St Agatha 245–6
  Chapel of St Nicholas 245
  Chapel of St Roque 244
  Corte Capitanale/Courts of Justice 239
  Dungeons 77, 237–8
  eating out 250–1
  Fontanella Tea Garden 243
  getting to and around 235
  Herald's Loggia 239
  history 235–7
  House of Notary Bezzina 243
  Howard Gardens 246
  Magazine Street/Greeks' Gate 245
  Mdina Experience 245
  Medieval Times Adventure 244
  Nunnery of St Benedict/ chapel of St Peter 245
  Palazzo Falzon/the Norman House 235, 243–4
  Palazzo Gatto Murina 244–5
  Palazzo Santa Sophia 244
  Palazzo Vilhena/Museum of Natural History 235, 238–9
  St Paul's Cathedral 235, 240–3, 241
  Torre dello Standardo 238
  tourist information 250
  Villegaignon Street 243
  where to stay 250
  Xara Palace 239
media 84–5
Mediterranean Film Studios 133–4
Mediterraneo Marine Park 77, 166
Mellieħa 72, 170, 180–2
  eating out 189–90
  festa 188
  getting around 181
  Our Lady of Ransom chapel 181
  Our Lady of Victory church 181
  Selmun Palace 181
  Shrine of Our Lady of Mellieħa 181–2
  where to stay 188–9
Mellieħa Bay 88, 180–1, 189, 190
Mesquita, Don 236
Mġarr (Malta) 185, 186, 188, 190

Mġarr (Gozo) 89, 293–5
  eating out 299–300
  Fort Chambray 295
  Harbour 295, 301
  history 294–5
  where to stay 299
Mintoff, Dom 38, 41–3, 144, 187–8
Mistra Bay 175, 178
Mnajdra 200–1, 202–4, 203
mobile phones 92
money 62–3
Monserrat, Nicholas 266, 282
Moorish invasions 174
Mosta 233, 234, 252–3, 255
motorcycles 69
mountain biking 90
Mqabba 206, 208, 209, 210
MSC (Marsa Sports Club) 89
Msida Creek 147, 148, 149
MTA (Malta Tourism Authority) 60, 62, 72, 89
museums 85, 86
Mussolini, Benito 35–6, 37
Mustapha Pasha 27, 140, 174
Napoleon Bonaparte 32–3, 107, 112, 159, 174, 180–1, 213, 237
national holidays 85
National Park 253
National Swimming Pool 222
Naxos 316, 319
Naxxar 253–4, 255
Naxxar Gap 166
Nelson, Horatio, Lord 159, 214
newspapers 44, 85
nightlife 80, 164, 165, 179, 251
  Gozo 293
nude bathing 87
opening hours 85–6
Paceville 159
  bars 164–5
  eating out 163–4
  nightlife 80, 164, 165
packing 86
Paola 224, 225–6, 232
Paradise Bay 182
parasailing 90
parking 67
passports 61
Paul, St 49–52, 111, 169, 171–3, 177, 180, 308
Paule, Grand Master Antoine de 30, 124, 257
Perellos, Grand Master 31, 110
Peter of Aragon 25
Peter's Pool 88, 219
pets 93
pharmacies 81, 86
Phoenicians 23–4, 235–6, 300

Pieta Creek 148
Pinto Battery 217
Pinto, Grand Master 32, **103**, 106, 175
Pinto Redoubt 175
Pisani, Carmelo Borg 194
playgrounds 78
Playmobil Fun Park 77
pleasure cruises **66**, 176
police 80
political parties and politics 38–9, 41–4
polo 90
Popeye Village 78, **183**
postal services 86–7
Publius, Roman governor 172–3, 177
Qawra 170, 175, 176
    eating out 178–9
    where to stay 177–8
Qrejten Point 166
Qrendi 206, **208**, 209, 210
quarantine station (*lazzaretto*) 150–1
Qui Si Sana 156
Rabat 233, *234*, 235, 246–9, *247*
    catacombs 235, **248–9**
    eating out 251
    Empire Arts and Crafts Centre 83, **250**
    nightlife 251
    Roman *Domus* 235, 246
    St Paul's Chapel and Grotto 235, **247–8**
    tourist information 250
    where to stay 250
    *see also* Victoria (Rabat) (Gozo)
radio 84
rail travel
    from the UK 64–5
    Ionian Sicily 315
rambling 72
Ramla tal Mixquqa 184
Ramon Despuig 32
Ras il Qammieħ 183
Ras il Raħeb 188
Razzett tal Ħbiberija 77
Red Skorba 187
religion 87
Rhodes 26–7
rock climbing 91
Roger the Norman, Count **25**, 139, 141, 174, 236
Rohan, Grand Master de 32, 111, 217, 260
Roman Baths 185
Romans 24

Royal Malta Yacht Club 93–4, **150**, 151
Safi 206, 209
St George's Bay 160–5
    beaches 161
    eating out 162–3
    entertainment and nightlife 78, **164**
    getting to and around 160
    where to stay 161–2
St Julian's Bay 147, *153*, 159–65
    Dragonara Palace casino 80, 160
    eating out 162–3
    entertainment and nightlife 164
    *festa* 161
    getting to and around 160
    Palazzo Spinola 159–60
    sports and activities 161
    where to stay 161–2
St Paul's Bay 171–9, *172*
    Buġibba **176**, 177, 178, 179
    church of St Paul's Shipwreck 171, 174, **175**
    church of San Pawl Milqi remains 172
    eating out 178–9
    *festas* 177
    getting around 174
    history 171–4
    nightlife 179
    San Pawl Milqi church 176–7
    services 177
    where to stay 177–8
    Xemxija 175, 178
St Thomas Bay 88, 221, **222**, 223
Salina Bay 169–70
salt industry 170, 180
    Gozo 281
San Anton Palace gardens 257
San Pawl Milqi 176–7
San Pawl tat Tarġa 254
Sannat 72
Scott, Sir Walter 105, 150–1
sea travel *see* boats; ferries
Second World War **35–7**, 131, 133, 184, 224, 228, 237
self catering 74
Selum Bay 72
Senglea (L'Isla) 97, 130, 131, 132, **134–5**, *134*
    Dockyard Creek 134, 135
    Fort St Michael 132, 134
    French Creek 134
    Safe Haven Gardens 135
    Victory Street 135
shooting **46–7**, 91
shopping 82–4

shopping (*cont'd*)
    antiques 84
    Birkikara 261
    clothes **83**, 156
    crafts and souvenirs 83–4
    food **83**, 156–7
    Gozo 275–6, 287, 292, 299
    markets 83
    Mdina 250
    opening hours 85
    Rabat 250
    shopping malls/centres 83
    Sliema **154**, 156–7
    Three Villages 261
    Valletta 128
    Victoria (Gozo) 275–6
Sicily *see* Ionian Sicily
Siġġiewi 195, 196, **198–200**, 205
    chapel of Our Lady 199
    chapel of St John the Baptist 199
    Inquisitor's Summer Palace 199–200
    Madonna Tal Providenza 199
    St Nicholas Church 199
Sinan Pasha 26
Skorba phase 22
Skorba Temples 186, **187**
skydiving 91
Sliema 147, 152, *153*, **153–8**
    beaches 155–6
    car parking 67, 154
    church of the Sacred Heart 155
    Dragut Point 154–5
    eating out 158
    *festas* 156
    Marsamxett ferry 65–6, 98, 154
    private lidos 156
    services 156
    shopping **154**, 156–7
    Sliema Creek cruises 154
    Sliema Creek promenade 154
    sports and activities 157
    Tigne Fort 155
    where to stay 157–8
Slug's Pool 219
snooker 90
snorkelling 78, 88–9
    Comino 303
    Gozo 283
souvenir shops 83–4
speedboats 87
Splash and Fun Park **77**, 166
sports and activities 87–91
Starkie, Walter 316
Suleyman the Magnificent **27**, 47, 49

Sweethaven (Popeye) Village
78, **183**
Syracuse 307–12
basilica and catacombs of St
John 310
crypt of St Marcianus 310
Duomo 311
Ear of Dionysius 309
eating out 312
Fontane Bianche 311
Fonte Aretusa 311
Foro Italico 311
getting around 309
Greek Theatre 309
Grotta dei Cordari 309
history 307–8
Latomia del Paradiso 309–10
Museo Archeologico Paolo
Orsi 307, **310**
Museo Regionale d'Arte
Medioevale e Moderna 311
Neapolis Archaeological Park
307, 309
Ortygia 307, 310–11
Palazzo Beneventano del
Bosco 311
Piazza del Duomo 311
Roman amphitheatre 310
Santuario della Madonnina
delle Lacrime 310
tourist information 312
Tyche 310
where to stay 312
Ta'Ċenċ 72
Ta'Hagrat Temples 186
Taormina 307, **316–19**
beaches 319
Castelmola 319
church of San Giuseppe 318
church of Santa Caterina 318
Duomo 318
Greek Theatre 317–18
history 316–17
Palace of the Dukes of St
Stephen 318
Palazzo Corvaja 318
Piazza del Duomo 318
Piazza IX Aprile 318
Porta di Mezzo 318
Public Gardens 318–19
Sanctuario Madonna della
Rocca 319
Saracen fort 319
Torre dell'Orologo 318
tourist information 319
where to stay and eat 319
Ta'Qali
Aviation Museum 77–8
Crafts Village 77, **83**

Tarxien Cemetery phase 22, 23
Tarxien phase 22, 23
Tarxien Temples 224, 225,
**226–8**, 227
Tas Salib 200
Tas Silg 218
Ta'Xbiex 147–8
taxis **69**, 98
Gozo 266
telephones 76, **79**, 91–2
television 84
Temple phase 22
tennis 90
theatres 80
Manoel (Valletta) 80, 98, **120**
Third Crusade 26
Three Cities 130–44
Cospicua (Bormla) 97, 130,
131, **134**
Cottonera Lines 133
eating out 144
*festas* 144
getting to and around 131
Great Chain 132–3, **135**
history 97, 130, **132–5**
Margherita Lines 133
Mediterranean Film Studios
133–4
Senglea (L'Isla) 97, 130, 131, 132,
**134–5**, *134*
tourist information 144
Vittoriosa Wharf 97
yacht marina 131
Żabbar Gate 133
*see also* Vittoriosa (Birgu)
Three Villages **257–9**, 261–2
Tigne Beach 156
Tigne Fort 155
time 76, 92
timeshares 74
tipping 92
toilets 92
Torri and Exiles Beach 155–6
Torri tal Kapitan 254
tour operators 72–3
tourist information 60
Comino 304
Gozo 299
Mdina and Rabat 250
Syracuse 312
Taormina 319
Three Cities 144
Valletta 127
traveller's cheques 63
Turks **26–7**, 30, 31, 98, 118, 134,
184, 230
Valletta 29, **95–130**, *96*, *102*
Admiralty House/Museum of
Fine Arts 122–3

Valletta (*cont'd*)
Archbishop's Palace 120
Auberge d'Aragon 119
Auberge de Bavaria 119
Auberge de Castile et Leon
102–3
Auberge de Provence 121
Auberge d'Italie 103
bars 130
Bibliotheca 111–12
building and architecture
98–100
bus terminus 69
cafés 130
car parking 67, 98
Carmelite Church 120
Casa Rocca Piccola 116
Castellania 104
Centre for Creativity 77, **101**
Church of St Catherine of
Italy 101–2
City Gate 69, 100, 101
eating out 129–30
*festa* 127
Floriana 124–7, *125*
Fort St Elmo 98, 100, 118–19
General Post Office 86, 103
getting to and around 98
Grand Harbour 97, 101
Grand Master's Palace 62, 97,
99, **112–15**, *114*
Great Siege of Malta and the
Knights of St John 112
Great Siege Square 111
Hastings Gardens 123
history **96**, 124
Il Belvedere d'Italia 103
Knights Hospitallers display
117
Lascaris War Rooms 124
Law Courts 111
Lower Barracca Gardens 116
the Malta Experience 117
Manoel Theatre 80, 98, **120**
Marsamxett Ferry 65–6,
98, 154
Marsamxett Harbour 101, 147
Mediterranean Conference
Centre 98, 117
Merchants Street 100
Merchants Street market 97
Mount Sceberras 99
Museum of Archaeology 97,
121
National War Museum 119
Old Bakery Street 100
Old Opera House 101
orientation 100–1
Our Lady of Victory 101

Valletta (cont'd)
  Palace Armoury 97, 115–16
  Palace Square 97, 112
  Palazzo Bonici 120
  Palazzo di Città 110–11
  Palazzo Ferreria 101
  Palazzo Parisio 103–4
  Republic Square 98, 111
  Republic Street 100
  Sacra Infermeria 117
  St James's Cavalier 77, 98, **101**
  St James's Church 104
  St John's Cavalier 123
  St John's Co Cathedral and
    museum 62, 87, 97, 99,
    **104–10**, *106*
  St Paul's Anglican Cathedral
    87, **119–20**
  St Paul's Shipwreck 51, 111
  Second World War Memorial
    117
  services 127
  shopping 128
  Siege Bell Monument 117
  Sovereign Military
    Hospitaller Order of St
    John of Jerusalem of
    Rhodes and Malta 123
  Strait Street 120–1
  street signs 67
  tourist information 127
  Triton Fountain 101
  Upper Barracca Gardens 103
  the Wartime Experience 116
  where to stay 128–9
Vasconcellos, Grand Master de
  30
VAT 92
Vaubois, General 33, 159
Verdala Palace 197–8
Verdalle, Grand Master de 30,
  197
Verres, Governor of Syracuse
  308
Victoria Lines **169**, 254
Victoria (Rabat) (Gozo) 269–76,
  *271*
  Archaeological Museum
    272–3
  Banca Giuratale 273
  basilica of St George 273–4
  Cathedral of the Assumption
    270–2
  Cathedral Museum 272
  Cathedral Square 271
  Citadel 270–3, *271*
  Citadel Theatre 273
  Collegiate Basilica of St
    George 269

Victoria (Rabat) (cont'd)
  eating out 276
  *festas* 275
  Folklore Museum Museum
    272
  getting to and around 270
  Governor's Palace 271–2
  Law Courts 271
  Natural History and Science
    Museum 272
  Old Prisons 273
  Post Office 86
  Public Registry 272
  Rundle Gardens 274
  shopping 275–6
  tourist information and
    services 274–5
  where to stay 276
Vilhena, Grand Master de 31,
  126, 151, 236, 238–9, 273, 295
Villa Bettina 229–30
villas 74
visas 61
Vittoriosa (Birgu) 97, 130,
  **135–44**, *137*
  Advanced Gate 136
  Armoury 136
  Auberge d'Allemagne 138
  Auberge d'Angleterre 138
  Auberge d'Auvergne et
    Provence 138
  Auberge de Castile et Leon
    138
  Auberge de France 138
  Auberge d'Italie 140
  Bishop's Palace 136
  church of St Lawrence 135
  Collegiate Church of St
    Lawrence 139
  Couvre Porte Gate 136
  Dockyard Creek 132, 133
  Fort Rinella (Kalkara) 135,
    **143–4**
  Fort St Angelo 131, 132, 133,
    135, **140–2**
  Freedom Monument 139–40
  Gate of Provence 136
  Infermeria Sally Port 136
  Inquisitor's Palace 135, 142–3
  Maritime Museum 131, 135,
    140
  Naval Bakery 140
  Norman House 138
  Posta d'Allemagne 136
  Posta d'Angleterre 136
  Posta de Genoa 136
  Poste d'Aragon 136
  Poste de Castile 136

Vittoriosa (Birgu) (cont'd)
  Residence of Conventual
    Chaplains 143
  Sacra Infermeria 136, **137**
  St James's Cavalier 136
  St John's Cavalier 136
  St Joseph's Chapel 138–9
  St Lawrence statue 138
  Site of Slaves' Prison 142
  Victory Monument 138
  Victory Square 138
  Wharf 136
von Hompesch, Grand Master
  Ferdinand 32–3, **225**
walking 72–3, 184–5
  Gozo 266, 288
Wardija Ridge 176
water 81
water polo **91**, 176, 222
water skiing 91
Waugh, Evelyn 97
when to go 58
where to stay 73–4
  *see also under individual
    places (where to stay)*
Wied iż-Żurrieq (The Blue
  Grotto) 205, 206, **207–8**,
  210
Wignacourt, Grand Master Alof
  de **30**, 140, 175, 297, 301, 302
Wignacourt Tower museum 175
windsurfing 91
wine 56
women travellers 86, **92**
work permits 82
Xarolla windmill 209
Xemxija 175, 178
Ximenes, Grand Master 32
Xlendi 72
Xwieni 72
yachts
  marinas 131, 147, 149
  Royal Malta Yacht Club **150**,
    151
  yachting information 92–4
Youth Hostels Association
  (YHA) 74
Żabbar **223–5**, 232
  Our Lady of Graces church
    224–5
Żebbieħ 187
Żebbuġ 259–61
Żejtun 224, **230–2**
Zondadari, Grand Master 31
Zonqor Point 222
Żurrieq **205–7**, 209

## About the Updater

**Lucia Mizzi**, an osteopath and naturopath, was born in Malta but grew up in Saudi Arabia and England. In 1996, she returned to Malta, where she now lives.

## 4th edition published 2007

**Cadogan Guides** is an imprint of
New Holland Publishers (UK) Ltd
London • Cape Town • Sydney • Auckland

| | | | |
|---|---|---|---|
| New Holland Publishers (UK) Ltd | 80 McKenzie Street | Unit 1, 66 Gibbes Street | 218 Lake Road |
| Garfield House | Cape Town 8001 | Chatswood, NSW 2067 | Northcote |
| 86–88 Edgware Road | South Africa | Australia | Auckland |
| London W2 2EA | | | New Zealand |

*Cadogan@nhpub.co.uk*
*www.cadoganguides.com*
**t** 44 (0)20 7724 7773

Distributed in the United States by Globe Pequot, Connecticut

Copyright © Simon Gaul 1993, 1998, 2003, 2007

Cover photographs: © Hugh Sitton/Getty, © Carole Hewer/Alamy
Photo essay photographs © Kicca Tommasi
Maps © Cadogan Guides, drawn by Maidenhead Cartographic Services Ltd
Cover and photo essay design: Sarah Rianhard-Gardner
Editor: Tim Locke
Proofreading: Elspeth Anderson
Indexing: Isobel McLean

Printed in Italy by Legoprint
A catalogue record for this book is available from the British Library

ISBN: 978-1-86011-365-9

The author and publishers have made every effort to ensure the accuracy of the information in this book at the time of going to press. However, they cannot accept any responsibility for any loss, injury or inconvenience resulting from the use of information contained in this guide.

Please help us to keep this guide up to date. We have done our best to ensure that the information in this guide is correct at the time of going to press. But laws and regulations are constantly changing, and standards and prices fluctuate. We would be delighted to receive any comments. Authors of the best letters will receive a copy of the Cadogan Guide of their choice.

# Malta, Gozo & Comino touring atlas

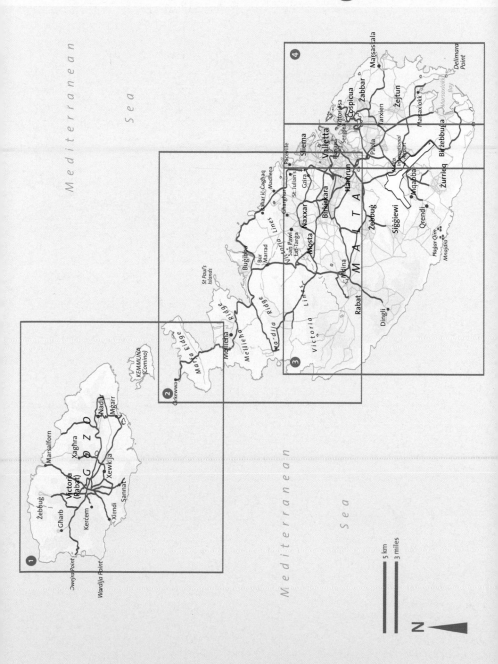

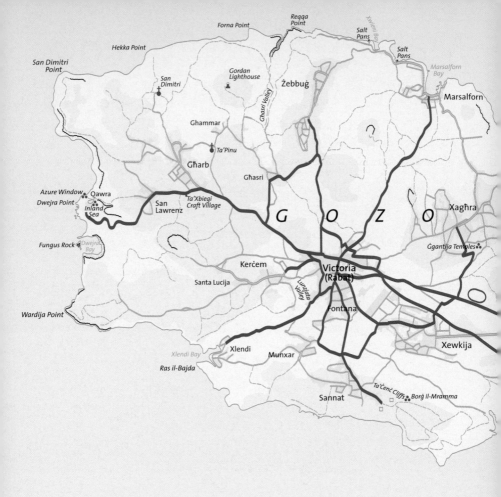

San Dimitri
Point

Hekka Point

Forna Point

Reqqa
Point

Xwieni Bay

Salt
Pans

Salt
Pans

Marsalforn
Bay

Marsalforn

San
Dimitri

Gordan
Lighthouse

Żebbuġ

Ghammar

Għasri Valley

Ta'Pinu

Għarb

Għasri

Azure Window
Dwejra Point

Qawra

Inland
Sea

San
Lawrenz

Ta'Xbiegi
Craft Village

G  O  Z  O

Xagħra

Ġgantija Temples

Fungus Rock

Dwejra
Bay

Kerċem

Victoria
(Rabat)

Wardija Point

Santa Lucija

Lunzjata Valley

Fontana

Xewkija

Xlendi Bay

Xlendi

Munxar

Ras il-Bajda

Ta'Ċenċ Cliffs

Borġ il-Mramma

Sannat

M  e  d  i  t  e  r  r  a  n  e  a  n

S  e  a

N

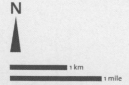

1 km

1 mile

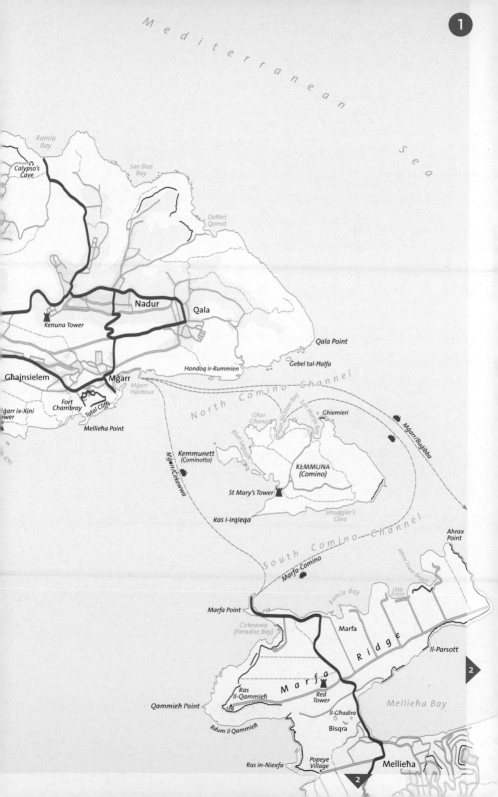

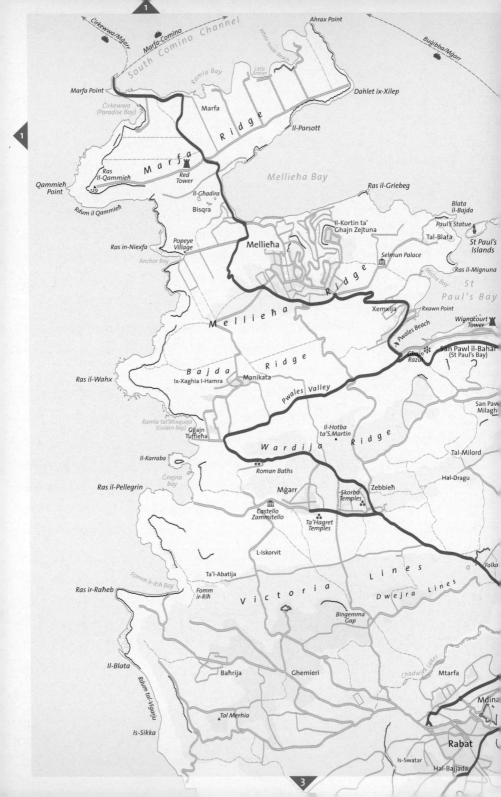

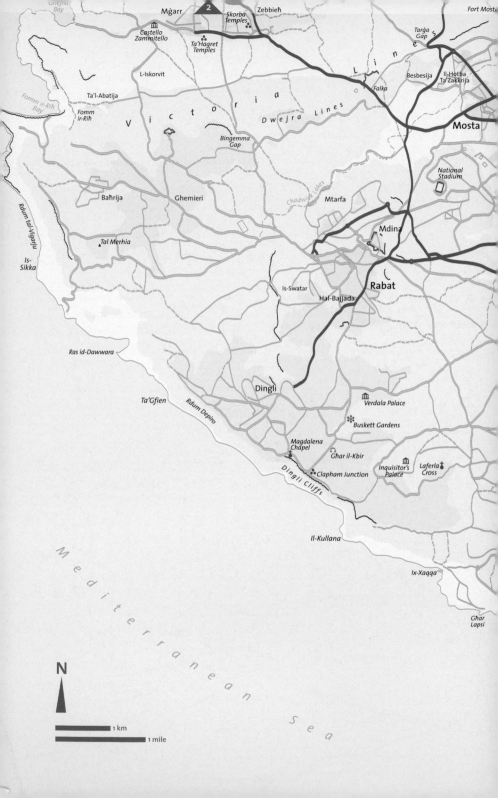

Il-Qaliet

Spinola Palace
Spinola Point
St Julien's Tower
St Julien's Point

Bugibba/Sliema

1 km
1 mile

N

Il-Fortizza
Sliema Point
Ggar id-Dud

Sliema

Baluta Bay

Tigne Fort
Dragutt Point
St Elmo Point

Sliema Creek

Manoel Island
Fort Manoel

Fort St Elmo

St Elmo Lighthouse

Lazzaretto Creek

Ta'Xbiex

Marsamxett Harbour

Valletta

Ricasoli Point
Ricasoli Fort

Fort Rinella

Catania/Genova/Palermo/Pozzalo/Reggio diCalabria & Siracusa

Tripoli

Mediterranean Sea

Msida Creek

Pieta Creek

Pieta

Floriana

Fort St Angelo

Rinella Creek

Gwardamanga

Grand Harbour

Dockyard Creek

Senglea

Vittoriosa

Kalkara

Xghajra

Ras il-Gebel

Ħamrun

Ras Hanzir

Il-Kortin

French Creek

Kalkara Creek

Cospicua

Marsa

Kordin

Zabbar Gate

Il-Hofra

Fort St. Leonardo

Żabbar

Ghajn Dwieli

Airport (Manoel Ct.)

Rahal Gdid
Hypogeum
Tal Borg
Fgura

Ta'Grazzia

Zonqor

Marsaskala

Fort St Thomas
Zonqor Point

Ħal Saflieni Temples

Paola

Tarxien Temples

Wied ta' Mazza

Wied il-Ghajn

Marsaskala Bay

Il-Kappara

Il-Hamrija

Il-Ġzira Point

Luqa

Santa Lucia

Tarxien

Il-Minzel

Wied iz-Ziju

Il-Minzel

Tal-Barrani

Mamo Tower

Mignuna Point

St Thomas Bay

St Mary

Ta' Bir Miftuh

Malta International Airport

Gudja

Għaxaq

Bir id-Deheb

Żejtun
St Gregory's

Tas Silg

Tas Silg Battery

Island Bay

Xrobb Il-Ghagin

Il-Munxar

Marsaxlokk

Ras il-Fenek

Ghar Dalam

Il-Blez

Il-Hofra z-Zghira

Borg in-Nadur

St Lucian's Tower

Kbira Point

Delimara

Peter's Pool

Tumbrell Point

Birżebbuġa

Pinto Battery

Pretty Bay

Marsaxlokk Bay

Fort Delimara

Long Bay

Slug's Pool

Mizieb

Ħal Far

Tal-Papa

Kalafrana

Delimara Lighthouse

Delimara Point

Ħal Far Industrial Estate

Benghisa Point

Fort Benghisa

Ghar Hasan Cave